THE
REAL-WORLD
LINGUIST:

LINGUISTIC APPLICATIONS IN THE 1980s

Editors

PETER C. BJARKMAN and VICTOR RASKIN

Purdue University

ABLEX Publishing Corporation
Norwood, New Jersey

P
129
.R4
1986

Library of Congress Cataloging-in-Publication Data
Main entry under title:

The Real-world linguist.

Predominantly papers presented at the Symposium on "Linguistic Applications in the 1980's," held during the 1981-1982 academic year, Purdue University.
Includes bibliographies and indexes.
1. Applied linguistics—Addresses, essays, lectures. I. Bjarkman, Peter C., 1941-   . II. Raskin, Victor, 1944-   . III. Symposium on "Linguistic Applications in the 1980's" (1981-1982: Purdue University)
P129.R4 1986   410   85-46067 ISBN 0-89391-357-X

Ablex Publishing Corporation
355 Chestnut Street
Norwood, New Jersey 07648

Contents

iii

Contributors

Myrdene Anderson, Department of Sociology and Anthropology, Purdue University, West Lafayette, Indiana 47907.

Peter C. Bjarkman, Department of English, Purdue University, West Lafayette, Indiana 47907.

Victor A. Friedman, Department of Slavic Languages and Literatures, University of North Carolina, Chapel Hill, North Carolina 27514.

Georgia M. Green, Department of Linguistics, University of Illinois, Urbana, Illinois 61801.

Shaun F. D. Hughes, Department of English, Purdue University, West Lafayette, Indiana 47907.

Judith N. Levi, Department of Linguistics, Northwestern University, Evanston, Illinois 60201.

James D. McCawley, Department of Linguistics, University of Chicago, Chicago, Illinois 60637.

Sergei Nirenburg, Department of Information and Computer Science, Colgate University, Hamilton, New York 13346.

Victor Raskin, Department of English, Purdue University, West Lafayette, Indiana 47907.

Háj Ross, Department of Linguistics and Philosophy, Massachusetts Institute of Technology, Cambridge, Massachusetts 02139.

Robert E. Sanders, Department of Rhetoric and Communication, State University of New York, Albany, New York 12222.

Herbert F. W. Stahlke, Department of English, Ball State University, Muncie, Indiana 47306.

Robin Thelwall, Department of Linguistics, The New University of Ulster, Coleraine BT52 1SA, Northern Ireland.

Ronnie B. Wilbur, Department of Audiology and Speech Sciences, Purdue University, West Lafayette, Indiana 47907.

Arnold M. Zwicky, Department of Linguistics, Ohio State University, Columbus, Ohio 43210.

Acknowledgments

The editors would like to thank the Dean's Office of the School of the Humanities, Social Sciences, and Education, Purdue University, as well as the Heads of the Departments of Audiology and Speech Science, Communication, Education, English, Foreign Languages and Literatures, Philosophy, Psychology, and Sociology/Anthropology, for their support and funding of the Symposium on Linguistic Applications in the 1980s, at which most of the papers in this volume were first reported.

The editors are also grateful to the contributors for their cooperation, especially to those who submitted their papers promptly and waited patiently for the others, but also to those others who finally came through when there seemed to be no more hope.

Ann Moore, the word-processing secretary at the Department of English, deserves a great deal of credit for her competent handling of the manuscripts and her patience. Cherylynn K. Horváth, the Head Secretary of the Department of English, was very helpful in authorizing the high priority which the secretarial work on the book always needed. Judy Ware's word-processing expertise, readiness to help, and endless patience were also an important asset.

Peter Bjarkman was greatly assisted in his editorial duties by Ronnie B. Wilbur, who was extremely generous with her time and intimidatingly fast and competent as editor.

Victor Raskin would like to thank the Center for Applied Linguistics for the permission to use in the Preface the material of his article, "Linguistic careers and linguistic applications in the 1980s—One man's view," *The Linguistic Reporter* 24:9, 1982. (He would like to think that it was not the publication of that article which caused the demise of the *Reporter* immediately thereafter.)

Both editors were impressed by the Ablex people, from the president, Walter Johnson, to the editors and staff, who made their decisions quickly, negotiated in good faith, and contributed greatly to the speedy execution of the book. The anonymous reader who responded promptly and positively to the Ablex inquiry about the worthiness of the project also earned our appreciation.

Linguistic Applications in the 1980s

Victor Raskin

In recent years some of the best departments of linguistics in this country, and for that matter abroad, have been having trouble placing even their best graduates, with brand-new Ph.D.s and master's, in academic positions in linguistics. Apparently, part of the problem is the nature of these graduates' training, which was exclusively 'pure linguistics' and made them virtually unemployable in any alternative professional capacity. At the same time, graduate enrollments in linguistics in many departments have been on the decline.

This situation has been correlated with an academic change of attitude taking place within linguistics. Since the early 1970s, some of the best representatives of the 'transformational' generation have been experiencing crises in their own linguistic ideology as they were discovering that there was much more out there, in real human language, than what met the transformation, or rather what the transformation met.

Both processes, curiously enough, have led to a similar result—the emergence of articles devoted to various linguistic applications and written, often somewhat shamefacedly and self-consciously, by former 'pure' linguists. Many, if not most, of these often interesting essays are somewhat ad hoc, anecdotal, and atheoretical in nature; some even contain renunciations by the authors of their own former adherence to formal and scientific methods of linguistic research.

It seems to be obvious that the time of meaningful linguistic applications has come, and the future of linguistics as a discipline now depends to a large extent on the successful training and placement of linguists in those areas of academia and professions in which people with linguistic expertise can be usefully and gainfully employed.

Facing the problem of job placement in linguistics, the Linguistic Society of America created an ad hoc committee on careers in linguistics (and this author was appointed to it in its first year). There have also been sessions on careers outside academia at a few recent annual conventions of the Society. While there is no doubt that these efforts are timely and laudable, we cannot hope to achieve significant results until a critical mass of linguistic educators and researchers realizes the importance of linguistic applications for the prosperity and, indeed, survival of the discipline.

Ironically, there have been many more non-linguists than linguists writing on linguistic applications, and with all due respect to these authors, false expectations from, and subsequent bitter disappointments in, what linguistics can offer its adjacent fields have emerged in various areas. I believe that the linguists should bear the blame for that rather than dismiss those attempts as ignorant, superficial, and incompetent raids on the treasury of linguistic knowledge.

This preface to a collection of articles on linguistic applications authored predominantly by practicing linguistic researchers makes the following claims.

First, research in linguistic applications to various adjacent fields can be carried out successfully only on the basis of the same theoretical framework, complete with theory and concerns for adequacy, explanation, and justification, as the one developed for theoretical linguistics in the last decades.

Second, the new generation of students should be offered a kind of linguistic education which combines thorough preparation in 'pure' linguistics with a systematic and *theoretically based* treatment of goals and techniques of linguistic applications. It is believed that graduates with such skills will be able to compete very successfully, both inside and outside universities, with graduates in psychology, sociology, communication, education, anthropology, philosophy, computer science, public relations, and in a number of other fields. All of these fields have acute language-related problems and needs which their own specialists, lacking linguistic training, are unable to cope with.

Third, if the first two claims are true, they set a goal for linguistics which cannot be achieved before a significant body of knowledge on linguistic applications is obtained through research and made available to the linguistic community through publication. Such linguistic publications are very scarce, to say the least, and this volume is an attempt to start filling the gap.

By linguistic applications we will mean here the use of data, methods and/or theories accumulated or developed in linguistics, to solve the problem from a different field of study, any language-related field of study which might need linguistic expertise. The only difference between research in pure linguistics and research in applied linguistics is viewed as exactly this—that the problem which is solved in a linguistic application does not come from linguistics but rather from another field.

Let us consider three simplistic (and not necessarily absolutely realistic) examples of such problems from three different fields which require a linguistic application for their solution.

Problem 1, from computer science, or rather from automatic language-data processing: How to teach the computer to summarize a text?

Problem 2, from teaching English as a second language (ESL) or, for that matter, from teaching any language to non-native speakers (the field traditionally denoted by a misnomer, 'applied linguistics'): Should one teach one's students the difference between some two 'difficult' sounds?

Problem 3, from speech therapy: How to help a stuttering child who sometimes does stutter on a certain sound and sometimes does not?

The first problem involves basically linguistic semantics and syntax. In order to summarize a text (or to translate it into a different language, or to answer questions about the text) the computer must understand it first. This means that all the relevant syntactic and semantic information which is necessary to approximate, or model, the understanding of the text by the native speaker should be introduced into the computer. To make this possible, a complete and adequate syntactico-semantic description of the language of the text should be available. A graduate in pure linguistics knows that no such description is available in full, and the parts which are there are fragmentary, controversial, and very complex. Even worse, such a graduate may be familiar with just one theory which may be unsuitable for the application. If such a linguist is asked for help by an expert in information processing, this is the answer the linguist is likely to come up with. However, it is obviously not good enough for the customer who needs the problem solved, anyway. The expert in automatic language-data processing begins doing it without linguists and sometimes practically without linguistics, taking short cuts and, with luck, producing an acceptable (though almost always partial) ad hoc solution of one particular problem.

The second problem involves phonology. A good phonologist knows all about traditional phonology, structural phonology, generative phonology, and natural phonology. A not so good phonologist will know all about the one school in which he or she happened to be reared. Both, however, realize the enormous complexity of the involved phenomena and of the rules which are needed to describe them. The ESL expert who faces the practical problem is likely to be turned off by the complexity and/or controversiality of the available linguistic information. However, since the problem does need to be solved anyhow, the unsatisfied customer will try to play it 'by ear,' also in the literal sense of the phrase, and solve it, once again, without a linguist and perhaps without linguistics. As a result, the ESL person may end up spending a considerable amount of time teaching a non-speaker of English the difference between the aspirated and unaspirated /p/ or between the pronunciations of the diphthong in *ride* and *right*.

The third problem may involve more than what seems to be obvious. If the linguist attempts a purely phonetical or phonological solution, it is likely to be falsified by the fact that the child can pronounce the sound very well in some cases but not in others. Unless the linguist is there and is knowledgeable and innovative, a very important observation can be missed, namely, that the stuttering occurs more on syntactic boundaries. If the linguist is there and has everything it takes to make this discovery, he or she may still not be forthcoming with a solution to the practical problem because various syntactical theories draw some syntactic boundaries in different places. If, however, competent linguistic help is not available to the speech therapist, much if not all of the treatment may be completely wasted.

These examples describe, probably without much exaggeration, what actually happens in the fields to which linguistics can be fruitfully applied and in which linguists can be gainfully employed. In most cases, however, the experts in those fields do not even try to solicit the linguist's help either because they do not know anything about linguistics and its possibilities or because somebody tried it once long before them and was burnt, or because somebody else, from an adjacent field, gave linguistics a bad name (of an arrogant, 'ivory tower' discipline) with regard to its usability for practical purposes. The result is clear enough: the fields go without linguists and pay the serious consequences; the linguists go without jobs and cannot pay anything only because they are broke.

The question is, Do the fields need those linguists and do those linguists need those jobs? The answer is an emphatic "yes" to both, but with a very important qualification.

The applied fields need linguists only if the linguists can help them. The linguists need the jobs only if they can fill them qua linguists. Both of the results seem to be attainable.

If the linguists want to be useful for an applied field, they do not have to forget all they know about the complex linguistic data, methods, and theories which have to be applied to the field, and to deal with the applied problem simplistically and condescendingly—what would result from that is the shame-faced, anecdotal, ad hoc essays mentioned above.

On the other hand, the linguists should not try to apply their knowledge in all its complexity to the field—many have tried that and failed.

What the linguists should do is try to translate the best theory, method, or technique they have at their disposal in theoretical linguistics into a *usable applied theory*. As every other linguistic theory, such an applied theory would consist of a general part, universal for all fields of application, and particular parts, special for each field of application. The general part would contain principles of simplification and reduction of linguistic theories for practical pur-poses without compromising or distorting the linguistic truth. The particular parts would take into account the specific requirements of every particular field of application. The applied theory would, therefore, bridge the often existing gap between linguistic theory and potential fields of application, and it would do this while always maintaining the high scholarly level attained in linguistics, com-plete with concerns for adequacy, explanation, and justification.

Thus, in the case of Problem 1, the computational problem, the linguist should perhaps realize that the text is written in a sublanguage, not in the entire natural language, as it were, since in most cases when such problems arise practically, the texts to be summarized come from a narrow field of science or technology, and therefore many syntactical and semantic problems are sim-plified. The applied theory adapts the syntactico-semantic equipment available for the whole language to the utilized sublanguage. Another strategy is to simplify the available theory through realizing that some parts of it are irrelevant for the field in question. A good example is something Terry Winograd (*Understanding Natural Language*, New York: Academic Press, 1972) did in the early 1970s in SHRDLU, his artificial intelligence system based on natural language: he realized that transformational grammar was too complex for the limited syntax he needed in the system, and he deliberately opted for a simpler though inferior syntactic theory to apply. His decision was correct to the extent that the other theory was adequate on the syntax of the system, and he did not use it in the parts which were less adequate than transformational grammar. However, because his approach was not based on a usable applied syntactical theory, his approach could not be automatically extrapolated to similar cases and thus remained largely ad hoc.

In the case of Problem 2, the ESL problem, the linguist should realize that all the ESL expert really wants to know (and to convey to his/her students) is the important distinction between sounds that distinguish words and sounds that do not. No matter whether this distinction is captured by the notion of phoneme, or by rules, or processes, what counts in ESL is that the distinction between the two variants of /p/ or between the two variants of the diphthong /ay/ is not word distinguishing and therefore is less worthy of an effort than, say, the distinction between /b/ and /p/ or /ay/ and /oy/.

In the case of Problem 3, the speech therapy problem, similarly, the linguist should come up with an applied theory which will put forward a notion of syntactical phrase helpful for the speech therapist in determining where the stuttering is likely to occur. In fact, this problem is especially interesting because if it is established that stuttering is likely to occur on syntactic boundaries, the places where it does occur may be recognized as such, and this would be valuable feedback for linguistic theory. If there are two competing syntactic theories which analyze sentences into phrases differently, then if stuttering occurs where one of the theories sees a syntactic boundary and the other theory does not, the former theory would seem to be justified by speech therapeutical practice.

In general, the linguist can only do applications well if they are maintained at the high theoretical and descriptive level which will make it possible for the linguist to continue his or her search for the linguistic truth. Good applications will provide the linguist with valuable feedback and can, in fact, be used as verification tests for various theories. All this, and desirable jobs in applications, will materialize only if and when the profession and its practitioners are ready.

Mainly because of the prevailing ignorance about linguistics, but also because of the unfortunate recent and not so recent histories of various linguistic applications, the burden of the proof of their usefulness for various applications lies now with linguists. Fully equipped with their theories and methods, they have to go aggressively for a targeted applied field, and prove to the expert in the field that linguistics brings over the knowledge without which the field cannot be successful. This will either create jobs for linguists where now there are none, or vacate the existing jobs, now occupied by non-linguists who are incapable of providing the necessary service to the applied field, for linguists who will be able to do so.

Obviously, in order to combine these two objectives—to be useful for applied fields and therefore marketable, on the one hand, and to be able to combine fruitfully their work in applications with their 'pure' linguistic research, on the other—linguists should be educated accordingly.

Under the present system, departments of pure linguistics hardly ever have anything to do with departments of applied linguistics (which deal with teaching languages only) and have very little to do with departments of literatures, sociology, psychology, communication, computer science, etc., which all deal with language-related areas and have corresponding needs. This system is hardly satisfactory.

One way of cutting through territorial boundaries is establishing interdepartmental programs in linguistics, especially at the undergraduate level. A few such programs have been set up recently, including one at Purdue, which is six years old and doing well. One clear academic advantage of such an arrangement is an easy access for students enrolled in interdepartmental programs to courses in areas of possible linguistic applications. Another is that such a program is an easy channel for interdisciplinary cooperation in teaching and research. A clear non-academic advantage is, of course, that such a program does not have to be concerned about its enrollment nearly as much as a regular department.

An established department of linguistics, interested in broadening its base in the direction of applications, would have to find ways of opening its doors for both incoming and outgoing students; i.e., students from other departments should be attracted into linguistics courses and linguistics students should be steered into some courses in other departments. This purpose would, however, be served better by the development of application-oriented interdepartmental offerings.

Again, a movement towards facing these problems can be clearly detected in the linguistic community. Thus, the 1984 Chairs Meeting at the LSA Annual Convention was devoted to the issue of undergraduate training, and the interdepartmental approach was prominent on the agenda.

The surviving skills of this generation of linguists are being severely tested, and applications may be the key to success.

The concerns expressed above led the Purdue Linguistic Group, the informal forum of the Interdepartmental Program in Linguistics, to coordinate its internal and visiting speakers' program over a few recent years around the theme of linguistic applications. Taken together, the sponsored presentations made up a symposium entitled "Linguistic Applications in the 1980s."

Eleven out of the fifteen contributors to this volume made their presentations at the Symposium and wrote them up (sometimes with modifications) for the book. Four other chapters were solicited by the editors, primarily to cover important areas of potential or actual linguistic applications which were not mentioned at the Symposium.

The fifteen chapters are somewhat loosely grouped into four parts. The title of each part is an attempt to capture the common trait of its chapters.

Thus, the four chapters of Part One deal with various manifestations of non-casual language: dictionary entries (McCawley); well-written essays, literary texts, verbal humor (Raskin); poetry (Ross); lyrics (Zwicky).

The next four chapters, in Part Two, deal with language use outside the ordinary speech community: by non-native speakers (Bjarkman); by computers (Nirenburg); by primates (Stahlke); by the deaf (Wilbur).

Societal usage brings together the four chapters of Part Three. Anderson's studies an application of linguistics to anthropology; Green's to reading; Levi's to the language of the law; Sanders's to the study of human communication.

Part Four stands somewhat apart from the first three parts, in which the chapters share a usage-related facet. Instead, the three chapters of the last part view language in history and examine linguistic applications to national policies and language planning (Friedman); to the philosophy of science and, generally, the affiliation of ideas (Hughes); to the study of undocumented history (Thelwall).

While within each part the chapters are arranged alphabetically by author, there is no rational explanation for the numeration of the parts themselves, and their order should be considered arbitrary.

We would like to believe that the list of areas of application dealt with in the volume is quite representative though, naturally, not exhaustive. We also hope that the response, criticism, and feedback to this practically unprecedented venture into linguistic applications by a group of authors, almost all of whom are full-time theoretical linguists (and the remaining small minority are part-time theoretical linguists with highly respectable linguistic credentials), will be more talk and more published work by linguists on this important and sorely neglected subject.

PART ONE
NON-CASUAL
LANGUAGE

What Linguists Might Contribute to Dictionary Making If They Could Get Their Act Together

James D. McCawley

1. Introduction

This article is concerned with ways in which the kinds of results obtained by linguists in their research on particular languages and the conceptual machinery that they employ can be of use in the compilation of dictionaries intended for purchase and use by non-specialists.

My qualifications for writing such an article are not overwhelming, a fact that I note at the outset simply to give the reader an idea of how seriously to take what I say. My only experiences in the compilation of dictionaries intended for publication are a one-week stint as a consultant to a general-purpose dictionary; the work that I have done on the highly specialized glossary that comprises the bulk of McCawley (1984); and the work that I put into the short glossary of technical terms that appears in McCawley (1976). In addition, in my linguistic research on the relationship between syntax and semantics, I have devoted considerable attention to the contributions of the meanings of words to their syntactic behavior, e.g., the fact that the sentences that figure implicitly in many paraphrases of semantically complex lexical items can support adverbs or serve as the scopes of quantifiers and negations:

(1) a. Bill lent me his bicycle until next Tuesday.[1] (The adverb modifies *I have Bill's bicycle*, corresponding to *lend* = allow to have temporarily.)

b. John dissuaded Mary from writing any sonnets. (*Dissuade* = cause-become-not-intend, and the scope of the understood *not* is *Mary intends to write some (>any) sonnets.*)

In connection with this research I have taught courses entitled ''The Lexicon and Grammar'' and ''Practical Lexicography,'' the latter involving considerable critical examination of existing published dictionaries.

The bulk of this paper will be devoted to describing and illustrating common sorts of deficiencies in existing dictionaries for which work in linguistics is relevant not merely to remedying these deficiencies but to remedying them in a way that could well increase the number of persons willing to shell out $19.95 plus tax for a copy of a dictionary.

2. Omissions in Dictionaries

There are a number of cases in which well-known and reasonably well understood differences among words are largely ignored by dictionaries other than some such as ALD and LDCE[2] that have been compiled with non-native learners of English in mind. Take, for example, the difference between count nouns (such as *job, poem, board, steak, operation*) and mass nouns (such as *work, poetry, lumber, meat, surgery*). This distinction distinguishes words of a given language not only from one another but often also from their closest equivalents in other languages, e.g., the closest Spanish equivalent of the English mass noun *advice* is the count noun *consejo*, perhaps best translated as 'piece of advice,' and *advice* must often be translated into Spanish by the plural *consejos*. It can be argued (as in McCawley 1975) that the meanings of count nouns differ systematically from those of mass nouns, the former including an individuation (e.g., *steak* = slice of meat cut in such-and-such a way while raw) while the latter are unspecified for individuation. If that claim is correct, definitions could be worded in such a way as to specify indirectly whether a word is a count or mass noun, by respectively including or omitting an individuation. I know of no dictionary, however, in which this is systematically done, e.g., the following definitions provide no clue to the reader that *bean* is a count noun and *rice* a mass noun rather than vice versa:[3]

(2) *bean* (AH) 1. Any of several plants of the genus *Phaseolus* . . .
2. *The edible seed or pod of any of these plants.*

rice (AH) 1. A cereal grass, *Oryza sativa*, . . . 2. The starchy edible seed of this grass.

A large number of words and expressions are known to be negative polarity items (that is, to occur only in the scope of negative elements) or positive polarity items (that is, to be excluded from appearing in the scope of negative elements), e.g.,[4]

(3) a. John doesn't *hold a candle* to Mary.
a'. *John holds a candle to Mary.

b. I *would rather* be in Philadelphia.
b'. *I wouldn't rather be in Philadelphia.

Published dictionaries generally take no note of these restrictions except to the limited extent that they treat a handful of negative polarity items as if they were parts of idioms that involved *not*, which is an error, since *not* need not be the device by which the negation is expressed.[5] A much less well-known restriction (discussed in Hinds 1974) to which some lexical items are subject is that they be used in performing or referring to a particular type of speech act, e.g., *delicious* can be used only in expressing or reporting a positive reaction to something:

(4) a. This meatloaf is delicious!
     b. *This meatloaf isn't delicious.
     c. *Is the meatloaf delicious today?

Violations of such restrictions are common errors in non-native speech, as when a Japanese, mistakenly identifying English *delicious* with Japanese *oisii*, utters (4b) or (4c), and the failure of dictionaries to take note of them is a respect in which the interests of non-native users are poorly served.

A final example of the omission by dictionaries of information that linguists deal with is that, aside from the fact that dictionaries generally mark verbs as 'transitive' or 'intransitive,' they typically provide no information about what adjuncts a word allows or requires. While the noun *husband* demands a NP adjunct to fully the same extent as does the verb *buy*, dictionaries typically register the latter fact by marking *buy* 'v.t.' but make no allusion to the former fact:[6]

(5) a. *John is a husband.
         John is Mary's husband.

     b. *John bought.
         John bought a new hat.

The traditional transitive/intransitive distinction is a special instance of a far more general set of distinctions, and it is to the credit of linguists that they have identified the dimensions in this realm on which words differ from one another and have investigated in considerable detail how the various distinctions apply to a fairly large set of vocabulary items. Only LDCE makes a real attempt to record such information, and the information cannot be recovered from the definitions given in the other dictionaries, e.g., (6a) provides no information that would distinguish the 'transitive' noun *husband* from the 'intransitive' expression *married man:*

(6) a. *husband* (AH) 1. A man joined to a woman in marriage . . .
     b. John is a married man.
     b'. ??John is Mary's married man.[7]

This last fault of omission is in fact closely related to some systematic positive respects in which existing lexicography misrepresents vocabulary. I now turn from omissions, which can be corrected by supplementing existing dictionary entries in fairly obvious ways (though to do the corrections satisfactorily, one must have reasonable familiarity with what is omitted), to faults whose correction calls for some substantial changes in lexicographers' attitudes towards the dictionary entries that they compose.

3. Faults in Dictionaries

The failure of lexicographers to indicate that *husband* is a 'transitive' noun reflects two ubiquitous characteristics of lexicography: (i) that the dictionary entry specifies information that is internal to the word and omits information about the syntagmatic and paradigmatic relations in which it stands, and (ii) that a description of the referent of a word is regarded as a satisfactory definition of the word. One is in fact not justified in assuming that an accurate description of the sorts of individuals that can be referred to as husbands necessarily tells what the contribution of the word *husband* to the meaning of a sentence is. The more general point being made here is brought out nicely by an example due to Richmond Thomason (cited in Gupta 1980:16), who points out that every integer (positive, zero, or negative) is both a successor (of something) and a predecessor (of something), but that doesn't make *successor* and *predecessor* semantically vacuous when applied to integers: *3 is the successor of 2* means something quite different from *3 is the predecessor of 2*. The contribution of *husband*, as well as that of *successor* or *predecessor*, to the meaning of a sentence has to do not just with what kind of object it refers to but with the relationship of that object to another object that is generally mentioned elsewhere in the sentence.

The definitions typically given to the word *bride* illustrate respects in which descriptions of referents are inadequate as definitions:

(7) *bride* (AH) A woman who has recently been married or is about to be married.

Like the definition of *husband* in (6a), this definition fails to indicate that *bride*, like *husband*, is 'transitive':

(8) *My sister is a bride.
John's bride wore an exquisite gown.

In addition, (7) indicates in a very inaccurate way the relationship between the meaning of *bride* and the wedding that the word alludes to. While, for obvious and uninteresting reasons, a wedding is most frequently spoken of shortly before and shortly after it takes place, *bride* and all the other words that allude to the ceremony can be used perfectly well with reference to ceremonies that are in the distant past or future, e.g., the fact that the ceremony in question took place over 2000 years ago doesn't stop one from saying *Julius Caesar's bride*. What makes it appropriate to say *John's bride* (or even *the bride*, with reference to a wedding that is already under discussion) is not how far in the future or past the woman's wedding is but whether the wedding is being used as a reference point in identifying her. *Bride* differs from *wife* in that with the latter it is not the wedding but the married state that serves as the reference point, an observation that is confirmed by the striking difference that emerges when each word is combined with *recent:*

(9) a. John's recent bride = the woman that recently became John's wife
     b. John's recent wife = the woman that recently was John's wife (but no longer is, as a result of divorce or death)

John's recent bride isn't his recent wife unless they got divorced awfully quickly. The style of lexicography used in Wierzbicka (1971, 1980), in which clauses like 'who is thought of as . . .' abound, allows for much more accuracy here than does the style currently typical of dictionaries; the word *bride* contributes to the meaning of a sentence not just a description of a person but a description of her in terms of a role that she plays in a certain event.

4. Definitions in Dictionaries

Another ubiquitous characteristic of existing lexicography that has worked to its detriment is (iii) that lexicographers cling to the classical 'genus plus differentiae' formula ('X which is Y,' with X the genus and Y the differentiae) for definitions without at the same time trying very hard to get the genus right. For example, the following definition of the technical baseball sense of *ball* (10a), if taken literally, appears to put balls in that sense in the genus of spherical physical objects rather than in the genus of events; it is accordingly less accurate than stigmatized sentences such as (10b), in which the use of *when* points fairly clearly to events as the genus:[8]

(10) a. *ball* (AH) 4. A pitched ball not swung at by the batter that does not pass through the strike zone.
      b. A ball is when a pitch doesn't go through the strike zone and the batter doesn't swing at it.

Closely related to characteristic (ii) is the fact that (iv) dictionary definitions are presented as if all their content is part of the meaning of the word defined, when in fact the 'encyclopedic information' that makes up a large part of many definitions is not part of the meaning of the word at all but merely serves to fix the reference either of the word or of something alluded to in the word. Some definitions of *horse* illustrate this point well:

(11) a. *horse* (W3) A large solid-hoofed herbivorous mammal (*Equus caballus*) domesticated by man since a pre-historic period and used as a beast of burden, as a draft animal, or for riding, and distinguished from the other members of the genus *Equus* and the family Equidae by the long hair of the mane and tail, the usual presence of a callosity on the inside of the hind leg below the hock, and other less constant characters (as the larger size, larger hooves, more arched neck, small head, short ears).

   b. *horse* (SO) A solid-hoofed perissodactyl quadruped (*Equus caballus*), having a flowing tail; its voice is a neigh. In domestic state used as a beast of burden and draught, and esp. for riding upon.

The bulk of these definitions is information about the species *Equus caballus* that one in fact need not know in order to knew what *horse* means (I know what *horse* meant before I read W3's definition, even though it was from that definition that I first learned of the callosity on the inside of the hind leg), but which serves to distinguish that species from other species. Any satisfactory definition of *horse* amounts to 'member of species X' plus information that serves to specify what species X is (possibly including the information that X is called *Equus caballus*). I reject as mistaken the popular belief that some specific choice of that information serves to define *horse* (or any other species word). Only by historical accident can any list of facts describe exactly one species. The history of this planet could perfectly well have turned out in such a way that besides horses there was another species of large herbivores that also had been used as beasts of burden since prehistoric times, had long manes and tails, had callosities on the insides of their hind legs, etc., but were biologically distinct from horses and were called by a separate name. Likewise, historical accident is responsible for the fact that some of the pieces of information given in definitions like (11) serve to distinguish the species in question from other species; the reference to the long mane is probably there in order to distinguish *horse* from *donkey,* and the history of the world could perfectly well have turned out in such a way that no such species as the donkey evolved but *Equus caballus* did evolve.

   Existing dictionary definitions of words like *horse* are inaccurate in that, first, they do not make clear how the notions of member and species play a role in the meaning of the word, and second, they do not make clear that the encyclopedic information is an aid to identifying the reference of the word rather than part of its meaning. As the definitions stand, they make it sound as if the encyclopedic information provided criteria for an object to be a horse when they in fact provide only criteria for a species to be *Equus caballus*. When you say that Dobbin, the beast on your grandfather's farm, is a horse, you are not saying that Dobbin has been used as a beast of burden since prehistoric times or that Dobbin has a long mane. Dobbin did not exist in prehistoric times and need not have been used as a beast of burden ever in order to be a horse, and if his mane were shorn off, he would remain a horse and not become a donkey. To typically have a long mane is a property of the species *Equus caballus,* not a condition that an individual beast must meet in order to qualify for membership in that species.

The applicability of words like *horse* to particular beasts depends not only on information that serves to identify the particular species but also on the notion of species itself and the factual knowledge that governs the applicability of that notion, a point that is brought out in an interesting way by a consideration of such questions as, What does a two-headed unicorn look like? I have received a considerable variety of answers from the persons to whom I have asked this question, including the following:

(12)   What does a two-headed unicorn look like? (Answers:)

   a.   It has two heads, each with a horn in the middle of the forehead.
   b.   It has two heads, one with a horn in the middle of the forehead and one without.
   c.   It has two heads and a single horn that is rooted in the middle of both foreheads.

The most common answer is some version of (12a), in which *unicorn* is treated as denoting a biological species (albeit a nonexistent one) that is subject to the same sorts of genetic and embryological pathology as are extant species, notwithstanding the fact that beasts with two horns would then be describable as unicorns. (These interviews are even more amusing when conducted in German, where the question is *Wie sieht ein zweiköpfiges Einhorn aus?*). The far less common answers in (12b–c) reflect adherence to a 'classical' definition that involves 'one horn,' plus either ignorance of how biological species work or willingness to divorce the use of (ostensibly) biological terms from one's knowledge of biology. From the point of view taken by those who answer as in (12a), the answer in (12b) describes a beast that is doubly a freak: it is a freak by virtue of its extra head, and it is a freak by virtue of the absence of a horn from that head.

I note in passing that biological species nouns do not have accurate definitions that fit the classical 'genus plus differentiae' formula ('X which is Y,' with X the genus and Y the differentiae). An accurate definition must amount to something of the form 'member of species X'; the only part of such a definition that could plausibly serve as a classical 'genus' is 'member'; but since 'of species X' is not the equivalent of a restrictive relative clause (that was the point made above regarding *predecessor/successor of Y*), the remainder of the definition does not have the syntactic role that classical differentiae must have.[9] While the encyclopedic information in definitions like (11) plays a role that could reasonably be called "differentiae," what it differentiates is not different instances of the genus (here, different kinds of 'members') but rather a term that the classical formula, interpreted literally, does not provide for.

Encyclopedic information is by no means restricted to biological species words, nor even to words (such as *Glaswegian* or *shortstop*) whose meanings involve references to things (here, the city of Glasgow and the game of baseball) that exist only by historical accident. The following definitions illustrate the use of encyclopedic information in distinguishing the terms of a universal contrast:

(13) a. *right* (AH) 10a. Of, pertaining to, or toward that side of the human body in which the liver is normally located. 10b. Of, pertaining to, or toward the corresponding side of something relative to the observer's point of view.

   b. *left* (AH) 1. Designating, belonging to, or located on the side of the body to the north when the subject is facing east. 2a. Designating or located on the corresponding side of anything that can be said to have a front. 2b. Designating or located on the side nearest to the left hand of the subject or agent.

   c. *left* (SO) Distinctive either of the hand which is normally weaker, and of the other parts of the body on the same side of the body . . . hence also of what pertains to the corresponding side of anything else.

   d. *left* (RH) Of, pertaining to, or belonging to the side of a person that is turned to the west when the subject is facing north.

The words *right* and *left* presuppose a division of certain things into two 'sides,' and to specify which of the two sides is called right and which one left, it is necessary to make use of encyclopedic information about objects that have an asymmetry between their two sides.[10] Which object and which asymmetry are brought into the definition doesn't matter much, as long as information about the asymmetry is fairly accessible to the reader. What is objectionable about the definitions in (13) is not the sometimes quaint choice of encyclopedic information but their failure to indicate what notion of 'side' is relevant. We speak of objects not only as having a right side and a left side but also as having a front side and a back side, and only with the former understanding of 'side' does the definition accord with the lexicographer's intentions. The relevant notion of 'side' presupposes an object that has a front and a back,[11] and refers to the halves into which the object is divided by a vertical plane running from its front to its back. Since any encyclopedic information is as good as any other encyclopedic information, as long as it draws the distinction accurately and is not too obscure, a lexicographer could legitimately utilize encyclopedic information about the dictionary itself, e.g., by referring to a diagram as in (14):

(14)   *left* The half indicated below (the diagram represents an object having a front and a back, viewed from above):

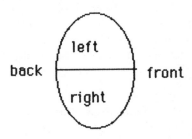

I conjecture that the fact that diagrams as in (14) have not been exploited in dictionaries results from lexicographers' mistaken beliefs that encyclopedic information in definitions is part of the meaning of words and that the meanings of words in all cases can and ought to be expressed in words.

A further deficiency of the definitions in (13) is that they do not indicate how the meanings of *right* and *left* figure in the meanings of expressions containing them. For example, while the definitions make extensive use of the expression 'the corresponding side,' they give no clue as to which correspondence one is to employ in which cases, e.g., they say nothing from which one can predict that if John and Mary are facing the speaker, the configuration described by (15a) can alternatively be described not by (15b) but rather by (15c):

(15)   a.   John is on Mary's right.
       b.   John is to the right of Mary.
       c.   John is to the left of Mary.

Occasionally definitions of other terms indicate the appropriate way to combine *right* or *left* with the spatial configuration alluded to, e.g.,

(16)   *right field*   (AH)   The part of the outfield that is to the right as viewed from home plate.

To the right and *to the left* relate to the division of an observer's visual field into two halves, and a definition must indicate the observer's vantage point if *to the right/left* is to contribute anything to the definition.[12]

5. Definitions of Grammatical Terms

I turn now to a vocabulary area that has been especially poorly served by existing dictionaries and will suggest that the quality of definitions in that area could be improved greatly if lexicographers were to heed the morals drawn above in connection with *horse*. Ironically, the most inaccurate definitions to be found, even in highly prestigious dictionaries, are those of grammatical terms. It is rare when a dictionary's definition of a grammatical term accords with the way that that term is used in that same dictionary. For example, SO's definition of *adjective* does not accord with SO's labeling of words like *former, potential,* and *total,* as in *former wife, potential murderer,* and *total idiot,* as adjectives:

(17)   *adjective*   (SO)   A word added to the name of a thing and signifying an attribute of the thing.

Former, potential, and *total* do not express attributes of individuals that one refers to as a wife, a murderer, or an idiot (*Gee, Tom, your wife is awfully former these days!*). The ubiquity of definitions like (17) even in highly respected dictionaries like SO is the result of lexicographers' uncritical acceptance of definitions offered by grammarians.[13] The definitions of grammatical terms that grammarians have offered in fact bear very little relation to the grammarians' professional work and are in most cases merely rationalizations by which a grammarian discharged the supposed obligation to define terms before using them and thereby freed himself to get down to the real business of doing grammar without fear of being lynched by upholders of the ideology that recognizes such an obligation. When, as has usually been the case, the ideology that makes an unwilling lexicographer out of the grammarian is combined with a reductionist ideology, grammarians will define the vocabulary of grammar in extragrammatical terms, thereby forcing themselves to abstain from definitions that presuppose grammatical notions such as 'part of speech' or 'grammatical relation,' even where such presuppositions are very much in order.

Parts of speech are much more like biological species than has generally been recognized. Within any part of speech, or any biological species, there is considerable diversity. Parts of speech can be distinguished from one another, just as biological species can be distinguished from one another, in terms of characteristics that are typical for the members of that part of speech (or species), even though none of those properties need be instantiated by all members of the part of speech (or species). The most prototypic representatives of the category 'adjective' do in fact serve as modifiers of nouns (I take it that in SO's definition, 'added to' and 'name of a thing' are euphemisms for 'modifying' and 'noun') and do in fact express properties of the denotatum of the noun (more accurately, the denotatum of the NP of which the noun is the head), though these characteristics are neither necessary nor sufficient for membership in the category 'adjective.' Examples have already been given of adjectives that do not denote properties of objects. Predicate adjectives as in (18a) are adjectives even though they do not, strictly speaking, serve as modifiers in that construction, and words such as *bitch, breeze, beauty*, as used in (18b) denote properties of objects and serve as modifiers of nouns but are not adjectives:

> (18) a. I am happy.
>   b. Definitions are a bitch of a problem.

Each part of speech is a fuzzy category (cf. Rosch 1973) whose core consists of items possessing semantic, syntactic, and morphological characteristics that are typical of the part of speech, and whose periphery consists of items having some but not all of the properties that characterize the core of the category. An accurate definition of a part-of-speech word like *adjective* must amount to 'member of part-of-speech' plus encyclopedic information distinguishing that part of speech from other parts of speech. It presupposes the notion 'part of speech' in the same way that a definition of *horse* or *elm* presupposes a notion of species, and the encyclopedic information about the particular part of speech does not embody necessary or sufficient conditions for a word to belong to that part of speech. Once in a while, published definitions of grammatical terms take a form similar to that which is used in definitions of biological species terms, e.g.,

> (19) *adjective* (W3)   A word belonging to one of the major form classes in any of a great many languages, typically used as a modifier of a noun to denote a quality of the thing named . . . to indicate its quantity or extent (as *five* in *five cows, every* in *every word*) or else to specify or designate a thing as distinct from something else (as *these* in *these wheels*), and in many languages declined for gender, number, and case and agreeing in all these respects with the noun it modifies but in English having no such inflections (except for *this*, plural *these*, and *that*, plural *those*).

I regard this definition as exemplary. Note that it presupposes the notion of 'part of speech' (= '(major) form class'), makes clear that the encyclopedic information given consists of criteria for distinguishing one 'form class' from other form classes, not for determining whether a particular word belongs to that form class, and represents the relation of an adjective to the part of speech 'adjective' as parallel to that of a horse to the species *Equus caballus*.

Grammatical relation words like *subject* also demand a treatment parallel to that of biological species words and also usually do not get it:

(20) a. *subject* (W3) A word or group denoting that of which something is affirmed or predicated: a term that is construed with or without modifiers as the nominative of a verb and is grammatically either a noun or a word, phrase, or clause used as a noun equivalent.

     b. *subject* (SO) The member or part of a sentence denoting that concerning which something is predicated (i.e., of which a statement is made, a question asked, or a desire expressed); a word or group of words constituting the 'nominative' to a finite verb.

The information contained in the first clause of each of these definitions characterizes not the notion of subject but that of topic.[14] The subject of a clause (more generally, of a 'nexus' in Jespersen's (1924) sense) need not even denote anything, let alone anything of which something is predicated, as illustrated by *there* in (21a), and the thing of which a statement is made, a question asked, or a desire expressed need not be the subject, as illustrated by *the proof* in (21a), *Frank* in (21b), and *some coffee* in (21c):

(21) a. There is an error in the proof.
     b. Is anything the matter with Frank?
     c. Get me some coffee.

Moreover, a subject need not be in the nominative case and the verb of which it is the subject need not be finite, as illustrated by the genitive subject of *quitting* in (22a) and the accusative subject of *to quit* in (22b):

(22) a. His quitting his job came as a complete surprise.
     b. For him to quit his job would be ridiculous.

The things mentioned in the definitions in (20) are indeed relevant to distinguishing 'subject' from other grammatical relations, but an accurate definition would have to take a form unlike that in (20), say, something beginning "a word or expression standing in that grammatical relation for which, typically . . . ," with the information embodied in (20) presented not as conditions under which an expression is the subject of something but as characteristics distinguishing the subject relation from other grammatical relations (e.g., if there is a topic, it will most typically stand in the subject relation, though not all clauses have topics and not all topics serve as subjects).

6. Individuation and Organization of Lexical Information in Dictionaries

One further, and for the purposes of this chapter, final, respect in which linguistics has something of value to contribute to lexicography is that linguists take questions of individuation and identity much more seriously than lexicographers generally have, and in particular, they take more seriously than lexicographers do the sorts of units that lexicographers have set up (lexical item, lexical entry, sense of a lexical item, etc.) and have made significant, albeit fragmentary, contributions to the general question of how one can justify particular organizations of lexical information. For example, Zwicky and Sadock (1975) provides a critical evaluation of proposed tests of ambiguity that can be used in determining whether putatively different senses of a lexical item are really different. Green (1969) provides discussion of the conditions under which distinct senses of a lexical item are related though distinct. Weinreich (1964) criticizes W3 for its failure to exploit parallelisms among the senses of related lexical items, noting, e.g., that had W3 exploited the correspondence between intransitive uses of *turn* and parallel causative senses of transitive *turn,* they could have avoided the inaccuracy in their definition (23a) of a sense of intransitive *turn* that corresponds to transitive *turn* in the expression that it defines as in (23b):

(23) a. *turn* v.i. . . . 8. to become nauseated (of one's stomach)
      b. *turn one's stomach* to disgust completely; to nauseate, sicken

The use of *turn* in (23a) (as in *My stomach turned*) refers not to a stomach becoming nauseated but to a person becoming nauseated, exactly as in (23b). Had W3 explicitly related *X's stomach turned* to turn X's stomach, they wouldn't have confused the roles of the stomach and the person as they did in (23a). Weinreich points out that by devoting appropriate attention to the individuation and relatedness of lexical entries, W3 could have significantly increased the accuracy of their definitions while at the same time decreasing their bulk, a point that illustrates the complaint I voiced earlier in this paper, that dictionary entries are typically constructed without regard to the paradigmatic and syntagmatic relations in which the item defined stands. I am heartened by the sharp break with that tradition that is manifested in LDCE, which contains cross-references galore, integrated into the definitions by the simple and effective device of printing in capitals (with parenthesized numerals to indicate subentries) the words in the definition to which the reader is referred for additional information.

There are many other things about LCDE that I find heartening, including the highly efficient system that it employs for indicating the syntactic characteristics of each sense of each item (compared to LDCE, the other dictionaries with their 'v.t.' and 'v.i.' are still in the stage of counting 'one, two, three, many'), but I am especially heartened by the not coincidental circumstance that LDCE has made more extensive use of the services of linguists than has any of its predecessors. In saying this, however, I do not wish to be taken as implying that I think improved dictionaries will necessarily result if the publishers of dictionaries hire more linguists. The amount of serious detailed study of extensive bodies of vocabulary done by linguists is quite small,[15] and until such research becomes less rare than it has been, publishers of dictionaries have little motivation to make greater use of work by linguists than they have so far. LDCE's linguists had their act together (many were participants in Randolph Quirk's remarkably productive Survey of English Usage), and LDCE's success is due in large part to Longmans's wise choice of whom to exploit and how to exploit them. I hope this chapter will be of some benefit to potential exploitees looking for ways to be exploited to the mutual benefit of themselves and their exploiters.

NOTES

1. This example was brought to my attention by Masaru Kajita.
2. The following abbreviations are used here in references to and citations from dictionaries:

> AH = *American Heritage Dictionary of the English Language.* New York: American Heritage, 1969.
> ALD = A. S. Hornby, E. V. Gatenby, and H. Wakefield, *The Advanced Learner's Dictionary of Current English,* 2nd edition. Oxford: Oxford University Press, 1963.
> LDCE = *Longman Dictionary of Contemporary English,* London: Longman, 1978.
> RH = *Random House Dictionary.* New York: Random House, 1966.
> SO = *Shorter Oxford Dictionary,* revised and corrected 3rd edition. Oxford: Clarendon Press, 1977.
> W3 = *Webster's International Dictionary,* 3rd edition. Springfield, MA: Merriam-Webster, 1961.

3. AH does, however, usually give definitions of count nouns in a form that begins with *a* and a singular noun, thereby conveying that it is in fact a count noun, e.g.,

> *expert* (AH) 1. A person with a high degree of skill in or knowledge of a certain subject.

Strictly speaking, this is a definition not of *expert* but of *an expert.*
4. These statements are considerably oversimplified. Negative polarity items differ with regard to how strongly negative a context they demand or whether some sort of conditional or interrogative structure will suffice in lieu of a negation, and positive polarity items can be combined with normally negative elements if the element either does not express a real negation or is combined with other negative elements in such a way as to be semantically 'canceled':

> Did John *lift a finger* to help me?
> *Did John arrive *until* 5:00?

You *wouldn't* *rather* be in Philadelphia, would you?
I know of no one who *wouldn't* *rather* be in Philadelphia.

5.   Holisky (1974) notes that there are relatively few instances like the following in which an idiom involves one specific negative item:

Your brother will *stop at nothing*.
*Your brother won't stop at anything.

6.   In both instances, it is in fact possible to use the word without an overt NP adjunct, though in such cases there is an understood anaphoric or generic NP adjunct:

John earns his living buying for Macy's.
A husband shouldn't be condescending to his wife.

7.   Were (6b′) ever uttered, *Mary's married man* would probably be interpreted as referring not to Mary's husband but to someone else's husband, with whom Mary was having an affair.

8.   One can avoid both the literal inaccuracy of (10a) and the stigmatized form of (10b) by recasting (10a) as 'a pitch not swung at. . . .' The problem of identifying the genus correctly is in a large part the problem of identifying what Gupta (1980) calls the 'principle of identity' that (according to Gupta, a point in which I concur in McCawley 1982) is part of the meaning of a common noun. Different senses of *ball* differ with regard to what they allow one to describe as 'the same ball'; similarly, different senses of *pitch* differ with regard to what counts as 'the same pitch' (the batter struck out on three pitches, all of which may have been instances of the same pitch, e.g., a knuckleball).

9.   The role of encyclopedic information in definitions is fairly close to that of *non-restrictive* relative clauses.

10.   It would be nice, though, to have the same asymmetry figure in the definitions of both words. I conjecture that one person defined words beginning with 'L' for AH and another person defined words beginning with 'R' and the two persons did not communicate much.

11.   This presupposition is alluded to in AH's definition of *left* but not of *right*.

12.   From the center fielder's vantage point, right field is to left. In defining *right field* as in (16) rather than as 'the part of the outfield that is to the left as viewed by a person in the outfield who is facing home plate,' the lexicographer indicates not only what *right field* refers to but also its relation to *right*.

13.   I assume that the task of lexicographers in giving definitions of technical terms is to report what the relevant specialists mean by those terms, not what those specialists mistakenly say or even think they mean by them. The lexicographer's primary concern should be with semantic fact, not with semantic folklore or semantic myth.

14.   There is a deplorable tradition, not only among grammarians and lexicographers, but even among linguists, of giving the terms 'subject,' 'topic,' 'agent,' and some-times also 'nominative' definitions appropriate to one of the other terms in the list, thus obscuring the fact that the first term refers to a grammatical relation, the second to an 'informational' relation, the third to a semantic relation, and the fourth to a

morphological relation. For extensive and highly illuminating discussion of the notion 'subject,' see Keenan (1976) and Perlmutter (1982).

15. This observation is made with particular force by Gross (1979), who notes that transformational grammarians typically make do with one or two examples of each phenomenon that they study, remaining oblivious to how large or small a set of lexical items participates in the phenomenon. For example, Raising-to-subject and Raising-to-object are generally treated on a par despite the fact that (according to Gross's count) 3 French verbs participate in the former and over 600 in the latter. Gross' conclusions can be summarized as: If transformational grammarians are so smart, why aren't they rich?

REFERENCES

Green, Georgia 1969. "On the notion 'related lexical entry.' " CLS 5, pp. 77–88.

Gross, Maurice 1979. "On the failure of generative grammar." *Language* 55, pp. 859–85.

Gupta, Anil 1980. *The Logic of Common Nouns*. New Haven, CT: Yale University Press.

Hinds, Marilyn 1974. "Double plusgood polarity items." CLS 10, pp. 259–68.

Holisky, Dee Ann 1974. *Negative Polarity*. Unpublished master's thesis, University of Chicago.

Jespersen, Otto 1924. *The philosophy of Grammar*. London: Allen and Unwin.

Keenan, Edward 1976. "Toward a universal definition of 'subject.' " In: Charles Li (ed.), *Subject and Topic*. New York: Academic Press, pp. 303–33.

McCawley, James D. 1975. "Lexicography and the count-mass distinction." BLS 1, pp. 314–21. Also in: James D. McCawley, *Adverbs, Vowels, and Other Objects of Wonder*. Chicago: University of Chicago Press, 1979, pp. 165–78.

McCawley, James D. (ed.) 1976. *Syntax and Semantics*, Vol. 7. *Notes from the Linguistic Underground*. New York: Academic Press.

McCawley, James D. 1982. Review of Gupta 1980. *Journal of Philosophy* 79, pp. 512–7.

McCawley, James D. 1984. *The Eater's Guide to Chinese Characters*. Chicago: University of Chicago Press.

Perlmutter, David 1982. "Syntactic representation, syntactic levels, and the notion of subject." In: P. Jacobson and G. K. Pullum (eds.), *The Nature of Syntactic Representation*. New York: Academic Press, pp. 283–340.

Rosch, Eleanor. 1973. On the internal structure of perceptual and semantic categories. In: T. Moore (ed.), *Cognitive Development and the Acquisition of Language*. New York: Academic Press, pp. 111–44.

Weinreich, Uriel 1964. "*Webster's Third:* A critique of its semantics." *IJAL* 30, pp. 405–9. Reprinted in: U. Weinreich, *On semantics*. Philadelphia: University of Pennsylvania Press, 1980, pp. 361–7.

Wierzbicka, Anna 1972. *Semantic Primitives*. Frankfurt: Athenäum.

Wierzbicka, Anna 1980. *Lingua mentalis*. Sydney and New York: Academic Press.

Zwicky, Arnold, and Jerrold M. Sadock 1975. "Ambiguity tests and how to fail them." *Syntax and Semantics*, Vol. 4. New York: Academic Press, pp. 1–36.

CHAPTER TWO

On Possible Applications of Script-Based Semantics

Victor Raskin

1. Encyclopedic Knowledge and the Scope of Semantic Theory

One of the most crucial problems of modern linguistics, as well as of the philosophy of language and cognitive psychology, is the existence of a boundary between our knowledge of language and our knowledge of the world. This problem seriously affects the possibility of meaningful applications of linguistics to other language-related fields. By drawing that boundary too close to its own central core, linguistics has come up with 'isolationist' theories and descriptions, which are not applicable outside of it and, it may be argued, not too much applicable inside, either. By pushing the boundary too far out, linguistics would make itself accountable for everything that can be expressed in language or, in other words, for everything there is in the world and thus render its own task unfeasible and its applications impossible.

Over twenty years ago, worrying about the feasibility of high-quality automatic translation, Bar-Hillel came up with this example (1964):

(1) Little John was looking for his toy box. Finally he found it. The box was in the *pen*.

In order to disambiguate the final word correctly, one should, of course, take into account the relative measurements of *box, pen*₁ ("an implement for writing"), and *pen*₂ ("a small enclosure for animals and children"). The problem as it presented itself to Bar-Hillel was how to introduce this information, which is not contained in any ordinary or formal dictionary, into the computer. There are two obvious strategies in this situation: either to decide that this cannot be done in principle (for instance, by calling this kind of information 'encyclopedic' and thus implying that it is not part of the dictionary and excluding it from the proper domain of linguistics) and abandon any problem whose solution depends on the availability of this semantic information; or to decide that if this and similar problems cannot be solved, linguistic semantics would lose its raison d'être, and to look for a solution of the problem.

Most recently, the problem of the boundary between our knowledge of language and our knowledge of the world has assumed still another guise. The former kind of knowledge is now assigned to the proper domain of semantics while the latter is delegated to pragmatics. In a somewhat half-hearted follow-up to the interpretive-generative battle of the late 1960s, Katz (1980) is attacked as an 'autonomous semanticist' by his adversaries who adhere to 'non-autonomous semantics' (Chomsky 1977; Jackendoff 1981).

Autonomous semantics presupposes a clear-cut distinction between semantic competence and semantic performance. Semantic competence includes meaning proper and should be studied by semantics. Semantic performance goes beyond semantics and actually belongs in pragmatics. Semantic competence is the knowledge of linguistic meaning. Semantic performance is the knowledge of extra-linguistic meaning. Non-autonomous semantics "claims that no clean point of separation exists where logical or semantic inference leaves off and pragmatic or knowledge-based inference begins; rather, the two kinds of inference are interdependent, or based on the same principles, or both" (Jackendoff 1981:425). According to Chomsky, only a very small part of meaning, the one he refers to somewhat misleadingly as 'logical form,' belongs to his sentence grammar. The rest of it, 'meaning' proper, incorporates information from the speakers' knowledge of the world.

The fight between the two sides reveals a surprising lack of difference with regard to the feasibility of semantic research. Katz wants to discard most of semantics and study the uninteresting remainder. Chomsky and Jackendoff strive to broaden the scope of semantic phenomena by claiming that more and more information should be included in semantics and that this information is basically of a pragmatic nature. In doing this, they exclude almost every single semantic phenomenon from Chomsky's sentence grammar and therefore from his linguistics in general, for Chomsky does not have any non-sentence grammar to offer.

If Katz's position is vacuous, Chomsky and Jackendoff's is outright defeatist and not really distinct from the spirit of Bloomfield's notorious anti-semantical statement in which he claimed that in order to know the meaning of any simple word one has to possess precise information about everything that surrounds one, and since the state of human knowledge is not sufficient for this kind of information to be available, Bloomfield concludes that one cannot know the meaning of any word with the exception of technical and scientific terms (see 1964:Chapter 9). Similarly, Chomsky and Jackendoff declare every semantic phenomenon and issue to be dependent on pragmatic factors related to "the speakers' belief systems" (Jackendoff 1981:425) and, therefore, also inaccessible, even if they do not say so explicitly.

The goal of the script-based semantic theory proposed here is to account for the meaning of every sentence in every context it occurs. The theory does not incorporate our entire knowledge of the world and does not claim that it is possible to do so. It subscribes to the view shared by most if not all sciences and propounded by a highly defensible philosophy of language that the ultimate impossibility or infinity of the problem should not prevent one from trying to get as near its solution as possible. The theory recognizes the existence of a boundary between our knowledge of language and our knowledge of the world and, being a linguistic theory, does not account for what is on the other side of the boundary. However, it pushes the boundary much further out than any other available formal semantic theory. As a result, it becomes capable of accounting for contextual meaning and, therefore, applicable to those adjacent language-related areas for which the notion of context is crucial.

The next two sections contain a brief exposition of a contextual semantic theory while the final two sections, preceded by a section touching on linguistic applications in general, deal—equally briefly—with its applications.

For further and more detailed discussion of linguistic and encyclopedic knowledge see Raskin (1985a,b); of the script-based semantic theory, Raskin (1984:59–98; in press); of linguistic applications in general, Raskin (1982; 1984:45–58; 1985); to rhetoric and composition, Raskin (1981b); and to humor, Raskin (1984).

2. Script-Based Lexicon

The lexicon of the proposed semantic theory is based on the notion of 'script.' The script is a large chunk of semantic information surrounding the word or evoked by it. The script is a cognitive structure internalized by the native speaker, and it represents the native speaker's knowledge of a small part of the world. Every speaker has internalized rather a large repertoire of scripts of 'common sense' which represents his/her knowledge of certain routines, standard procedures, basic situations, etc., for instance, the knowledge of what people do in certain situations, how they do it, in what order, and so on. Beyond the scripts of 'common sense' every native speaker may, and usually does, have individual scripts determined by his/her individual background and subjective experience and restricted scripts which the speaker shares with a certain group, e.g., family, neighbors, colleagues, and so forth, but not with the whole speech community of native speakers of the same language.

What is labelled here 'script' has been called 'schema,' 'frame,' 'demon,' etc. On the other hand, the term 'script' has been sometimes reserved for a temporal sequence of frames. The notion has been used extensively in a number of adjacent fields such as psychology, sociology, anthropology, artificial intelligence, education (see, for instance, Bartlett 1932; Bateson 1972; Charniak 1972, 1975; Schank 1975; Schank and Abelson 1977; Minsky 1975; Goffman 1974; Chafe 1977; Tannen 1979; Freedle 1977, 1979). I will not elaborate here on the terminological differences between the use of the term 'script' here and the use of the same or similar terms elsewhere.

Formally or technically, every script is a graph with lexical nodes and semantic links between the nodes. In fact, all the scripts of the language make up a single continuous graph, and the lexical entry of a word is a domain within this graph around the word in question as the central node of the domain. Somewhat tentatively and simplistically, (2) represents a domain of the continuous graph which (partially) contains two lexical entries—for *color* and *artifact.*

(2)

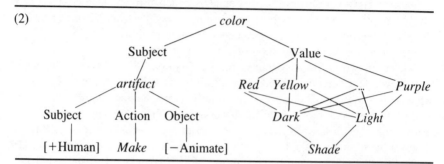

As shown in (2), the links characterize the relations between the nodes, often but not necessarily in terms of the roles assigned to one node with regard to the other. Two important features of the scripts not shown in (2) are the distance and the emphasis. The first feature involves the relative length of the links between the nodes—thus the link between *color* and *artifact* is, in fact, much longer than those between *artifact* and the three nodes under it, which reflects the fact that the idea of color is much less related to the meaning of *artifact* than the situation of a human producing something inanimate. The second feature emphasizes certain nodes with respect to others—thus in the domain of the graph which is the lexical entry for *artifact* the node [−Animate] should be emphasized to reflect the fact that it is this node which is actually the central part of the meaning in question.

The fact that the constituents of the sentence evoke pieces of semantic information which go beyond the usual lexical entries for these constituents in the existing ordinary dictionaries or in the lexicons of the existing formal semantic theories can be illustrated by the examples of (3), especially when compared to (4).

(3) (i)   John was a dime short and had to do without milk.
     (ii) Mary saw a black cat and immediately turned back home.

(4) (i)   John was a dime short and had to do without family.
     (ii) Mary saw a black cat and immediately bought a bicycle.

Similarly, the native speaker will understand (5i) and (5ii) differently—the former will not raise any question as to the reason for John's failure while the latter will:

(5) (i)   John tried to eat his hamburger with a spoon but did not succeed.

    (ii)   John tried to eat his hamburger with a fork and knife but did not succeed.

The semantic difference between the two sentences cannot be accounted for in terms of an ordinary lexicon, whether formalized or not. Thus, a typical dictionary such as Webster (1976) would describe the appropriate meanings of the key words as (6):

(6)   (i)   EAT vt: 1.   To take in through the mouth as food: ingest, chew and swallow in turn

     (ii)   HAMBURGER n: 2.   A sandwich consisting of a patty of hamburger [ground beef] in a split bun

    (iii)   SPOON n: 1.   An eating or cooking implement consisting of a small shallow bowl with a handle

Neither these lexical items nor the ones in terms of which they are described, e.g., *sandwich, beef, bun,* contain any information about the fact that hamburgers do not belong to the class of liquid or dry substances that can be eaten with a spoon. However, it is exactly this piece of semantic information which makes the speaker's perception of (5i) different from that of (5ii). Since this semantic information is obviously available to the native speaker its source is a script which includes a small domain like (7i). The full script for *spoon* will also include additional links and nodes such as (7ii–iv):

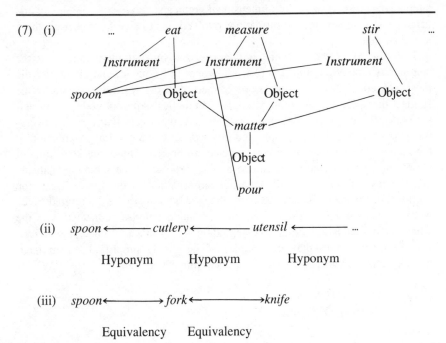

(ii)   *spoon* ⟵———— *cutlery* ⟵———— *utensil* ⟵———— ...

       Hyponym   Hyponym   Hyponym

(iii)   *spoon* ⟷———— *fork* ⟷———— *knife*

       Equivalency   Equivalency

(iv)

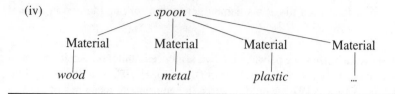

The names assigned to the links both in (2) and (7)—'object,' 'subject,' 'action,' 'instrument,' 'material,' 'hyponym,' 'equivalency' [membership in the same category], 'value'—can be treated simply as convenience terms for the purposes of this book. Generally, the theory resorts to two alternative ways to accommodate this type of information: 1) postulating a number of standard semantic relations along these lines and trying to keep them at a limited number and at roughly the same level of abstractness in order to avoid the arbitrariness and unwieldiness of Mel'čuk's 'sense ↔ text' model (1979); or 2) postulating abstract, non-lexical nodes corresponding each to one type or subtype of link and having all the pertinent lexical nodes connected with those non-lexical nodes by the same unnamed link. According to the latter alternative, each verb, for instance, will be connected by an unnamed link to one of the non-lexical nodes marked 'Subject,' which will contain exactly the kind of subject the verb takes, e.g., [+Animate] for *sleep*. Both alternatives are interestingly compatible with, though clearly distinct from, Fillmore's early idea of deep cases (1968). Both alternatives presuppose a multidimensional graph and, given the complexity and heterogeneity of semantic information involved, it is naive to expect anything less than that.

Every word of the sentence is characterized by a limited domain of the continuous semantic graph. Every word evokes this domain, and obviously, the most adjacent nodes, i.e., the nodes connected to the word-itself node by the shortest links, are evoked more strongly than the less adjacent nodes. In principle, since the graph is continuous and all-inclusive, every word evokes everything which is there in the graph, and this seems to be a good approximation of the native speaker's semantic performance. In practice, however, the limits of the evocation process are determined by the purposes of the semantic analysis, and the rest of the potentially evocable information is disregarded. For the purposes of the analysis outlined here, the evoked domain can be limited to the word-itself node and to one 'circle' of surrounding nodes connected with the word by a limited number of such essential links as 'subject,' 'object,' 'activity,' etc. (8i–ii) are representative examples of the greatly simplified, streamlined, and discretized concept of script as used in this paper.

(8)   (i)   DOCTOR
       Subject: [+Human] [+Adult]

Activity: > Study medicine
         = Receive patients: patient comes or doctor visits
                             doctor listens to complaints
                             doctor examines patient
         = Cure disease: doctor diagnoses disease
                          doctor prescribes treatment
         = (Take patient's money)
Place: > Medical School
         = Hospital or doctor's office
Time: > Many years
         = Every day
         = Immediately
Condition: Physical contact

(ii) LOVER
Subject: [+Human] [+Adult] [+Sex: x]
Activity: Make love
Object: [+Human] [+Adult] [+Sex: x̄]
Place: Secluded
Time: > Once
       = Regularly
Condition: If subject or object married, spouse(s) should not know

The scripts of (8) are not very elementary in the sense that they themselves utilize the material of other scripts, which is usually the case with scripts. It is important to understand that in the full-fledged script-based semantic theory, the scripts are constructed from the elementary level up in order to avoid the typical lexicographic circularity.

3. Combinatorial Rules

Every word of the sentence evokes a script or scripts with which it is associated. Obviously, the node for an ambiguous word will be the center of two or more domains of the continuous graph, and, in principle, each of these domains will be evoked when the word is uttered. The main function of the combinatorial rules in the script-based semantic theory is to combine the scripts evoked by the words of the sentence into one or more compatible combinations. An unambiguous sentence will be associated with just one compatible combination of evoked scripts, an *n*-way ambiguous sentence with *n* compatible combinations. The semantic interpretation of the sentence does not coincide with the compatible combination(s) of evoked scripts but is determined by it/them. (9i) below is a blend of two hackneyed examples from semantic works of the last two decades, the word *bachelor* and the sentence *the man hit the colorful ball,* first discussed by Katz and Fodor (1963) and then by their friends and foes alike. With another potentially ambiguous word, *paralyzed,* thrown in, (9i) is a representative example of the ambiguous sentence treated in terms of the evoked scripts by the combinatorial rules. In (9ii), the evoked scripts are assigned tentative and almost arbitrary but self-explanatory names for the sake of this discussion. (9iii) lists all the potentially compatible combinations of the evoked scripts (with the script for *the,* DEFINITE, deliberately omitted):

(9) (i)   The   paralyzed   bachelor   hit   the
    (ii)   1. DISEASE   1. MARRIAGE   1. COLLISION
                 2. MORAL   2. ACADEME   2. DISCOVERY
                                3. KNIGHT
                                4. SEAL

             colorful   ball
             1. COLOR   1. ARTIFACT
             2. EVALUATION   2. ASSEMBLY
    (iii)   11111, 11112, 11212, 11222, 12111, 12112, 12212, 12222,
             13111, 13112, 13212, 13222, 14111,
             21111, 21112, 21212, 21222, 22111, 22112, 22212, 22222,
             23111, 23112, 23212, 23222

The 12 scripts listed in (9ii) can be theoretically combined in 64 ways. The combinatorial rules will reduce this number to the 25 potentially compatible combinations listed in the obvious way in (9iii). Thus 11212, for instance, is a combination of Script 1 for *paralyzed,* Script 1 for *bachelor,* Script 2 for *hit,* Script 1 for *colorful* and Script 2 for *ball,* and it is paraphrased below as (10i). 14111 and 23222 are paraphrased as in (10ii) and (10iii), respectively:

(10)   (i)   A never-married man who cannot move (some of) his limbs discovered (found himself at) a large dancing party abundant with bright colors.
       (ii)   A fur seal which cannot move (some of) its limbs pushed (with its nose?) a spheric object painted in bright colors.
       (iii) A young knight who serves under the standard of another knight and who finds that he is unable to act (a pacifist?) discovered (found himself at) a large and picturesque dancing party.

While it does follow from (9) that (9i) is potentially 25-ways ambiguous, for most native speakers it would be hard to discover all these ambiguities without their being prompted by the appropriate obvious contexts (see Raskin 1977). Whenever (if ever) (9i) is actually used, the actual linguistic and extralinguistic context will disambiguate it for any native speaker, and the combinatorial rules should be able to do the same, otherwise the theory will lose its adequacy. This is one of the many requirements on the combinatorial rules, and (11) is an example on which the functioning of the combinatorial rules will be non-technically illustrated:

(11) I got up in the morning, took a shower and made myself some breakfast.
Then I went out and started the car.

(12) Then I went out and started the car.

(11) is a short discourse, and the combinatorial rules will be applied to its second sentence, repeated as (12) for a convenient reference. First, let us list the scripts evoked by the words of (12)—for the sake of simplicity again, they are not really listed but rather alluded to in an informal and self-explanatory way:

(13) (i)   THEN adv: 1. At that time
                          2. Next in order of time
                          3. In that case
      (ii)   I pron: 1. Speaker or writer
      (iii) GO OUT v: 1. Leave shelter
                          2. Entertain oneself outside one's home
      (iv)   AND conj: 1. [Connection or addition]
      (v)   START vt: 1. Cause to move
                          2. Bring into being
                          3. Begin the use
      (vi)   THE det: 1. Definite
                          2. Unique
      (vii) CAR n: 1. Horse carriage
                          2. Automobile
                          3. Railway carriage
                          4. Cage of an elevator

At Stage Zero of the process of semantic interpretation of (12), the scripts evoked by its words will include a few more scripts unlisted in (13), e.g., the adjective script for *then* as in *the then secretary of state* or the intransitive script(s) for *start* as in *he started when he heard the shot*. The combinatorial rules filter these syntactically inappropriate scripts on the basis of the syntactic structure associated with (12):

(14)

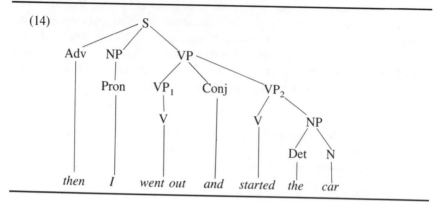

The part of the scripts which is most related to the syntactic information of (14) is a set of named links or, alternatively, non-lexical nodes, such as 'subject,' 'object,' 'instrument,' etc. Combining this information from the scripts with (14), the combinatorial rules get rid of those scripts evoked by the words in (12) which are syntactically incompatible with (14).

At Stage One, the combinatorial rules have to determine which mode of communication (12) is uttered in. If there are no clues to the contrary or, most often, no explicit clues at all, the combinatorial rules introduce the bona fide communication mode (cf. Grice 1975; Searle 1969; Raskin 1979:328), viz., the 'ordinary,' information-conveying mode (no lying, acting, joking, etc.). In this mode, unlike Katz and Fodor's projection rules, the combinatorial rules are geared not to come up with all the potential ambiguities, as was done in (9), but on the contrary, to disambiguate a (-n always) potentially ambiguous sentence to exactly one, most probable meaning. For this purpose, all the scripts evoked by a word are divided into two parts. The first part contains exactly one unmarked script; the second part contains all the other, marked, scripts—the marking there can be hierarchical, from the least marked to the most marked. Unless some clues to the contrary are present in the context, the combinatorial rules will always push the unmarked script for the word forward. If it turns out to be impossible (see below), the combinatorial rules change the marking of the scripts for the word temporarily, for the purposes of the processed discourse, and declare another script unmarked. It is assumed here that the scripts with underlined numbers are treated as unmarked in (13). The combinatorial rules can then be expected to come up with a semantic interpretation for (12) which can be loosely paraphrased as (15):

(15)   After having done something else, the speaker left a shelter and brought (the engine of) some definite car to move.

After having used the unmarked scripts for the words of the sentence, the combinatorial rules have to check whether those scripts involve any conditions on their use and, if so, whether these conditions are satisfied. Thus, in the case of *then* there should be a mention of a previous action in the discourse, and (11) satisfies this condition. However, in the case of *the*, the script DEFINITE can only be used if the discourse contains a previous reference to an object of the class denoted by the noun following *the*. This condition is not satisfied, and the combinatorial rules switch to the other script of *the* concluding that the car in question is unique for the speaker, i.e., the only car the speaker has at his/her disposal.

The combinatorial rules will do some remarking of the scripts on their own— if, for instance, the text is about railways, then at the beginning of its processing, some clue will indicate that the intended script for *car* is, in fact, Script 3 of (13), and then the combinatorial rules will declare that script unmarked for the current discourse. The marking of the scripts for a word also changes in the course of history—thus, some two hundred years ago, the unmarked script for *car* was apparently Script 1 of (13).

On the basis of other features of the involved scripts, the combinatorial rules will generate the statements of (16) as the presuppositions of (12) and the statements of (17) as the probable presuppositions of (12).

(16)   (i)   The speaker is human.
        (ii)   The speaker is able-bodied.
        (iii) The speaker is past infancy.
        (iv)   The speaker knows something about cars.

(17)   (i)   The shelter is the speaker's home.
        (ii)   The car is very near the shelter.
        (iii) The speaker started cars before.

The combinatorial rules will also generate the inferences of (18) as well as the probable inferences of (19):

(18)   (i)   The speaker had the use of the car and the (ignition) key to it.
        (ii)   The car was not inside the shelter.

(19)   (i)   The speaker intended to go somewhere by car.
        (ii)   The speaker did not come back in.

The combinatorial rules will also generate the question of (20). They will fail to answer it on the basis of the previous discourse and will attempt to answer it on the basis of the information about the world accumulated in the process of semantic interpretation of the previous discourse, if any, or of the semantic information postulated in advance (see below). If no answer is available to (20), the combinatorial rules will record (20) as unanswered and will attempt to answer it every time new information is obtained in or around the discourse.

(20)   Who is the speaker?

The combinatorial rules will list every lexical node which is contained within the selected scripts for the sentence, collect the scripts for those words, and put them in a special storage marked ASSOCIATIONS. In the case of (12), this will probably involve the scripts for such words as *you, he, she,* etc.; *time, shelter, move, in, bring, vehicle, engine.*

The combinatorial rules will also add the obtained semantic interpretation for (12) to another special storage marked WORLD KNOWLEDGE. The latter operation involves comparison of the information contained in the semantic information for (12) with the information already stored in WORLD KNOWL- EDGE. The main goal of the comparison is to use the information in this storage to disambiguate the sentence if the combinatorial rules have failed to do it so far. This will not be necessary perhaps for (12) in bona fide communication but it will be necessary for a syntactically ambiguous sentence such as (21) because the instruction to use the unmarked scripts in the process of its semantic interpreta- tion will still preserve the potential ambiguity as either(22i) or (22ii).

(21)   Flying planes can be dangerous.

(22)   (i)   It happens that flying planes is dangerous.
          (ii) It happens that flying planes are dangerous.

In the case of (21), if WORLD KNOWLEDGE contains some statement to the effect that planes are the subject of discourse, the combinatorial rules will disambiguate (21) as (22i). If, on the contrary, the discourse is on flying as an activity, they will disambiguate the sentence (22ii).

On the other hand, WORLD KNOWLEDGE may already contain any of the statements in (23), which, of course, will contradict (12). Then the combinatorial rules will have to opt for one of the alternatives in (24).

(23)   (i)   The speaker does not have a car at his/her disposal.
          (ii)   The speaker is outside.
          (iii) The car is already started.
          (iv) The car is a railway car.

(24)   (i)   Declare the sentence anomalous and list a conflict with one of the
                  statements in (23) as the reason
          (ii)   Change the mode of communication to non–bona fide
          (iii) Determine the scripts shared by (12) and the conflicting state-
                  ment in (23) and check whether the conflict can be resolved by
                  switching to another script of the same word

The last two options in (24) would involve going back to Stage One above and starting the process of semantic interpretation from there.

Option (24ii) would mean considerable changes in the described procedure, most important of which is the different goal with regard to disambiguation: the combinatorial rules would no longer be instructed to disambiguate each sentence to just one meaning by using the unmarked scripts. The marking may be kept, but the instruction will be to obtain all the compatible combinations of scripts and thus all the potential meanings of the sentence.

In various forms of non–bona fide communication, the combinatorial rules are instructed not to discard syntactically or semantically deviant sentences but rather to introduce minor changes in the scripts causing the deviance and calculate the semantic interpretations conditional on these changes. This will often lead to metaphors, implicatures, and language innovations. In other words, in the non–bona fide modes, the combinatorial rules will slightly modify their format with regard to the operations described above and also assume some additional responsibilities.

4. Applications of Script-Based Semantics: General Principles

Any application of script-based semantics is meaningful only if it conforms to the general principles outlined below.

When one field of study (the 'source' field) is applied to another (the 'target' field), a strict division of labor should be maintained. To simplify the situation for the sake of the argument, each field can be described as consisting of data, theories, methods, and problems as shown in (25):

(25)   *Source Field*   *Target Field*

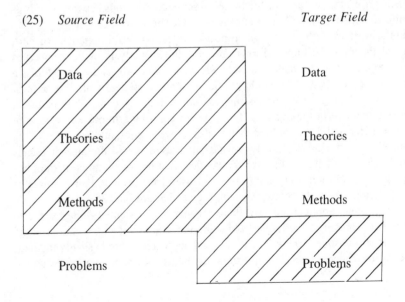

Data	Data
Theories	Theories
Methods	Methods
Problems	Problems

In a legitimate application of the source field to the target field the problems should come from the latter while the methods are supplied by the former. The data and the theories may actually overlap, but it is the source field which is primarily responsible for these as well. Any significant deviation from this normative situation of application as represented schematically by the shaded area in (25) is likely to lead to largely irrelevant research.

Thus, some two decades ago when the so-called mathematical linguistics came into fashion, various statistical methods were applied to linguistic material. Statistics was then the source field and linguistics the target field. Statistics turned out to be rather easily applicable to linguistics since in most cases the linguistic entities constitute identifiable, discrete, and countable objects, especially at such lower levels of linguistic structure as phonetics and morphology. The early applications led, for instance, to frequency tables of high reliability, generality, and validity, and there was nothing wrong with that. The only problem with many such applications was that there was no *linguistic problem* they were actually solving or, to put it differently, the statistical results could not be interpreted in a way which would yield any non-trivial conclusions about language. The fact that the word *the* tends to be the most frequent word in the English language, for instance, did not seem to signify much beyond itself, and in this and many similar cases, the statistical methods as applied to linguistic material at best corroborated what was well known in linguistics anyway and for which the heavy battery of statistics was hardly necessary. In this situation the owner of a method is much more interested in applying it to some new material than is the owner of the material. On the other hand, when a linguist came up with a real problem and statistics proved to be useful in providing a (partial) answer to that problem, the result was valid research and a valid application to linguistics, i.e., the problem of 'distance' in semantic relations between words as researched statistically by Šajkevič (1963) or Garvin et al. (1967).

Similarly, it would not really help poetics if the powerful apparatus of phonological theory were imposed on it and a detailed analysis of the phonemes making up a poem were made available when such an analysis did not address a valid issue in poetics itself or could not be interpreted poetically at all or at least non-trivially. Thus, we do not perhaps want to know the distribution of all distinctive features in the quatrain if it does not contribute to our knowledge of rhyme or meter and does not help distinguish between good and bad poetry. On the other hand, if we ask ourselves what alliteration is and the answer comes phrased in terms of the recurrence of identical distinctive features of the phonemes in the line, then it is again a piece of useful research and an example of valid application in full accordance with the shaded area in (25).

The legitimate applications are, therefore, problem-oriented—they strive to solve a real problem of the target field using the available facts, techniques and theories from the source field. The ill-advised applications are basically method-oriented—the interest is usually in extending the use of one's favorite method to some new material without much concern for the real need of the field to which this new material belongs. The result of a method-oriented application is not necessarily valueless—in fact, it can be quite interesting and informative as far as the method in question is concerned. However, it is highly unlikely to provide any fresh insights into the target field.

It follows then that if script-based semantics as part of linguistics is to be applied to anything, then the problems, questions, and needs should come from outside of linguistics.

5. Applications of Script-Based Semantics: Three Brief Examples

In this section, I will try to demonstrate that script-based semantics is able to help various fields of study solve their meaning-related problems. For the sake of brevity and simplicity, this will be done on the example of just one meaning-related problem shared by three different disciplines, the study of literature, rhetoric and composition, and artificial intelligence. One meaning-related problem all the three fields of research share is the problem of comprehension based on inference. Somewhat simplistically, the problem can be stated as (26):

(26)   How do we comprehend a text with many parts missing from it?

(27) is a good example of such a 'cryptic' text, while (28) is a much more 'complete' version of it.

(27)   Jimmy was really embarrassed by Billy's dealings with the Libyans. That loan remained unpaid for a long time.

(28)   President Jimmy Carter was embarrassed by his brother Billy's dealings with the Libyan government. While the relations between the two governments were extremely strained, the Libyans had approached Billy Carter and lent him a large sum of money in the hope that he would influence the president in their favor. Such lobbying is not considered ethical, and no president wants to be suspected of unethical practices. The loan accepted by Billy Carter remained unpaid for a long time.

Obviously, (27) is almost totally incomprehensible to anyone who does not possess the background information supplied in (28). On the other hand, (28) is almost entirely self-contained and does not require any (or at least as much) background information for its comprehension. Without begging the question whether script-based semantics can, or should, provide such specific background information as contained in (28), we can easily see that much more general and simple background information is necessary for the comprehension of 'incomplete' texts in various fields.

Let us take literature first. Comprehension and interpretation of texts is, obviously, the most important problem in this target field. (29) contains one of the simplest (and shortest) possible examples of a literary text, written by Dorothy Parker and reprinted here by kind permission of Viking Press:[1]

(29)   Men don't make passes
       At girls who wear glasses.

An interpretation of (29), albeit sexist and obsolete but clearly intended by the woman author many years ago, is given in (30):

(30)   Men make passes at women when they are attracted to the women. Women are interested in attracting men. In order to attract a man a woman has to try and make herself as attractive as possible. If men do not make passes at girls who wear glasses, it means that they are not attracted by all those girls. Since the common feature all those girls have is wearing glasses, it can be concluded that glasses are an unattractive thing to wear.

No current semantic theory can provide the extralexical information which is contained in (30) and which is indispensable for comprehending (29). Since we take it for granted here that (29) should be accounted for by a valid semantic theory if the native speaker is capable of comprehending (29), such a theory should be made available. Script-based semantics, with its elaborate script-evoking mechanism and the combinatorial rules capable of inferencing, is believed to be such a theory.

Similarly, in rhetoric and composition, a semantic theory should be available to explicate the fact that (31) is too cryptic, (32) is too detailed, while (33) is acceptable.

(31)   Next winter I am going to Florida. I hate shoveling snow.

(32)   Winters bring much snow here. In order to make the pavements and driveways passable one has to shovel snow all the time. I hate doing it, so I am going to spend next winter in Florida instead of here. The climate is warmer in Florida, and one does not expect snow at all there, or at least not as much as here, in winter. Therefore, it is likely that I will be able to avoid shoveling snow in Florida and thus save myself from doing something I don't like doing.

(33)   There has been so much snow here lately. I have been shoveling it all the time, and I don't like doing that. Next winter I am going to Florida.

What we are dealing with here is apparently a relevant meaning-related phenomenon on which a criterion of rhetorical acceptability is based: too much inference is unacceptable, too little is also unacceptable, but a certain (variable) amount of it in between is just right. Script-based semantics is, of course, the only available semantic theory which can supply the conceptual apparatus and the methods for measuring the amount of inferencing.

Similarly again, in natural-language artificial intelligence, the computer is programmed to communicate intelligently in human language. For this purpose, a formal semantic description of the language of communication should be developed and introduced to the computer prior to its use. Such examples as (34) show that the inferencing mechanism should be an important part of this theory. Otherwise, the computer will be unable to infer the simple facts in (35) from (34) and therefore to process the information in any useful way (see Charniak 1975 for more examples).

(34)   Jill hid the magazine under her cardigan and hastily left the library.

(35)   (i)   Jill did not want anybody to see her hiding the magazine.
        (ii)   Jill needed to have the magazine outside the library.
        (iii) Jill could not or did not want to charge the magazine out in the
               usual way.
        (iv)   Jill stole the magazine from the library.
        (v)   Jill left the library hastily because she was afraid of being caught.

In this case again, script-based semantics is the only available formal semantic theory which makes it possible for the computer to inference in a systematic, non–ad hoc way aiming to approximate the inferencing ability of the native speaker.

6.   Applications of Script-Based Semantics: One Long Example

The longer example is an application of script-based semantics to the study of humor. The purpose of the study is to formulate the semantic conditions, both necessary and sufficient, for a text to be funny. The main hypothesis on which this approach is based can be formulated as (36):

(36)   A text can be characterized as a single-joke-carrying text if both of the
       conditions in (37) are satisfied.

(37)   (i)   The text is compatible, fully or in part, with two different scripts.
        (ii)   The two scripts with which the text is compatible are opposite in a
               special sense defined below.

The two scripts with which some text is compatible are said to overlap fully or in part on this text.

According to (36), therefore, the set of two conditions in (37) is suggested as the necessary and sufficient conditions for a text to be funny.

Thus, the simple joke in (38) is at least partially compatible with both of the scripts DOCTOR and LOVER (8i–ii), i.e., the two scripts overlap on (38) in part. The first sentence of (38) evokes and corroborates the script DOCTOR. The second sentence loses some of the compatibility with this script and acquires a strong compatibility with the script LOVER instead:

(38)   "Is the doctor at home?" the patient asked in his bronchial whisper. "No," the doctor's young and pretty wife whispered in reply. "Come right in."

The two overlapping scripts are perceived as opposite in a certain sense, and it is this oppositeness which creates the joke. Obviously, an overlap is not a sufficient condition for a text to be funny—in fact, any ambiguous text is compatible with two or more scripts but certainly not every ambiguous text is funny. According to the main hypothesis, a script overlap is a necessary condition for a text to be funny, and any joke which can be demonstrated not to evoke two distinct scripts should be considered a counterexample to this approach to the analysis of verbal humor.

Joke (38) chosen here for a full though non-technical script analysis is typical in many ways. Its script analysis is based on the following components (39):

(39)   (i)   A continuous lexical graph with domains corresponding to the lexical entries (i.e., words) of the text
       (ii) Combinatorial rules combining those domains (scripts) into one or more larger scripts compatible with the script
       (iii) A system for marking certain scripts as opposite

Every word of the sentence evokes one or more scripts. Each script is a limited domain of the single continuous multidimensional graph which is the lexicon of the language. If a word is polysemous, as is often the case, the surrounding domain will consist of a number of subdomains, or areas of the graph with close links inside each area and few links with the other areas. Thus, *bachelor* will be surrounded by a domain which can be presented, without any further structuring, as (40):

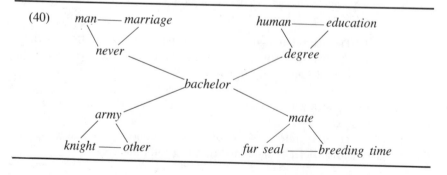

Assuming the availability of such a script-based lexicon (cf. Raskin 1981a), (41–45) list the scripts evoked by the text of joke (38) clause by clause using Webster (1976) as a source of reference. As in (13), the numbers of the scripts considered unmarked are, of course, marked, i.e., underlined.

(41) (i)   IS = BE v   1. Equal or belong to a set
                       2. Exist
                       3. Spatial
                       4. Must
     (ii) THE det   1. Definite
                       2. Unique
                       3. Generic
     (iii) DOCTOR n   1. Academic
                       2. Medical
                       3. Material
                       4. Mechanical
                       5. Insect
     (iv) AT prep   1. Spatial
                       2. Target
                       3. Occupation
                       4. State
                       5. Cause
                       6. Measure
     (v)   HOME n   1. Residence
                       2. Social
                       3. Habitat
                       4. Origin
                       5. Disabled
                       6. Objective

(42) (1)   THE (see (41ii))
     (ii) PATIENT n   1. Medical
                          2. Object
     (iii) ASK v   1. Interrogative
                          2. Request
                          3. Selling
     (iv) IN prep   1. Inclusion
                          2. Instrument
                          3. Circumstance
                          4. Purpose
                          5. Mathematical
     (v)   HIS pron   1. Belonging to *he*
     (vi) BRONCHIAL adj 1. Bronchi or lungs
     (vii) WHISPER n   1. Utter
                          2. Communication

(43)   No adv   <u>1.</u>   Negation
           2.   Surprise

(44)   (i)   THE (see (41ii))
    (ii)   DOCTOR (see (41iii))
    (iii) 'S pron   <u>1.</u>   Belonging
    (iv)   YOUNG adj   <u>1.</u>   Age
                      2.   New
                      3.   Experience
    (v)   AND conj   <u>1.</u>   Connection
                      2.   Logical
    (vi)   PRETTY adj   <u>1.</u>   Beauty
                      2.   Terrible
                      3.   Considerable
    (vii) WIFE n   <u>1.</u>   Marriage
    (viii) WHISPER v (see (42vii))
    (xi)   IN (see (42iv))
    (x)   REPLY n   <u>1.</u>   Answer
                      2.   Legal

(45)   (i)   COME v   1.   Move
                      <u>2.</u>   Arrive
                      3.   Sexual
                      4.   Become
    (ii)   RIGHT adv   1.   Propriety
                      2.   Direct
                      <u>3.</u>   Orientation
                      4.   Immediate
                      5.   Truth
    (iii) IN (see (42iv)

Just as in (13), the items numbered by Arabic numerals are loose shorthand for the scripts evoked by the words of the text. However, they are assumed, for the limited purposes of this analysis, to represent accurately the areas of the continuous graph potentially activated by the utterance of each word. Even this loose notation reveals the interconnected nature of various lexical items. Thus, items (41i-1), (42v), and (45iii) contain the same node *belong,* and a detailed presentation of them would also reveal this node within the domains evoked by (41v-1) and (42iii-3); (41iii-2) and (42ii-1) coincide; (42iii-1), (42iii-2), (42vii-1), and (44vii-1) share the same node *utter.* These and similar connections are very important for the proper functioning of combinatorial rules.

The combinatorial rules start out by calculating the phrasal and sentential meaning on the basis of the available syntactic structure and the scripts in (41–45). Leaving the syntax aside, along with other more or less obvious technicalities, let us follow the order of semantic operations performed by the combinatorial rules.

Within each clause, they will look for the script or scripts which are evoked by two or more words. (Actually, at the technical level, the rules will be looking inside the scripts and go for the ones which contain the common domains.) Thus, in the case of the first clause of the text, the combinatorial rules will notice the common script denoted as SPATIAL in (41i-3) and (41iv-1). They will consequently shift the feature of unmarkedness from (41i-1) to (41i-3) and adopt SPATIAL as a working hypothesis. Accordingly, they will reject (41v-2), (41v-3), (41v-4), and (41v-6) as not easily compatible with the script SPATIAL. Some additional syntactic and idiomatic information within the graph will select (41v-1) over (41v-5), i.e., *at home* will be correctly interpreted as *in the residence* rather than as *in a home for the disabled*. This choice will then lead to the selection of the two human scripts of *doctor*—(41ii-1,2) over the other three possibilities. The selected meaning of *home,* (41v-1), will have a semantic recursion node within its script which will require information on the owner. Both the medical and academic scripts for *doctor* (41iii-1,2) will be recognized as appropriate fillings for the node. Finally, in this clause, the unmarked script for *the* (41ii-1) will be rejected in favor of (41ii-2) because of a similar semantic recursion trigger within the script (41ii-1) requiring a filling from the previous discourse. Since none is available, the combinatorial rules will reject the script. In other words, the combinatorial rules will thus accommodate the fact that *the* can only be understood as 'definite' if there is a preceding reference to its head (*doctor*) in the text—since there is no preceding text, such an interpretation is unacceptable. As a result of this procedure, the first clause of (38) will be formally interpreted as two-way ambiguous. The two possible meanings can be roughly paraphrased as (46):

(46) (i) Question: The unique proprietor of a family residence, who is a physician, is physically present in the residence

     (ii) Question: The unique proprietor of a family residence, who has a Ph.D., is physically present in the residence

At this stage, since the first sentence is not complete, the combinatorial rules will register the ambiguity and will go for the second clause of the sentence. Following a similar path, they will pick out the script MEDICAL in *patient* (42ii-1) as well as within *bronchial* (42vi-1). The duly registered interrogative feature of the first clause (46) will disambiguate *ask* as (42iii-1), which will, in its turn, disambiguate *whisper* as (42vii-1); *his* will be easily related to *patient* with the help of a semantic recursion node; and *the* will be interpreted in its unmarked meaning of 'definite,' with the semantic recursion trigger node mentioned in the analysis of the first clause above filled, somewhat non-trivially though quite simply, with 'the questioner of the previous question.' The doubly corroborated script MEDICAL will disambiguate the first clause and reject (46ii).

The entire first sentence of (38) will then be interpreted roughly as the paraphrase in (47):

(47)   Somebody who was previously treated for an illness wants to know whether the unique proprietor of a family residence, who is a physician, is physically present in the residence

At this point, the combinatorial rules are ready to come up with the presuppositions, inferences, and questions concerning the entire first sentence of (38) (see Section 3, especially (16–20)).

The non-trivial presuppositions of the first sentence are listed in (48) and its probable presuppositions in (49):

(48)   (i)   The patient is human
        (ii)   The doctor is human
        (iii) There is a hearer

(49)   (i)   The patient is at the door of the doctor's residence
        (ii)   The patient does not know the answer to the question

Some inferences from (47) are listed in (50) and probable inferences in (51):

(50)   (i)   The patient is male
        (ii)   The patient whispers because of a problem with his bronchi or lungs
        (iii) The patient is temporarily unable to speak normally

(51)   (i)   The patient is adult
        (ii)   The patient has been treated by the doctor before
        (iii) The patient wants to see the doctor
        (iv)   The patient has a problem with his bronchi or lungs
        (v)   The patient wants the doctor to correct the problem

The question the combinatorial rules produce in relation to (47) is, of course, (52):

(52)   Who is the hearer?

(48–52) go to the special component closely associated with the combinatorial rules and called WORLD KNOWLEDGE. The component may already contain some elements of information which the theory assumes at the outset of the analysis of any text. The newly obtained information supplements the previously contained information if it is compatible with it and signals a conflict if it is not. One important element of information the combinatorial rules are interested in from the very beginning is the mode of communication, and the usual path to take is to assume that it is bona fide.

The second sentence of (38) will be processed similarly, clause by clause, the one significant difference being that the combinatorial rules will keep relating the obtained results to the first sentence. Thus, the first clause will be disambiguated as negation (43-1) in view of the preceeding question and will be interpreted accordingly as (53):

(53)   The doctor is not at home

In the next clause, *doctor* will, of course, be disambiguated automatically as medical and *the* as definite; *wife* will be related to *doctor* by *'s,* and *wife* will also disambiguate *young* and *pretty* in their unmarked scripts, i.e., as (44iv-1) and (44vi-1), respectively; *whisper* and *reply* will pick out the compatible scripts within each other's domains, namely the ones which share the node *utter,* i.e., (44viii-1) and (44x-1), respectively; *reply* will disambiguate *in* as instrumental (44ix-2).

Finally, the third clause will be interpreted in the physical-motion sense of the three constituent words on the basis of the overlapping scripts (45i-1), (45ii-2), and (45iii-1).

The combinatorial rules will again come up with a (smaller) number of usual presuppositions and probable presuppositions. More importantly, it will make a few significant inferences (54), one of them (54i) being, of course, the answer to the question (52) asked by the combinatorial rules after having processed the first sentence.

(54)   (i)   The doctor's wife is the hearer
         (ii)   The doctor is male
         (iii) The reply refers to the patient's question
         (iv)   The patient and the doctor's wife are talking to each other
         (v)   The doctor's wife wants the patient to come into her home
         (vi)   The doctor's home is the doctor's wife's home

A significant probable inference will be (55):

(55)   The patient and the doctor's wife are alone

At this stage, a very important set of derivative inferences (56) will be produced by the combinatorial rules on the basis of all the inferences stored so far in the world knowledge component, i.e., (50–51) and (54–55).

(56)   (i)   If the patient does come into the doctor's home he will not see
                the doctor
         (ii)   If the patient comes into the doctor's home he will not achieve
                his purpose
         (iii) The patient does not need to come into the doctor's home

Next, the combinatorial rules will come up with the crucial question (57):

(57)   Why does the doctor's wife want the patient to come in?

The only answer the combinatorial rules will be able to come up with on the
basis of further inferencing is (58):

(58)   The doctor's wife does not understand that (56iii)

Since one of the basic assumptions stored in the world knowledge component
will be that any human being, unless otherwise specified, has the same inferencing ability as the combinatorial rules, the only explanation which will be available to the theory is that the doctor's wife's interpretation of the situation is
different from the one obtained by the combinatorial rules.

An important decision will be made by the combinatorial rules at this stage.
Since there is no further explanation of the situation in the text, the registered
misunderstanding cannot be treated as a genuine sample of bona fide communication. The combinatorial rules will, therefore, reject the first default value of
the mode of communication adopted earlier and switch to the next default value,
namely that of joke telling, which is, of course, non–bona fide. This switch will
command the combinatorial rules to start looking for a competing script analysis
of the entire text or part thereof in view of the main hypothesis.

The strategy of the search built into the combinatorial rules can be presented
schematically as (59):

(59)   (i)   Go back to the text and, beginning from the end, look for another
              script or node evoked by more than one word; go to (ii).
       (ii)   If such an additional common script is found go to (v); if not found,
              go to (iii).
       (iii) Go for the oppositeness directions: if there are still directions there
              which have not been applied, apply the next direction; if there are no
              directions left, register defeat and go to (iv).
       (iv)   Characterize the text as not belonging to the joke-telling mode of
              communication and switch to the next default value of non–bona fide
              communication (probably lying).
       (v)   Check the compatibility of the discovered additional common script
              with the text: if it is compatible with at least a part of the text, go to
              (vi); if it is not, register defeat and go to (iv).

(vi)   Go to the oppositeness directions and check the suitability of one of them for the obtained pair of scripts, i.e., the one compatible with the first interpretation of the text and the script discovered in (ii); if a suitable type of oppositeness is discovered, go to (vii); if not, register defeat and go to (iv).

(vii)   Recognize the analyzed text as a joke characterized by the opposition of the type determined in (vi) between the two obtained scripts.

In the case of joke (38), the first interpretation of the text established above puts forward the script MEDICAL or DOCTOR. In general, the process of script analysis of a sentence leads to the recognition of such a macroscript characterizing the entire situation. There are at least two alternative ways of getting at the macroscript. The process of interpretation as described above suggests one of the alternatives, namely, adopting the most frequently recurring script as the macroscript. This route implies a sequence of rather complicated trial-and-error checks. The other way is almost identical technically but more subtle conceptually. It is based on the recognition of a difference between those scripts which are regular 'static' semantic descriptions of the kind which have been described and used so far, on the one hand, and those which describe a process stage by stage. The first kind of script can be referred as atemporal, i.e., not incorporating the notion of time or chronological sequence, while the other will then be temporal. Basically the same distinction is captured by Schank's (1975) usage of the terms 'frame' and 'script.' In script-based semantics, the term 'scenario' is usually reserved for the temporal scripts. It is typical for a temporal script to be a chronologically (and perhaps otherwise as well) ordered sequence of atemporal scripts.

The script MEDICAL is then the scenario evoked by the text of joke (38). As has been demonstrated on this example, in script-based semantics, the semantic interpretation of the text is a function of the scenario discovered in the process of script analysis, and an ambiguous sentence will, of course, be associated with two or more scenarios. Beginning to look for another scenario, the combinatorial rules will be instructed first to go back to those words of the second sentence of the text which do not evoke the script or node MEDICAL. Those include at least *young, and, pretty, wife, whisper, come, right,* and *in.* The combinatorial rules will soon discover the concealed script of SEX, evoked—much less obviously perhaps but no less persistently than the script MEDICAL by other words—by at least the words *pretty* and *wife* as well as the inferences and probable inferences of (50i) and (51i); *whisper* in combination with the probable inference of (55) will then match the scenario ADULTERY.

Since the search of a competing scenario is successful in the case of joke (38), the next step is to carry out (59v). The scenario will, in fact, turn out to be perfectly compatible with the second sentence and not contradicted by anything in the first sentence either.

The next step (59vi) requires a set of oppositeness instructions. From the study of a large corpus of simple jokes the list of (60) can be obtained and easily formalized for use by the combinatorial rules.

(60)	If Script (Scenario) 1 is:	then Script (Scenario) 2 is:
(i)	actual	non-actual
(ii)	normal	abnormal
(iii)	possible	impossible
(iv)	goodness-related	badness-related
(v)	life-related	death-related
(vi)	non-sex-related	sex-related
(vii)	non-money-related	money-related
(viii)	high-stature-related	low-stature-related

The list in (60), though perhaps not exhaustive, is representative and clearly sufficient for most, if not all, simple jokes.

The two scenarios of joke (38) will then be associated with (60i) and (60vi), and the last step, (59vii), will then lead to the following result (61) of the entire script analysis:

(61)   Analysis of: Text (38)
       Result: Joke
       Script 1: MEDICAL (DOCTOR)
       Script 2: ADULTERY (LOVER)
       Type of oppositeness: Actual–Non-actual; Sex-related

Script-based semantics has thus determined that a certain text is indeed a joke. In other words, applied to the target field of the study of humor, it has helped solve the central problem of the field, namely the problem of telling a joke from a non-joke.

NOTE

1. From *The Portable Dorothy Parker Reader*, edited by Brendan Gill, copyright 1926, renewed 1954 by Dorothy Parker. Reprinted by permission of Viking Penguin Inc. and Gerald Duckworth Co. Ltd.

REFERENCES

Bar-Hillel, Y. 1964. "A demonstration of the non-feasibility of fully automatic high quality transla- tion." In: Y. Bar-Hillel, *Language and Information*. Reading, MA–Jerusalem: Addison-Wesley–Magnes, pp. 174–9.
Bartlett, F. G. 1932. *Remembering*. Cambridge: Cambridge University Press.
Bloomfield, Leonard 1964 (1933). *Language*. New York: Holt, Rinehart and Winston.
Bateson, G. 1972. *Steps to an Ecology of Mind*. New York: Ballantine Books.

Chafe, W. L. 1977. "Creativity in verbalization and its implications for the nature of stored knowledge." In: Freedle 1977, pp. 41–56.

Charniak, E. 1972. "Towards a model of children's story comprehension." AI TR-266, MIT.

Charniak, E. 1975. "Organization and inference in a frame-like system of common knowledge." In: R. C. Schank and B. L. Nash-Weber (eds.), *Theoretical Issues in Natural Language Processing*. Cambridge, MA: Bolt, Beranek, and Newman, pp. 42–51.

Chomsky, Noam 1977. *Essays on Form and Interpretation*. New York: North Holland.

Cole, P., and J. L. Morgan (eds.) 1975. *Syntax and Semantics*, Vol. 3. *Speech Acts*. New York: Academic Press.

Fillmore, C. J. 1968. "The case for case." In: E. Bach and R. T. Harms (eds.), *Universals in Linguistic Theory*. New York: Holt, Rinehart and Winston, pp. 1–88.

Freedle, R. O. (ed.) 1977. *Discourse Production and Comprehension*. Norwood, NJ: Ablex.

Freedle, R. O. (ed.) 1979. *New Directions in Discourse Processing*. Norwood, NJ: Ablex.

Garvin, P., J. Brewer, and M. Mathiot 1967. *Predication-Typing. Language* 43, Supplement to No. 2, Pt. 2.

Goffman, E. 1974. *Frame Analysis*. New York: Harper and Row.

Grice, H. P. 1975. "Logic and conversation." In: Cole and Morgan 1975, pp. 41–58.

Jackendoff, Ray 1981. "On Katz's autonomous semantics." *Language* 57, pp. 425–35.

Katz, J. J. 1980. "Chomsky on meaning." *Language* 56, pp. 11–41.

Katz, J. J., and J. A. Fodor 1963. "The structure of a semantic theory." *Language* 39, pp. 170–210.

Mel'čuk, I. A. 1979. *Studies in Dependency Syntax*. Ann Arbor, MI: Karoma.

Minsky, M. 1975. "A framework for representing knowledge." In: P. H. Winston (ed.), *The Psychology of Computer Vision*. New York: McGraw-Hill, pp. 211–77.

Raskin, Victor 1977. "Literal meaning and speech acts." *Theoretical Linguistics* 4:3, pp. 209–25.

Raskin, Victor 1981a. "Script-based lexicon." *Quaderni di semantica* 2:1, pp. 25–34.

Raskin, Victor 1981b. "Scripts and the composing process." ERIC Clearinghouse on Language and Linguistics, ED 207 329.

Raskin, Victor 1982. "Linguistic careers and linguistic applications in the 1980s—One man's view." *The Linguistic Reporter* 24:9, pp. 3, 11–12.

Raskin, Victor 1984. *Semantic Mechanisms of Humor*. Dordrecht–Boston: D. Reidel.

Raskin, Victor 1985a. "Linguistic and encyclopedic knowledge in text processing." In: M. Alinei (ed.), *Quaderni di semantica's Round Table Discussion on Text/Discourse. Quaderni di semantica* 6:1, 92–102.

Raskin, Victor 1985b. "Once again on linguistic and encyclopedic knowledge." In: M. Alinei (ed.), *Quaderni di semantica's Round Table Discussion on Text/Discourse. Quaderni di semantica* 6:2, 377–83.

Raskin, Victor 1985c. "Preface." In this volume.

Raskin, Victor, in press. "Script-based semantics." In: W. A. Donohue and D. G. Ellis (eds.), *Contemporary Issues on Language and Discourse Processes*. Hillsdale, NJ: Lawrence Erlbaum Associates.

Šajkevič, A. Ja. 1963. "Raspredelenie slov v tekste i vydelenie semantičeskix polej v jazyke" (Word distribution in the text and distinguishing semantic fields in language.) *Inostrannye jazyki v škole* 2, pp. 94–102.

Schank, R. C. 1975. "Using knowledge to understand." In: R. C. Schank and B. L. Nash-Weber (eds.), *Theoretical Issues in Natural Language Processing*. Cambridge, MA: Bolt, Beranek, and Newman, pp. 42–51.

Schank, R. C., and R. Abelson 1977. *Scripts, Plans, Goals and Understanding*. New York: Wiley.

Searle, J. R. 1969. *Speech Acts*. Cambridge: Cambridge University Press.

Tannen, D. 1979. "What's in a frame?" In: Freedle 1979, pp. 137–81.

Webster's New Collegiate Dictionary 1976. Springfield, MA: Merriam.

CHAPTER THREE

Poems as Holograms*

Háj Ross

1. Introduction

The standard view of communication is that it consists of a transfer of objects from one being (the sender) to another (the receiver), through a channel. Diagrammatically, a communication event proceeds as follows: the sender A takes ideas, seen as physical objects, out of her or his head, puts them into containers B (e.g., words, phrases, sentences, paragraphs, and so on), and moves these containers through a conduit C. When the containers arrive at D, they are unpacked and the ideas go into the head of the receiver.

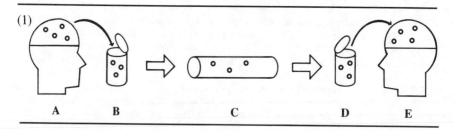

(1)

A   B   C   D   E

This view of communication is argued for by the analysis of conventionalized metaphors, as is demonstrated brilliantly in a recent paper by Michael Reddy (1979). Reddy found that about 70% of the expressions that are used in English to describe acts of communication can be seen to derive from highlighting one or another aspect of the schematic characterization in (1). Some examples:

(2)   a.   Mildred *packs* a lot of meaning *into* her words.
       b.   We couldn't *get anything out of* this phrase.

This work was supported in part by a grant from the National Institute of Mental Health, to which I am very grateful.

I would like to thank Jim Harris for the many insights into the structure of Spanish which he has given to me, and to us all.

This paper originally appeared in *Poetics Journal* 2 (1982), and is also being republished in Thomas Ballmer and Roland Posner (eds.) *Nach-Chomskysche Linguistik (Freundesschrift für Helmut Schnelle),* Verlag Walter de Gruyter, Berlin, West Germany, 1985.

    c.   That idea doesn't *come across/through* clearly.

    d.   I may have *given* you the wrong idea.

    e.   An emotion-*laden* plea, *empty* threats/promises/words.

Reddy observes that this is not the only logical possibility—that there are other ways of structuring the concept of communication metaphorically. He gives an extended example of one alternative view, and I wish to present yet a third.

It is a commonplace that poetry differs from "normal" language in that poems do not assert. Poems are not normally viewed as being true or false—rather, I will say, following a suggestion of Charles Pyle, that poems *point*. It is hard to say what they point to—typically, they are used to evoke in the reader feelings or emotions that arose in the poet, that the poet wishes to reawaken in the reader.

Feelings are notoriously hard to convey in plain language. In a study of the language used at funerals, one researcher found that the most commonly used type of expression was "I don't know what to say." A feeling of harmony with the universe, or of grief, or of rage, may not allow itself to be decomposed, technically, as would the description of how to build a patio.

1. Dig a level hole six inches deep. 2. Spread a thin layer of half-inch gravel. 3. Cover with 2 inches of sand . . .

Typically, then, feelings are wholes, gestalts. They do not fit comfortably into a process like that implied in (1), which requires the transfer of a succession of containers—which would necessitate breaking a feeling into a number of smaller parts.

What to do? I will attempt to show that poets, who have to use language as a point of departure, nonetheless structure it in such a way that it becomes a hologram—that is, an entity in every part of which the message (more accurately, the pointing) is contained. That is, the poet does not put an idea in one place in a poem—she or he puts it everyplace.

2. Hologram

Since probably not all of the readers will have personally experienced holograms, I beg the indulgence of those who have to digress a moment to explain what they are. Basically, holograms are a kind of twentieth-century magic. There is a way of photographing a three-dimensional object, using the beam of a laser, and capturing the resultant image on a photographic plate, or piece of film, in such a way that when the resulting negative is developed and reilluminated by two laser beams, the three-dimensional image is regenerated. If the original object was a pair of dice, one can stand on one side of the regenerated image and see a die showing 3 spots, and one showing 2 spots. When one walks behind the image, one sees a die with 4 spots, and one with 5 spots, exactly as would be the case if one were to walk behind the original dice.

So far, so good. An unforgettable experience, mysterious, but somewhat similar to perspective in painting, or to the illusion of three dimensions with only two in use—close enough, at any rate, so that one is fascinated, but not staggered. But now to the reason for calling such laser-produced negatives "holograms."

If one takes a glass hologram of our pair of dice, and shatters it into thousands of splinters of glass, one can take the smallest particle of glass and illuminate it with two laser beams and *the entire image of the two dice will be recreated.* This is a fact of the twentieth century which flies in the face of our intuitions. How can the entire image of both dice be located everywhere in a glass plate? It seems miraculous. There is an explanation—an easily readable version appears in Itzhak Bentov's *Stalking the Wild Pendulum,* and I will not go over it here. I mention the experiential facts of encountering a physical hologram only to make clearer what my claim about poetry is. Just as the dice 'are everywhere' in the glass plate, shot through it, one might say, so also is that which a poem communicates located everywhere in the poem.

3. Example

A concrete example may make the point clearer. Let us consider the following poem by Octavio Paz.[1]

> *Viento, agua, piedra*
> A Roger Caillois

A. *El agua horada la piedra*
   el viento dispersa el agua
   la piedra detiene al viento.
   Agua, viento, piedra.

The water bores through the stone
the wind disperses the water
the stone stops the wind.
Water, wind, stone.

B. *El viento esculpe la piedra*
   la piedra es copa del agua
   el agua escapa y es viento.
   Piedra, viento, agua.

The wind sculpts the stone
the stone is a goblet of the water
the water escapes and is wind.
Stone, wind, water

C. *El viento en sus giros canta*
   el agua al andar murmúra
   la piedra inmóvil se calla.
   Viento, agua, piedra.

The wind in its turnings sings
the water as it goes murmurs
the immobile stone is silent.
Wind, water, stone.

D. *Uno es otro y es ninguno:*
   entre sus nombres vacíos
   pasan y se desvanecen
   agua, piedra, viento.

One is the other and is neither:
among their empty names
pass and disappear
water, stone, wind.

The interpretation of this poem that makes the most sense to me is the following, which seems to be pretty clearly stated in the fourth stanza.

Although the three states of matter—gas, liquid, and solid—seem entirely separate, the poem shows them to be interconvertible. Their different names—wind, water, stone—are empty, without force. They differ in appearance only: they have the same underlying nature. They are merely three different manifestations of the same primordial stuff, which is formless and nameless.

In the order given in the title, the three ''elements'' increase in fixity, in solidity. However, the opposite order is the one followed by the verses of the poem—that is, the poem makes a transition from order and rigidity and differentiation to disorder, fluidity, sameness. In a way, the poem takes us on a journey of piercing the veil of appearance—what appears to be different is finally seen to be the same, the same old wine in different, transitory, changing bottles. The poem is thus highly consonant with a Buddhist, Hindu, or Taoist view of the world, or, for that matter, with the view of subatomic physics (cf. Fritjof Capra, *The Tao of Physics*).

Assuming that this is in fact what the poem conveys, how does it do it? In many many ways—the poem holograms this interpretation. The basic method, proceeding from the first to the fourth stanza, is for a clear pattern, which is established early in the poem, to suffer decay and disruption as the poem proceeds, thus mirroring the decay of the appearance of differentiation, as we penetrate to the core of reality.

4. Syntax

Let us take as a first case the broad-brush characterization of the syntax. The poem's stanzas, except for D, consist of one sentence which runs from the first to the third line of each stanza, containing three independent clauses, one to each line. This three-clause sentence is closed by a period. The second period follows the three nouns listed in the fourth line of each stanza.

The first stanza contains exactly three verbs, one per line, all transitive. This pattern seems to continue at the start of B, but the second line already shows the first wrinkle: an instance of the copula *es,* which is not a transitive verb, and which is not followed by a single definite noun, in the pattern set up so far, but by *two* nouns, forming an indefinite noun phrase. Furthermore, while all of the preceding verbs have been trisyllables, *es* is not.

The next line shows an even greater perturbation: two verbs, of which the first, *escapa,* is also a departure from the previous transitive pattern, in that it is the poem's first intransitive. And the last noun of this line evidences the same departure from the definite direct object pattern of A: *viento* is another indefinite noun phrase—moreover, it is the first indefinite noun to end a line other than the last line of a stanza.

A strong pattern that has been set up by the first two stanzas is that each line will begin and end with a noun phrase based on one of the three nouns in the title.

The first line of C breaks this pattern, but at least it contains two noun phrases: *el viento* and *sus giros*. The second line of C contains one clear noun—*el agua*—and the verbal noun *el andar*, 'the going,' object of the preposition *a*, 'to,' in an idiomatic nominal construction that translates as an English *as*-clause. We might stretch a point and say that this second line of C still conforms to the two-noun pattern of A and B, but it is clear that the nouns are fading. In the third line of C, only one noun remains. The line also contains the first adjective in the poem, and the first (non-copular) stative verb.

In D, no trace of the two-noun pattern remains. In fact, the only noun of this stanza is the abstract *nombres*, 'names,' modified by *vacíos*, 'empty.' The first two verbs are instances of the copula, in line 13, and the last two verbs, the poem's only plural verbs, are the two intransitives of line 15. Thus the pattern of one transitive verb per line preceded by an agentive subject and followed by an affected direct object, which is set up in A, perturbed slightly in B, and seriously in C, has been abandoned entirely in D. The second line of D is the first line of the poem which contains no verb, and the third line is the first which contains no noun phrase.

The global structure of D is an even greater disruption. Each of A, B, and C consists of one long sentence, spanning the first three lines and a (conjoined?) list of the three elements on the last line. D is inverted: this stanza consists of one long sentence, divided by a colon into two clauses, a one-line clause (*first* in the stanza, instead of last), followed by a three-line clause. Note that the first line of D also contains three noun phrases (the only three-noun-phrase line in the first three lines of any stanza), thus making it parallel to the three-noun lines 4, 8, and 12.

The final rug to be pulled out from under our feet is the fact that the poem's last clause (lines 14–16) is inverted—the last three nouns of D are the subject of the two verbs in line 15. This is the only sentence in the poem that ends with its subject.

There is more to be said about the syntax of the poem, but from what I have said thus far, I hope my main thesis has emerged clearly enough: that syntactically, the poem progresses from the highly constrained, rigid, repetitive structure of A, in a gradual way, along a number of axes, to the highly fluid, and in fact *inverted*, structure shown in D. Thus we proceed from a syntactic order to its inverse—mirroring the series of perceptions that would accompany a reseeing of the nature of reality, a new seeing in which differentiation has given way to a realization of formlessness.

5.   Meter

Another facet of the poem's structure which points in a parallel, holographic, way, is the meter. Jim Harris has called to my attention that given two conventions of syllable counting, the poem can be shown to have an absolutely regular eight-syllable meter. The conventions are (a) that two adjacent vowels with no intervening consonant can count as one syllable for metrical purposes, and (b) that the diphthong *ie* [ye] can count as one or two syllables for metrical purposes. Both of these conventions are standard for Spanish. I will indicate a scansion in (3) below, linking cases of two adjacent vowels to be counted as one syllable with the sign ⏑, and drawing vertical lines after every two syllables.

(3)   El a‿gua hora|da la| piedra,
                  el vien|to dis|persa‿el | agua,
                  la pie|dra de|tiene‿al | viento.
                  Agua, | vien|to, pi|edra.

                  El vien|to‿escul|pe la | piedra,
                  la pie|dra‿es co|pa del | agua,
                  el a|gua‿esca|pa y‿es | viento.
                  Pie|dra, vi|ento, | agua.

                  El vien|to‿en sus | giros | canta,
                  el a|gua‿al an|dar mur|mura,
                  la pie|dra in|móvil | se calla.
                  Vien|to, a|gua, pi|edra.

                  Uno‿es | otro | y‿es nin|guno:
                  entre | sus nom|bres va|cíos
                  pasan | y se | desva|necen
                  agua, | pie|dra, vi|ento.

Thus in terms of an abstract metrical pattern, the poem is perfectly regular. However, superimposed upon this scaffolding, there is a meter which is closer to the phonetics, and which shows the same sequence of progressively greater perturbations which we have seen to characterize the syntactic structure.

This 'concrete' meter can be characterized as three amphibrachs per line for the first three lines of each stanza, followed by a fourth line of three trochaic feet. An amphibrach is a foot of the form weak-strong-weak. In (4) below, I will scan each of the first three lines of each stanza as a sequence of three occurrences of W-S-W, drawing lines to indicate foot boundaries, and marking stress.

(4)   El água | horáda | la piédra,|
                  el viénto | dispérsa | el água,|
                  la piédra | detiéne | al viénto.|
                  Água,| viénto,| piédra.|

                  El viénto | escúlpe | la piédra,|
                  la piédra | es cópa | del água,|

→   el água | escápa | y es viénto.|
     Piédra,| viénto,| água.|

→   El viénto | en sus gí|ros cánta,|
→   el água | al andár | murmúra,|
     la piédra | inmóvil | se cálla.|
     Viénto,| água,| piédra.|

→   Úno es | ótro y es | ningúno:|
→   éntre | sus nómbres | vacíos|
→   pásan | y se dès|vanécen|
     água,| piédra,| viénto.|

As can be seen, this amphibrachic meter is followed without exception in A. In B, there is one (small) wrinkle: the third line contains ten phonetic syllables, which necessitates the postulation of a third foot with two weak syllables before the stressed syllable. I emphasize that the line is not unmetrical; it is merely more marked than the preceding lines of A or B. I indicate this markedness by the arrow to the left of the line.

There are arrows to the left of the first two lines of C, because the stressed syllable of the second foot of each of these lines falls not in the middle of the foot, on the fifth syllable of the line, as has been the case in A and B, but rather on the sixth syllable. This is a more severe departure from the pattern of A than is line 7.

Now let us examine D. In the first line, only the third foot has the stress in the expected middle position. The first two feet have initial stress, which makes this line the most marked to be encountered thus far, since the previously arrowed lines only exhibited wrinkles in one of their three feet. Note in addition that the middle foot of line 13 requires an application of convention (a) above, resulting in a middle foot with an extra phonetic syllable.

The following line contains only eight phonetic syllables, and can only be matched to an amphibrachic trimeter structure by assuming that the first weak syllable of the first foot need not be realized. Again, a departure from the perfectly regular nine-syllable lines of A, hence the arrow.

Line 15 is the most marked of the entire poem. Again, its eight syllables require that we allow one of the positions of the first amphibrach not to be realized—once more, as in line 14, the first position. And the situation is also complex with the second foot of line 15: we are confronted with another final-stressed foot, as in lines 9 and 10, but with the additional wrinkle that for the first time in the poem, the maximal stress in a foot is not the main stress of a word, but only a secondary stress.

To sum up, it is clear that the meter becomes more fluid, less rigid, as the poem progresses: in only one foot in B, in two lines in C, where both violations are of the same type, and in three lines in D, where the *types* of violation, or markedness, differ from line to line, with line 15 being the biggest departure of all from the regularity imposed in A.

One final perspective on the meter of the poem. In general, each line of the poem can be segmented into three phrases (there is one important exception, to which we will return shortly), in such a way that the boundaries of these phrases correspond to the boundaries of the three amphibrachic feet in each line. In (5), I have drawn carets under each line to break it into syntactic phrases. Where these phrases between carets correspond to boundaries between amphibrachs, as is uniformly the case in A and B, I have made no further notation. But in one line in C, and in two in D, there is a conflict between syntactic and metrical boundaries. I have in these cases indicated the metrical boundaries by vertical lines.

(5)
El agua∧horada∧la piedra,
el viento∧dispersa∧el agua,
la piedra∧detiene∧al viento.
Agua,∧viento,∧piedra.

El viento∧esculpe∧la piedra,
la piedra∧es copa∧del agua,
el agua∧escapa∧y es viento.
Piedra,∧viento,∧agua.

→   El viento∧en sus gi|ros∧canta,
el agua∧al andar∧murmura,
la piedra∧inmóvil∧se calla.
Viento,∧agua,∧piedra.

→   Uno∧es|otro∧y es|ninguno:
entre∧sus nombres∧vacíos
→   pasan∧y se des|vanecen
agua,∧piedra,∧viento.

The first clash is in line 9, in only one foot. A sharper clash is in line 13, in two feet. The sharpest clash of all can be seen in line 15, which is syntactically bipartite, not tripartite like all of the other lines. Thus again, we see a pattern of order in the earliest stanzas yielding to progressively greater disruptions in later stanzas—another hologramming.

Passing on to rhyme, we find the last vowels of each of A and B to fall into the pattern *a-a-o-a*. In C, this pattern is slightly perturbed—instead of an *o* in line 3, we find a fourth *a*, but still all four lines end in vowels. But when we reach D, we find *no* lines in *a,* and two lines ending in consonants. Again, another progression towards chaos.

If we consider the categories of the line-final words, we get the following pattern,

(6)   A, B: N,N,N,N
       C: V,V,V,N
       D: Pronoun?, Adj, V,N

which again shows the typical progression: tightest constraints early in the poem, relaxing in C, anarchy in D.

6. Phonology

While it would take us too far afield to examine the phonological patternings with the requisite care, it is possible to point to a few suggestive areas. Let us examine first the stressed vowels in the first three lines of each of the four stanzas.

(7) A.	água	horáda	piédra	a a e
	viénto	dispérsa	água	e e a
	piédra	detiéne	viénto	e e e
B.	viénto	escúlpe	piédra	e u e
	piédra	cópa	água	e o a
	água	escápa	viénto	a a e
C.	viénto	gíros	cánta	e i a
	água	andár	murmúra	a a u
	piédra	inmóvil	cálla	e o a
D.	úno	ótro	ningúno	u o u
	éntre	nómbres	vacíos	e o i
	pásan	dèsvanécen		a e e

Inspection of these vowels reveals that the amount of diversity per stanza increases. That is, for earlier stanzas, the vowel space is less fully utilized than it is for later stanzas. This will emerge somewhat more clearly, possibly, by summing over vowel types.

(8)	A	B	C	D
	6 e	4 e	2 e	3 e
	3 a	3 a	4 a	1 a
		1 u	1 u	2 u
		1 o	1 o	2 o
			1 i	1 i

It is clear that the four stanzas move monotonically towards the maximally homogeneous situation, where all vowels are used with equal frequency.

It may even be possible to claim that the transition towards greater diversity happens over a smaller expanse than the whole poem. Let us consider the 9 syllables of the first line.

(9) *1st foot*   *2nd foot*   *3rd foot*

    e   lá ɣwa   o   rá ɗa   la pyéðra

$\left[\begin{array}{c}\text{Mid}\\V\end{array}\right]$ Lá Spirant Glide a $\left[\begin{array}{c}\text{Mid}\\V\end{array}\right]$ Lá Spirant a

Note how closely these first two trisyllabic feet resemble each other phonetically—and how the third foot does not conform to the pattern set up by the first two feet: its stressed vowel is no longer *a,* it contains the first stop, the first voiceless segment, the first consonantal cluster in syllable onset.

It would be very important for my thesis, that the transition from order to chaos is hologrammed throughout this poem, to be able to cite many such cases. At present, however, I cannot, and thus can only claim that this type of phonetic hologramming is done over larger stretches of text.

7. Semantics

When we turn to semantics, however, it is not difficult to find many transitions of the desired kind within a single stanza. Let us first consider C. Its three verbs all pertain to sound. The first, *canta,* refers to sound which is highly structured; the second, *murmura,* to sound which is less organized, and also of lower amplitude; and the third, *se calla,* a stative, to the negation of sound.

In C, there are three other predicates, all denoting motion. The first, *giros,* refers to a repetitive structured motion; the second, *andar,* to the most general and colorless kind of motion; and the third, *inmóvil,* to the absence of motion.

Thus we could generalize and say that C shows us two transitions from positive to negative, or from existence to non-existence, or from actions to states.

This latter progression mirrors the global transition from action to state: in A, all three verbs are volitional activities; in B and C, only two of the tensed predicates in each stanza are activities (*esculpe* and *escapa,* on the one hand, and *canta* and *murmura* on the other). And in D, which begins with two stative copular predications, the two verbs in line 15 denote events, not activities, and the second, *desvanecen,* is more negative than the first, *pasan.*

And a close examination of the meaning of the poem's first three verbs reveals a parallel increase in negativity. The result of *horada* is to make the surface of the stone non-continuous: the stone will continue to exist, but with a topological change of its surface.

The result of *dispersa* (note the presence of the negative prefix *dis-*) is to make the water non-contiguous, possibly even to induce it to change to a different form, to vaporize it. Clearly, then, *dispersa* can imply more destruction than *horada* does.

And finally, the result of *detiene* (again, with a negative prefix *de-*) for the wind is the absolute vanishing, the destruction, of the wind. For if wind does not move, it does not exist.

So already in the first three verbs we can find a preview of the poem's meaning: the coming not to be of the three elements, the loss of their appearance of differentness.

If the arguments I have made for hologramming in this poem are found to be convincing, and if the general claim, that all (or only almost all?) poems exhibit such holographic organization, can be established, through the microscopic study of other poems, then it may be wise to reexamine the almost axiomatic picture of "normal" communication that Reddy has so aptly characterized. One can point to many factors in a communication even which would seem to be obviously hologrammed: sex, age, and socio-economic status of the speaker; the intimacy of the relationship between speaker and hearer; the formality of the situation; the amount of stress, or anger, etc., under which the speaker is conveying meaning. . . .

Typically, all such holistic properties of a communicative event are abstracted away from. The study of poetry makes one wonder whether some baby may not be being thrown out with the bath water.

NOTE

1. Octavio Paz, *A Draft of Shadows and Other Poems.* Copyright © 1979 by the *New Yorker* magazine, translated by Mark Strand. Reprinted by permission of New Directions Publishing Corporation.

REFERENCES

Capra, Fritjof 1977. *The Tao of Physics.* Bantam Books, New York.
Paz, Octavio 1979. *A Draft of Shadows.* New Directions, New York.
' Reddy, Michael 1979. "The conduit metaphor—A case of frame conflict in our language about language." In: Andrew Ortony (ed.), *Metaphor and Thought.* Cambridge: Cambridge University Press, pp. 284–324.

CHAPTER FOUR

Linguistics and the Study of Folk Poetry*

Arnold M. Zwicky

1. Poetic Systems and Linguistic Systems

I will begin with some general remarks about the relationship between poetic systems and linguistic systems proper, using a single folk song to illustrate my points. Then I will turn to some comments on what linguists can have to say about poetry; in so doing, I will introduce a couple of poetic topics that have recently interested me.

My exemplar is the first verse of the "Irish Rover,"[1] reproduced below as it appears in a collection of Clancy Brothers and Tommy Makem songs (but with my line divisions):

(1)   In the year of our Lord, eighteen hundred and six,   1
          we set sail from the Coal Quay of Cork,   2
      We were sailing away with a cargo of bricks   3
          for the grand City Hall in New York.   4
      We'd an elegant craft, It was rigged 'fore and aft,   5
          And how the trade winds drove her.   6
      She had twenty-three masts and she stood several blasts   7
          And they called her the Irish Rover.   8

In discussing this example, I will want to distinguish between linguistic systems proper and what I shall call, for want of a better term, *(linguistic) overlay systems*. With this latter term I will refer to poetic forms, language games, secret languages, systems of expressive word formation, codes and ciphers, writing systems, and some conventional schemata for borrowing words from one language into another (this is a representative, and not necessarily an exhaustive, list). The characteristics of linguistic overlay systems are, first, that

* This paper is dedicated to the memory of Roman Jakobson, who got me into the study of poetry in the first place. An earlier version was presented at the University of California, Santa Cruz, in May 1982. This paper is a lightly edited version of a Linguistic Institute Forum Lecture (University of Maryland, College Park, August 1982). I began work on it at the Center for Advanced Study in the Behavioral Sciences; I am grateful to the Spencer Foundation for financial support and to the Ohio State University for sabbatical leave.

58   ARNOLD M. ZWICKY

they are in an important sense *detachable*—it is possible to talk about the
linguistic system with which they are associated without referring to the overlay
systems (but it is not possible to talk about the overlay systems without reference
to the linguistic systems with which they are associated)—and second, that the
principles that appear in these overlay systems are, at least in part, significantly
unlike the ones that appear in linguistic systems. My claim here is that an overlay
system embraces a set of conventional principles involving linguistic material,
but that these principles differ in type, as well as in detail, from the (equally
conventional) principles by which a linguistic system is organized. The class of
cases I have in mind here is, of course, poetic forms, in particular the forms of
folk poetry.[2]

A side issue I must deal with before passing to the main events is the distinction between linguistic overlay systems, as I have just characterized them, and
varieties of a language—dialects, styles, and registers. Overlay systems and
varieties have properties in common: both are conventional and structured, and
varieties differ from one another in some of the same gross ways that overlay
systems differ from one another and from linguistic systems proper—in particular, in the frequency of use of certain items or constructions. But the touchstone
in distinguishing overlay systems, which are in a sense outside of a linguistic
system, from varieties, which are themselves linguistic systems, is the second
criterion I mentioned above, according to which we expect overlay systems to
exhibit principles that are, at least in part, different in character from the principles in *any* variety.

Consider the first verse of the "Irish Rover." It divides into eight *lines*,[3] as
do the remining verses of the poem. The line unit is roughly comparable to the
linguistic unit *sentence*, though the two units are not coextensive: lines can be
shorter than a sentence or can comprise several sentences or parts of several
sentences. Moreover, the lines of "Irish Rover" are regulated according to the
number of strongly accented syllables they contain. The pattern appears to be
4-3-4-3-4-3-4-3 (later I will argue that this is mere appearance, that there is a
sense in which all eight lines have four strongly accented syllables). Now this
sort of patterning is simply never seen in linguistic systems; no variety of any
known language requires that its sentences have some fixed number of strongly
accented syllables.

As the poetic unit the *line* and the linguistic unit the *sentence* are roughly
comparable, so are the poetic unit the *verse* and the linguistic unit the *paragraph*.
Again, they are not identical, only comparable. And again the poetic unit is
regulated in what is from the linguist's point of view an unexpected way: in the
"Irish Rover," various lines rhyme in pairs (lines 1 and 3, 2 and 4, 5 and 7, 6
and 8). Rhyme—the requirement of phonemic identity between segments in
specified positions in lines—is a common organizing principle governing verses
of poetry (especially folk poetry), but nothing similar to it ever seems to govern

paragraphs in any variety of ordinary language; no variety requires phonemic identity between segments in specified positions in sentences.

2. Relating Poetic Systems to Linguistic Systems

With this side issue out of the way, I consider the abstract form of the relationship *between* the two systems I am considering, a linguistic system and a particular overlay, a poetic system.[4] The general scheme I propose is diagrammed in Figure 1. On the one hand, we have the language system, with its units and structures and with the rules that describe these units and structures. Here I have in mind phonological units like features, segments, and syllables; phonological structures like those within syllables and those in which syllables are combined into larger prosodic units; grammatical units like words, phrases, and sentences; grammatical structures both below and above the word level; and a variety of rules describing how these various units are combined into these various structures.

On the other hand, there are poetic units, structures, and rules. Some of these—the syllable, for instance—are also part of the language system, but most have no simple correspondent in the language system: this is the case for the poetic units the foot, the line, and the verse, and for the poetic structure the accentual foot type (iamb, trochee, dactyl, anapest, and their ilk), and in general for poetic rules regulating the form of lines and verses.

A very important part of the picture in Figure 1 is the sub-box responsible for *relating* the linguistic system and the poetic system. Following the usage of Halle and Kiparsky, among others, I have labeled this the *mapping function*. The task of this piece of the poetic system is to match poetic structures to linguistic structures, and there are many ways one could imagine this task being done. For English folk poetry, the mapping function has three things to do:

(1) a. It must match phrases and sentences of the language with poetic lines and verses.

b. It must match prosodic structures (of syllables, words, and phrases) with metrical structures (of feet and lines).

Figure 1. Poetic systems as related to linguistic systems

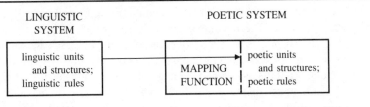

    c. It must pick out certain portions of certain lines as relevant for rhyming principles, and it must define what is to count as matching for the purposes of rhyme.

(In other poetic traditions, the mapping function might have less work; rhyme is not a necessity, of course, and even metrical regulation is absent in some types of free verse, and, according to Hymes (e.g., 1977:sec. IV), in many oral narratives that nevertheless show line and verse structure.)

I must stress here that both the units and the rules in the linguistic system and the units and the rules in the poetic system are conventional. They are different, but they are both conventional. They are two interlocked systems.

Consider the first line of the "Irish Rover," repeated here:

(3) In the year of our Lord, eighteen hundred and six

If you read this line out loud (especially if you know the music that goes with it), you will see that its metrical pattern is a very common one—what is technically called *anapestic tetrameter:* four feet, each of the anapestic (weak-weak-strong) foot type:

(4) Ĭn thĕ yéar | ŏf oŭr Lórd, | ĕightĕen hún | drĕd ănd síx

I will want to say, in fact, that the whole poem is anapestic tetrameter, even though there are deviations, or apparent deviations, from the abstract anapestic tetrameter pattern in these eight lines:

(5) ˘ ˘ ´ | ˘ ˘ ´ | ˘ ˘ ´ | ˘ ˘ ´

That is, I will say that the poetic system calls for four-foot lines, each foot of the weak-weak-strong type. So much for meter.

Now consider the divisions between what are written as lines, and certainly perceived as separate poetic subunits (whether or not these verses are written down). The divisions between these lines come at major constituent breaks. This is signaled by the fact that there is a major mark of punctuation at the end of most of them (a visual indication of a major constituent break). Line 7 ends in a division between two whole clauses, and could perfectly well have been punctuated with a comma. The remaining line is line 3, which ends in a noun phrase *bricks,* separated from a long modifying prepositional phrase (the whole of line 4)—again, a major constituent break. There is clearly a fairly close fit between the large chunks of the syntax and the major divisions of the poem. This fit is not perfect, again: notice that there is a division between clauses in the middle of line 5, so that not all the major breaks between syntactic constituents are located exactly at line breaks.

With respect to segmental matching—(2c) above—observe that the whole poem falls into two sub-pieces, each with four lines. Within each half-verse, the even-numbered lines must match one another and the odd-numbered lines must match one another (an ABAB rhyme scheme), and what must match within any pair of such lines are the last accented vowel nuclei and everything that follows them in their lines: *six–bricks, Cork–York, aft–blasts, drove (h)er–Rover*. The first two pairs here 'match' by virtue of having their relevant parts (phonemically) identical, and perhaps the last pair does as well, as it will if *her* is pronounced without an /h/. The third pair, *aft–blasts*, has /æft/ matched with /æsts/, or in British English, /aft/ matched with /asts/—not phonemic identity, but not gross disparity either, so perhaps this is a kind of 'match,' too. We shall have to see.

3. Details of the Matching Function

I now return to the metrical matching in the "Irish Rover." In (6) below, I've given a relatively straightforward example of a prosodic structure (part of the linguistic system) assigned to a phrase, along with a metrical structure (part of the poetic system) assigned to the same phrase, *in the year*, from line 1.

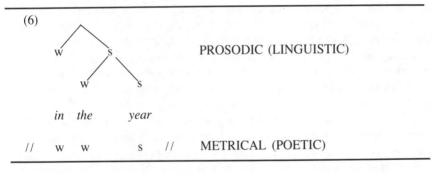

(6)

w   s   PROSODIC (LINGUISTIC)

w   s

in   the   year

//   w   w   s   //   METRICAL (POETIC)

The prosodic structure (which here follows the syntactic phrase structure) has a weak, relatively unaccented preposition followed by its object, a strong, relatively accented noun phrase; and within that noun phrase, there is a weak, relatively unaccented article followed by a strong, relatively accented noun. On the metrical side (annotated also with *w*s and *s*s, but enclosed within double slash lines to distinguish them from the *w*s and *s*s of the prosodic structure), at the point in the poem at which *in the year* occurs what is required is an anapest, w-w-s.[5] In this case the prosodic structure is also w-w-s, exactly what the meter requires.

This is as direct a matching as one could hope for. Now look at a more complex case, the phrase *eighteen hundred and six*, also from line 1. The prosodic structure is built on the accent patterns of the individual words (*eighteen* and *hundred*, both with accent on the first syllable) and their syntactic phrase structure (as before, function words are the weak members of their constructions, and otherwise a weak modifier combines with a strong head). The metrical requirement is for two anapests in sequence:

(7)

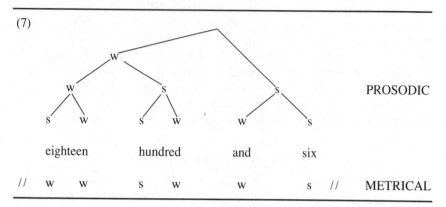

eighteen		hundred		and		six

Notice first that in (7) the division between words does not always correspond to the division between feet; *hundred* ends one foot and begins another. In general, the two types of units are quite separate from one another.

The exciting, and complicated, part of this business is the treatment of the word *eighteen,* which is stressed on the first syllable but nevertheless counts as two weaks for the purposes of the poetic meter. It turns out that people with some experience of particular metrical traditions are able to make fairly firm judgments about the metricality or unmetricality of individual lines. (These judgments are parallel in many ways to grammaticality judgments, and subject to some of the same problems.) An example like line 1 of the "Irish Rover" would be uniformly judged to be perfectly metrical, so that there must be some sense in which *eighteen hundred and six* is composed of two anapests, even though its first syllable is linguistically strong. It follows that the matching function cannot be as gut-simple as you might want it to be, prosodic weak matching metrical weak, prosodic strong matching metrical strong. Sometimes weak can match strong, and sometimes strong can match weak—without any sense of violation. In the case at hand, the relevant principle is not hard to see: the metrically strong syllable should be the linguistically *strongest* syllable in its foot. The first syllable of *eighteen* is linguistically strong, but it is part of a weak unit, while the first syllable of *hundred* is linguistically strong within a strong unit.

This is far from the whole story, of course. Kiparsky (1975, 1977), in particular, has explored matching functions that permit *w* corresponding to *s*, or *s* corresponding to *w*, without any accompanying sense of unmetricality.

A few words about segmental matching. I have already remarked that two of the four pairs of syllables (or sequences of syllables) that are required to match by the ABAB rhyming principle do so unproblematically, and that a third probably does so as well. This leaves *aft–blasts,* identical in vowel but not in the following consonantal offset. The pairing is /ft/ against /sts/, consonant clusters that differ in *two* respects:

(8)

f	t	Ø	*aft*
s	t	s	*blasts*

In (8), /f/ is paired with /s/, and zero with /s/. The question is now whether these are really mismatches, or whether they are parallel to the prosodic-metrical relationships in (7), where a prodosic *s* is paired with a metrical *w*. I will return to this question below.

Next, there are apparent deviations from the gross metrical pattern for whole lines. Lines 2 and 4 are apparently short one whole foot, a very unlikely event in verses set to music. In fact, all the remaining verses of the "Irish Rover" also show an apparent 4-3-4-3 pattern in the first half-verse. To detect what is going on here, you have to read the lines out loud, or (better) sing them. If you do this, you will see that in the place of the last foot of lines 2 and 4 there is a pause, a *rest.* The lines are all, in fact, four feet long.

Lines 6 and 8 are more clearly deviant. Line 6, with three short (weak-strong) feet followed by one supershort (one-syllable) foot is wildly off the anapestic pattern:

(9)   Ănd hów thĕ tráde wĭnds dróve hér

while line 8, ending in a short foot followed by a supershort one, has a deviant second half:

(10)   Ănd thĕy cálled hĕr thĕ Írĭsh Róvér

The feeling of deviation in these lines is much increased by the fact that the supershort foot in each case is a syllable that is linguistically unaccented, or weak—the anaphoric object pronoun *her* in (9) and the final unaccented syllable of the word *Rover* in (10). The second of these is not a small, permissible variation within a larger pattern, like the prosodic *s* matched with a metrical *w* in (7), but a genuine violation.

Finally, a few words about line divisions. I have already remarked that the line divisions fall at major phrase boundaries throughout this verse of the "Irish Rover." The half-line divisions are rather more interesting. In the odd-numbered lines (1, 3, 5, and 7), there is a clear syntactic break halfway in the middle of each line:

(11)   a.   In the year of our Lord,   eighteen hundred and six
         b.   We were sailing away   with a cargo of bricks

    c. We'd an elegant craft,   It was rigged 'fore and aft
    d. She had twenty-three masts   and she stood several blasts

(In lines 5 and 7, in fact, there is an S boundary in the middle of the line.) Most of the even-numbered lines are quite different, though line 4 has a reasonably large break at its midpoint:

(12) for the grand City Hall   in New York

Lines 2, 6, and 8, however, divide words: compound nouns in 2 and 6 (*Coal Quay, trade winds*), the one-word adjective *Irish* in 8.

It turns out that the differences between odd and even lines in the first verse are repeated in the other three. The even lines are metrically deviant and usually do not divide naturally into half-lines. On the other hand, the odd lines rhyme only in the first verse; in the later verses, the rhyme pattern for half-verses is ABCB, with rhyme between even lines only. But overall, the odd lines are normal, the even lines peculiar, with line 6 constituting a kind of crisis of deviation.

4. Poetics and Stylistics

I now turn away from this particular folk song, to make some general remarks, stressing particularly what I think is an important distinction in the sorts of things that linguists have to say about poetry.

Linguists are, naturally enough, often interested in poetry for their own sectarian reasons. We might say that they are seeking linguistic uses of poetic facts; being interested, say, in the psychological reality of linguistic units like the syllable, the segment, the distinctive feature, the syntactic phrase, prosodic structures, and the like, they hope to mine poetry for its evidential nuggets. But there are also poetic uses of linguistic facts, and it is in this realm that we can properly speak of ways in which linguists can contribute to the study of poetry. What I have in mind here is the use of linguistic terminology, formalization, and concepts to illuminate poetry itself.

There are two ways in which this particular enterprise can go ahead. One approach might be called *narrow poetics,* or just *poetics* for short. Here we deal with the rule-governed, the conventional, aspects of poetic systems—for instance, principles requiring that each line must have some specified number of syllables, or a specified number of feet, each of a specified form, with allowable variants of certain sorts. We can think of these principles as *defining* what is a poem of a certain type, and therefore as being analogous to grammatical rules specifying the sentences in the linguistic system proper.

Poetics in this narrow sense deals with what is expected, with what is predictable, given a particular poetic scheme. Some of the things I've mentioned in dealing with the "Irish Rover" clearly belong to poetics in this sense. In general, my remarks about the fit of the poem to a linguistic analysis deal with the requirements of the poetic form (having to do with the nature of lines, rhymes, line divisions, and so on).

But some of what I said above is of a rather different sort, treating what you might call *broad poetics*, though its proper name is *stylistics*. Stylistics concerns itself with those aspects of a poem (or, indeed, of any other linguistic production) that are unexpected, unpredictable, *strategically placed* rather than determined by rule. These aspects of the poem manifest the intents of the author or performer and (perhaps) produce certain effects in the audience.

(The distinction between stylistics and narrow poetics is quite parallel to that between perlocutionary effect and illocutionary force in the theory of speech acts: again, a distinction between the strategic allocation of linguistic resources to achieve certain ends or effects, on the one hand, and rule-governed, conventional behavior on the other.)

Failure to observe this distinction has led to a certain amount of ill will and misunderstanding between linguists and literary critics. The linguist has, in a sense, something absolute to say to the literary critic with respect to (narrow) poetics. In this area, the linguist and the literary critic have a common interest— but the area is not very great in extent, and what linguists have to say here is not of enormous interest to literary critics. The fact that the expected line form in a particular poetic scheme is one with, say, ten feet in it is background information so far as the literary critic is concerned; it's all the other stuff that the literary critic is interested in.

The linguist's standing in stylistics is less secure than in poetics, and much more is at stake. What the linguist can offer is some *facts* about poems, couched in terms of the vocabulary appropriate to discussions of linguistic structure. What the linguist isn't in a position to supply is an *interpretation* of those facts. We have observed that in the "Irish Rover" the odd-numbered lines are very regular, and the even-numbered lines are irregular. That's a fact about this particular piece of language, a fact which a linguist like me could provide to a literary critic who's interested in the "Irish Rover" (should there be such a person), and which could then be used in spinning some further story about what that fact means, in particular about how one might interpret the poem in light of that fact (and other facts, of course, many of which the linguist has no responsibility to supply and no special insight about). A description of the stylistics of a poem is not an analysis of it.

What sorts of facts do we talk about in the field of (poetic) stylistics?

• mismatches, as when the poetic form calls for a strong syllable at some point in a line, but an unaccented syllable occurs at that point (as in line 8 of the "Irish Rover" verse, where the second syllable of *Rover* fills a strong slot in the poetic pattern)

- deviations from poetic rules, for instance, lines with the wrong number of feet
- deviations from linguistic rules, for instance, word orders not otherwise permitted in the language

That is, deviations from matching principles, deviations from poetic rules, or deviations from linguistic rules. But not all style is deviation. There are also:

- frequency effects, the high-frequency *or* low-frequency use of material that is not otherwise governed by some sort of rule and therefore is open for free choice (as when high vowels appear with extraordinary frequency in a poem, or when some set of lexical items is emphasized or avoided)
- co-occurrence effects, in which elements of different types occur together and in some sense reinforce one another.

A particularly nice example of two of these effects in one package is a famous bit of eccentric word formation on the part of the Latin poet Ennius. Ennius might have written *cerebrum comminuit* 'he smashes the brain,' but he chose instead to formulate the idea as *cere–comminuit–brum,* so breaking up the noun *cerebrum* 'brain' by inserting the verb *comminuit* 'he smashes' in the middle of it. The result is nonsense, because it violates the rules of word formation in Latin. This striking deviation of linguistic rules is accompanied by a particular bit of semantic content, namely the reference to smashing in the inserted verb form. The co-occurrence itself is striking and (at least to my mind) effective.

5.   Illustration: Types of Rhyme

Now I should like to turn to two cases that have interested me, one from poetics narrowly understood, the other from stylistics.

In poetics, among the issues that naturally attract the linguist's eye is the question of what it is that rhymes—or, in the terms I developed above, what the segmental matching function is. (There are similar questions about meter and about line divisions; for the latter question I especially recommend Kiparsky (1975) for its discussion of differences in line divisions between different poets at different times.) All kinds of different systems of rhyme can be discerned in the practices of the world's poets. That is to say, there are different matching functions at different times and places.

The function we've been looking at is usually called *full rhyme.* It is not the only one that's available, for 'high' poetry or for folk poetry. One alternative scheme is represented in the literature primarily by the extraordinary system of rhyme in Old Irish. According to standard descriptions of this system (Murphy 1961, for instance), it worked in terms of *classes* of consonant segments that count as equivalent for the purposes of the rhyming system: any consonant in one class counts as equivalent to any other consonant in that class and doesn't count as equivalent to any other consonant in a different class. For instance, the voiced stops form a class, so that any voiced stop counts as matching any other, but a voiced stop doesn't match a voiceless stop, even one at the same point of articulation. This system allows more matches than full rhyme, obviously, but only those within its set of six 'equivalence classes.' I will call this type of scheme *equivalence class rhyme*.

A system that is superficially similar to equivalence class rhyme is that of Turkish traditional poetry, as discussed by Malone (1982). In the traditional Turkish system there are four classes:

(13) a. i ü u ï
      b. a e
      c. o
      d. ö

That is, the four high vowels all count as matching one another, while of the nonhigh vowels, only /a e/ count as matching one another; and each of the phonemes /o/ and /ö/ matches only another occurrence of the same phoneme. It's significant in this case, as Malone points out, that the groups of vowels that count as equivalent for this matching function are exactly those that play a role in the vowel harmony of the language. Indeed, in an abstract representation for Turkish words (at least for affixes) the vowels of (13a) would be assigned a single representation, say *I*, while the vowels of (13b) would be assigned another, say *A,* and the isolated vowels of (13c) and (13d) would represent third and fourth entities.

It is a consequence of these facts that one way to see Turkish rhyme—indeed, the way Malone encourages you to see it—is not in terms of phonemic identity, but rather in terms of *morphophonemic* (or, at least, somewhat abstract) identity. Here Malone is pushing a proposal that has been advanced in several places by Kiparsky (especially 1968, 1972), with respect to the Finnish Kalevala and the Sanskrit Rigveda. The claim is that non-surface, more abstract than phonemic, representations are relevant in determining which segments count as rhyming.[6] In any case, Turkish might represent an example where there is some *sense* to the equivalence classes, where the equivalence classes are a surface manifestation of some more abstract unity.

Rather different from equivalence class rhyme is a type of rhyme for which there is no good standard name, but which I will call *half rhyme* (despite the fact that any two dictionaries of poetics will differ wildly in what they describe under this heading). The scheme that I'm talking about here is discussed in Zwicky (1976), the title of which illustrates the phenomenon:

(14) This rock and roll has got to stop,
       Junior's head is hard as rock.

Stop ends with /p/, and *rock* ends with /k/, but they count as rhyming, at least in the practice of many folk and popular poets. There is, in fact, a very large body of lyrics using this looser matching function. Representative lyricists are Bob Dylan, Paul McCartney, Paul Simon, James Taylor, Judy Collins, and Warren Zevon.

What characterizes half rhyme is that the rhyming parts of words don't have to be phonemically identical—only close, in several specific senses: (a) a stressed vowel can be matched with a different vowel one feature different from it, /i e/ or /i I/, for instance; (b) a postvocalic consonant can be matched with a different consonant one feature different from it, /s z/ or /m n/, for instance; or (c) a single postvocalic consonant can match a cluster containing that consonant, /d nd/ or /d dz/, for instance.

Recall again the first verse of the "Irish Rover," which has one failure of perfect rhyme, *aft–blasts* (see (8) above). Where you would expect perfect identity in consonants after the stressed vowel, you have instead /f/ matched with /s/—a single-feature difference between the two consonants. And where you would expect the same number of consonants after the stressed vowel, you have instead an extra /s/ at the end of *blasts*, /t/ matched with /ts/. What we have here is a (not uncommon) case of a compound of two types of half rhyme, types (b) and (c).

Many traditions of folk rhyme follow patterns very similar to those in the rock lyrics—half rhymes of all three types are to be expected. The operative matching function is less demanding than in most familiar rhymed verse, but still quite constrained.

Half rhyme and equivalence class rhyme are distinct from one another. They do not group together the same kinds of divergences from full rhyme. Notice that in the Old Irish case, the corresponding voiced and voiceless stops do not count as rhyming, though they would in a system of half rhyme; on the other hand, the Old Irish grouping together of /v/ and /r/ goes well beyond what a half-rhyme scheme will allow, since the two phonemes are more than one feature apart, in anyone's feature system.

(It is also true that both half rhyme and equivalence class rhyme are distinct from a fairly common scheme of 'high' poetry, namely *assonance*. The differences are discussed in Zwicky 1976.)

6. Illustration: Regularity and Deviation

I turn now from poetics in the narrow sense to stylistics, as applied to poetry. Here we are concerned with questions like the following: How can linguistic form and meaning reinforce one another? How are mismatches and deviations distributed throughout a poem? What does it mean if a certain element of linguistic form appears very often in a poem? And so on.

For several years now my wife and I have been exploring the second of these questions, about the distribution of mismatches and deviations in a poem. We began with folk verse, broadly understood, although our interest has recently extended itself to the poetry of W. H. Auden. Folk poetry is a natural starting point, because it is composed, learned, and performed according to unconscious canons of what 'sounds right,' rather than by adherence to explicitly formulated rules;[7] in addition, primarily oral transmission insures that the verse is free of effects intended for the eye only, or calculated as a kind of obscure puzzle for the reader or hearer. That is, for folk poetry it is essentially guaranteed that linguistic structure—or at least those aspects of linguistic structure that have some psychological reality—will be relevant to analysis.

Our first research (Zwicky and Zwicky to appear) involved three sources of verse: (dirty) limericks, traditional American folk songs, and lyrics by Bob Dylan and the various Beatles. In verse from all three sources, as in folk poetry in general, line divisions are quite regular, so that the stylistic interest of these works lay in how rhythm and rhyme are used in them. It occurred to us when we first examined these materials that it would be reasonable to expect that the beginning of a poem would, in general, be more regular than its continuation, especially in oral poetry: the audience (or the reader) is required to discern a pattern fairly early on in the poem, in order to be able to interpret what follows.

As it happens, folk poetry does not tend to come in lines with the same number of feet or with the same foot type throughout. There is a fair amount of variation from one poem to another: the lines are mostly four feet long, but three-foot and six-foot lines also occur, and the dominant foot types include iambs, trochees, and anapests, and occasionally other types as well. The rhyme schemes are frequently ABAB, but there are a number of other patterns. What this means is that if you listen to the beginning of a folk poem, you simply don't know what foot type will be the norm, how many feet per line to expect, or where rhyming words will mark off verse structure. Consequently, if you are the poet and hope that your audience will perceive (however unconsciously) the pattern that lies behind your creation, you will do well to concentrate on keeping deviations in portions away from the very beginning.

Now there is a great deal of tedious technical detail involved in how one makes precise, and then tests, the proposal that the beginning of a poem is more regular than what follows. Fortunately, I can simply refer you to the discussion in Zwicky and Zwicky (to appear).

A brief summary of the studies and their results: (a) for the limericks, we compared their first halves to their second, with respect to the number of mismatches between the (linguistic) prosodic patterns of lines and the patterns required by the metrical scheme, and found these mismatches to be significantly less frequent in the first half than in the second; (b) for the folk songs, we compared the first verses of the songs to later verses in the same way, and found the first verses to be significantly more regular than the others rhythmically; and (c) for the pop/rock lyrics, we compared the first verses to later verses, with respect to the use of half rhyme or no rhyme versus full rhyme, and found that first verses showed significantly more full rhyme than later ones.[8]

A particularly nice incidental result fell out of this last study, which used a set of Dylan lyrics and all the usable lyrics from the Beatle's *White Album*. The Dylan lyrics fell naturally into two groups of unequal size: a large number of songs with four-line verses, mostly rhymed ABAB, and a few songs with very complex rhyme schemes in each verse. We examined five songs with extraordinarily complex requirements on segmental matching, among them "Like a Rolling Stone."[9] Below I provide the first verse of one version of this poem:

(15)   Once upon a *time* you dressed so *fine,*
        You threw the bums a *dime* in your *prime, didn't you?*
        People'd *call,* say "beware *doll*
        You're bound to *fall,"* you thought they were *all kiddin' you.*
        You used to laugh *about* everybody that was hangin' *out,*
        Now you don't talk so *loud,* now you don't seem so *proud,*
            About having to be scrounging for your next *meal.*
        [Words or phrases subject to rhyme requirements are italicized.].

Each verse of the poem comes in three pieces, each piece consisting of two lines with an appended phrase. Each of these lines has internal rhyme, so that there is a requirement for four matches in two lines. The phrases appended to the first two couplets rhyme with one another, and the phrase appended to the third couplet rhymes with a repeated line of the refrain, *How does it feel?* The scheme is then:

(16)   A+A A+A B
        C+C C+C B
        D+D D+D E

Notice that in (15) not all of the rhymes are full: *fine* is a half rhyme to *time, dime,* and *prime; doll* is a half rhyme to *call, fall,* and *all;* and *about* and *out* half-rhyme with *loud* and *proud. Didn't you* and *kiddin' you,* despite appearances on the printed page, were perfect rhymes in the recorded performance we used as the basis for our calculations. *Meal* in the last phrase matches the refrain word *feel* perfectly. In other verses full rhymes appear in place of some of these half rhymes, half rhymes appear in different places, and some matched words don't rhyme at all.

    Schemes of the complexity of (16) are hard to pull off in verse that is performed rather than printed, especially if the words are to be sung, and especially if you sing like Bob Dylan. We expected ahead of time that if there was a tendency towards regularity at the beginning of folk poems, it would show up in sharp relief in complex cases like (15). And, in fact, with only five 'complex' Dylan poems in our analysis, we got a very strong statistical effect for regularity in the rhyming of the first verses versus later ones.

7. Conclusion

I have now illustrated some of the ways in which a linguist might assist the study of poetry, especially folk poetry. In one narrow domain—poetics proper—it is the linguist's constructs that are the very objects of study. In another, much larger, domain, the linguist has the role of one adviser among many, offering observations about the language of poetry that might be interpreted and combined with other sources of insight into a work's effects. I hope to have shown you that a linguist examining folk poetry can serve both roles, elucidating poetic form itself (as in my discussion of the metrical matching function of half rhyme) and also suggesting paths in interpreting the poem's effects (as in my discussion of regularity and deviation in the rhyme and rhythm of folk verse).

NOTES

1. From "The Irish Rover" in *The Clancy Brothers and Tommy Makem Song Book*, p. 39, copyright 1964, Tiparm Music Publishers.
2. By 'folk poetry' I refer to verse transmitted primarily by oral, rather than written, means. I include nursery rhymes, limericks, mnemonic rhymes, nonsense verse, the words to folk songs, and the lyrics of popular music, even when the authors of these are known (as is the case for Gelett Burgess's nonsense poem "The Purple Cow" and all popular song lyrics), even when written versions of the words are widely distributed (as is the case for much nonsense verse and all nursery rhymes), and even when the verse is known to be of recent composition (as is the case for popular song lyrics).
3. Following the general custom in the study of folk poetry, I use the term *line* even for units of oral verse. The reader must not attribute any unintended orthographic interpretation to the word.
4. What follows is largely based on the work of Paul Kiparsky (especially Kiparsky 1975, 1977). See O'Connor (1982) for some discussion of this framework and of the Jakobsonian viewpoint it grows from.
5. In a fuller treatment the metrical feet would also have internal structure, which I have suppressed here for simplicity.
6. Churma (1979) stresses throughout his discussion of 'external' evidence in phonology, as does Sommerstein (1977:218–20) in his treatment of poetic schemes as evidence in phonology, that poetic equivalences like those of Turkish, Finnish, Sanskrit, or (Sommerstein's example) Icelandic cannot be used directly to argue for phonological analyses in which the equivalent segments have the same (morphophonemic) source. The alternative is simply that the equivalences are poetic conventions, part of the matching functions in the languages in question (historically, they are archaisms, reflexes of earlier full rhymes: earlier identities are present equivalences). The natural objection to *this* proposal is that these matching functions are unnecessarily complex, and that simpler matching functions (referring to abstract levels of representation) are available. However, nothing says that simplicity arguments applicable to linguistic analysis should carry over to the poetic domain (or, indeed, to the domain of any other overlay system).

7. This observation is as true of pop music lyrics as of traditional folk verse: "pop music is made by ear-musicians, not eye-musicians" (Mellers 1973:28). Elsewhere in this book on the Beatles' music and lyrics, Mellers refers to the 'empirical' processes governing the Beatles' harmonic progressions; that is, the Beatles tried a number of things and then stuck with effects they liked. Surely much the same can be said for the Beatles' lyrics. In the case of Bob Dylan, with his roots in folk music and blues, it it perhaps more obviously true that composition is a matter of choosing what 'sounds right'; performance (rather than a given text) is stressed, and there are many variants of individual songs on different occasions (see Bowden 1982 for an extended discussion of these points).

8. We do not propose that earlier portions of poems are more regular than later ones in all cases, in all poetic traditions. In 'high' poetry, especially in forms usually encountered visually, the tendency might on occasion be absent, or even reversed. And in any case the tendency is a statistical one. A particular poem might be aberrant, even interestingly aberrant.

9. From "Like a Rolling Stone," by Bob Dylan (copyright 1965 by M. Witmark and Sons), in *Bob Dylan,* pp. 4–6 (copyright 1974 by Warner Bros.).

REFERENCES

Bowden, Betsy 1982. *Performed Literature: Words and Music by Bob Dylan.* Bloomington, IN: Indiana University Press.
Churma, Donald G. 1979. *Arguments from External Evidence in Phonology.* Unpublished dissertation, Ohio State University.
The Clancy Brothers and Tommy Makem Song Book 1964. New York: Oak Publications.
Freeman, Donald C. (ed.) 1981. *Essays in Modern Stylistics.* London: Methuen.
Hymes, Dell H. 1977. "Discovering oral performance and measured verse in American Indian narrative." *New Literary History* 7, pp. 431–57. Reprinted in: Hymes 1981, pp. 309–41.
Hymes, Dell H. 1981. *"In Vain I Tried to Tell You."* Philadelphia: University of Pennsylvania Press.
Kiparsky, Paul 1968. "Metrics and morphophonemics in the Kalevala." In: Charles E. Gribble (ed.), *Studies Presented to Professor Roman Jakobson by His Students.* Cambridge, MA: Slavica, pp. 137–48.
Kiparsky, Paul 1972. "Metrics and morphophonemics in the Rigveda." In: Michael K. Brame (ed.), *Contributions to Generative Phonology.* Austin, TX: University of Texas Press, pp. 171–200.
Kiparsky, Paul 1975. "Stress, syntax, and meter." *Language* 51, pp. 576–616. Reprinted in: Freeman 1981, pp. 225–72.
Kiparsky, Paul 1977. "The rhythmic structure of English verse." *Linguistic Inquiry* 8, pp. 189–247.
Malone, Joseph L. 1982. "Generative phonology and Turkish rhyme." *Linguistic Inquiry* 13:3, pp. 550–3.
Mellers, Wilfrid 1973. *Twilight of the Gods: The Music of the Beatles.* New York: Macmillan.
Murphy Gerald 1961. *Early Irish Metrics.* Dublin: Royal Irish Academy.
Obler, Loraine K., and Lise Menn (eds.) 1982. *Exceptional Language and Linguistics.* New York: Academic Press.
O'Connor, M. P. 1982. " 'Unanswerable the knack of tongues': The linguistic study of verse." In: Obler and Menn, pp. 143–68.
Sommerstein, Alan H. 1977. *Modern Phonology.* London: Edward Arnold.

Zwicky, Arnold M. 1976. "Well, this rock and roll has got to stop. Junior's head is hard as rock." CLS 12, pp. 676–97.

Zwicky, Arnold M., and Ann D. Zwicky to appear. "Patterns first, exceptions later." In: Robert Channon and Linda R. Shockey (eds.), *A Festschrift for Ilse Lehiste*.

PART TWO
EXTENDED
SPEECH
COMMUNITIES

CHAPTER FIVE

Natural Phonology and Strategies for Teaching English/Spanish Pronunciation

Peter C. Bjarkman

1. Introduction

A theory of Stampean natural phonology which I have been promoting (see Bjarkman 1975, 1976, 1978a, 1978b) and which was conceived and developed by David Stampe (1969, 1973a; Stampe and Donegan 1979) has had growing impact as a system of phonological analysis.[1] And it may well be "one of the most important developments, if not *the* most important, since Generative Phonology itself" (Sommerstein 1977:235). Wider utilizations of this theoretical viewpoint within 'applied' realms, in such fields as language pedagogy, have yet to be fully demonstrated, however. The concluding three chapters of my forthcoming book (Bjarkman in preparation) attempt what I believe is the first extensive and principled effort at such an assessment. This present chapter, by contrast, provides what is a necessarily brief yet highly representative sketch of essential arguments and conclusions reached in that more elaborate study. My narrower subject here is the application of Stampe's principles to formal classroom language instruction. I am especially interested in the notions of a 'natural phonetic process' and its implications for our acquisition of native-like pronunciation in both English and Spanish.[2] The acquisition I will be focusing on is that done by those 'non-native' adults whose goal is native-like competence in some target second language.

There has been at least one earlier attempt made at assessing some of the implications of Stampe's novel theory for language pedagogy. In his sketchy yet sufficiently insightful article, William J. Daniels (1975) argues for his own interpretations of natural phonology as an approach that can overcome certain long-recognized inadequacies of taxonomic theory, as well as of generative theory, as a basis for the teaching of Russian pronunciation. But unfortunately for applied linguists, as well as Russian teachers, Daniels offers only some exceedingly tentative steps in this direction, and the effort is finally somewhat mitigated by his own inadequate (at best) understanding of the natural phonologist's distinctions between *morphophonemic* and *allophonic*-type natural processes.[3] Daniels is certainly to be commended for an initial apprehension of the possible applications of natural phonology in the realm of language teaching. In spirit, he is essentially correct in his observation that all phonological processes are neither of identical teleology nor acquired in a similar direct fashion, and therefore are not to be taught identically. His distinction between the substitutions which are 'rules' and those which are the innate natural phonological 'processes' is overly simplistic, however, and should be drastically revised before full application of this theory for language teachers is altogether transparent—or even mildly approachable.

My purpose in this present paper is necessarily twofold. At first, I aim to correct Daniels's portrait of natural phonology, at least insofar as such systems might be applied to the teaching of pronunciation, and in the process to clarify and even expand on the original discussion of formal distinctions between types of phonological processes and the related dichotomy between types of teaching strategies. Relying on English, American Spanish, and Korean as my primary data sources, I will next sketch briefly here some implications of natural phonology for the teaching of English as a foreign language.[4] An expanded Stampean model of natural phonology to be presented here will, among its other advantages, allow for several more serviceable applications than the more limiting model advocated by Daniels. And there will be some additional payoffs—in terms of fresh explanations of observable phonological performance—to be derived from a streamlined Stampean model as well.

I begin with the following minimal set of working hypotheses about natural phonology, and therefore about all language systems. It may be necessary at this point to ask my reader to keep in mind that all such tentative postulates still fall very much within realms of what might be called 'slippery speculations.' That is, they represent only very loosely formulated and somewhat incomplete proposals. In all cases the claims seem to be intuitive, and they do find some empirical validation; still none has yet proven to be adequate beyond any shadow of doubt.

Claim One: Contrastive Analysis.   Natural phonology provides a more satisfactory basis, both for a contrastive analysis of English and Spanish and for the practical teaching of pronunciation, than does either taxonomic phonology or the standard forms of generative phonology. This is precisely so because natural phonology recognizes two distinct types of phonological substitutions: 'innate,' physiologically motivated phonological processes versus abstract and learned phonological rules (for the primary and assumed distinctions here, see Bjarkman 1975).

Claim Two: Free Variation.   What have been viewed in traditional phonology as being 'free' variations are not 'free' at all, but rather represent the manifestations of extensions of processes, or the limitations on natural phonological processes, operating in the native language system. The piling on of additional processes results in the stylistic variation we have come to label as 'rapid' or 'casual speech' pronunciation.

Claim Three: Cognitive Instruction.   The fact that phonological 'processes' are teleologically different from phonological 'rules' carries a subtle implication that they must also be differently (if at all) taught. In fact, processes might be more properly imparted (where they do not already exist as the tacit carryover from the learner's infant language system) through some form of blind mechanical drill than through any type of more cognitive instruction, to which we more frequently appeal.

Claim Four: Predictability.   Since 'processes' relate to the teaching of pronunciation and 'rules' to the teaching of formal grammar, for the pronunciation teacher contrasts between processes will indeed imply potential error sources (viz., the failure to suppress native processes or the total failure to acquire new non-native ones) whereas the contrasts between true rules do not predict such phonological interference. In the latter case, such errors are due only to inadequate and improper formal learning on the student's own part. Processes are only acquired through painstaking practice, whereas the formal 'rules' of the grammar simply must be 'learned' and replicated without error. Process 'errors' lead only to detectable 'accent.'' Errors with rules lead to miscommunication (at the very worst) and a faulty linguistic competence (at the very best).

The final two claims here, while in one sense clarifying and thus simplifying the instructional task, at the same time place an added and rather imposing burden upon the shoulders of the classroom ESL teacher (or at least upon the author of classroom programs of instructional materials). Essentially, the ESL teacher must now turn into something of a natural phonologist. That is, he must himself know the distinctions drawn here between phonological processes and phonological rules, as well as the particular manifestations of productive and recurrent processes in both the targeted instructional language and the language which is native for his students—the linguistically naive language learners. And yet, with the elementary school or secondary school foreign language classroom, as most of us have always known it, such knowledge has rarely if ever been in any formal sense a part of the planned instructional program.

2.   A Natural Phonological Model

The model of natural phonology in question incorporates a series of assumptions about the native phonological system. Such assumptions are merely restated here for simplicity's sake from the inventory of parallel assertions drawn from Stampe (1973a), then later catalogued more thoroughly in my own work (Bjarkman 1977). It is precisely assumptions such as these which seem never to be an integral part of those tools of the trade which we, as theoretical linguists, should be attempting to impart to our colleagues who labor, often blindly, in the pedagogical field.

Assumption One: Processes versus Rules.   Phonological substitutions made by the child (as well as by his adult counterparts) should be recognized as consisting of two distinct types of alternations of contrasting purpose: a restricted set of learned and arbitrary (in the sense that they are not very well motivated phonetically) phonological rules (which are by and large the exclusive set of substitutions discussed by Chomsky and Halle throughout *The Sound Pattern of English* as comprising the true phonological component), and a far more comprehensive set of the innate and physiologically or 'mentally' motivated natural processes (these being defined by natural phonology in a way that encompasses a good deal more than simply phonetic-detail rules admitted into the grammar by Chomsky and Halle and other transformational or generative phonologists). The first set here ('rules') functions to assure the necessary grammatical complexities we associate with allophony and allomorphy; the second, to facilitate the most facile articulations. Processes are thus innate, productive, and unordered (among other characteristics); the rules seem to be learned and often apparently 'ordered', at least in the sense that they do not apply indiscriminately and repeatedly throughout derivations (see Bjarkman 1975 for the complete catalogue of characteristics).

Assumption Two: Adult Speech Residues.[5]   To quote Stampe here: ". . . The phonological system of language is largely the residue of an innate system of these phonological processes, revised in certain ways by [each speaker's own] linguistic experience" (1969:443). This is to say that the child spends most of his time 'unlearning' natural tendencies, and a more restricted block of time learning or mastering unnatural ones (i.e. those not highly motivated by phonetic environment).

Assumption Three: Conflicting Constraints.   These innate processes inevitably comprise contradictory sets of speech reduction mechanisms, and such oppositions result from the conflicting restrictions on our innate phonetic system (e.g., obstruents tend naturally to become voiceless by processes of linguistic change and in child language (i.e., strengthening) regardless of context, while a normal reflex is to voice obstruents, and later even to spirantize them, when they occur intervocalically (i.e., weakening)). Furthermore, these contradictions in processes are resolved by native speakers through (a) the suppression of one of the contradictory processes; (b) a limitation, which is a suppression of some part of one of these contradictory processes; and/or (c) the ordered or reordered application of such processes.

Assumption Four: Phonetic Change.   Linguistic change—as it is manifested in the altered pronunciation of new generations of speakers—results not from the addition of rules to the grammar, but rather from the child's failure to suppress some characteristic process, such failures to suppress or to restrict a process inevitably appearing on the surface as an actual 'addition' of a rule to the grammatical component (Stampe 1969:448). For example, if the English speaker were to fail in continuing to suppress final obstruent devoicing (which is not relevant in English where we continue to distinguish word-finally between voiced/voiceless pairs), it would appear that he had suddenly *added* a 'rule' devoicing final obstruents. Natural phonology here assumes that such processes as final devoicing are innately present across all languages, that all speakers of some languages simply learn to suppress them, and that linguistic change occurs usually (there are admittedly some few other types—such as adult borrowing) when whole generations of speakers make such drastic alterations as this failure to retain such a well-learned suppression.

Assumption Five: Non-Abstractness. The child does not in essence possess an abstract phonemic system of his own devising, but rather his phonological representations will closely conform to the phonetic system recognized for adult speech. More abstract forms are postulated by the child (it is assumed) only to account for cases of 'absolute neutralization'—that is, cases in which the posited form has no actual phonetic manifestation, never appearing as a pronounced form. Evidence is again found for such a claim in Stampe (1969, 1973a), and we will turn to it again briefly below.

Assumption Six: Process Types. Innate processes are taken to be of three distinct types: 1) those unrestricted paradigmatic (context-free) processes which apply (most especially with child language) to eliminate numerous impermissible segments from the lexicon (e.g., it is assumed here that English, as a case in point, has no underlying nasal vowels, since paradigmatic processes would remove any such segments from a child's inventory); 2) morphophonemic syntagmatic (or context-sensitive) processes that convert one 'underlying' segment into another and thus account for cases of absolute neutralization; and 3) the allophonic syntagmatic processes, which reestablish at the phonetic level sounds eliminated from underlying representation by earlier paradigmatic processes. If English does not carry nasalized vowels in its lexicon, such phonetic vowels are thus established by process in nasalizing environments (preceding a nasal segment).

Since learned phonological rules capture for the most part the abstract relationships between individual morphemes, while innate phonological processes state constraints on articulation and operate on the basis of purely phonetic (mental/physiological) conditions, it is a general principle of natural phonology (though not such an absolute irrevocable law as some earlier writings mistakenly took it to be) that processes naturally apply after rules. (There is unfortunately little space here for details about exceptions—but more on the matter below.) Moreover, paradigmatic processes, which will function to eliminate the inner complexities of single segments, stand clearly distinct in their function from syntagmatic processes, which will eliminate complexities arising from sequences of segments. It is therefore quite understandable that the former (paradigmatic processes) are largely restricted to child language, since massive neutralizations of segments which they produce would be most intolerable in any adult speech. Finally, since morphophonemic processes manipulate underlying segments— while allophonic processes serve to introduce what are only permissible surface segments (e.g., nasalized vowels in English)—it is apparent that the latter type

Figure 3.0.1.   Taxonomic Phonological Derivations

(.......)	morphophonemic	/......./	allophonic	[.......]
morphemic	rules ——————→	**phonemic**	rules ——→	**phonetic**

will as a matter of principle apply to outputs of the former. Allophonic properties of sounds (those introduced by the allophonic processes) are by definition, after all, barred from the phonemic or 'underlying' level of representation.

Although far from offering a complete picture of the type of evolving grammar now projected for the child by the natural phonologist (cf. Stampe 1973a), the above list of assumptions should suggest enough of what may be remiss about traditional generative or taxonomic phonology to make altogether apparent what necessary revisions in our language-teaching methodology might be in order. Before we move to pedagogical questions, however, some further speculations about implications of natural phonology seem to be in order.

3.   Implications of Natural Phonology

3.0.   In taxonomic phonology, separate and autonomous morphemic and phonemic 'levels' are mediated by the morphophonemic rules, and rules of allophonic distribution relate phonemic representations to phonetic ones.[6] See Figure 3.0.1 for a graphic representation.

In generative phonology, by contrast, the autonomous morphemic level (here 'systematic phonemic' or 'underlying') is realized as the phonetic output through a single set of mediating rules. This follows from an arbitrary decision at the inception of generative grammar to assume that no alternations which govern actual substitutions can be taken to constrain the phonological (as opposed to the phonetic) form (Stampe 1968). The relevant phonological level of representation is thus the systematic phonemic level, which in turn corresponds to the distinction between lexical redundancy conditions and phonological rules (P-rules), rather than the autonomous phonemic, which corresponds to a distinction between morphophonemic and allophonic substitutions. Of course, the generative model does not admit any autonomous phonemic level of representation. Tenuous psychological distinctions by speakers were abandoned in the latter model in favor of an economy criterion.

To assist the reader at this point by clarifying more graphically the three contrasting notions of a phonological derivation (natural phonology vs. generative phonology vs. taxonomic phonology), we have below the sample derivations for a well-worn sample English word *electricity* according to all three models of analysis. The issue at hand, of course, is what kind of psychologically real deep structures the speaker is assumed to have (see Figure 3.0.2).

Figure 3.0.2.   Derivations for English 'Electricity'

STAMPEAN NATURAL PHONOLOGY

		ilēktrɪk+ʊti	Systematic Phonemic
RULES	-ɪ ti-Stressing	ilɛktrīkʊti	
	Velar Softening	ilɛktrīsʊti	Natural Phonemic Form
PROCESSES	Aspiration	ilɛktrʰīsʊti	
	Vowel Reduction	əlɛktrʰīsʊti	
	Tap Formation	əlɛktrʰīsʊɒi	
	?-Insertion	?əlɛktrʰīsʊɒi	Surface Form

TAXONOMIC PHONOLOGY

		ilēktrɪk+ʊti	Lexical Representation
		ilɛktrīk+ʊti	MORPHEMIC
Morpho-	Velar Softening	ilɛktrīsʊti	Autonomous Phonemic
phonemic			
RULES			
Allophonic	Aspiration	ilɛktrʰīsʊti	
RULES	Vowel Reduction	əlɛktrʰīsʊti	
	Tap Formation	əlɛktrʰīsʊɒi	
	?-Insertion	?əlɛktrʰīsʊɒi	PHONETIC

GENERATIVE PHONOLOGY

		ilɛktrɪk+ʊti	MORPHEMIC
Phonology	Stress Shift	ilɛktrīkʊti	
RULES	Velar Softening	ilɛktrīsʊti	
	Aspiration	ilɛktrʰīsʊti	
	Vowel Reduction	əlɛktrʰīsʊti	
	Tap Formation	əlɛktrʰīsʊɒi	
	?-Insertion	?əlɛktrʰīsʊɒi	PHONETIC

Paul Kiparsky is one generative phonologist who has at points returned to the psychological reality of something like the autonomous phonemic representation as the level on which the 'alternation condition' is determined. In establishing a principle working against the occurrence of absolute neutralization (viz., underlying forms that never have surface realization), Kiparsky observes that "one of the effects of restricting phonology like this is to enter non-alternating forms in the lexicon in roughly their autonomous phonemic representation . . . that is, if a form appears in a constant shape, its underlying representation is that shape, except for what can be attributed to low-level, automatic processes" (1968:18). It easily follows from this that Kiparsky's notion of phonetic form minus the low-level automatic processes (Stampe's allophonic natural processes?) is reasonably equivalent to Stampe's own natural phonemic form. Richard Rhodes has already examined the near equivalence between Stampe's notions of phonemic representation and Kiparsky's similar notions of this alternation condition (see Rhodes 1973)—thus the conclusion is not entirely a unique one. Yet we will see below that in several important senses Stampe's notion of a 'phonemic representation' for phonetic outputs is still altogether different in essence from the notion of generative phonologists (even that of Kiparsky), with their assumptions of static levels in a derivation and their precise categories of ordered blocks among the rules of any phonological derivation.

3.1. The Stampean natural phonologist (and Stampe's model should be kept quite distinct here from others like Vennemann's and Hooper's, which appropriate terms like 'natural generative phonology' and then offer derivations with little if any phonetic basis for the articulation of human speech) is thus a generative phonologist, in the sense of adopting abstract phonological representations, derivational rules and processes, and the crucial organizational and articulatory role of distinctive features. But the parallels almost end here. The Stampean phonologist takes the division (which is simply metaphorical here) or distinction between morphophonemic and allophonic process types to be a crucial one—yet one which represents a classification of the type of output that an operation produces, rather than any fixed division between two separate and autonomous blocks of rules or processes. And this is a very real distinction for Stampe, since exclusive ordering of rules is not employed within his account of phonological derivations of utterances. Abstract underlying representations are real for speakers; morphophonemic- and allophonic-type natural processes have different rationales and different effects within the grammar; and learned rules are quite distinct—as we emphasize in the latter half of this paper—from the innate and universal processes of speech. Yet it is the output of a process (does it neutralize or introduce phonemic units?) which determines its allophonic or morphophonemic status, not where it is ordered with respect to other rules/processes. And it is the phonetic motivation of substitutions (the ease of articulation or facilitation of phonetic perception) which keeps the processes quite distinct from those 'learned' and morphologically conditioned phonological rules.

As we established above, generative phonology historically has recognized only two 'levels' of distinctive representations: these have been labeled consistently as the phonetic and the systematic phonemic levels of derivation. The assumption implicit in this decision about dividing up the grammar is that the distinction between static redundancy conditions and phonological rules is precisely the proper distinction and the only distinction between which type of process may and which may not constrain phonological as opposed to phonetic representation.

This distinction between phonological rules and redundancy rules, of course, is in no way intrinsic to the forms of the rules themselves; rather, it is imposed in an extrinsic manner by separating them arbitrarily into distinct components or divisions of the phonology. Phonological rules are taken to govern actual substitutions and therefore not to govern lexical representation; redundancy rules determine the lexical shapes, yet never make substitutions (Chomsky and Halle 1968). In cases like that of Spanish nasal assimilation, of course, (just to pick a most obvious case among dozens in the processes of any grammar), such an artificial division simply does not exist: it can only be maintained by admitting a considerable duplication of labor among rules. Thus the process which makes nasals homorganic to the following obstruents in Spanish constrains the phonological representation of forms like *nombre, lente,* and *crianza* (there could not be any form **fwemte,* for example), while at the same time it must govern alternations in forms like *un burro, un chico,* and *un gato* where such assimilations apply in derivations across word boundaries (after the same fashion in which they apply within a stem in the former cases).

As Stampe called to our attention a decade and a half ago, under this hypothesis (let us call it the 'systematic phonemic hypothesis') it is true that no processes which govern alternations, either morphophonemic or allophonic in type, can ever be taken to constrain lexical representation. There is a slight but irrelevant difference in generative phonology between a 'lexical representation' and the systematic phonemic form which follows from it (after the application of redundancy rules); there is never any difference in substance, however, since redundancy rules do not cancel or even change representations but merely fill in the previously unspecified redundant features of such representations.

The practical result of just such a hypothesis, notice, is that for those forms which do not display alternations to reveal all features of phonological representation, the 'lexical representation' as opposed to systematic phonemic representations (those following only the redundancy rules) will have some segments unspecified for certain phonetic features (i.e., it will contain archisegments). Here, as an example, we have the classical cases of final devoicing in Germanic, with non-alternating forms like *unt* 'and' beside the alternating forms like *Bun[t]/Bun[d]e* 'association(s).' Since German *unt* is never inflected, just how do we go about reasonably determining under the systematic phonemic hypothesis what the true voicing status of its underlying obstruent is? We might, as the generative phonologists have usually done, simply appeal to some system of 'markedness' and assume a voiceless consonant. But then how do we determine what should be the 'marked' and 'unmarked' segments of any inventory in the first place? We have done this presumably on the basis of what segments have greatest universal occurrence, or appear to be physiologically the easiest articulations. We are therefore only talking about which segments apparently *do* or *do not* occur throughout the languages in question. In the German case just cited, Stampe notes that a resolution to our problem quite conveniently appears in events of historical change, when some of the German dialects lose the final devoicing process. It is in just these cases, of course, that the final voiced obstruent reemerges in all forms with alternations (*Bunt/Bunde*) where it apparently was underlying, and does not reappear in the non-alternating forms (*unt*) where it was obviously not (Stampe 1968).

We should also note the revealing fact that when speakers of German or Dutch or other languages with such final devoicing rules are asked about the admissibility of forms in their language, they will repeatedly brand the nonsense forms or foreignisms they might be given—where this process is not applied—as non-native (Shibatani 1973). That is, they hold abstract representations for such forms at no deeper than a phonemic level (in other words, after a morphophonemic process like *devoicing* has applied). Often such phonemic representations have reality in the spelling system adopted. Notice Dutch *duif* versus *duiven* 'dove(s)' as one illustrative case in point.

3.2.   The system of phonology which Stampe proposes, then, and the one which I have been advocating in earlier work, resolves such apparent contradictions by acknowledging that speakers take the distinction between what processes constrain phonological representations and what processes do not as the distinction between morphophonemic-type processes and allophonic-type processes.

In effect, speakers must record two different types ('levels,' if that term is more compatible with the current linguistic jargon) of phonological forms, depending on the types of processes applying in a given derivation. The underlying representation for the English plural *cats* would be taken as //kætz// since a phonemic representation /kæts/ (after the application of a cluster voicing assimilation) would obliterate for native speakers the true voicing status of the final obstruent of the lexical form ///kæt+z///.

This is another way of saying that if any condition of biuniqueness were to be taken as relevant for phonology (and I have argued at some length in Bjarkman 1978c that it probably should not be), it would be relevant only as a condition mediating between the phonemic and the phonetic levels, but never between the morphophonemic and phonetic levels. In forms like German *unt,* however, since the speaker does not have to account for any apparent alternation with /d/, the abstract representation is taken to exist no deeper than phonemic /unt/. No morphophonemic representation is needed since no neutralizations are apparent. Hence, morphophonemic processes are taken to be those which govern phonemic representation, and all allophonic processes are those which introduce (by starting with a phonemic representation) non-phonemic segments into a derivation.

All this seems important for establishing the inadequacies as a pedagogical model of what will be presented here in subsequent sections as Daniels's overly simplistic version of natural phonology, based as it is solely on a single rule/process dichotomy. I have suggested here already that a hierarchy of processes themselves is a good deal more complex than Daniels would maintain. In fact, I argued in an earlier paper (Bjarkman 1978d) that morphophonemic and allophonic processes might be hopelessly intermixed in fast speech derivations (e.g., an English rapid speech pronunciation of the word *question*); see Figure 3.2.1.

A process will thus apply whenever its input is available, and if a process with

Figure 3.2.1.   Fast Speech Derivation for 'Question'

Underlying Form	kwɛstyən	
PROCESSES		PROCESS TYPES
T-Palatalization	kwɛst'yən	ALLOPHONIC
Glide Deletion	kwɛst'ən	MORPHOPHONEMIC (?)*
T-Affrication	kwɛsčən	MORPHOPHONEMIC
S-Palatalization	kwɛščən	MORPHOPHONEMIC
Phonetic Form	[kwɛščən]	

*No impermissible segment is introduced (actually a segment is lost)

an allophonic effect creates the new environment in casual speech for a neutralizing or morphophonemic effect, then that will also again occur.

The issue in careful speech derivations, by contrast, is simply what depths of representation (morphophonemic or phonemic) any speaker maintains for each formative in his language. The natural phonologist contends that this is a direct function of the processes involved. First, note again that while English *cats* has an underlying morphophonemic representation //kætz// (with the phonemic /kæts/ dismissed as irrelevant), the form for the plural of *knife* is morphophonemically //nayvz// (Wojcik 1980). Here morphemic neutralization is still not resolved even at the morphophonemic level, since it is apparently introduced by a learned 'rule' which precedes all phonological processes of both morphophonemic and allophonic types. The real evidence for this is that speakers do not take the alternation involved to be a restriction on native pronunciation (i.e., it is not an allophonic process), since one can easily say [nayfs], which is in fact the expected form of the plural.[7]

4.   Applications of a Natural Phonology Model

4.0.   Daniels has argued rather persuasively that, whereas generative phonology fails as a pedagogical tool since it denies countenancing any psychologically real 'level' intermediate between morphophonemics and phonetics, taxonomic phonology will disappoint us equally, though for a very different reason. Although the taxonomic model pays lip service to such a level, it makes no clear-cut and practical applications of the distinctions between actual morphophonemic and allophonic substitutions to be mastered by the language learner. Daniels contends that the foreign language teacher (a teacher of Russian in this particular case) is normally quite aware of differences between rules types as sources of pronunciation errors and linguistic interference. But while one available model (the generative) will not acknowledge any such distinction in rules, the other model (the taxonomic) marks that distinction in precisely the wrong place. Generative phonology simply does not have room for morphophonemic/allophonic distinctions which it takes as redundant and uneconomical but which, as I have been suggesting here, may after all actually have psychological validity for speakers. On the other hand, statements about contrastive systems based on taxonomic theory remain mechanical and almost useless, primarily because such statements have never been founded in any theoretically valid way on the actual articulatory mechanisms that individuals speakers seem to employ.

One important observation about phonological systems that is missed by the taxonomic framework is that languages (and hence the individual dialects of languages) are characteristically identified most readily by their allophonic peculiarities. In a valuable earlier discussion of implications of dialect radicalism for Spanish language instruction, Jorge Guitart (1978) notices that while certain Hispanic dialects are by matter of course classified as more conservative than others, no dialect fails to display its own distinctive allophonic features; dialects in the Hispanic world can in fact be classified in a wholly useful way precisely in terms of just how much their pronunciation differs from standard orthographic code. One of Guitart's most interesting observations here, and one that also has implications for selection of formal classroom models for teaching Spanish, is that when conservative and radical dialects come into contact, the radical speakers tend to be more conservative in their articulations (they suppress weakening and deletion processes) while conservative speakers never seem to attempt the more radical speech of the less prestigious dialects.

Guitart's speculation is that it is not merely a matter of prestige involved, but one of fear of being misunderstood: radical speakers compensate in order to assure intelligibility.[8] Based on the notions of natural phonology offered so far in this discussion, I would suggest another contributing factor which would help explain this phenomenon. In order to be more conservative, radical speakers must suppress natural weakening and deletion processes which one also normally has learned to suppress much of the time in order to speak any standard version of the language as mastered by an adult speaker. Most children learning any dialect of Spanish natively (all except those speaking the most radical dialects) suppress such processes. Conservative speakers, by contrast, in order to delete and weaken must reinstitute processes they have long since (as children) suppressed. The latter activity—resurrection of suppressed processes—is apparently a much more difficult one. Once 'natural' patterns have been done away with, it is not at all a natural matter once again to recapture them. (See my more elaborate treatment of this principle and my response to Guitart's analysis of radical Hispanic dialects in Bjarkman 1985.)

4.1. Addressing himself to the teaching of Russian and assuming (as have other generative phonologists) that Stampe's model advocates a distinct division between the processes, which are psychological and physiological, and rules, which are acquired, Daniels proposes a radical yet potentially useful (if not fully articulated) formal pedagogical program. This program depends crucially on the psychological reality for speakers of a 'natural phonemic level' which is the actual output of the phonological rules and, at the same time, the level of input for innate phonological processes.

An initial motivation for the kind of instructional program which Daniels has in mind is found in the very nature of Stampe's theory of phonology. Since natural phonology makes a basic claim for articulatory features motivating the pronunciation of lexical items, it follows that certain underlying forms (phonemics) and processes (allophonics) have a direct application in a way in which they do not in other forms of process phonology, particularly in generative phonology. With the generative model, on the other hand, redundancies and other formal mechanisms such as morpheme structure constraints would seem to have no such pedagogical relevance, if only because of generative phonology's fundamental assumption (the systematic phonemic hypothesis discussed above) that alternations governing actual substitutions will not in turn constrain the phonological representation.

Daniels's starting point has been to observe that no distinction is made in Russian teaching grammars (and the same would be true for standard grammars of English, Spanish, etc.) between those types of substitutions to be mastered that would correspond to anything like the dichotomy between learned rules and innate phonetic (i.e., allophonic) processes. That rules are ordered prior to processes in derivations (that is, that they apply at a deeper pre-phonemic level) is not to be taken to suggest that students must learn rules first: they simply must learn them differently and learn them all. Learning rules is part and parcel of learning the grammar of Spanish, or of Russian, and complete mastery of such rules is the logical goal. Acquiring the processes is a matter of acquiring native pronunciation, which is not always the sole or even the desired target. Thus, imperfect grammar is not an outcome which either the student or the teacher will likely tolerate; but imperfect pronunciation may well be something both teacher and learner tolerate well. The first goal is always the ability to communicate in the new target language; rarely if ever do we have the expectation of creating native-like speakers with not even the slightest trace of foreign accent. Nor would we have any reasonable excuse for such an expectation.

Since phonological rules as opposed to processes are morpheme-specific, they are rightfully treated in the textbook and the classroom as part of inflectional and derivational morphology. The complex alternations of Spanish thematic and stem vowels in the conjugations of verbs would fall into this category. So would numerous morpheme-specific alternations in the grammar of English. Such rule types are illustrated for Spanish in Figure 4.1.1. Figure 4.1.2 provides an illustration of corresponding rule samples for English.

Phonological rules like those in Figures 4.1.1 and 4.1.2 have little if anything to do with 'pronunciation' of a language; they are matters of grammatical knowledge, not of native accent. To acquire (or at least to improve) his pronunciation, as opposed to a grammatical mastery of the foreign/second language, the learner must face a very different task. And this task is at least threefold.

Figure 4.1.1.   Some Spanish Phonological Rules

DIPHTHONGIZATION OF STEM VOWELS

PHONOLOGICAL RULES are unproductive, applying to select morphemes or select classes of morphemes within the language. Lexical entries must therefore be specially "marked" for the particular rules they undergo. Such, in this case, is true of certain Spanish verbs marked for stem diphthongization.

contar / cuento   (to count / I count)
pensar / pienso   (to think / I think)

Note that this rule applies to selected verb stems (i.e. it is "lexically" marked), and also that it is reflected in the Spanish spelling. There are numerous similar verbs where the rule is not at all applicable.

reñir / riña   (to quarrel / a quarrel)
teñir / tintura   (to tint / a dye)

OBSTRUENT TENSING RULE

The obstruent tensing rule changes some instances of underlying "lax" voiced /b,d,g/ to the "tense" voiceless segments [p,t,k], but again this rule is highly restricted, applying only to a small subset of the Spanish lexicon.

TENSING RULE   [+obstr] → [-tense] / V _____ [-obstr]
                (under certain conditions)

EXAMPLES   natación   nadar   (swimming)
                recipiente   recibir   (receiving)
                persecución   perseguir   (persecuting)
                (noun)   (infinitive)

4.1.3.   Steps in Acquiring Native Pronunciation

Step One: The learner must master the relevant phonetic processes of a target language (and I will assume, for the illustrations below, the target languages to be English and/or Spanish). Or at least he must master (as a minimum requirement) those processes which provide the language with its unique phonetic identity. If the target is Spanish, then processes such as nasal assimilation, vowel nasalization, spirantization, non-strident obstruent deletion, aspiration, and deletion of final /s/ and /f/, etc., would be among the minimal requirements for mastery. For English, vowel reduction (the schwa rule), nasal assimilation (within word boundaries), partial aspiration of the initial voiceless stops, and vowel lengthening before voiced consonants would be characteristic minimal expectations.

Step Two: The learner must also acquire sufficient knowledge about where to apply these characteristic phonetic processes. That is, he must recognize the phonemic representation for lexical items and learn to apply (as the native speaker naturally does) all the relevant allophonic processes to the output of the

Figure 4.1.2.   Some English Phonological Rules

VELAR SOFTENING
electri[k] vs. electri[s]ity
recipro[k]al vs. recipro[s]ity
opa[k]ue (opaque) vs. opa[s]ity

That this is a lexically "marked" rule and not a productive process for English is seen with a nonsense word like

persni[k]ity   (not persni[s]ity)

PRE-VOCALIC y-GLIDE
PURE (versus POOR)
use
habitual
presidential
residual

TRISYLLABIC LAXING
serene vs. serenity   (ser[i]ne vs. ser[ɛ]nity)
divine vs. divinity
profane vs. profanity

VOWEL SHIFT RULES
1) non-back Vs become back and round
   cling/clung   tell/told   bind/bound

2) back Vs become non-back and non-round
   run/ran   hold/held

3) back Vs become non-back and non-round in irregular plurals
   mouse/mice   foot/feet

---

phonological rules (like those represented in Figures 4.1.1 and 4.1.2) and the morphophonemic natural processes (as in the case of German final devoicing or the case of English cluster voicing, where one permissible underlying segment becomes neutralized with another—e.g. when English morphophonemic //kæt+z// becomes phonemic /kæts/). To apply allophonic processes, the learner must both recognize them, and recognize the phonemic forms to which they are relevant.

Step Three: The learner must acquire information about which native processes (i.e., those from his own native language) will cause interference problems with the target language and are therefore to be suppressed. The recognition of such interference situations is crucial to the learner, though not always entirely simple to detect, as we will see below.

The acquisition of native pronunciation, then, is largely a matter of (1) acquiring native (target) processes which may not be part of the speaker's own first language; (2) acquiring knowledge about the appropriate level of phonemic

Figure 4.1.4. Sample Regular English Allophonic Processes (see Appendix 1 for additional processes) (Processes given in abbreviated Standard Notation)

(Processes given in abbreviated Standard Notation)

1) BG DELETION

[+stop   ] → Ø / [+nasal]_____$ *except when the
 +voice   αposition   segment to be
 αposition   deleted is [+alveolar]

accounts for deletion of final obstruent in
sing, song, lamb (but not in lamp)

2) PALATALIZATION

[+obstruent] → [+palatal] / _____y
 +alveolar

president/presidential
reside/residual
influence/influential

3) NASAL ASSIMILATION

[+nasal] → [αposition] / _____ [+obstruent]
                                                       αposition

nasal consonants assimilate place of articulation to following obstruents within English words in careful speech. The same process occurs across word boundaries in fast, sloppy speech (with i[m]bed for in bed, or o[ŋ]guard for on guard)

representation (which is the input on which processes apply); and (3) suppressing processes from the native language which are irrelevant to (or will interfere with) native-like articulation of the language to be learned. Since Daniels presents, at his very best, a distorted version of Stampe's notion of phonemic representation, it is on the second task above that his suggestion will fail us as a guide to effective steps in overcoming difficulties for the foreign language learner. This is a point which will be taken up again at much greater length below. The first and most challenging task for the foreign language teacher, clearly, is that of developing at least a working familiarity with essential natural processes (the allophonic processes especially) of the target language being taught. Some minimal knowledge of basic processes in the learner's own native language (those that might be in conflict with target processes and need to be eliminated in order to master native-like speech) is also helpful if not always practical. The latter might not even be feasible, of course, for the teacher faced with learners speaking a wide variety of different (and perhaps even exotic) languages. A partial list of some characteristic English allophonic processes is given in Figures 4.1.4 and 4.1.5, with a fuller list provided in the Appendices to this chapter. Such pro-

Figure 4.1.5. Sample Radical English Allophonic Processes (see Appendix 2 for addition processes)

1) DENTAL s
     sθs → ş
     sixths
     sɪksθs → sɪkş

2) TAP DELETION
     PHONETICS   fənɛDɪks → fənɛɪks
     BETTER   bɛDər → bɛər

3) w-DELETION
     w → Ø / œ_____l
     foul ball
     fœwl bɔl → fœl bɔl

cesses provide a minimal working list for any teacher of English pronunciation. (A sample list of regular processes is found in Figure 4.1.4 and an extended list in Appendix 1; a sample list of radical processes is given in Figure 4.1.5 and an extended list in Appendix 2.)

4.2. Faced with an instructional approach based on acquisition of native target-language processes and suppression of interfering processes from a learner's original native tongue, the teacher must eventually make some decisions about what non-standard utterances by his pupils are to be corrected, about the manner in which such corrections are to be carried out, and also about whether or not some 'incorrect' pronunciations are to be 'corrected' at all.

A rule of thumb is available: when errors are rule-related (that is, if they are grammatical), then they must be corrected, and they must be corrected forthrightly. If errors consists instead of not suppressing a native process from the speaker's own language (the regular case of phonological interference), then more drills on applying the correct process (e.g., the English process with ESL students) in the correct environment are called for. If we are here dealing with a native English speaker learning Spanish, we would have the following illustrations. The wrong thematic vowel in the third conjugation verb form should never go uncorrected; nor should the failure to diphthongize theme vowels in conjugated stems which admit such a rule (in *contar* ~ *yo cuento* or *pensar* ~ *yo pienso,* for example). English aspiration superimposed on initial voiceless stops before stressed vowels (i.e., [pʰepe] or [pʰƐype] for *pepe*) demands more drill of Spanish forms without such aspiration. A third type of error is also possible: extension of native Spanish processes to improper environments, that is, the learner of Spanish acquires the target process but then proceeds to apply it indiscriminately even in those environments where native speakers don't. For example, learners of Spanish may conceivably begin to aspirate initial as well as syllable-final /s/, a process which is in fact now emerging in some Caribbean dialects of Spanish.[9] Daniels suggests for this final type of error that nothing be done by the pronunciation teacher monitoring native acquisition of, in this case, Spanish. Discussing as he is the teaching of Russian pronunciation, Daniels contends that if student pronunciation errors come from extending some Russian processes in non-canonical ways, then no correction is called for, since students are speaking like Russians. To quote: "There is an obvious rule here which is not new: correct only those errors due to transferred processes; *noncanonic* application of Russian processes calls, at most, for some comments on style of pronunciation" (1975:71). A parallel case from English will ascertain the wisdom of Daniels's point here. While English speakers normally apply the native process of nasal assimilation only within formal word boundaries (we have words like *pumpkin* and *lamb* but never *punkin* or *lanb*)[10]—in contrast with Spanish which has this process even across word boundaries (*u[m] burro* or *u[ŋ] gaucho* versus *u[n] burro* or *u[n] gaucho*)—yet in rapid speech English natives regularly produce phrases like [ImbƐd] for 'in bed' and [waŋken] for 'one cain/cane.' Such extensions of native processes clearly are matters of style (see Stampe 1973a) and should always be treated as such.

Daniels's review of the application of natural phonology and the recognition of natural processes (versus learned rules) to teaching Russian pronunciation therefore leads him to a practical formula for classroom pedagogy.

4.2.1. *Daniels's Conclusions about Teaching Russian Pronunciation*

1. The student cannot be expected to obtain sound mastery of Russian pronunciation without at the same time obtaining a degree of lexical and grammatical mastery in the language. In brief, pronunciation mastery always follows and supplements mastery of the grammar of the language.
2. For almost any conceivable normal purpose, it is never necessary to demand perfect native Russian pronunciation from our students, who will always at any rate be detected as foreigners no matter what their mastery of the language (as physical appearance and cultural knowledge are almost always dead giveaways).
3. For any stage in the learning of a language, the goal of the instructor should be to provide students with at least a minimal need for adequate pronunciation of Russian at that stage (i.e., beginner, tourist, graduate student traveling within a foreign country, etc.). Minimal needs, of course, are determined by how the students intend to use their Russian.

All of Daniels's observations about proper teaching of Russian can, quite obviously, be extended to the teaching of any other target languages. And the three notions about teaching above lead to a formal program which Daniels refers to as a 'pronunciation hierarchy' for language instruction. Such a program will advocate propositions which together can be satisfactorily labeled as the 'pronunciation hierarchy for effective language teaching.'

4.2.2. Assumptions Basic to Daniels's Pronunciation Hierarchy for Effective Language Teaching

Daniels's thesis is that Russian literary pronunciation (a reasonable goal for first-year college courses in Russian) is the result of applying a set of natural processes to the Stampean (natural) phonemic level of phonological representation. Processes to be applied may be ranked in descending order of importance, and a final acquisition of such processes is dependent upon precisely this ranking.

Processes which are identical to English ones are removed from the learning task, since these contribute nothing to the learning difficulty. (English speakers acquiring Spanish have to learn to extend nasal assimilation beyond word boundaries even in careful speech, while Spanish speakers acquiring English have to learn the opposite task, that of restricting this process to a smaller word-interval environment. But neither set of learners needs to be drilled on the process of nasal assimilation, which is second nature for speakers of both languages.) Russian texts designed for English-speaking learners need not drill voice assimilation in consonant clusters, even though it is needed in Russian; but they must treat phrase-final devoicing, since the English speaker does not have such a process in his own native inventory.

The student then proceeds from top to bottom on the list of native Russian processes in order to acquire the remaining inventory of processes represented by the hierarchy. A student can stop anywhere along this hierarchy, if he is not interested in polishing or perfecting a native-like pronunciation.

Daniels's assumptions about the 'pronunciation hierarchy' lead him to conclude that textbook organizers and curriculum specialists can effectively "integrate the progression through the grammatical and lexical materials with selected stages on the pronunciation hierarchy" (1975:71). This means we begin instruction by familiarizing students with a natural phonemic level of lexical representation, in which stress has already been placed, consonants are fully specified as hard or soft (both by lexical entry and by rule), other rule-governed substitutions (vowel-zero alternations, etc.) have been applied, and place and manner of articulation are implemented (some of which, of course, will be in contrast with English). After the establishment of such a level for lexical items, process-governed substitutions (palatalizations, processes reassigning vowel stress, syntagmatic sequential processes like assimilations, contractions, or syncopes, etc.) are then presented for mastery. Extensions of these processes, as noted above, lead to non-literary but still Russian pronunciation (fast speech articulations, for example), and for these only some comment of styles of Russian pronunciation is necessary.

One reason that errors in the applications of learned phonological rules (as opposed to natural phonetic processes) can be treated quite differently is that speakers themselves treat rules differently. Notice that we have not mentioned another possible error type: the English speaker applying a native English rule while trying to pronounce proper Russian or Spanish, etc. Such rule substitutions, as opposed to improper substitutions of processes, are simply not done. Rules, like the English trisyllabic laxing rule, do not transfer the pronunciation of target Spanish words, or Russian target words, or any foreign target words. Processes will readily transfer, however, such as the one which would cause the native English speaker to try diphthongization of Spanish vowels he perceives as tense (thus [pʰƐype] for [pepe]).[11] Or the related one which will cause Spanish speakers to tense all English vowels, producing (with humorous effect) English *sheet* for *shit,* etc.

Daniels has observed that good language teachers often intuit the methods being suggested here; that is, natural phonology merely provides us with a theoretical rationale for assumptions that our better language teachers have from the beginning been making anyway, even if in a rather haphazard way. In this light, we might return briefly to the article on Spanish pronunciation by Guitart mentioned above. Here two further proposals are now of considerable interest. First is Guitart's suggestion that American students of Spanish ought to be given some exposure to radical dialects so they might "at least acquire the same degree of receptive competence in radical dialects that native conservatives have" (1978:58)—in other words, so that they might understand a Puerto Rican neighbor to the same extent as they can a refined Castilian radio announcer. Guitart believes such exposure comes best only through systematic listening to recordings of radical speakers, or better still, listening to them *en vivo* in the classroom. This idea of a systematic exposure (even simple listening for considerable periods) rather than formal classroom instruction on the particular features of radical dialects is quite consistent with the notion that processes are to be drilled and practiced in real-life language situations, while rules are to be formally learned, perhaps even through a deductive rather then purely inductive method.[12]

Also, Guitart takes up problems of teaching Spanish pronunciation to Spanish ethnics who speak radical dialects of their own native tongue. Here he advocates an opposite approach: their pronunciation should not be corrected at all, not even by drilling, but rather they should be made more highly literate through being made more text-oriented. Guitart suggests that emphasis should fall on correcting non-standard lexical forms in writing (like *entodavía* for *todavía*) and not at all on correcting a Puerto Rican speaker with l/r confusion, which is after all a matter of allophonic processes and not of inaccurate lexical representation. Here again Guitart's suggestion will be given a greater formal legitimacy in light of assumptions of natural phonology. Radical speakers (those speaking dialects featuring radical deletion and weakening processes, such as the dialects of Caribbean Spanish), like the child learning the adult forms of a language, must simply be made more aware of systematic or underlying representation and existence of their own phonetic (allophonic) weakening processes. Such is accomplished by establishing greater awareness of the standard orthographic code (which almost always parallels, if not duplicates, the systematic level of representation). And as I have argued extensively elsewhere (Bjarkman 1985), it is far easier for radical speakers to suppress their allophonic processes and thus acquire a conservative pronunciation (one approximating systematic representation) than it is for conservative speakers to reinstitute such radical weakening processes once they have been suppressed in the earliest stages of language acquisition. The radical speaker here, given the hint found in the orthographic representations of the language, needs only to do what conservative speakers have already done in earlier stages of language acquisition—suppress radical childhood processes. And the rule/process distinction of Stampe, along with natural phonology's assumptions about the nature of speech acquisition, again aid in clarifying the actual task facing the adult language learner.

Incorporating Stampe's notion of rules and processes as it does, Daniels's model for foreign language teaching provides us with a promising start. It suggests, if nothing else, the crucial distinction between acquisition of grammar and acquisition of pronunciation, a distinction which has clouded previous pedagogical models. Yet there are several major flaws which tend to magnify once we examine actual language interference situations and which therefore render Daniels's model less than fully useful. Of greatest difficulty, there is Daniels's assumption that natural processes of Stampe's type are all allophonic in nature and in function. And connected with this issue is an equally fallacious view of Stampe's actual notion of systematic phonemic or natural phonemic representation. The pronunciation hierarchy model for acquisition of pronunciation rests on an assumption that a fixed and regular natural phonemic representation is as obvious and recoverable as Daniels claims it is,[13] as well as on the assumption that all processes are of an identical teleology. Application of Daniels's model in its present form leads to a number of immediate problems with the actual data of language acquisition cases. It is easy to find examples, citing one obvious problem, where applications of what must be taken as natural processes from the speaker's own native language (ones not equally relevant in the target language) actually cause lexical confusions and misunderstandings in the same fashion as misapplication of rules. Other complications also set in. The rules/processes distinction itself may not prove to be entirely sufficient; among even processes, contrasting types may need accounting for: viz., regular vs. radical, prosodic vs. segmental, fortitions vs. lenitions, and morphophonemic vs. allophonic. Also, a far less rigid interpretation of Stampe's notions of deep structure may be a preliminary requirement.

In the concluding section of this chapter I will attempt to clarify these issues further and, at the same time, suggest modifications of Daniels's model which might be sufficient to salvage such a pedagogical framework for pronunciation based on Stampe's notions of natural phonology. Most important, I will further articulate some immediate applications of Stampe's model which make it, despite the problems of detail, perhaps still the most viable theoretical model available for clarifying issues and for constructing curricula in the pedagogical treatments of foreign language pronunciation.

5. Natural Phonology and Language Acquisition

5.0.   Our current theory of phonology, and the preceding one to boot, suggest that children learn information of only a single type when acquiring the pronunciation systems of language. It is this subtle implication of both generative phonology and its forerunners which the natural phonologist finds least palatable.

Within generative phonology the organization of human sound production is truly monolithic: the level of underlying form (called 'autonomous morphemic' or 'systematic morphemic') is related to actual articulations by a single set of phonological rules. Both 'lexical redundancy rules,' which fully specify matrices that have remained unspecified in the lexicon, and phonetic-detail rules, which clean up infelicitous articulations or maximize sloppy speech, are seen as largely peripheral to any phonological system itself. While the former are mechanisms for economizing lexical representations, the latter are dismissed as stylistic variations unrelated to normal language usage. If distinct rule types have different roles or different impacts on the learner or his grammar, this fact is never made evident in standard versions of the theory.

In contrast to the generative models, taxonomic phonology (see Figure 3.0.1 above) lends credence to several distinct types of phonological processes, but the distinction found there between rules with morphophonemic or neutralizing effect and those with allophonic or phonetic effect is found, on closer inspection, to be largely a sophisticated formalism almost devoid of any real substance. While Chomsky and Halle's (1968) notion of generative phonology has straightaway ignored a possible psychological reality for distinct levels of phonological representation (or separate types of phonological processing with highly distinct grammatical effects), taxonomic phonology in turn rigorously separates morphophonemic and allophonic substitutions without any principled theoretical account of their roles, or the rationale behind such a division of labor in the mechanisms of speech articulation.

Generative grammars, from Chomsky right down to the autosegmentalists, have never claimed much for their model as a hypothesis about language acquisition mechanisms. Child language theory from the outset has been for generative grammarians more of a testing ground for speculations about their own grammatical models rather than a practical laboratory for implementing linguistic applications to child development research.

Taxonomic phonology, in its turn, has been at the same time both more bold in its claims about applications and more dramatic in its failures to contribute significantly through contrastive analyses between native languages and target languages. A major application for language pedagogy has been that approaches to contrastive analysis of language systems drawn on this model reflect a division of the grammar into levels based on distinct analyzable types of sound substitutions. In any language course built on taxonomic principles, basic sounds are first introduced, along with observations on pronunciation, which usually translates into statements about allophonic distribution. Since all such courses strive, however, to avoid theoretical subtleties and circumvent hopeless controversies, little space is left for any serious exploration of distinguishable process types. While taxonomic theory and the contrastive studies based on it rigorously separate allophonic processes from the morphophonemic ones, no evidence is provided (nor even is any attempt made to provide such evidence) that one will have any greater effect on learning than the other. Structural contrasts seem to predict interference (the 'strong contrastive analysis hypothesis') and learning difficulties, regardless of the level of contrast or the types of processes involved.

Generative phonology assumes that because the identical substitution (for instance, nasal assimilation) can have both allophonic effects (e.g., as it applies across word boundaries in Spanish utterances) and morphophonemic effects (e.g., within Spanish lexical items), no such distinction of process types can hope to hold any important reality. Following the lead of Halle in the early 1960s, generative grammarians abandoned such a distinction altogether, as both redundant and unwarranted within any grammar based on some type of economic metric. Taxonomic phonology, in turn, never consistently applies the distinction in process types it sets up, nor does it clearly define the rule types and their implications for both acquisition and articulation. And since neither model effectively articulates a distinction among contrastive types of phonological distinctions, neither is able to codify the types of learning tasks facing either the child or the adult in his or her respective role as language learner.

Another version of this popular notion in acquisition studies, that acquisition of a phonological system is a narrow and even singular type of learning task, takes a more sophisticated if equally damaging form. Such an assumption seems to underlie the viewpoint summarized by Moskowitz's (1978) popular account of child language systems, that the operation of phonetics in the child's acquisition of language is totally separate from the operation of phonology. For Moskowitz, phonetics and phonology are totally distinct phenomena: "In learning to pronounce, then, a child must acquire a sound system that includes the *divergent* [emphasis added] systems of phonology and phonetics . . . and the acquisition of phonology differs from that of phonetics in requiring the creation of representation of language in the mind of the child. . . . This representation is necessary because of the abstract nature of the units of phonological structure" (op. cit.:201). What is lost to such a view is the integral role of phonetic phenomena in much childhood phonological processing.

5.1. Stampe's model of natural phonology draws some very different conclusions about the relationships between phonetics and phonology for the acquisition model of language structure. Unlike the generative model or the taxonomic model, Stampe's phonology assumes that the child in learning speech 'acquires' two very different types of phonological operations. This assumption is in direct contradiction to the generative notion that all pronunciation rules are essentially of the same type. And further, these distinct types of phonological operations hold different implications for the learning tasks faced by either adult learners of second languages or the child mastering his native speech. In the latter approach, we find significant improvement as well over a taxonomic model (and the contrastive analyses based on such a model), which maintains distinctive types of phonological processes (morphophonemic and allophonic) but then takes all structural contrasts between two language systems to imply the same order of 'acquisition' problems for the adult second language learner.

The model which I am advocating here is the one which distinguishes between learned phonological rules (which make up the smallest and most unproductive part of the adult phonological component) and innate natural phonological processes left over from the earliest stages of child language acquisition (which account for most of the pronunciation or accent difficulties when adults attempt to master a second, contrasting language system). This model is outlined in considerable detail in Bjarkman (1975, 1976) and the reader should turn to those sources for fuller explication. The essential distinctions are summarized for our purposes here in Figure 5.1.1.

The primary implication of adopting such a model for the native phonological component is that we now, as a direct consequence, need to reorganize teaching materials and teaching procedures in something like the following dramatic ways:

(1) *Rules,* like diphthongization connected with vowel stress in Spanish (*contar/cuento*) or the velar softening of English (*electri[k]* versus *electri[s]ity*) and all other similar morphologically conditioned substitutions, are part of the derivational morphology or inflectional morphology of any language system. Although this fact is often implicitly recognized and reflected by language textbook materials, this is not always done systematically. And in the face of previous linguistic models, there has never been any sound theoretical rationale for such an organizational decision.

That rules generally apply in derivations of individual morphemes and sentences before processes apply does not mean that such rule substitutions must be learned *first,* with all processes being learned later. (Note here, of course, that the native speaker does not *learn* processes but already possesses them from the first; in fact, the child usually must *learn to suppress* such processes.) The point is that *all rules* (like those in Figure 5.1.2) *must be learned,* and such learning involves teaching activities of a particular and familiar type.

Figure 5.1.1. Summary of Rule/Process Dichotomy for Stampean Natural Phonology

CHARACTERISTICS OF NATURAL PROCESSES
(which hold true for Paradigmatic/Fortition Processes as well as Syntagmatic/Lenition Processes, of both Morphophonemic and Allophonic types)

INNATE	Part of the child's inherited native language mechanism—the child does not have to "learn" processes, but only to learn to suppress and modify the ones he starts with.
PRODUCTIVE	They apply whenever a correct phonetic environment is satisfied, to all native and nonnative words.
UNORDERED	Processes reapply in a derivation whenever their environment is satisfied.
PHONETIC	They are physiologically or mentalistically motivated efforts at reducing the task of articulation.
EXAMPLES are:	English initial voiceless stop aspiration German final obstruent devoicing Spanish nasal assimilation (both progressive and regressive—with nasalization of vowels before nasal consonants, and assimilations of nasal consonants in place of articulation to following obstruents)

CHARACTERISTICS OF PHONOLOGICAL RULES

LEARNED	Must be acquired and properly generalized by the child during the activities of language learning.
NON-PRODUCTIVE	They do not apply to loanwords, nonsense-type words, or any native forms which are not of the class "marked" to undergo that rule.
ORDERED	At least to the degree that Bleeding Orders or relationships do exist, and rules may be blocked from application by other rules.
GRAMMATICAL	They apply to particular morphemes or sets of morphemes that are specified to undergo that particular rule (as well as others).
EXAMPLES are:	English velar softening (opaque . . . opacity) Spanish stem diphthongization (pensar . . . pienso)

What the recognition of distinct rule types like those in Figure 5.1.2 suggests is not that we teach the hypothesized underlying forms maintained by native speakers, along with synchronically active vowel shift rules, maintaining for example (like Chomsky and Halle and other generativists) that *spa* [spaʌ] comes from /spæ/ through w-insertion, glide vocalization (w to u), rounding adjustment, and backness adjustment (Chomsky and Halle, 1968:205–6). What it does mean is that we must introduce students to all morphological alternations like

Figure 5.1.2.   Additional Learned Rules of English

1) PLURAL STEM FRICATIVE VOICING

$$\left\{ \begin{array}{c} /s/ \\ /f/ \end{array} \right\} \rightarrow \left\{ \begin{array}{c} [z] \\ [v] \end{array} \right\} \quad / \quad \underline{\hspace{1cm}} \quad \begin{array}{c} /z/ \\ \text{[+plural]} \end{array}$$

SINGULAR	PLURAL	
lapse	*lapses	(note lexical exceptions
knife	knives	to this rule, like:
wife	wives	chiefs
half	halves	waifs
roof	*roofs	safes
shelf	shelves	

*with [s]/[z] or [f]/[v] in free variation (alternation)

2) TD SOFTENING

$$\left\{ \begin{array}{c} /t/ \\ /d/ \end{array} \right\} \rightarrow \text{[s]} \quad / \quad \underline{\hspace{1cm}} \quad \begin{array}{c} \text{-ive} \\ \text{[+adjective]} \end{array}$$

VERB	ADJECTIVE
recede	recessive
conclude	conclusive
exclude	exclusive
preclude	preclusive
submit	submissive
permit	permissive

3) IRREGULAR VERB SUPPLETIONS

go / went / gone
do / does / did / done
see / saw / seen
be / is / are / am / was / were / been

those suggested by Figures 4.1.2 and 5.1.2 and their corresponding English spellings. Alternations like *mouse/mice* and *serene/serenity* are matters of English grammar (morphology) and not matters of stylistic (literary versus colloquial) pronunciation. They are really not pronunciation items at all, but word-formation items. Students are therefore introduced from the first to exercises (often writing) of the type that demonstrate all such morphological and spelling alternations:

(2) *Processes,* on the other hand, affect pronunciation and not grammar. Here the work is exclusively 'oral' and the *learning,* it follows, is of three related yet distinct types:

(2a) First, the learner must acquire processes which are native to the linguistic system to be mastered (the target language) but not at all native to his own phonological system. These processes are largely stylistic in implication (at least the allophonic ones are) and are, in the most general terms, a matter of colloquial or conversational as opposed to literary or formalistic speech. A Spanish speaker learning English must acquire the initial aspiration process for voiceless obstruents before stressed vowels (which is not relevant in Spanish). In fact, what this means is that such a learner has to resurrect a childhood process which was earlier suppressed in acquiring adult native pronunciation of Spanish. And as I have argued in Bjarkman (1985), such reacquisition of earlier suppressed processes is not altogether easy, requiring considerable exposure to the desired outputs, though it is ultimately possible to achieve (see also note 8 of this chapter).

(2b)   Second, native processes from the learner's own speech which are not applicable in the new target language must be fully suppressed. The German speaker learning English must therefore suppress final devoicing of obstruents. The Spanish speaker acquiring English must suppress his own native version of nasal assimilation (i.e., across word boundaries). The Korean speaker learning English has to suppress further lenition of the voiceless stop (i.e., producing [p^h] for /p/ in words like *spit* or *spat*). It is worth noting here that while it is most difficult for learners to resurrect processes already suspended in their own child language acquisition (the requirement in (2a) above), the suppression of native processes required here is apparently not all that difficult. The activities of child language acquisition, recall, have been largely an exercise in suppressing processes, once the data to which the child was exposed suggested sufficiently that the processes in question were not consistent with the adult speech model. It may be largely a similar matter of sufficient exposure here for the second-language learner, along with suggestions by the teacher about what transferred processes are indeed getting in the way of a native English pronunciation. And one further matter: the failure to limit native processes from the first language to their proper environments in the second language is not usually an error of any real consequence, since such processes are often extended in less formal speech in that language anyway. If the Spanish speaker does extend nasal assimilation across word boundaries in English, the result will sound like sloppy English, but English nonetheless, since in careless speech native English speakers extend this process in the same way ([wʌm#bUk] for *one book*).

(2c)   Finally, shared processes between the two languages are simply to be transferred; that is to say, they don't have to be of any concern to the language teacher or the textbook writer at all. If Spanish speakers are learning English (or vice versa), such processes as nasal assimilation within the word, vowel nasalization, and nasal deletion after nasalized vowels—being equally native to both language systems—will be transferred without any pedagogical effort. The failure to recognize the distinction between rules and processes, or to understand the shared processes of particular language systems, has often resulted in space being allotted in texts or teacher-prepared materials for presentation of linguistic processes to be acquired by the learner which are already second nature to that learner's own native speech outputs. In the worst case, such presentations are needlessly confusing to the learner; and in the best cases, they are simply wasted effort.

5.2. It is now plausible to formulate a principle governing foreign language instruction which I will label somewhat arbitrarily here the 'strong hypothesis on speech correction.' This hypothesis is drawn from Daniels's sketchy preliminary model for classroom language teaching.

5.2.1. *Speech Correction Principle: Rules must be mastered (students must be grammatical) but native-like pronunciation may not be crucial. Processes are merely constraints on articulation (pronounceability), and failure to suppress native processes or to acquire target-language processes leads to no more than problems of native accent. Rules are matters of formal grammar, whereas processes are matters of native pronunciation.*

A corollary to this principle is Daniels's formulation of the pronunciation hierarchy (given as 4.2.2): once processes shared by both languages are eliminated (since these would offer no threat of interference), all of the remaining processes which characterize the target language are ranked by importance (by frequency and by the degree to which they facilitate standard literary pronunciation), and students are free to master whichever and however many processes as time, motivation, special cultural interest, or other factors dictate.

Suggestions may also be formulated for the role of grammar correction in the second-language classroom, and the first observation of both authors who have previously written seriously on pedagogical implications of Stampe's model (Daniels, and Wojcik 1981) is that errors made by the foreign language learner most frequently translate as failures to *suppress* the non-applicable native processes. When errors are made with rules, these are not the province of the pronunciation teacher, or at least not of the pronunciation lesson (for the teacher himself often wears several hats simultaneously). While processes often transfer in this manner from one language to the next, rules never transfer in this fashion. Processes are constraints on linguistic production and perception, and we suspend those we have maintained from earliest childhood only with maximum mental effort. Rules, by stark contrast, are learned in association with particular words and morphemes and thus seem to be triggered only by those precise lexical environments with which they have become associated. The English teacher, then, needs to know almost nothing about Spanish rules or Korean rules, as helpful as familiarity with first-language *processes* might prove to be in predicting or diagnosing student cases of mispronunciation. The English speaker will diphthongize tense vowels in Spanish (a process) as a matter of course, saying [p€ydro] for *Pedro* or [pʰÍyto] for *pito*. But Spanish speakers simply will not perform the above-mentioned vowel alternations of *contar/cuento* or *pensar/pienso* when speaking English.

It follows from all this that you simply do not have to suppress wrong responses which are matters of misarticulations. And the reason should, at this point, be quite apparent. If a speaker makes certain substitutions in the target language, it is because they are already an ingrained part of his phonological/phonetic system. If this student is a Korean, for example, who says [sp^{h}It] for English *spit*, you will not teach him to make the 'proper sounds' with negative reinforcement for the articulations which he is already making by second nature.

If another student, native speaker of another language, hears these misarticulations that involve processes he does not share, he will never acquire these "cognitively," simply because of one or two exposures. Non-native processes are just not that easily acquired. If they were, after all, we would only have to play over and over again tapes of native speakers for our ESL students, featuring the articulations we want mastered. The daily experience of any classroom language teacher rules out any such hope.

Ultimately, then, there are three types of correction with which the teacher can acquaint himself. If an error is rule-oriented, we correct immediately, if reasonably (though space will not allow here a complete discourse on methods and strategies of correction). We of course will tolerate non-native pronunciation (for it may be unreasonable to expect almost anything else), but we do not tolerate ungrammaticality. In teaching English, we would correct *div[ay]nity*, or *poor* for *pure* (and notice the lexical confusion here), or a pronunciation like *electri[k]ity*.

Second, if an error comes in our view from a failure to suppress a native process of the learner's own language, then more practice time is to be found for drilling and practicing the English process(es). Such practice, it need not be stressed, must be oral and conversational, never written or too formalized. It makes little sense to 'correct' the Spanish speaker's rendering of English *milk* as *m[Iy]lk* or *m[i]lk* (without the lax vowel) until he has practiced and begun to acquire some semblance of the English lax vowel process. Otherwise, he most likely will be as incapable of hearing his error as he is of escaping it.

Lastly, if pronunciation errors seem to be the product of an excessive application (viz., expansion of environment or extension to a different stylistic level) with native target-language processes, then we have the most positive situation of all, and little or nothing is demanded of the teacher. Here the native process has been mastered articulatorily, i.e., the learner is now speaking like a native. Recall, of course, that most processes get extended after this fashion eventually by native speakers themselves. At most, the situation calls for a discussion of appropriateness of style. At any rate, what we have here is hardly an acquisition problem at all.

5.3.   I have argued throughout this article that Stampe's notions of natural phonology serve as a viable model both for explaining the mechanisms of first-

and second-language acquisition and for providing insight into the tasks and duties of the classroom second-language teacher. My purpose has been to explicate natural phonology as a working model, but also, in part, to propose an enticing and theoretically valid approach to perennial issues and obstacles confronting educational methodologists and classroom teachers alike. As we have seen, the appeal and the validity of the model of Stampean natural phonology derive primarily from the fact that this is the only modern theory of phonology which "models direct constraints on speech production and perception" (Wojcik 1981:24). As Wojcik maintains, this fact is fundamental, since acquisition of foreign language accent is essentially a problem involving the production mechanism of language learners, not their intuitions about what is phonologically acceptable in the acquired patterns of speech. The controlling thesis, throughout this chapter, has been that acquisition of phonology is deeply constrained and controlled through the ever-present mechanisms of childhood phonetics (and the residue of childhood phonetics found in the active natural processes of adult speech).

The model drawn here is not a complete and fully articulated one, quite obviously, and many problems arise with it, only a small number of which have emerged from this discussion. For the sake of balance, I wish to conclude by calling attention to two such interesting complications for the model I have been advocating. One has to do with proper interpretation of the mechanisms of natural phonology and is, once recognized, easily enough resolved. The second will prove a bit less tractable for the theory of natural acquisition, at least as that theory now stands.

First, the pronunciation teacher must be careful not to confuse, when comparing competing language systems, what might be (a) the application of the learner's native language processes in speaking the target language, with (b) the non-canonical extension of processes within the target language. The issue has more than moderate import here, since we have suggested that failure to suppress native processes which cause interference is a legitimate concern for the pronunciation teacher (requiring more intensive practice in applying the proper target language process). Extension, non-canonically, of the native processes in the target language is not, in the same fashion, a teaching issue. It is a matter of style more than a matter of native accent: native speakers themselves extend processes after this fashion in more careless and rapid speech. But to decide which issue we are facing, the classroom teacher (in his role as natural phonologist) must judge properly the source of mispronunciation. And sometimes the phonological behavior of the language learner is more subtly masked than we have so far suggested. Since Korean, for example, has a three-part distinction in stops between voiceless lenis (p), voiceless lenis aspirated (p^h), and fortis (pp), in contrast with the English voiced/voiceless opposition, an obvious confusion potentially results. When the Korean speakers says [sp^hIt] for the English *spit*, this is in fact an imposition of his own native system on the English, not merely an improper extension of English aspiration with voiceless stops. The teacher of pronunciation must remain vigilant for such subtleties. We see again clearly here why the pronunciation teacher not only must familiarize himself with major tenets of Stampe's theory, but also must become something of a practicing natural phonologist himself.

A further obstacle to a practical pedagogical application of Stampe's model emerges from the sophistications of the model itself. As is now evident from the discussion up to this point, natural processes (phonetically and mentally moti-vated substitutions) are not solely of the allophonic type. Nor are possible errors in applying the necessary native processes to be taken exclusively as matters of native accent, or variations in style, as Daniels has assumed throughout. While the great bulk of evident phonetic substitutions may be of this order, others also exist, and some have impact on the foreign language learner. Daniels's model is simply too primitive to serve us very well at this juncture.

Some processes of the native linguistic system are paradigmatic (context-free) as we earlier noted, and function in this capacity to constrain segmental represen-tations in the lexicon. Since there is no persuasive evidence that English has nasalized vowels at the lexical or underlying level, such a gap is explained in terms of an active denasalization of all vowels in the basic inventory, a paradig-matic 'process' which actively eliminates a nasalization feature in some cases of linguistic borrowing but has only vacuous application in most adult grammars.[14] There is indirect evidence for such context-free substitutions in the data of child language (Stampe 1979:17ff); and it might be noted that their frequency in child rather than adult phonology is to be expected, since the massive neutralizations that result would be highly unacceptable in the more mature and varied adult speech. Empirical evidence for the actuality of such substitutions (does lack of nasalized vowels imply mere gaps or actual substitutions?) is sketchy and their justification is for many the most unconstrained and unacceptable of Stampe's notions. Paradigmatic neutralizations of this type are also taken to operate in tandem with complementary syntagmatic ones (while English does not permit lexical nasalized vowels, nasalization is reintroduced in nasalizing environ-ments—preceding a nasal consonant); and a later version of the theory now classifies paradigmatic substitutions as *fortition* or strengthening tendencies which intensify salient features of individual segments, while syntagmatic sub-stitutions are, by clear contrast, lenitions or weakening which make segments or sequences easier to pronounce by reducing articulatory 'distance' between fea-tures of the segment and those of its adjacent members (Stampe and Donegan 1979).

Among the more evident of contextual weakening processes, again some have allophonic effects and others are clearly morphophonemic in effect. The same word-external assimilation of nasals in the rapid speech utterances of the phrases *in bed* [Imbɛd] and *one cain* [wʌŋkɛyn] has morphophonemic impact in one case (one phoneme neutralized with another) and introduces an allophonic segment [ŋ] in the other. To put this in another context, the failure of such nasalization in one case would have little noticeable impact (the mispronunciation of a word like *engulf*) but in the other might cause semantic breakdown (*in bed* contrasted with *imbed*).

To take still a more dramatic and more illustrative example, a process which serves a purely allophonic role in the native language of the learner may in fact turn out to have unintended neutralizing or morphophonemic effect when extended into the target language being learned. We can again here turn to Korean, and again to the Korean inventory of lenis and fortis voiceless stops discussed above. Because no contrast exists for Koreans between p/f, or p/v, or p/b, [p] becomes the target sound (substitution by process) for all these closest segments from English. While such a substitution constitutes allophonic variation for the Korean, in his own language, the effect in English is to neutralize perfectly good lexical distinctions (*pine* for *vine,* or *pan* for *van/ban,* etc.). And even more spectacularly, Korean features a number of stop/nasal assimilation rules which wreak havoc with Korean pronunciation of English strings containing these sequences.[15] With one of these rules (i.e., phonetic assimilation processes), voiceless stops (p/t/k) take on the feature [+nasal], while maintaining the original place of articulation before a nasal consonant. That is, $p/p^h/pp$ become [m] before a nasal, while $t/t^h/tt$ become [n] in the same environment, etc. This leads the Korean, by merely transferring a native allophonic process, to produce *king Mary* for *kick Mary, hung me* for *hug me,* or *bean Mary* for *beat Mary.*

It is clear enough that these final cases are stark counterexamples to Daniels's proposal: viz., that transfer of native allophonic processes will result only in foreign (here Korean) accent and need cause no concern unless polishing of native-like accent is the goal. Here morphological errors result and "pronunciation" is no longer the issue. Such cases are the clear minority, yet they are after all real, and not exceedingly rare.

Modification of the strong hypothesis on speech correction now seems in order: for the original principle stated as 5.2.1., we might now substitute 5.3.1.

5.3.1. *Modified Speech Correction Principle:*
Rules must *be mastered (students* must *be grammatical), but native-like pronunciation may not be crucial.* Most *natural processes are constraints on articulation only, and failure to suppress native process or to acquire target-language processes in a majority of cases will lead only to noticeable foreign accent.*

Generalizations about processes (versus rules) and pronunciation (versus grammar) have referred, then, throughout this article, to processes which have allophonic function in the target language or native language systems. This seems to be still the vast majority of cases, even in light of the counterexamples offered here and others like them. The weaker version of the speech correction principle cited in 5.3.1 is built on a broader notion of natural phonology and a more accurate interpretation of Stampe's work than the model for pedagogy offered by Daniels. But even where we encounter exceptions like those discussed above, correction work with such students is to be oral and not cognitive—it is still a matter of supplanting interfering native processes with more appropriate target-language processes, and extensive exposure to native processes is still the solution, even if the malady here (where lexical errors are the result) is more severe. What processes are to be drilled in the target language again depends on the shared inventory of processes between the two languages. It still holds, then, that the most effective teacher of pronunciation is the teacher who is at least in part a natural phonologist as well.

Appendix 1 Regular English Natural Processes

Below is a minimal listing of Regular English Allophonic Processes, drafted in large part from the more extensive catalogue presented in HILL (1973). The list is comprised of a minimum set of natural processes that must be mastered as part of full native pronunciation of English, across almost all dialects of the language. All are drawn from English rapid speech phenomena. If a native accent is a concern in the classroom, then attention must be paid to natural processes such as these, and the list here could easily be expanded three or four-fold.

1) AFFRICATION
   alveopalatal stop becomes affricate
   did you do it?
   dɪjəduət → dɪǰəduət

2) an-SELECTION
   an form of the indefinite article inserted before a vowel
   an (h)eretical doctrine
   ə hərɛtɪkəl daktrɪn → ə ərɛtɪkəl daktrɪn →
   ən ərɛtɪkəl daktrɪn

3) ASPIRATION
   voiceless initial stops before stressed syllabics/vowels
   pɪg → pʰɪg

4) d-DELETION
   between nasal and consonant, unless d begins a syllable
   endgame
   ɛndgem → ɛngem

5) g-DELETION (I)
   between velar nasal and word boundary (following nasal velarization)
   sɪng → sɪng → sɪŋ

6) g-DELETION (II)
   between nasal and word boundary, when this syllable has an unstressed vowel
   dárlɪng → dárlɪn

7) VOWEL LENGTH
   before voiced obstruent
   BUZZ   BUD   bʌz → bʌ·z   bʌd → bʌ·d
   BED   bɛd → bɛ·d
   BET   bɛt → bɛt

Appendix 1 (Continued)

8) STOP INSERTION
voiceless epenthetic stop homorganic with preceding
nasal
PRINCE   prɪns → prɪnts
ANXIOUS   æŋšəs → æŋkšəs

9) TAP FORMATION
non-initially under certain circumstances when not next to
consonants (extremely complex environment)
BETTER   bɛtər → bɛɒər
AT HOME   æt hom → æɒ hom

10) t-DELETION
between obstruent and consonant
most people
most pʰipəl → mos pʰipəl

11) VELAR NASAL
optional if the n̲ is in unstressed syllable and velar precedes
the main stress
congressional
kəŋgrɛšənəl OR   kəngrɛšənəl

12) VOWEL REDUCTION
unstressed vowel reduced to SCHWA (usually followed by
ə-Syncope (deletion)
manual
mæ̲nuwæl → mæ̲nəwəl
stressed vowel underscored

Appendix 2 Radical English Natural Processes

These processes are less important and even (in some cases) unimportant to the pronunciation teacher, since they do not represent crucial and regular features of a recognizable English accent. 1) Some of these processes are peculiar to a particular dialect or speaker (idiolect). 2) Others apply only in more rapid and careless speech and are highly optional. 3) A final group are processes whose effects would be practically indistinguishable to most native ears, let alone to the ear of a nonnative/foreign speaker.

1) č-SIMPLIFICATION
   č becomes a š after another š
   question
   kwɛščǝn → kwɛššǝn

2) DEGEMINATION
   C¹C² becomes C¹ in fast speech
   BOOKKEEPER   bʊkkipǝr → bʊkipǝr
   UNKNOWN   ʌnnon → ʌnon

3) fθ-SIMPLIFICATION
   fθ changes to θ before vowels and to f before consonants
   Fifth Avenue vs. Fifth Street
   fʊfθ ævǝnu → fʊθ ævǝnu
   fʊfθ strit → fʊf strit

4) DENTAL t/d/n
   alveolar closure becomes dental before any dental
   TENTH and EIGHTH
   tɛnθ → tɛn̪θ
   etθ → et̪θ

5) PALATALIZATION BEFORE r
   alveolars become alveopalatals before r
   TRY   traj → čraj
   DRILL   drʊl → jrʊl

6) r/l COLORING
   SCHWA becomes a SCHWAR before r
   BETTER or BUTTER   bɛtǝr → bɛtǝrr
   BIRD   bǝrd → bǝrrd

NOTES

1. The best introductory sources for natural phonology are still the short review in Sommerstein (1977:234–7) and Stampe's revised thesis included in Stampe (1979). Stampe and Donegan (1979) provide elaborate readjustments and extensions of the original model. My own book-length study (Bjarkman in preparation) promises to be the first published separate monograph on the subject.

2. The final chapter of Bjarkman (in preparation) will look more exclusively at acquisition of English as a second language—especially the acquisition of English by native speakers of Spanish. The lists of English rules and processes given here provide only an approximate outline of the learning task, which will be more exhaustively examined in my forthcoming chapter. Among works presently or soon available, Bjarkman (1986) will emphasize *learning* and *acquisition* (the internal mechanisms of the speaker) as opposed to the teaching procedures themselves. Following the currently popular model of Stephen Krashen, this latter work attempts to articulate more precisely a distinction between 'learning' (= rules) and 'acquisition' (= processes), another task for which Stampe's model proves particularly adaptable.

3. For the most thorough examinations and explications of the notion of 'allophonics' versus 'morphophonemics,' the reader is directed to Bjarkman (1975 or 1978d). Profitable additional sources on this crucial distinction within natural phonology are also Stampe (1979), Rhodes (1973), and Wojcik (1979), the latter article offering something of a contrasting viewpoint to that expressed in my own work.

4. I will not distinguish carefully in this paper between the designations of English as a second language (ESL) and English as a foreign language (EFL). I am most interested throughout this work (and my other writing on the subject) in those learners who acquire English—or any other idiom—as a second 'first' language, i.e., another language of primary communication. Throughout the literature, ESL is used to distinguish this type of learner from those who may aim at only partial usage of a foreign idiom (EFL)—for reading in the sciences, for example.

5. That the adult grammar consists largely of the residues of a complete set of infant speech reduction processes (as Stampe claims) rests of course firmly on the evidence that can be mustered for the cognitive and physiological reality of such a system of processes in the infant. Here perhaps the evidence from infant babbling is the most persuasive defense of such a hypothesis. If any child makes all the vocalic and consonantal sounds of the human inventory in the pre-linguistic stage (cf. Moskowitz 1978:102), then how might this fact be reconciled with the child's inability to produce anything but the first basic vowel sound [a] at the onset of speech acquisition? Chomsky's notion that the child must learn rules to acquire a pronunciation system is not as helpful here as Stampe's notion that, at the onset of infant language acquisition, the child begins suppressing the full range of inborn or innate articulation reduction processes. Speech acquisition here is taken to be a matter of process loss (fewer processes allow the larger inventory of vowel articulations) rather than rule acquisition. The child makes a full range of vowel sounds in the babbling stage precisely because no reduction processes have yet been activated in this pre-linguistic period.

6. The notion here is essentially the same as the one later adopted by Stampe and the

natural phonologists, in the sense that morphophonemic rules (processes) are those which substitute one potential underlying segment for another (thus causing neutralizations or phonemic overlap). Allophonic rules are those which introduce only segments (aspirated voiceless stops in English, for example) which are absent from or impermissible in the underlying inventory of sounds.

7. Wojcik (1980:22) points, as well, to several additional English pairs which stand as incontrovertible evidence that the substitution here is not a constraint on articulation, i.e., pronounceability. Note the pairs, among others, *chief/chiefs, waif/waifs,* or *oaf/oafs.*

8. I argue against this intelligibility claim in Bjarkman (1985). My position is essentially the one outlined briefly here, but argued more extensively in that earlier article on radical Hispanic dialects. The issue here seems to be not so much one of social constraint as it is one of the physiological and mental difficulties of reinstituting natural processes already suppressed in the earlier stages of child language acquisition.

9. Cases of syllable-initial /s/-aspiration are cited for Dominican Spanish by both Nuñez-Cedéño (1980) and Hammond (1976). The point here is that native speakers often extend such native processes in rapid or sloppy speech by relaxing restrictions on the environments in which they apply.

10. *Punkin* [pʌnkIn] is, of course, possible in English and is usually heared as an affectionate term of endearment, or even a nickname (*my little Punkin*). But note that this form occurs in highly informal speech, or as an imitation of childlike speech or baby-talk. That is, it is taken by native speakers as a clearly exceptional form. The fact that we pronounce it in English when we want to, however, again demonstrates that such constraints on pronounceability are highly mentalistic and not at all physical (physiological).

11. Note that actually two processes transfer in the example given. In addition to the diphthongization, the English speaker would also be expected to transfer aspiration of the initial voiceless stop.

12. The child's approach in native speech acquisition is largely inductive—he is exposed to large bodies of unorganized primary language data from which he draws generalizations in order to hypothesize the appropriate linguistic rules. Classroom approaches to language instruction are usually deductive in strategy: the formalized statement of a rule is first offered to the learner, who then generalizes to the proper examples (creates sentences utilizing or applying the rule). We may, in part at least, find a clue here to the partial failure of the classroom approach to language acquisition.

13. As I suggested at the outset, the drawback to Daniels's article is that his program is overly simplistic, addressing as it does only the processes or phonetic substitutions of the allophonic type. It makes, for one thing, a false assumption that in natural phonology a phonemic representation is always the same. And yet Spanish speakers may perceive a word like *apto* as being phonemically either /abto/ or /agto/, depending on which morphophonemic processes they have applied (see Bjarkman 1978b for analysis of this case). The point seems to be that, faced with such neutralization, speakers will maintain morphophonemic and not autonomous phonemic representations for such forms.

14. Another example of paradigmatic fortition is the syllable-initial constraint on nasals

in English. All syllable-initial nasals must be [+anterior] (i.e., /n/ or /m/, but never /ñ/ or /ŋ/), which explains the English-speaker's attempts at pronouncing something like the Vietnamese name *Nguyen* (see Stampe 1973a: Chapter One), where spelling leads to the conclusion that a velar nasal appears word-initially (in actuality, the Vietnamese word begins phonetically with a labialized velar stop [gʷ] which in turn was misperceived by the French who produced the current spelling).

15. Another example (among several more that could be cited) of a Korean process that has allophonic effects in the native tongue but morphophonemic effect when transferred to English is a process governing nasal-plus-liquid sequences. In Korean, /l/ becomes /n/ when it immediately follows either /m/ or /ŋ/. Thus, *Hamlet* would be pronounced as *Hamnet*, *home run* as *home nun*, *King Lear* as *King Near*, etc. Of course, again, context would usually disambiguate these utterances.

REFERENCES

Bjarkman, Peter C. 1975. "Towards a proper conception of processes in natural phonology." CLS 11, pp. 60–72.

Bjarkman, Peter C. 1976. *Natural Phonology and Loan-Word Phonology*. Unpublished dissertation, University of Florida at Gainesville.

Bjarkman, Peter C. 1977. "The role of autonomous phonemics in natural phonology." Paper read at the 1977 International Phonetic Sciences Congress (IPS-77), Miami Beach.

Bjarkman, Peter C. 1978a. "Natural phonology and applied linguistics: On theoretical phonology and English as a second language methodology." Paper read at the 53rd Annual Meeting of the Linguistic Society of America, Boston.

Bjarkman, Peter C. 1978b. "Reassessment of the role of natural phonology in the analysis of Cuban Spanish." Paper read at the Annual Convention of the Modern Language Association, New York.

Bjarkman, Peter C. 1978c. "The phonemic hypothesis and some related issues in natural phonology." In: Donald M. Lance and Daniel F. Gulstad (eds.), *Proceedings of 1977 Mid-America Linguistics Conference*. Columbia, MO: The Area Program in Linguistics, The University of Missouri, pp. 303–19.

Bjarkman, Peter C. 1978d. "Allophonics, morphophonemics, and the so-called 'natural' phonemic level." *The CUNY Forum* 5–6, pp. 133–44.

Bjarkman, Peter C. 1985. "Conservative and radical Hispanic dialects: Theoretical Accounts and pedagogical implications." In: Robert M. Hammond and John B. Jensen (eds.), *Actas del VIIIº Simposio de dialectología del Caribe Hispánico*. Washington, DC: Georgetown University Press.

Bjarkman, Peter C. 1986. "Natural accounts and strategies for second language acquisition." In: Allan R. James and Brian Wenk (eds.), *Phonetics and Phonology in Second Language Acquisition*, to appear.

Bjarkman, Peter C. in preparation. *An Introduction to Natural Phonology (With Examples from Native Phonology and Loanword Phonology)*.

Chomsky, Noam, and Morris Halle 1968. *The Sound Pattern of English*. New York: Harper and Row.

Chu, Harold S., and Young-Hee Park 1977. *Contrastive Analysis between Korean and English for ESL Teachers*. Arlington, VA: Bilingual Education Project of the Arlington (Virginia) Public Schools.

Daniels, William J. 1975. "Natural phonology and the teaching of pronunciation." *Slavic and East European Journal* 19, pp. 66–73.

Gandour, Jack, and Marc Fey 1979. "Problem-solving in early phonological acquisition." Paper read at the 54th Annual Meeting of the Linguistic Society of America, Los Angeles.

Guitart, Jorge M. 1978. "Conservative versus radical dialects in Spanish: Implications for language instruction." *The Bilingual Review* 5, pp. 57–64.

Hammond, Robert M. 1976. *Some Theoretical Implications of Rapid Speech Phenomena in Miami-Cuban Spanish.* Unpublished dissertation, University of Florida at Gainesville.

Hill, Kenneth C. 1973. "Fast speech rules I." Unpublished manuscript, University of Michigan Phonetic Laboratory.

Kiparsky, Paul 1968. "How abstract is phonology?" Bloomington, IN: Indiana University Linguistics Club.

Kiparsky, Paul, and Lise Menn 1977. "On the acquisition of phonology." In: John MacNamara (ed.), *Language Learning and Thought.* New York: Academic Press, pp. 47–78.

Moskowitz, Breyne Arlene 1978. "The acquisition of language." *Scientific American* 239:5, pp. 95–108.

Nuñez-Cedéño, Rafeal 1980. *La fonología moderna y el español de Santo Domingo.* Santo Domingo: Editora Taller.

Rhodes, Richard 1973. "Some implications of natural phonology." CLS 9, pp. 530–41.

Shibatani, Masayoshi 1973. "The role of surface phonetic constraints in generative phonology." *Language* 49, pp. 87–106.

Sommerstein, Alan H. 1977. *Modern Phonology.* Baltimore: University Park Press.

Stampe, David L. 1968. "The acquisition of phonological representation (or Yes, Virginia . . .)." Paper read at the 4th Regional Meeting of the Chicago Linguistic Society.

Stampe, David L. 1969. "The acquisition of phonetic representation." CLS 5, pp. 443–54.

Stampe, David L. 1973a. *A Dissertation on Natural Phonology.* Unpublished dissertation, University of Chicago.

Stampe, David L. 1973b. "On Chapter Nine." In: Michael Kenstowitz and Charles W. Kisserberth (eds.), *Issues in Phonological Theory.* The Hague: Mouton, pp. 44–52.

Stampe, David L. 1979. *A Dissertation on Natural Phonology* (including "The acquisition of phonetic representation"). Bloomington, IN: Indiana University Linguistics Club.

Stampe, David L., and Patricia J. Donegan 1979. "The study of natural phonology." In: Daniel A. Dinnsen (ed.), *Current Approaches to Phonological Theory.* Bloomington, IN: Indiana University Press.

Wojcik, Richard 1975. "Remarks on natural phonology." *The Columbia University Working Papers in Linguistics* 3, pp. 1–12.

Wojcik, Richard 1977. "The interaction of syllables and morpheme boundaries in natural phonology." Unpublished manuscript, Columbia University.

Wojcik, Richard 1979. "The phoneme in natural phonology." In: P. L. Clyne et al. (eds.), *Papers from the Parasession on the Elements.* Chicago: Chicago Linguistic Society, pp. 273–84.

Wojcik, Richard 1980. "Natural phonology and generative phonology." Unpublished manuscript, Columbia University.

Wojcik, Richard 1981. "Natural phonology and foreign accent." Unpublished manuscript, Barnard College.

CHAPTER SIX

Linguistics and Artificial Intelligence: An armchair drama in 3 acts, with a prologue and an epilogue

Sergei Nirenburg

1. Prologue

Let us imagine a meeting between a linguist and a specialist in artificial intelligence. There is a common understanding that each field may and will profit from closer contacts with the other. But so far little has been done to overcome the all too human feelings of apprehensiveness and resentment against each other's 'misrepresentation' of, 'immateriality' to, and 'failure' with, the problems of the study of language. Our characters are resolved, if not to alleviate this friction, then at least to clarify the respective positions and look for mutually acceptable ways of cooperation.

The artificial intelligence researcher is primarily interested in natural language processing, unlike many of his friends who work in such fields as computer vision, game playing, theorem proving, etc. A diligent person, this researcher— let us call him AI, for convenience—once set out to read all the linguistic materials he could find that might have shed light on the ways to construct a computer system for processing natural language. Had he found ready-made answers he would have simply represented the linguistic rules and structures in LISP (or another suitable programming language) and thus would have obtained a self-contained 'linguistic' module to be used in any natural language-related application, such as a knowledge-based 'expert' system, a translating machine, etc. Rather unexpectedly, AI discovered that linguistics cannot offer certified answers, that it is a complex field of study in which a number of hypotheses about the language structure and meaning compete for recognition and priority, and that even the better ideas and theories are being refuted on a regular basis. (We can only guess what AI's confusion would be if he were told that what he observed was but a tip of the linguistic iceberg: namely, the transformationalist theories; and that linguistics can offer more insights at the philosophical and meta-theoretical level than suggested there.) After attempting halfheartedly to follow the arguments of all the sides in the linguistic dispute and trying (with results worse than expected) to use the transformational grammars (Chomsky

1957, 1965) directly for computer generation (cf. Petrick 1965) and analysis (e.g., Kuno and Oettinger 1963; Zwicky et al. 1965), AI then concluded that the best linguistics could offer at the moment for extensive use in artificial intelligence research was the idea of case grammars (Fillmore 1968, 1971). (There were some attempts at using dependency grammars (e.g., Hayes 1964) and systemic grammars (Halliday 1970), but they were lone, if well-known, attempts and were not pursued widely.) The case grammars were modified slightly (Simmons 1973) or significantly (Schank 1973, 1975); and used in various computer systems (cf. Samlowski 1976; Bruce 1975; Winograd 1983, for three surveys).

AI brought himself to accept the obvious incompleteness of the current versions of case grammars by convincing himself that for the purposes of intelligent computer systems nothing more was necessary. Some more ideas (notably, the notion of 'natural logic') were picked up in the linguistic realm, but AI effectively decided to be self-sufficient in dealing with problems of language. The prevalent position was: "Linguistics, as it is at the present time, cannot help us to build intelligent machines." Incidentally, many of AI's best friends are linguists.

The linguist, L, has been bred on (though does not necessarily strictly adhere to) the transformationalist approach. He recognizes semantics as a vital component of linguistics and does not divorce language from its communicative function. Therefore, pragmatics, the field that studies language carriers in their relationship to the world they inhabit, as well as to each other, is one of the aspects of the study of language that interests him most. He is not sure that there is still any sense in staunchly defending the emphasis on the study of linguistic competence at the expense of performance, though he admits that the former approach has come up with more detailed formalisms. The historically 'post-Chomskian' or independently pursued topics of pragmatic presupposition, speech acts, conversational postulates, natural logic, language formulae, etc., have been more or less central to his studies. He was even for some time toying with the idea of borrowing the notion of frame (from artificial intelligence or directly from psychology) for use in language analysis.

He has an open mind towards computers and their application in linguistic research. As a matter of fact, he used to take part in building concordances and thesauri with the help of a computer. Of course, he has always understood the proper place of the computer: it is a tool, not unlike a pen or a pocket calculator. Artificial intelligence does not employ 'smart' computers; there is no such thing: computers are nothing but behemoth number-crunchers. Computer programs are being built that simulate 'intelligent' behavior, but these are more products of ingenious craftsmen than results of the application of scientific theories. In short, the linguist believes that artificial intelligence is an art. (We can only guess at what L's reaction would be if he heard that there is a lively discussion in the field of computer science as to whether computer programs may be regarded as theories.) At the same time L welcomes the thought that computers may be useful in more than the one simple way he is aware of. Needless to say, many of L's best friends are computer scientists.

Obviously, AI and L have a great deal to discuss. The most important thing for each of them to learn is what bearing his own discipline exerts on the other and, conversely, what use the other field has for his own. Ironically, AI and L hold very restrictive and unflattering views of each other's positions. In reality, however, neither is as narrow-minded as the other side believes.

2.   Act One. Mostly Definitions

AI: If we are to discuss the relations between our fields, then the best starting point will be to clarify whether we have a common understanding of the scope and goals of these disciplines. In my understanding, linguistics is a field whose object of study is natural language, especially the rules governing the construction of correct texts in natural language. Of course, not only may sincerity frighten the boy, but also my pet amoeba believes that I am a lousy cook. In general, though, the emphasis is on syntactic studies since the bulk of the formalisms for natural language is syntactic rather than semantic, to say nothing about the connection with the models of the real world in which language is a phenomenon. Also, linguists speak exclusively about structures, with a complete blackout on processes involved in language comprehension and production.

L: I think I must first of all thank you for just considering linguistics a scientific discipline. This is a welcome change from Wilensky's claim that "artificial intelligence is the real psychology, linguistics and philosophy" (Brachman and Smith 1980:109). Seriously, it is quite difficult to present a noncontroversial definition of a scientific field in a couple of sentences. Your definition tends to be closer to that of microlinguistics in the sense of Lyons (1981:36). First of all, people who work on comparative grammars of Semitic languages or on the intonation patterns in Burushaski are still linguists. The emphasis on language at the expense of languages is mostly a feature of just one influential stream in linguistic science that has come to be known as the Chomskian or transformationalist approach. Note that I use these names only as a rough reference, since many modern linguists would reject any association of their work with either Chomsky or the notion of transformations. Still, they share the basic attitude towards linguistic study and, at least for an outsider, constitute a group.

AI: For me this theoretical part of linguistics is the most interesting or even the only linguistics there is.

L: This is a restrictive position: pre-Chomskian linguistics is not necessarily nontheoretical. Linguistics as the study of language long predated Chomsky. Moreover, the status of the linguistic 'field work' is not unlike that of the numerous computer systems dealing with language. A grammar of Mohawk may carry as much (or as little) theoretical message as a system of augmented transition network–based parsing of Hebrew.

Back to the attempt at definition. Based on the idea that humans possess an innate language ability, linguistic competence, the linguists proceed to build theories about what makes a language entity (an utterance or a text) grammatical, meaningful, and appropriate. If an entity does not possess at least one of the above properties, it is considered 'incorrect,' or, more properly, not a language entity at all. And this is the sense in which I can agree with your usage of the word 'correct.' As an illustration, (1) is ungrammatical, (2) is grammatical but meaningless, and (3) is grammatical and meaningful, but inappropriate if uttered at noon.

(1) *Done have homework he been his.

(2) *Colorless green ideas sleep furiously.

(3) This is the happiest night of my life.

One tradition is to connect grammaticality with syntax, meaningfulness with semantics, and appropriateness with pragmatics. Another understands grammaticality as the sum of all three.

AI: I have several questions to ask. The first concerns the problem of completeness: Can it be proved that still further constraints on the notion of grammaticality will not be necessary, that is, that the above triad adequately describes the notion of 'correctness' underlying much of the theoretical work in linguistics? Second, what are the criteria that permit us to judge a theory's verdict about the 'correctness' of a language element? Do these belong to the field of linguistics or is there a need to borrow them from another field, possibly psychology or philosophy? Third, where does the competence assumption fit in here, or, in other words, why should the notion of the 'innate linguistic faculty' be the foundation of the whole edifice of the linguistic theory? And, finally, a simple observation: Does the notion of grammaticality need to be concentric? Isn't it possible, say, for an utterance to be meaningful and appropriate but 'ungrammatical'; I mean, syntactically unacceptable, and, at the same time readily understandable?

L: The first and the second questions would warrant book-length answers. In a sense, this is what linguistics is all about. I hope we shall return to a discussion of the second question, because the problem you mention, justification, is a methodological cornerstone not only of linguistics but also of artificial intelligence, cognitive psychology, and, as a matter of fact, science in general. The notion of competence, or rather the distinction between competence and performance, has been a very useful methodological tool that was also an expression of a hypothesis about human cognitive processes. True, it could not provide a basis for a universal linguistic theory, and it is for a long time now that some linguists have considered the study of performance at least as important as the study of competence.

Your fourth question, however, seems to be an expression of a certain assumption that I'd like to clarify. By questioning the 'concentricity' of the composite grammaticality notion you proclaim the primacy of semantics and pragmatics over syntax. First, the suggestion that since 'irregular' syntactic constructions are habitual in language use, syntax is largely irrelevant for the study of language, rests on false premises. Let me suggest that it may well be a fault of the theories of syntax that they became to a certain extent prescriptive: a certain class of structures was declared 'grammatical' and the discrepancy between this class and the existence of a larger set of structures judged to be proper and applicable by native speakers was explained in terms of the competence/performance dichotomy, which implied that performance may vulgarize the 'true' theory of competence understood as the structure of the well-delineated notion of an innate 'language faculty' in man.

AI: Yes, this state of affairs was, to a certain extent, inherited by the natural language analysis within the artificial intelligence paradigm. Consider, for example, the necessity of introducing weakening extensions, such as 'relaxation techniques' of Kwasny (1980) or systems for treating 'unparsable inputs' (cf. Weischedel and Black 1980) to the ATN parsers for English that were programs processing language within theoretically 'prescribed' syntax (cf. Woods 1970).

L: Arguably, ATN parsers themselves are not exactly products of a linguistically sound research, largely because they were never seriously meant to be more than frameworks for the applications of linguistic theories (cf. the claimed ability of ATNs to accommodate multiple linguistic approaches in Bates 1978; cf. also the discussion in Winograd 1983:Chapters 5 and 7).

The notion of competence, however, has played a singularly important part in making the theories of syntax within the transformational framework possible. This role resembles, for example, that of the notion of 'ideal gas' for physicists. The abstraction was necessary as an initial simplification. There may be a theory that will classify the previously rejected elements as correct.

AI: But what about the following opinion: ''The theory of linguistic competence is a proper subpart of a theory of performance, not some first approximation of one'' (Dresher and Hornstein 1977a)?

L: As you may have guessed already, this position can be defended only by somebody who desperately needs to maintain the original distinction between competence and performance. Remove this distinction, and the domino effect will immediately follow: most of the proposals within this particular approach will fall with it. At present, almost two decades after Chomsky's *Aspects,* it is only a minority in the linguistic community that suscribes to this idea in its original formulation. It may be erroneous to speak about language entities that satisfy pragmatic and semantic requirements but fail at the syntactic level. There might be a better, weaker linguistic theory, in which today's irregularities will cease to be such. It remains to be seen whether such a theory will seriously rely on semantics and pragmatics for its explanatory force, but so far nobody has produced a framework, let alone the formalism for such a theory, certain claims to the contrary notwithstanding. (The lexical-functional grammar of Kaplan and Bresnan 1982 is inspired by the all-encompassing Chomskian universal grammar, e.g., Chomsky 1975, which in its most cautious definition is weak enough; but the lexical-functional grammar itself is still a 'strong' claim.)

In artificial intelligence, the initial dissatisfaction with what linguistics had to offer for syntactic analysis led to the quick opinion that since semantic processing is to be done anyway in the process of language comprehension or generation (and procedural thinking prevails in artificial intelligence), then one might dispense with syntax or demote it to the status of a poor relative who does not deserve a full-fledged treatment. (Schank and Birnbaum 1980 is a very forcefully expressed statement to this effect; Raskin 1971 may well be the earliest such claim.) To be sure, this might be the description of an extreme position. But it reflects many a theoretical position and the mainstream of current knowledge-based language understanding practice. This is a reaction against the 'autonomy of syntax' hypothesis, which was erroneously perceived by most in artificial intelligence as a claim that semantics (and phonology, and pragmatics) should play only a supporting role to syntax.

In fact, the claim was that it is possible to study syntax in isolation from semantics, etc., and carried a methodological significance: if accepted, it brought along hope that a theory of syntax could be built in the observable future. This methodological device need not be considered relevant only to linguistics. Winograd (1983:151–3) discusses this hypothesis in terms of a "nearly decomposable system" in which the relations between different components (in our case, syntax and semantics) are in a certain sense weaker than the relations between elements and phenomena within each single component. The perception mistake made by artificial intelligence workers was confounded by the fact that, indeed, after making the methodological assumption of the above autonomy, many (if not most) linguists attacked specifically syntax—so that it appeared that this is the only thing they were interested in. This reaction notwithstanding, the artificial intelligence people should not have been drawn to the opposite extreme: after all, syntactic ambiguity is one of the most widespread and common phenomena (remember *old men and women, flying planes*, and scores of other famous examples).

AI: Let us go on with our agenda. It is time now to learn what you mean by 'artificial intelligence.'

L: Artificial intelligence is a collection of computer techniques and programs that desires to make the computer carry out tasks previously done by humans. The main idea is to explore the ways in which such a powerful tool as the digital computer may become an extension of the brain. So understood, the task of artificial intelligence products is not unlike that of the alphabet, the abacus, the book, and the pencil. This is the latest entry on the list of 'mental work implements,' just as, say, the space shuttle is one of the newest transportation means. Once man had to retain in his own memory all the information he had to process; then he invented cuneiform tablets and papyrus. Once man had to understand mass spectrograms manually; now DENDRAL does it for him.

AI: Well, isn't this a restrictive definition! I am sure you include more in the notion of artificial intelligence than you just said. You know, in an argument people tend to slide towards more extreme and irreconcilable positions than they really hold. Tell me, would you describe our field in the same way if you were talking with another linguist?

L: This is quite immaterial to our discussion.

AI: In the short history of artificial intelligence one can find descriptions of its object of study similar to the one you suggested. Thus, Newell offers three possible views of artificial intelligence: 1) as the science concerned with the answer to the question, "What mechanisms can accomplish what intellectual functions?" (1973:2); 2) "as a field devoted to the discovery and collection of a set of methods," where the methods have three components: the problem statement, the procedure, and, most notably, the justification, "the reasons for believing that if the conditions of the problem statement are satisfied, then the procedure may result in a solution" (op. cit.:9); and 3) as a field "that serves as theoretical psychology if one adopts the view of man as a processor of information, represented as a system of discrete symbols" (op. cit.:26). He then goes on to state that the first view is "closest to the historical truth in terms of the motivations and fascinations of the men who have worked and dabbled in the field of artificial intelligence" (op. cit.:2).

He also admonishes that "sciences are not defined, they are recognized." Perhaps this is a reason why the authors of major artificial intelligence textbooks often seem reluctant to present a definition of the subject, choosing instead to delve immediately into the description of specific methods or subfields (cf. Bundy 1978, Nilsson 1981, Raphael 1976, though the latter may be considered a 'popular' introduction to the discipline).

L: Come to think of it, this state of affairs is not surprising. The thoughts about defining a subject usually follow the accumulation of facts in it. In the meantime, the 'working' definitions make do. Indeed, one would imagine that a course in, say, foundations of mathematics, would be offered to students only after they have had a couple of thousand hours of elementary and advanced calculus, algebra, etc.

AI: Yes, this might be one of the reasons for those authors who did include a definition not to pursue the discussion of it any further. Here is an assorted set of definitions:

"Artificial Intelligence is concerned with the creation of computer programs capable of performing tasks normally considered to require intelligence—from chess playing to medical diagnosis. Many such tasks involve the use of natural language and by this route Artificial Intelligence adds itself to the list of disciplines concerned with the problems of language comprehension'' (Charniak 1976:1).

"The central goals of Artificial Intelligence are to make computers more useful and to understand the principles that make intelligence possible" (Winston 1977:1).

"The goal of Artificial Intelligence is commonly considered to be making machines intelligent" (Schank and Riesbeck 1981:1).

L: Notice that these definitions beg the question of what is intelligence, and that notion remains undefined.

AI: Right. More. "Artificial intelligence is the study of complex information processing problems that often have their roots in some aspect of biological information processing. The goal of the subject is to identify interesting and solvable information processing problems, and solve them" (Marr 1977:37).

Charniak's, Winston's, and Schank and Riesbeck's definitions can be classified as the 'brush-off' type. Marr, however, attempts to put artificial intelligence in some sort of perspective by defining a subject which is (or can be) claimed by linguistics, psychology, philosophy, computer science, neurophysiology, etc. Marr also goes on to distinguish between two kinds of endeavors: the 'what-and-why' and the 'how' approaches. The former, called 'Type 1 theories,' are assigned the task of characterizing the underlying nature of a particular computation and its basis in the physical world. 'Type 2 theories' consist of particular algorithms for implementing computations.

Your definition of artificial intelligence describes just the latter approach. This position is hardly defensible on methodological grounds and is easier to attack. Marr himself has the following criticism to offer: "Most AI programs have hitherto amounted to Type 2 theories, and the danger with such theories is that they can bury crucial decisions . . . beneath the mound of small administrative decisions that are inevitable whenever a concrete program is designed" (1977:39).

In a rather uncharacteristic mood, Schank declared: "Artificial intelligence is a field that is not exactly sure what it is about" (1979:196). Is this statement strange coming from one of the foremost authorities in AI? No. It is a request for postponement of (possibly negative) judgment on AI—until the time it becomes a full-fledged scientific discipline.

Having seen some of the views of the 'insiders,' let's now present a view on artificial intelligence held by a philosopher. Ringle (1979:7) divides artificial intelligence into four streams: technology, simulation, modelling, and theory. Technology constructs systems that demonstrate intelligent behavior "irrespective of whether its data structures relate in any way to human data structures." Simulation does essentially the same, but claims an affinity between the behavior of the program and that of human beings. Models are simulations that are less concerned with imitation of behavior and that stress the claimed similarities between the man and the machine as regards the data structures, internal states, and information processes. This is obviously the home turf of cognitive psychologists, who often feel robbed of their own subject of study by the villainous artificial intelligence people just as acutely as you feel about linguistics (cf., e.g., Longuet-Higgins 1981).

Theory is "interested in principles of knowledge and intelligence which may be used to account for concrete, physically-instantiated, time- and perspective-dependent cognition" (Ringle 1979:10). It is quite transparent that the latter part of this definition serves the purpose of preventing artificial intelligence from claiming the home turf of yet another (Ringle's own) discipline—philosophy, or, more concretely, epistemology.

L: Thank you. This has been an enlightening survey. I think it's time to discuss in great detail the attitudes linguistics and artificial intelligence have about each other.

AI: OK. One final remark. Roughly what Ringle calls artificial intelligence theory and modeling has recently acquired a new alias: cognitive science. By calling themselves cognitive scientists the new generation of researchers wanted to dissociate themselves from the technological heritage of their field. Winograd (1983:2) writes: "Much of the work in computer science has been pragmatic, based on a desire to produce computer programs that can perform useful tasks. But the design of computational systems also has a theoretical side, which is often called *cognitive science*. The same concepts of program and data that serve as a framework for building and understanding computer programs can be applied to the understanding of any system carrying out processes that can be understood as the rule-governed manipulation of symbols."

L: Yes, maybe the concepts of programming *can* be applied in manipulating any kind of symbols, but where is the proof that they *should?* Simply because there is a method or an approach that works in the field where it was first introduced does not necessarily mean that it will work in another field, or that this infusion will solve the problems better than the methods that had been acquired as a result of the efforts of many generations of workers in the 'recipient' field, in this case, linguistics.

3.   Act Two. Mostly Grievances and Prejudices

L: I should have noted last time that, though we have finally arrived at a definition of artificial intelligence that is much more palatable than I had supposed, it by no means reflects the majority position. Philosophical problems aside, most of the people in the field are still wary of the distinction among technology, modeling, and theory. They are driven by methodological inertia. Maybe public opinion is partly to blame, what with the spectacular encroachments of computers into our everyday life. Artificial intelligence is currently in vogue. It is this field that is currently entrusted with that elusive magician's wand which is supposed to help solve all problems of knowledge, language, and universal welfare. This may be one of the reasons why "the growth rate of the AI community seems to be faster than that of the population of some countries," to use Firdman's apt metaphor (1982:3).

AI: Why don't you mention the upsurge in linguistic research in the late fifties and early sixties—in the era of *Syntactic Structures?* Was the situation then dissimilar to what you observe in artificial intelligence now? Did you object to that instance of the same phenomenon?

L (paying no attention to AI's last words, reads from a prepared statement) The problem with artificial intelligence may be its sheer success. The field has been quite productive in accumulating various kinds of knowledge previously unavailable. The general mood has been quite upbeat, in part because so many palpable results in the form of new programs and systems have appeared. Less emphasis has been placed upon the justification of the solutions and those clusters of working decisions that can be upgraded to the status of theories. The amount of work invested in building extensive programs seemed to justify the exalted attitude towards 'working systems,' regardless of their theoretical merit. Essentially no criticism of any work in the field was accepted from the outside on the grounds that nobody who had not built a computer system had the right to express (unfavorable or critical) opinions. "Do some *real* work before you speak up!" was the general advice. Real work was writing computer programs.

AI research remains at present unchallenged in the sense that there is enough room for everybody. The AI 'economy' is still extensive: there are enough fields for everybody to plow. This can be exemplified by the history of the Yale AI project. There we had a succession of emphases: first on parsing, then on memory and inference making, which spawned a number of knowledge representation applications. Now Schank (1982) claims that it's time to look at learning. We are led to believe that the former problems have been already solved and the solutions verified, proved, and sealed. Of course, even Schank himself obviously cannot think so, but the edge that the curiosity of the kind "Will it work in learning too?" holds over the tenacity in justification and modification 'chores' is disconcerting. However, this cream skimming over a variety of fields is not unfortunate in itself. A less welcome thing is the almost universal conviction that anything that works is correct theoretically. One need not go far to find numerous assertions like: "Our two goals for SOPHIE's natural language processor are efficiency and friendliness" (Brown and Burton 1975:330); "The strongest support for procedural representation comes from the fact that is works" (Winograd 1975:190); "The justification for the representation is not at all a 'vague intuition' . . . but its demonstrable ability to be used as a basis for inference" (Schank and Wilensky 1977:100); "Rules [for manipulating conceptual dependency representations] are determined by the task at hand" (ibid.); "We were not as concerned with the ultimate correctness of the [conceptual dependency]

system as we were with its usability. No other canonical form existed, and the transformational   deep   structure   representations   and   predicate   calculus . . . neither adequately represented meaning nor were in any sense can-
onical'' (Schank 1980:251). One is immediately tempted to ask, What is can-
onical? What makes an approach canonical? Should the conceptual dependency theory become canonical, and why?

There are, however, other voices in the artificial intelligence community. Hayes (1980:242–4) has the following to offer: ''All too often, serious work on representational issues in AI has been diverted or totally thwarted by premature concern for computational issues. . . . It is tempting to make . . . demonstra-
tions [of working systems] from time to time. (They impress people; and it is satisfying to have actually *made* something that works, like building model railways; and one's students can get Ph.Ds that way.) But they divert attention from the main goal. . . . It is perilously easy to say that, because one has a program that *works* (in some sense), its representation of its knowledge must be more or less *correct* (in some sense).''

I fully agree with this position. Too much of 'theoretical' work in the field has been the process of very intelligent and ingenious groping in the dark in hope that 'something will click.' ''[In AI] one can try out ideas (to see if they 'work') at the terminal, without even having thought about them before'' (Ades 1981:13). Consider the following situation: if you face, say, a cryptarithmetic puzzle, your first impulse is to try to substitute the digits for letters at random—to see whether you could stumble on the solution without even attempting a systematic search. Only after being discouraged by several consecutive failures you start to contem-
plate a more systematic, theoretical approach. The same with a bundle of keys to try out on an unknown lock. The same with any other everyday activity that involves search. This generalization seems, incidentally, sufficient to postulate a special *try-at-random* plan-box for the goal D-SOLVE (cf. Schank and Abelson 1977:88–97; my apologies for the unsolicited suggestion). Such activities, however psychologically real and observable, cannot qualify as construction of theo-
ries. Not so, say Schank and Wilensky: ''. . . AI methodology—that is, building a program as a test of theory—has been extremely useful in pointing out deficien-
cies of theories, and uncovering problems that were not understood beforehand. For example, the problem of controlling the proliferation of inferences that occurred in programs like MARGIE (Schank et al. 1973) was not even recognized as a problem until we built a program that attempted to make inferences'' (Schank and Abelson 1977:138).

This example does not corroborate the point—it refutes it! If MARGIE is a program that carries out inference making, then, according to the methodological statement above, there was a theory of inferences that MARGIE was supposed to test. So, what was that theory like if such an important problem as proliferation control was not addressed in it? ''. . . It is just the fact that we don't know what the correct theory [of language] is that makes experimentation so useful'' (op.

cit.:139). Again, the impression is that experimentation is believed to be the process of building theories by 'groping' and not a means of justification and comparison. OK, you do not consider all the other theories of language or of knowledge representation and use adequate, but then the desire to implant your own hypothesis firmly in the AI–cognitive science–linguistics turf must compel you to come up with counterexamples, if not alternate theories, all by yourself, and at the very least, to emphasize the importance of the very job of 'doing justification.'

Moreover, it still needs to be shown that the empirical attitude of experimentation before theorizing is viable at all. In fact, I am sure that when faced with the question, "Is it possible for an experiment to be conducted without a certain (even not yet well-formulated) theory underlying it?" almost every AI researcher will take the Popperian anti-positivist viewpoint to answer in the negative. Why then are working programs considered to be on par with theories by so many? (For further discussion cf., e.g., Simon 1979, for a philosopher's view, and Winograd 1977:172, for that of a worker in AI.)

AI: It is quite interesting that the main topic of your critique has so far been methodological. I expected a different tune. Maybe something to the effect that we disregard the results of a generation in linguistics only to redo essentially the same research, or that our study of language does not in effect contribute anything to the study of language, or that our results are but very partial because of the insufficient generality of domains in our applications. Also, it seems strange that such criticism should come from a linguist: won't you agree with me that, to put it mildly, the concern for justification is hardly among the first items on the agenda of any linguist? Those few who address this problem specifically agree that justification, at least other than a simple and always very fuzzy reference to the notion of grammaticality, in any of the latter's meanings, is still largely a white spot on the linguistic map. Let me quote a linguist's views that corroborate this: "Very few linguists are explicitly concerned with justification, and attempts to consistently compare two alternative grammars on the basis of clearly postulated criteria are extremely rare" (Raskin 1979:154).

L: These words prove that linguists *are* concerned with justification. But a paraphrase of the above, I maintain, will be true for the field of artificial intelligence: "Very few AI researchers are explicitly concerned with justification and attempts to consistently compare two alternative proposals on the basis of clearly postulated theoretical criteria are practically non-existent," mostly because no such criteria have been suggested. Incidentally, Raskin suggests a number of such criteria for linguistics, which shows that it is quite erroneous to think that linguists tend to overplay the importance of grammaticality. "There are at least five more [in addition to grammaticality-awareness] manifestations of competence which the native speaker can be demonstrated to display in a no more unreliable way: . . . truth-value awareness, presupposition awareness, context awareness and appropriateness awareness" (op. cit.:156). Elsewhere (Raskin

1978), coherency awareness is also suggested. I disagree with Raskin that these are necessarily manifestations of competence, since the latter has come to be identified with the notion of grammar, which, in its turn, has never incorporated more than an (interpretivist) semantic level of description. I do not see why, for instance, context and appropriateness are not facets of the theory of linguistic performance, and I doubt that it is possible in principle to construct a 'pragmatic' grammar along the methodological lines familiar to all generative linguists. Raskin, however, shows that the methodological importance of the old competence/performance distinction is more or less obsolete in modern linguistics. So, we can substitute 'linguistic theories' instead of grammars. And we can use the above tools in consistent attempts at their justification.

AI: Excuse me, I think I need some more explanation of the nature of all the above 'awareness.'

L: OK, take a look at this. (A piece of paper changes hands; it contains the following:

(a)   Louis XV loved Madam de Pompadour.
(b)   Napoleon loved Brigitte Bardot.
(c)   The present king of France is bald.
(d)   There exists a unique person who is the present king of France.
(e)   I got up rather late. I washed and dressed and had some breakfast. It is intended as an introductory text. I barely managed to get to work in time.
(f)   Kissinger conjectures poached.
(g)   How do you think President Ford likes his eggs?

Truth value awareness makes the speakers assign 'true' to (a) and 'false' to (b); understanding of (c) necessarily presupposes (d); the third sentence in (e) does not pass the coherence test; (f) is understood only in the context of (g), or in a similarly revealing context. In clustering all these notions under one roof Raskin does not leave any stone unturned. The criteria involve the emphases maintained by most of the influential schools of thought in linguistics and philosophy of language over the last quarter of the century (and more). It is important to consider these tools as possibly applicable to justifying theories of language use.

AI: The problem with the above criteria, as I perceive them, is that they are not, as you say, tools. Just like the metric system is not a tool for measuring the width of this table. A ruler is still to be invented!

L: A linguist is not responsible for specifying concrete procedures for the application of these criteria, if this is what you imply. Raskin overtly leaves this job to psychologists: ". . . grammars can be directly evaluated in information-eliciting experiments with informants based on one of the natural manifestations of their linguistic competence" (1979:161). Once again, mind you, I object to the last word: I would use "knowledge and experience" instead. Of course, a possibility should be discussed of using computer models instead of informants.

AI: You are overly indulgent. No linguist will 'buy' any such judgment. Besides, justification in artificial intelligence is perceived along different lines. Consider the following view of how theories can be tested, where the first way is suggested for artificial intelligence: "One strategy in testing a theory (derived from the more traditional sciences) is to identify what phenomena it would exclude, and then to verify that the predicted ones indeed occur, and that the excluded ones do not. In linguistics this strategy often takes the following form: the grammars set out by proposed theories are tested to ensure that they reject so-called 'bad' sentences (those with syntax unacceptable to native English speakers). The purpose of making sure that theories exclude phenomena which do not occur is to guard against the construction of overly general (and therefore content-free) theories" (Brachman and Smith 1980:106).

L: Look how your colleagues misrepresent linguistic views! We have seen already that it is not only syntactic well-formedness that makes an utterance acceptable or unacceptable to the speakers of English.

AI: You should pay better attention to the newly found possibility of testing theories of language by predicting behavior of computer models. Also, it is a long way from being aware of the 'awarenesses' and actually putting them to use. Linguistics must elaborate on this point. Notice that Raskin does not suggest any kind of interaction among his criteria, nor a scale of 'weights' corresponding to their relative 'judgmental force.' In the meantime the artificial intelligence people will be best advised to be concerned about predictive verification. This is not a universal device, but it is probably the best to answer the (as yet) modest demand for justification theories in a field (AI) that is often considered as pre-theoretical even by its own practitioners (cf. Brachman and Smith 1980:106–7).

L: It seems to me, though, that when Winograd writes that "much of the work in AI is based on the methodological assumption that it is most profitable at this stage of the science to develop a body of alternative blueprints—to explore the possibilities before focusing on closely honed explanation" (1977:172), he risks being ostracized in his own community. Moreover, even such a prudent position is shaky, on the very 'no-observation-without-a-theory' grounds that we already discussed.

AI: OK, I grant you that the 'groping in the dark' has a theory behind it. The problem is, this is not yet acknowledged by the 'gropers' themselves. To be sure, some of them are but remotely interested in formulating such a theory. But others see no way of doing so without the accumulation of knowledge and experience in the area. This is what Winograd has in mind. Moreover, such admonitions may express one's reluctance to commit oneself to a theory 'before time.' Statements like, "This is too risky to undertake right now; it will be impossible to take into account X, find a theoretical measure of Y and provide a formal mechanism for Z—so let us postpone constructive work and think the whole thing over and over again," is one possible philosophy. It may be argued that had everybody always thought this way, not much would have been accomplished in the history of science. Another approach is to prod along and do 'the best you can' as regards explanations. Both approaches are appropriate at times. Now is the time to attempt the second approach in artificial intelligence. We might just as well concede that our work is pre-theoretical. Anyway, the problem of justification is one of the less transparent in any science. Let us simply agree not to disregard the concern for it in the future.

L: A good final remark on this topic will be the following quotation from Pylyshyn (1979:25–6), in which X is substituted for the name of a scientific discipline: "The delicate balance between rational systems and empirical observations which is the hallmark of mature science has been absent in much of X. . . . Among the consequences of this is that X is splintered with micromodels. . . The discipline is rather paradigm-driven, rather than being guided by major theoretical systems. Without such larger, formally structured systems the local puzzle-solving activities lack a convergent direction and may in fact degenerate into . . . a . . . task dominated by local maxima."

AI: You mean that X stands here for artificial intelligence, don't you?

L: No. It is not linguistics, either. It is psychology. But I doubt that our own fields can boast a different situation.

AI: It is with surprise that I discern an unexpected convergence course that our discussion takes. Don't let us forget a peculiar, at times dormant and at times turbulent history of relations between our subjects in the short lifetime of artificial intelligence. It is interesting that this discipline's relations with psychology and even with philosophy have been discussed rather abundantly (cf. Ringle 1979). The emergence of cognitive science, "the newest science of the artificial" (H. Simon), signifies the high degree of mutual interest. At the same time, there have been no comparable developments between AI and linguistics.

L: There was at least one memorable contact, or should I rather say, skirmish. I refer to the exchange between the linguists Dresher and Hornstein and artificial intelligence workers Winograd and Schank and Wilensky in *Cognition* in 1976–77. It all began with Dresher and Hornstein (1976). Schank and Wilensky (1977) and Winograd (1977) replied, and Dresher and Hornstein (1977a and b) were responses to the latter. Dresher and Hornstein criticize the work on natural language understanding within artificial intelligence, concentrating on the proposals of Minsky (the frame theory 1975), Schank (conceptual dependency theory 1975), Winograd (SHDRLU 1972) and the ATNs (they addressed Kaplan's and Wanner's work; we mentioned that of Woods and Bates above). They argue that all of the above proposals are essentially non-theoretical, limited in possible applications (that is, inextendable, not explaining anything), and that where they are 'coherent,' they do not contribute anything new to our understanding of human linguistic behavior. Thus, both Winograd and Schank were taken to task for providing no explanations of why they chose their approaches to parsing and representation, respectively. The stinging implication is that they overly relied on common sense at the expense of constructing a unifying theory. A unifying theory of Minsky's was claimed to be vacuous because it did not provide meaningful constraints, thus being reduced to the status of an alternative notation by allowing itself to express anything. Dresher and Hornstein discussed the details of the above proposals at some length. They argued, for example, that Winograd's decision to adopt the approach of the systemic grammar (Halliday, e.g., 1970) proved simplistic, that his semantic component was adequate only in a limited way, that conceptual dependency graphs were built uncritically and were largely arbitrary (if one did not consider the equally arbitrarily delineated set of possible inferences on an utterance to be complete and justified). In short, they discerned a number of low-level 'factual' deficiencies, and thus exposed the lack of 'linguistic culture' in artificial intelligence.

AI: This part of the criticism should have been rather welcomed by the community criticized. As a matter of fact, Winograd in his reply agrees with "many of the comments which deal with technical details" (1977:151–2). Your remark about the 'linguistic culture,' which I'd rather call 'experience,' may also be true. Of course, you might have forgiven us if you took into account the quite extensive knowledge from other fields that we had to master in order to build even these 'simple' systems. But the thrust of the matter is that, based on the technical comments, Dresher and Hornstein claim that "not only has work in AI not *yet* made any contribution to a scientific study of language, there is no reason to believe that the type of research that we have been discussing will *ever* lead to such theories, for it is aimed in a different direction altogether" (1976:377). This direction is, of course, technology. The implied meaning: stop any work other than building specific machines and build those without any claims as to their linguistic abilities or to their being models of human language use. I might add that the tone of the article was quite vitriolic, which, while reflecting the authors' 'unecumenical' state of mind and being distantly amusing, seemed to me quite excessive.

L: Leaving the modality aside for a minute, don't you agree that this criticism displayed the limitations in the approach of artificial intelligence to the science of language?

AI: I don't think that this point was appropriate in the given context. Dresher and Hornstein criticize the research in artificial intelligence as 'unscientific,' lacking explanatory power, and not based on general principles (this latter phrase crops up twelve times on the mere three pages of their response to Schank and Wilensky). But what about the linguistic theory itself? Is there a single proposal made in the framework of generative linguistics that has not yet been proven false or at least has not been contested with weighty evidence? Does this make linguistics unscientific? Let us rather see what strategy of rebuttal was chosen. Schank and Wilensky counterattack on the grounds that artificial intelligence is not interested in language in the same way as is linguistics: it is interested in processes, not in general principles and rules; there is no explanatory adequacy for a theory—only procedural adequacy; nobody in artificial intelligence is interested in grammaticality (they understand it as a purely syntactic notion); what does it take a person or a machine to understand the meaning of an utterance—this is what counts. In short, "their way is not our way."

L: We have already discussed the status of syntax. I was, however, surprised to find a line where Schank and Wilensky (1977:135) actually admit something: "In producing such [performance] theories, AI also tries to simplify the problems it studies. In fact, almost every AI model of language use is an ideal user." This is not, however, the impression one gets after studying Schank's works where one is made to understand that what one reads is the theory behind language use. No qualifiers. Also, at least outside the context of an argument, statements like "universal principles may constitute answers to transformationalists [but] they merely pose questions for AI researchers, who would find it necessary to account for the rules procedurally" (op. cit.:137) seem too empiricist. Moreover, Schank and Wilensky are not convincing in denying Dresher and Hornstein's claim that computer programs for natural natural language processing, in their present-day state, are not theoretically valuable since they cannot distinguish between competing theories.

AI: The key phrases in Schank and Wilensky's paper are 'processes' and 'programs as tests for theories.' Though they refer to the paradigmatic difference between linguistics and AI, it is Winograd who makes this the key phrase for this reply. He makes ample reference to Kuhn's *The Structure of Scientific Revolutions* (1962) in describing how Dresher and Hornstein's arguments are misled or outright invalid. The friction between linguistics (Winograd calls it the Chomskian paradigm) and artificial intelligence (the computational paradigm) is described as a most general phenomenon in the history of science understood as a succession of revolutions and periods of 'normal science.' In the case in point, the Chomskian paradigm represents the established 'normal science' and AI, the revolutionary new paradigm. Accusations of being unscientific are parried by quoting Kuhn: "The reception of a new paradigm often necessitates a redefinition of the corresponding science" (Winograd 1977:153). A rather detailed analysis of the Chomskian paradigm follows, in which it is shown rather convincingly that, to put it simply, its adherents use "a neat piece of intellectual legerdemain which gives the illusion that the detailed methodology of Chomskian linguistics must follow logically from any attempt to understand universal principles of language" (op. cit.:155). According to Winograd, the Chomskians start with proclaiming that all studies of language must be based on the notion of 'universal grammar' defined as "the system of principles, conditions and rules that are elements or properties of all human languages" (cf. Chomsky 1975:29), and then substitute the more familiar notion of grammar instead. This is followed by divorcing grammar from the study of linguistic processes, postulating that the 'innate linguistic faculty' of the language user creates this grammar and, finally, constricting the notion of grammar still further, identifying it with a formal syntactic system and making an inept attempt to justify this in terms of language learning.

After presenting an extensive and thoroughly entertaining biological metaphor of the Chomskian paradigm, Winograd goes on to present his understanding of the computational paradigm. He presents four major points central to this approach, in which the great influence of psychological and computational considerations are quite transparent: "(1) The essential properties of language reflect the cognitive structure of the human language user, including properties of memory structure, processing strategies and limitations. (2) The primary focus of study is on the processes which underlie the production and understanding of utterance in the linguistic and pragmatic context. The structure of the observable linguistic forms is important, but serves primarily as a clue to the structure of processes. (3) Context is of primary importance, and is best formulated in terms of cognitive structures of the speaker and hearer. . . . (4) It is possible to study scientifically the processes involved in cognition, and in particular in language use. Some parts of these processes are specialized for language, while other parts may be common to other cognitive structures" (Winograd 1977:169). Winograd's emphasis is on principle (2).

Another important strategic point discussed by Winograd is the one we referred to already: programs as theories. Here he makes several comments that stand in sharp contrast to the views of Schank and Wilensky: "A program which completely duplicates the processes of human language use would still not be a theory. But any program which is built can be viewed as a *hypothesized partial blueprint* and can be a step towards understanding . . ." (op. cit.:172–3). And later: "The state of artificial intelligence . . . is in some ways . . . akin to that of medieval alchemy. We are at the stage of pouring together different substances and seeing what happens, not yet having developed satisfactory theories. The analogy was proposed by Dreyfus (1965; see also Dreyfus 1972 for a more extensive criticism) as a condemnation of artificial intelligence, but its aptness need not imply his negative evaluation. Some work can be criticized on the grounds of being enslaved to (and making too many claims about) the goal of creating gold (intelligence) from base materials (computers). But nevertheless, it was the practical experience and curiosity of the alchemists which provided the wealth of data from which a scientific theory of chemistry could be developed" (op. cit.:174).

L: Well, this is indeed a very prudent description. I would say that this really makes many of the methodological accusations of Dresher and Hornstein invalid. Also, unlike Schank, Winograd is very careful to avoid declaring that the current achievements in the field are theories. By the way, what will be the X in the proportion: alchemy : chemistry = AI : X?

AI: It may well be called artificial intelligence! Or cognitive science. The name does not matter. They will come up with more than one anyway. It will be a science studying human intelligence through modelling the latter. The computer will, most probably, be the principal tool of this modelling for years to come.

L: Maybe we should ask Winograd. But I haven't got a chance to comment on the principle of the computational paradigm as presented by him. It really seems that Winograd speaks not about a linguistic science paradigm as seen by Chomskians like Dresher and Hornstein, but about a different science, which is interested in language only insofar as it sheds light on cognition. It is then small wonder that Dresher and Hornstein would find the approach 'non-linguistic' (they actually used the accusing epithet 'unscientific'). But not every linguist is an orthodox Chomskian, many do think that pragmatics is important. Still, we are concerned primarily with language. It indeed seems that the thrust towards broadening the limits of linguistics to include cognitive aspects is too strong. It also baffles me, in this connection, that Winograd still chooses to distinguish the 'linguistic' from the 'pragmatic' context in the small manifesto above. I'd assume that the computational paradigm of linguistics subsumes pragmatics. . . .

AI: It still remains to be shown that any viable linguistic theory can be put forward which does not take into account cognitive processes, and at a deep level, too.

L: It is interesting that in his *Language as a Cognitive Process* (1983) Winograd, after reiterating the paradigm differences, speaks about the similarities of the 'generative' and 'computational' paradigm, even uniting them tentatively in a 'cognitive' paradigm (cf. 20–21). This may be due both to the absence of overt polemical attitude that was so obvious in Winograd (1977) and to a reluctance to pursue the paradigm metaphor too far. If it serves to justify the lack of understanding on the part of the linguists, let me suggest that it is entirely unnecessary for the two people to belong to different scientific paradigms in order for them to be unable to engage in rational argument. The current scene in both linguistics and artificial intelligence can supply multiple examples. I must say that in the polemics we have discussed just now I tend to feel more at home on the artificial intelligence side. I am not alone among the linguists to think this way. I refer to George Lakoff and to his 'afterword' to the polemics in question. Quite predictably, Lakoff (1978:267) starts by criticizing both sides in the dispute for paying little attention to "the opinions of linguists, both generative and nongenerative, outside the interpretivist school."

AI: But he immediately proceeds to point out a most peculiar point: it appears that the background of the whole enterprise was not purely scientific, after all. "One thing that the exchange never mentioned but that seemed to be lurking in the background was money—in the form of research funding. With government funding sources running low and with a decision by the Sloan Foundation to pour millions of dollars into Cognitive Science, the competition for research funding has been keen. A number of people I have spoken to, both in AI and linguistics communities, viewed the timing and nature of the Dresher–Hornstein attack as being related to funding issues" (ibid.). What is your opinion on this? Do you feel deprived by the relatively high level of funding the research in my field?

L: Well, I think it would be fair to say that yes, I am. It hurts when the bright young people who would have become graduate students in linguistics fifteen years ago choose artificial intelligence instead. Also, some extra funding has never done any harm and is really needed now. But this is a different issue. Let's discuss it next time.

4. Act Three. Convergence

L: Lakoff's paper contains a perspective of the linguistic scene and linguistic problems vis-à-vis artificial intelligence. Since now we want to consider the areas of possible cooperation, Lakoff (1978) is as good a starting point as any.

AI: Lakoff actually attacks the narrowly Chomskian linguistics by challenging its very goals, and with all the fervor of a renegade. He cites four false assumptions that led to the definition of these 'gratuitous or implausible' goals. He maintains that a) one cannot speak about a 'language faculty' that is independent from "sensori-motor and cognitive development, perception, memory, attention, social interaction, personality and other aspects of experience"; b) language acquisition does not consist of "constructing grammars on the basis of purely linguistic data"; c) linguistic structure is dependent on linguistic function; d) it is preposterous to speak about phrase structure rules and transformations as the right (or only) devices in terms of which linguistic laws can be formulated (op. cit.:274).

L: Also, he shows that the mode of argumentation in the *Cognition* polemics was off mark, since it was assumed by Dresher and Hornstein (and quietly accepted by their opponents) that they possess a claim to the study of language universals and language acquisition. Lakoff correctly points out that most of the recent (and not so recent, too) research in both fields has been done outside the linguistic school that these authors represent.

AI: Both parts of the argument are taken to task for being too extreme in their views and hence too narrow in the choice of the problems discussed. "Nothing was said in the exchange . . . [about] linguistic phenomena which indicate that either processing models or AI-like representations are needed to account for empirical linguistic facts" (op. cit.:269).

L: Lakoff mentions several such facts: indirect speech acts, amalgams, interjections, correction and editing devices. More importantly, he also speaks about language formulae and, still more importantly, about the approaches to semantics. Every notion mentioned has been studied in linguistics, with varying amounts of effort. It will not be appropriate here to discuss them at length, but some comments may well be in order: after all, these are the first candidate areas of study where our disciplines can proceed jointly.

Speech acts in general and indirect speech acts in particular, have been studied quite extensively in linguistics and philosophy of language. Searle (1969) and Cole and Morgan (1975) are most frequently mentioned as useful references.

AI: Lakoff mentions this as a linguistic topic. But Wilks (1981:399) believes that linguistics failed with speech acts and that artificial intelligence can help: "[An] area of research, now booming in AI, [is] the analysis of conversations in terms of plan structures, beliefs and perspectives, loosely what has been known in philosophy and linguistics as *speech acts*. 'Speech acts are dead,'' said an eminent linguist to me the other day, which I interpret by saying that philosophy and linguistics encountered problems with the notion that their theoretical machineries did not allow them to solve.'' Incidentally, in the same paper Wilks warns researchers of natural language against the dangers of technology taking the place of science: "One danger to theoretically interesting natural language analysis in AI is the trend to expert systems: on that view, language about car repair or electrical circuits, say, becomes no more than a side effect . . . satisfying as it may be to commercial interests and Government sponsors'' (ibid.). This opinion alone should refute Dresher and Hornstein's position: it shows that artificial intelligence workers are at least as aware of the dangers of immediate technological thinking as are theoretical linguists.

L: Amalgams are sentences like *This is a present from you know who on we all know which occasion.* Parsers presently in use will have a difficult time consuming amalgams. And obviously no patchwork relaxation techniques will help. A sound linguistic proposal for treating amalgams is on the agenda. Treating interjections has long been neglected, but nobody can, uh, deny the contribution they make to the overall meaning of an utterance. Correction devices of various kinds, that is, from bona fide corrections as in *the people of Bolivia, I mean, Brazil* to such, well, quasi-corrections as in *the racial, or rather, racist, policies,* where the structure is used as a rhetorical device. Now, the topic of language formulae seems even more productive for a joint linguistic-AI study.

AI: The fact that both have been pointedly non-productive notwithstanding.

L: Exactly. It has been a point of interest for linguists for some time now that productive constructions in our speech are used at a much smaller scale than one would imagine. Any language is full of 'canned' phrases that are used in quite well defined situations. Tell me, wouldn't you immediately recognize the structure of a situation in which the notorious *Have a nice day!* is pronounced? Does this string of sounds really warrant the regular semantico-syntactic processing?

AI: Lakoff comments on the similarities between formulae and scripts (cf. Schank and Abelson 1977). "Both have the same form as productive structures—sentences on the one hand, and plans, on the other. Both are frozen forms of otherwise productive structures. . . . Both . . . seem to develop historically out of their productive counterparts'' (Lakoff 1978:272). Another peculiarity pinpointed by Lakoff is that both scripts and formulae are devices for saving mental energy.

L: There is, however, a flaw in Lakoff's comparison which relates to the discrepancies in perception of the two notions. Intuitively, a script is not an equivalent of a phrase. There is a clear difference of scale. Rather, a script is an equivalent for a text. Of course, one can speak of the almost non-scriptal 'instrumental' scripts (cf. Schank and Abelson 1977:65–6) as being parallel to sentences. But it seems promising to speak not about separate canned phrases but rather about the whole canned conversations. The productivity of such conversations will tend to be greatly restricted, to the point of filling a small number of slots. In the environment quite inevitable for such a discussion the following conversation can take place:

A: Good evening, sir. How many people in your party?
B: Just the two of us.
A: Please follow me.
. . .
C: Are you ready to order?
B: Yes. I will have X with Y and Z. Does it come with W?
C: Uh-huh.
B: OK. And for the lady here, P, medium rare, and no Q, please.
     (and so on)

I think that only X, Y, Z, W, P, and Q are the relatively productive slots to be filled. All the rest is not very informative conversation (it might be if something interesting, like a distraction or an obstacle, happens), it does not need a lot of mental energy for anybody familiar with the rules and goals of this kind of institutions; and the roles in the above conversation are too easily discernible to be even mentioned. In short, we have a canned text, a linguistic counterpart of a script of whose instance it is a perceivable manifestation.

AI: But what about paralinguistic behavior? The above text can be just as meaningful had it been:

A: (looks up inquisitively)
B: Two.
A: (motions A. and his companion forward with his hand)
     . . .
C: (approaches, and stands with his pencil poised on a notebook page)
B: (points in the menu) This here, and this. (gestures towards the companion)
     (and so on)

L: Let us study the paradigmatic context together, my friend. As they say in scientific jargon, let this be the topic of a separate study. On the notion of semantics, Lakoff suggests that "the idea that the processing of the sentence itself might have something to do with its meaning and its truth conditions is not considered" in linguistics. "The meaning of the sentence," claims Lakoff, "depends in an important way on how it is processed" (Lakoff, 1978:273). He quotes Fillmore's example, "If you want to save your life, press the little red button in front of you right . . . *now!*" and claims, correctly, that the time for executing the command depends on the processing of the sentence in real time, which is impossible when it is suggested that the sentence must be processed as a whole.

AI: The question of the use of semantics in knowledge representation within the artificial intelligence paradigm has been discussed along different lines. First of all, there is no unity as regards the meaning of the term 'semantics' itself. A recent survey of projects in knowledge representation (Brachman and Smith 1980) showed that one-third of all the respondents adhered to logical (denotational) semantics; one-fifth, to procedural semantics; and less than ten percent thought about using the notion as it is used by the linguists. Also, a number of other, more or less outlandish, kinds of semantics were quoted: relational, operational, referential, intentional, functional, conceptual, and analogical. I still have to learn exactly what most of these theories claim. An interesting statistic was the relative prominence of procedural semantics. You will say, of course, that 'procedural' is a catchword for anything computational, and as such, for any ex-postulations against the linguists.

Very roughly, and leaving all the development of the notion out, procedural semantics has its roots in the semantics of programming languages. The latter is concerned with the proofs that computer programs actually do exactly what they are supposed to. Programs are, as a rule, written in some high-level programming language, such as LISP or PASCAL, then translated (compiled) into a machine language of primitive instructions; the machine executes the code, and the results appear to be judged semantically correct or otherwise. The application of the 'compile–run–verify' strategy to natural language analysis was controversial enough; such loaded comparisons do not generally go unnoticed in scientific research. The journal *Cognition*—which seems to welcome the idea of becoming the arena for intellectual shootouts—featured a polemic between Johnson-Laird, a proponent of procedural semantics, and Fodor (Johnson-Laird 1977, 1978; Fodor 1978, 1979).

L: You could also mention Woods (1981:4), where procedural semantics is taken to be not a theory of meaning, but rather "a paradigm or a framework for developing and expressing theories of meaning." Just like the augmented transition networks are frameworks for expressing theories of syntax?

AI: This idea has more links to the old 'declarativist vs. proceduralist' controversy in knowledge representation, which has long been a prominent feature of the artificial intelligence scene. This is as much an organizational issue as a theoretical one. Anyway, Fodor dismisses procedural semantics on the grounds that, first, computer models do not provide any semantic theory in the sense of a theory of the relation between language and world; and, second, that procedural semantics is rooted in verificationism which "practically nobody except procedural semanticists takes seriously any more" (1978:229).

L: Note, however, that the term 'procedural' does have something to do with the context of the linguistics-AI debate. It is not by chance that Winograd, a prominent proceduralist in representation, also chides linguists for disregarding the importance of processes.

AI: Much more important is the statistic that only a small fraction of the artificial intelligence community considers linguistic semantics the right tool for their research.

L: My personal belief is that when the extensive economy I referred to is no longer possible—in the case at hand, when the procedural semanticists encounter first difficulties that cannot be solved with cleverer computational devices; or, if you wish, when the compiler metaphor wears itself sufficiently thin—the logical trend would be to look again at the linguists' work for possible insights. This is a natural 'division of labor.' Of course, if we take Woods' position, then such a trend is possible right now.

AI: So, you predict a convergence trend.

L: Yes, and my reasons are not only theoretical. It's not a secret that the linguistic community in this country and elsewhere no longer possesses the same clout it did some ten, fifteen years ago. This is reflected not only in the relative scarcity of research funding, but also in the number of students in the departments of linguistics. Artificial intelligence, on the other hand, has a good line of credit, so to say. Linguists should naturally desire to collaborate with artificial intelligence workers in mutually interesting projects. I believe that AI, in the sense of the term that we clarified here, did, does, and will benefit from contacts with linguistics, in applications such as information retrieval, computer-aided instruction, machine translation, etc. because linguistics is the only source for a body of knowledge about language to draw from and, peculiarly, to reject as a possibility in favor of newborn ideas.

AI: I think that departments of linguistics must become flexible enough in the philosophical sense to offer courses covering the 'computational' paradigm, just as they sometimes offer them in historical and structural linguistics, in addition to the generative paradigm topics. It is also important for the linguists to understand that the computer may well become the major tool for the justification of linguistic theories. Please understand that it is unnecessary (though it will not hurt) to become a first-class computer programmer to be able to use the computer not only for the storage of dictionaries and the calculation of frequencies.

L: And more recently, for word processing. Permit me one final comment on our principal controversy. Chaffin (1979) has conducted a number of experiments to shed light on whether people process knowledge of language differently from knowledge about the world (he checked the response times in making 'necessary' and 'invited' inferences—cf., e.g., Geis and Zwicky 1971). A necessary inference, made manifest in the acceptability of (lb) and unacceptability of

(1c) below depends on the meaning of the verb *make* and commits the speaker to
its conclusion

(1) (a) The trainer made the hungry lion wait before it ate its prey.
     (b) The lion waited before eating.
     (c) *But the lion did not wait.

The invited inference in (2) below, made manifest by the acceptability of both
(2b) and (2c), depends on factual knowledge about how lions behave and invites
(predicts) the conclusion that the lion did not wait. But the speaker is not
committed to this conclusion.

(2) (a) The trainer did not make the hungry lion wait before it ate its prey.
     (b) The lion did not wait before eating.
     (c) But the lion did wait.

The constraint that makes (1c) unacceptable is purely linguistic. The premise for
the experiments was that if the response time for 'necessary' inferences is shorter
than that for 'invited' ones, then language is distinct from the world.

   AI: Chaffin describes the two opinions as the 'formalist' and the 'naturalist'
positions but we can see that the formalists are what we called 'Chomskians':
they claim that linguistic and world knowledge are distinct, that language can be
studied independently of its use, etc. The naturalist position is that linguistic
abilities share the same underlying mechanisms as other cognitive abilities. Note
that Winograd's (1983) book is entitled *Language as a Cognitive Process,* and
that Chaffin also mentions Schank, Abelson, Norman, and Rumelhart (cf. Norman and Rumelhart 1975) as 'naturalists,' and you can see that we have the same
dispute, even thought the word *processing* has never been uttered.

   L: Chaffin mentions, though, that the formalist school dismisses the communicative function of language from the latter's scientific study. Also, he
perceives the debate as transcending the boundaries of linguistics, reaching into
philosophy (the formalist Carnap vs. the naturalists Austin and Grice) and psychology (where, according to Chaffin, the general trend was from the naturalism
of pre-Chomskian days to formalism roughly in 1957–66 (cf., e.g., Miller
1962), and then, gradually, back to naturalism). But the bottom line is that the
results of the experiments actually supported the formalist hypothesis (although,
in Chaffin's words, "equivocally"). In two of the four experiments Chaffin
conducted, necessary inferences were processed faster than invited inferences
and, moreover, attenuated the processing of those of the latter that were unnecessary for the task. In the other two experiments the response times were equal.
"This indicates that the distinction between world knowledge and linguistic
knowledge is more than just a heuristic convenience for linguists and philoso-
phers" (Chaffin 1979:327).

Wait, before you say that this conclusion brings us back to square one in our discussion. Let me say that, without questioning the set-up of the experiments themselves, we can try to provide another interpretation of their results. One might think of changing the status of the language processing as juxtaposed to world information processing from the two quite polar opinions to one that might be mutually acceptable. Norman (1980) draws a diagram of a cognitive system which (the diagram) becomes the basis for describing the issues that this field should tackle. Language is not specifically addressed there; and the impression is that it is considered important only as a tool in perception or, at the most, the interface between physical signals and memory structures (this is, of course, a strong simplification of the matter). Norman did not find a place for a 'language processes' module alongside those of 'thought processes,' 'emotions,' 'desires, intentions and motivations,' 'attention allocation,' etc., in the diagram of a cognitive system structure he uses in his paper.

Please don't tell me that Norman's 'issues' are not components: in the diagram they are components all right, even though these are treated as lines of research in the text. So what we have is a language module that is not at all autonomous, being a part of a complex cognitive system—indeed, we have criticized the autonomous 'innate language faculty' in sufficient detail; and at the same time, this module is distinguishable enough to be responsible, for instance, for the processing of 'necessary inferences' as well as many other phenomena that depend on the 'self-understanding' of language. To name just a few, what about the linguistic 'near misses,' such as *I look on you* in the speech of a non-native speaker of English; or why *Fantastic Faye* and *Terrific Terry* are not the same as *Terrific Faye*.

In short, I think that the consequences of the methodological tour de force I suggest, namely, to declare a 'linguistic processes' module alongside the 'thought processes' one, have to be explored.

AI: It may actually bring our sciences closer together by defining the area of efforts a linguist may undertake within the linguistic-philosophical-psychological-computational paradigm of cognitive science.

5. Epilogue

The discussion featured the following main points:

(1) Although linguists and the artificial intelligence community have a different approach to the study of language, this dissonance can be diminished, if not alleviated, if the emphasis is on the centripetal rather than on centrifugal forces within both communities. Both communities will profit from this. In fact, definitions can be found for both fields that will be acceptable for many people in both groups. The tendency for dispute tended to blur this understanding.

(2) At the theoretical level, the computational or procedural approach to the study of language should be recognized as a valid direction of studies, whether it

is considered a separate paradigm or just another variant of the established 'cognitive' one. In any case, this approach is to produce a general theory of language comprehension that will become the basis of future developments and, yes, a target of widespread criticism, a theory whose role will be not unlike that of Chomsky's a quarter of a century ago.

(3) At the methodological level, special attention must be paid, in both artificial intelligence and linguistics, to the problem of justification. In particular, it is crucial to study the question of when and which computer models can be considered valid means for justifying theories of language (and cognition, on a more general basis).

If we understand linguistics as our linguist does and artificial intelligence as our AI researcher does, then the following paraphrase of Pylyshyn's words about artificial intelligence and cognitive psychology will be quite appropriate: ''The field of AI is co-extensive with the field of linguistics. What I mean by this is that as intellectual disciplines they are concerned with the same problems and will stand or fall together because the same criteria of success must ultimately adjudicate them both'' (Pylyshyn 1979:25).

REFERENCES

Ades, A. 1981. ''Time for a purge.'' *Cognition* 10, pp. 7–15.

Bates, M. 1978. ''The theory and practice of augmented transition network grammars.'' In: L. Bolc (ed.), *Natural Language Communication with Computer*. Berlin–Heidelberg–New York: Springer-Verlag, pp. 191–249.

Brachman, R., and B. Smith (eds.) 1980. *Special Issue on Knowledge Representation. SIGART Newsletter* 70.

Brown, J. S., and R. R. Burton 1975. ''Multiple representations of knowledge for tutorial reasoning.'' In: D. G. Bobrow and A. Collins (eds.), *Representation and Understanding*. New York: Academic Press, pp. 311–350.

Bruce, B. 1975. ''Case system for natural language.'' *Artificial Intelligence* 6, pp. 327–60.

Bundy, A. (ed.) 1978. *Artificial Intelligence: An Introductory Course*. Amsterdam–New York: North Holland.

Chaffin, R. 1979. ''Knowledge of language and knowledge about the world: a reaction time study of invited and necessary inferences.'' *Cognitive Science* 3, pp. 311–28.

Charniak, E. 1976. ''Inference and knowledge I.'' In: Charniak and Wilks, pp. 1–22.

Charniak, E., and Y. Wilks (eds.) 1976. *Computational Semantics*. Amsterdam: North Holland.

Chomsky, N. 1957. *Syntactic Structures*. The Hague: Mouton.

Chomsky, N. 1965. *Aspects of the Theory of Syntax*. Cambridge, MA: MIT Press.

Chomsky, N. 1975. *Reflections on Language*. New York: Pantheon.

Cole, P., and J. L. Morgan (eds.) 1975. *Syntax and Semantics*, Vol. 3. *Speech Acts*. New York and London: Academic Press.

Dresher, B. E., and N. Hornstein 1976. ''On some supposed contributions of artificial intelligence to the scientific study of language.'' *Cognition* 4, pp. 321–98.

Dresher, B. E., and N. Hornstein 1977a. ''Reply to Schank and Wilensky.'' *Cognition* 5, pp. 147–9.

Dresher, B. E., and N. Hornstein 1977b. ''Reply to Winograd.'' *Cognition* 5, pp. 379–92.

Dreyfus, H. 1965. *Alchemy and Artificial Intelligence*. Santa Monica, CA: Rand Corporation.

Dreyfus, H. 1972. *What Computers Can't Do*. New York: Harper and Row.

Fillmore, C. J. 1968. "The case for case." In: E. Bach and R. Harms (eds.), *Universals in Linguistic Theory*. New York: Holt, Rinehart and Winston, pp. 1–88.

Fillmore, C. J. 1971. "Types of Lexical information." In: D. D. Steinberg and L. A. Jacobovits (eds.), *Semantics*. Cambridge: Cambridge University Press, pp. 370–92.

Firdman, E. 1982. "Towards a theory of cognizing systems." *Computer Science Lab* 7. Palo Alto, CA: Hewlett-Packard Corporation.

Fodor, J. A. 1978. "Tom Swift and his procedural grandmother." *Cognition* 6, pp. 229–47.

Fodor, J. A. 1979. "In reply to Philip Johnson-Laird." *Cognition* 7, pp. 93–5.

Geis, M., and A. Zwicky 1971. "On invited inferences." *Linguistic Inquiry* 2, pp. 561–6.

Halliday, M. A. K. 1970. "Functional diversity in language as seen from a consideration of modality and mood in English." *Foundations of Language* 6, pp. 322–61.

Hayes, D. 1964. "Dependency theory: a formalism and some observations." *Language* 40, pp. 511–24.

Hayes, J. 1980. "The naive physics manifesto." In: D. Michie (ed.), *Expert Systems in the Microelectronic Age*. Edinburgh: Edinburgh University Press, pp. 240–70.

Johnson-Laird, P. 1977. "Procedural semantics." *Cognition* 5, pp. 189–214.

Johnson-Laird, P. 1978. "What's wrong with Grandma's guide to procedural semantics: A reply to Jerry Fodor." *Cognition* 6, pp. 249–61.

Kaplan, R., and J. Bresnan 1982. "Lexical functional grammar." In: J. Bresnan (ed.), *The Mental Representation of Grammatical Relations*. Cambridge, MA: MIT Press, pp. 173–281.

Kuno, S., and A. Oettinger 1963. "Multiple path syntactic analyzer." In: *Information Processing 1962*. Amsterdam: North Holland 43–86.

Kwasny, S. 1980. "Treatment of ungrammatical and extra-grammatical phenomena in natural language understanding systems." Bloomington, IN: Indiana University Linguistics Club.

Lakoff, G. 1978. "Some remarks on AI and linguistics." *Cognitive Science* 2, pp. 267–75.

Longuet-Higgins, H. C. 1981. "Artificial intelligence—a new theoretical psychology?" *Cognition* 10, pp. 197–200.

Lyons, J. 1981. *Language and Linguistics*. Cambridge: Cambridge University Press.

Marr, D. 1977. "Artificial intelligence—a personal view." *Artificial Intelligence* 9, pp. 37–48.

Miller, G. A. 1962. "Some psychological studies of grammar." *American Psychologist* 17, pp. 748–62.

Newell, A. 1973. "Artificial intelligence and the concept of mind." In: R. Schank and K. Colby (eds.), *Computer Models of Thought and Language*. San Francisco: Freeman, pp. 1–60.

Nilsson, N. 1981. *Principles of Artificial Intelligence*. Palo Alto, CA: Tioga.

Norman, D. A. 1980. "Twelve issues for cognitive science." *Cognitive Science* 4, pp. 1–32.

Norman, D. A., and D. E. Rumelhart 1975. *Explorations in Cognition*. San Francisco: Freeman.

Petrick, S. 1965. "A recognition procedure for transformational grammars." Unpublished dissertation, MIT.

Pylyshyn, Z. 1979. "Complexity and the study of human and artificial intelligence." In Ringle (ed.), pp. 23–56.

Raphael, B. 1976. *The Thinking Computer*. San Francisco: Freeman.

Raskin, V. (V.) 1971. *K teorii jazykovyx podsistem* (Towards a theory of linguistic subsystems). Moscow: Moscow University Press.

Raskin, V. 1978. "Problems of justification in semantic theory." In: W. U. Dressler and W. Meid (eds.), *Proceedings of the Twelfth International Congress of Linguists*. Innsbruck: Innsbrucker Beiträge zur Sprachwissenschaft, pp. 223–6.

Raskin, V. 1979. "Theory and practice of justification in linguistics." In: L. Clyne et al. (eds.), *Papers from the Parasession on the Elements*, Chicago: Chicago Linguistics Society, pp. 152–62.

Ringle, M. 1979. "Philosophy and artificial intelligence." In Ringle (ed.), pp. 1–22.

Ringle, M. (ed.) 1979. *Philosophical Perspectives in Artificial Intelligence*. Atlantic Highlands, NJ: Humanities Press.

Samlowski, W. 1976. "Case grammar." In: Charniak and Wilks, pp. 55–72.

Schank, R. 1973. "Identification of conceptualizations underlying natural language." In: R. Schank and K. Colby (eds.), *Computer Models of Thought and Language*. San Francisco: Freeman, 187–248.

Schank, R. 1975. *Conceptual Information Processing*. Amsterdam: North Holland.

Schank, R. 1979. "Natural Language, philosophy, and artificial intelligence." In Ringle (ed.)., pp. 100–50.

Schank, R. 1980. "Language and memory." *Congitive Science* 4, pp. 243–84.

Schank, R. 1982. "Looking at learning." In: *Proceedings of ECAI*. Orsay, France, pp. 11–18.

Schank, R., and R. Abelson 1977. *Scripts, Plans, Goals, and Understanding*. Hillsdale, NJ: Lawrence Erlbaum Associates.

Schank, R., and L. Birnbaum 1980. "Memory, meaning and syntax." Research Report 189. Department of Computer Science, Yale University.

Schank, R., N. Goldman, C. Rieger, and C. Riesbeck 1973. "MARGIE: Memory, analysis, response generation, and inference in English." In: *Proceedings of IJCAI-3*, pp. 155–161.

Schank, R., and C. Riesbeck 1981. *Inside Computer Understanding*. Hillsdale, NJ: Lawrence Erlbaum Associates.

Schank, R., and R. Wilensky 1977. "Response to Dresher and Hornstein." *Cognition* 5, pp. 133–45.

Searle, J. R. 1969. *Speech Acts*. Cambridge: Cambridge University Press.

Simmons, R. F. 1973. "Semantic networks: their computation and use for understanding English sentences." In: R. Schank and K. Colby (eds.), *Computer Models of Thought and Language*. San Francisco: Freeman, pp. 63–113.

Simon, T. W. 1979. "Philosophical objections to programs as theories." In: Ringle (ed.), pp. 225–242.

Weischedel, R., and J. Black 1980. "Responding intelligently to unparsable inputs." *American Journal of Computational Linguistics* 6, pp. 97–109.

Wilks, Y. 1981. "A position note on natural language understanding and artificial intelligence." *Cognition* 10, pp. 337–40.

Winograd, T. 1972. *Understanding Natural Language*. New York and London: Academic Press.

Winograd, T. 1975. "Frame representations and the declarative/procedural controversy." In: D. G. Bobrow and A. Collins (eds.), *Representation and Understanding*. New York: Academic Press, pp. 185–210.

Winograd, T. 1977. "On some contested suppositions of generative linguistics about the scientific study of language." *Cognition* 5, pp. 151–79.

Winograd, T. 1983. *Language as a Cognitive Process*. Reading, MA: Addison-Wesley.

Winston, H. 1977. *Artificial Intelligence*. Reading, MA: Addison-Wesley.

Woods, W. A. 1970. "Transition network grammars for natural language analysis." *Communications of ACM* 13, pp. 591–606.

Woods, W. A. 1981. *Procedural Semantics as a Theory of Meaning*. Research Report No. 4627. Cambridge, MA: Bolt, Beranek, and Newman.

Zwicky, A., J. Friedman, B. Hall, and D. Walker 1963. "The MITRE syntactic analysis procedure for transformational grammars." In: *IFIPS Proceedings of the Fall Joint Computer Conference*. Washington, DC: Spartan Books, pp. 317–26.

CHAPTER SEVEN

Language Deprivation and Recovery in Lana Chimpanzee

Herbert F. W. Stahlke

1. Introduction

The Lana Project (Rumbaugh 1977) began computer-mediated language training with a chimpanzee (Pan) in January 1973. A skilled, creative group of researchers and technicians from Yerkes Regional Primate Research Center, Georgia State University, and the University of Georgia had prepared a computer-mediated environment in which Lana, a young female chimpanzee, was to become wholly dependent on her interaction with a computer for all of her needs, twenty-four hours a day, seven days a week.

Lana was first trained in a limited set of 'stock' sentences of the sort she would use to request food or services from the computer. The well-formedness of these sentences was evaluated by a software parser (von Glasersfeld 1977; Pisani 1977), and the computer would reinforce only exactly correct strings. Any deviation from the pattern of a stock sentence would not be reinforced and thus would extinguish. The computer was a much more accurate observer than any human interlocutor would prove to be, a fact that facilitated many of the more interesting developments in Lana's communicative behavior. As she began to interact with humans on the project, Lana's communication showed increasing deviation from stock sentence patterns in ways that could only be interpreted as contextually motivated (Rumbaugh and Gill 1977; Gill 1977). Her novel sentences appeared to be extensions of stock sentences, but the patterns were not consistently reinforced, as an extended example will show later.

On November 10, 1975, the first major period of language experimentation with Lana ended. The facility in which she had lived and been trained since 1973 was dismantled, and a new and larger facility was built. Lana moved into the new facility and resumed training on May 13, 1976, after a hiatus of six months. The most obvious innovations in the new facility were an expanded keyboard, allowing a larger vocabulary, and the addition of three display projectors, allowing an increase in sentence length of up to ten lexigrams.

During the hiatus, Lana's training shifted from language to non-linguistic tasks, leading researchers to ponder the effects of a six-month interruption of language use. This study reports the principal effects on Lana's language behavior of the half-year hiatus and investigates Lana's development during the thirty-day period following her return to the language training program. Given the relatively limited amount of linguistic work that has been reported on ape language use, and given the uniqueness of the Lana Project, this hiatus has provided an opportunity to ask a number of hitherto unapproachable questions. With the exception of Premack's work with Sarah (Premack 1972), all other ape language training has depended heavily on manual languages, rendering it impossible to remove a subject completely from a linguistic environment or to study the effects of a period of purely non-linguistic behavior on the subject's recall, use, and recovery of language.

This study investigates the effect of the hiatus on the ratio of well-formed to ill-formed strings in Lana's language production, the differential effect of the hiatus on stock sentences and on conversational sentences. Also, this study examines the occurrence of certain novel strings and explores in detail Lana's initial use of the longer sentences permitted by the new facility. In certain cases, data are considered from the beginning of 1977, a period approximately six months after Lana's reintroduction to language training.

2. On Analyzing Chimpanzee Language Data

A number of papers (Petitto and Seidenberg 1979; Savage-Rumbaugh, Rumbaugh, and Boysen 1980; Seidenberg and Petitto 1979; and Terrace, Petitto, Saunders, and Bever 1979) have discussed the apparently language-like character of the data from the Lana Project and from similar projects. Savage-Rumbaugh, Rumbaugh, and Boysen in particular criticize those who ". . . have presumed too readily that when an ape uses a symbol, it has some referential reason for doing so" (1980:51). Frequently, as they point out further (op. cit.:58), "the experimenters behaved as though they attributed intent to behaviors where it did not necessarily exist originally." Perhaps an extreme example of this would be the attempt to interpret a sentence Lana produced in the second year of the study: *Please give piece of behind.*

Any attempt to analyze such data with the methods of modern linguistics faces even more difficult problems. The linguist frequently includes as data the judgments of significant numbers of native speakers of a language that a particular string is grammatical and represents a certain meaning or range of meanings. In analyzing language-like data from an ape, no such judgments are obtainable. The discussion of paraphrase in Stahlke (1980) presents a conversation between Lana and Tim during which Lana requests Coke with a variety of strings, including *Question you give Coke in cup, Question give Coke, Question you give Coke to Lana, Question you give Coke to Lana in cup, Question you you give, Question you put Coke in cup, Question you give Coke in cup to Lana, Question you give Coke in machine,* and *Question you give Coke in cup to Lana in machine.* While this sequence of requests demonstrates considerable facility at string manipulation, there is little reason to believe that Lana actually intended different messages with each rearrangement of the string. Her capacity for syntactic behavior shows remarkably high development in that her rearrangements are not random but rather are limited to a small set of permutations of substrings, but the permutations appear not to be under either contexual or semantic control. In human language, a change in syntax normally signals a change in meaning, and syntactic structure is tightly controlled by semantics and by discourse context (Givón 1978). Since researchers cannot reliably call on the judgment of a speech community to assess the differences in meaning that correlate with differences in syntax in Lana's language use, one can only assume that such differences are inconclusive unless there are significant numbers of contexts in which the conditions governing the syntactic change are manifest. In the absence of evidence demonstrating that Lana's syntactic manipulations correlate with semantic or contextual differences, one cannot conclude that her highly developed syntactic facility is evidence of human-like linguistic competence.

Since we cannot rely on the judgements of a speech community, we must consider some other measure, such as the language training Lana underwent. This training, described in detail in Rumbaugh (1977), focused on a set of stock sentences, strings which permitted substitution of lexigrams in certain positions, but did not permit rearrangement of either lexigrams or strings of lexigrams. A number of these stock sentences were for use chiefly with the computer, to request that the computer supply some food or drink or perform some act. A few others, such as *Color of (object-name) (color-word)*, *(object-name) name-of this*, and *(object-name) (relational word) (object-name)*, were used in response to the questions *Question what color of this*, *Question what name this*, and *Question where (object-name)*. The computer identified as deviant any strings deviating from these stock patterns and did not reinforce such deviations. It is not surprising, then, that Lana should be much more accurate when communicating with the computer than when conversing with humans who inconsistently reinforce deviant strings and fail to reinforce well-formed strings. If we take the stock sentences as the standard of well-formedness, then we will have to reject as deviant the majority of the strings used in conversation with humans. In light of the facility for syntactic manipulation discussed earlier, this seems too stringent a measure, but any taxonomic measure other than the stock sentence is intrinsically arbitrary.

Another possibility is to reject the use of well-formedness judgments on the ground that any well-formedness judgment is guilty to some degree of the intentional fallacy. Instead of using the well-formedness criterion, we can look for differences between substrings in conversation and substrings in stock sentences. Thus a string like *Question you machine into drink what out* (11/9/75 10:39) is deviant since the strings *you machine*, *machine into*, *into drink* are not derivable from anything in stock sentences. However, *drink what* and *what out* are not clearly ill-formed, since they can occur in such strings as *Question Lana want drink what out room*.

The Derivability Criterion translates easily into an algorithm for determining well-formedness. The algorithm first assigns a boundary marker (##) to each end of the string in question. Thus the string presented above becomes ## *Question Lana want drink what out room ##*. The algorithm then scans the string for each connected pair, beginning at the left ## and proceeding to the right until it reaches another pair containing ##. The connected pairs in the string in question are ## *Question, Question Lana, Lana want, want drink, drink what, what out, out room,* and *room* ##. If any pair fails to match a pair in the list of well-formed pairs, the string is rejected as deviant; the system marks it so and does not reinforce that string. Single-word strings present a special problem, since an incorrect single-word response to a naming question may still be identified as well-formed by the derivability criterion. Thus the single-word response *Can* would become ## *Can* ##, which is scanned as ## *Can* and *Can* ##. Since the lexigram *Can* occurs both initially and finally in strings, the single-word response is well-formed. However, single word responses like *Color* and *Name* are ill-formed, since *Color* cannot occur in final position and *Name* can occur neither initially nor finally. It is often impossible to know from the printout whether a given single-word response is correct, since the experiment frequently makes no comment on a response. These problems have led us to regard single-word responses as well-formed as long as the word is from the set of words that could appropriately initiate a response to the experimenter's question. Thus an object name is acceptable in answer to the question *Question what name-of this*, but the lexigram *color* cannot initiate a well-formed response to a naming question. On the other hand, a color word is a well-formed response to the question *Question what color of this (object-name)*, as is a string such as *Color of (this) (object-name) (color-word)*. If we use the Derivability Criterion, we can avoid the intentional fallacy—the assumption that we can ascertain Lana's intent from what she has produced, we are freed from the strictures of the stock sentence criterion to deal with Lana's use of language in conversation, and we have an explicit, replicable criterion for well-formedness.

Two categories of error require discussion. Frequently during the first six weeks after the hiatus, Lana depressed the same key twice in succession. On 5/13/76, for example, repetition occurred 76 times. Approximately seven months later, only 34 repetitions occurred in an entire week. For the purposes of this analysis, all such repetitions must be regarded as artifacts of the software design. Before the hiatus, the software was designed to ignore repeated depressions of a single lexigram, and thus this behavior was unintentionally reinforced. After the hiatus, when the software was redesigned, repetition was no longer reinforced. The behavior, however, had not extinguished even seven months after Lana's return to language training. We will, therefore, not regard the repetition of a lexigram as sufficient grounds for rejecting a string, even though the computer consistently, and humans inconsistently, failed to reinforce that behavior. Before the hiatus, Lana had been conditioned to behave as if repeated key presses did not matter. When the software changed, there was no reason to believe that what she had learned changed as well. The second category of error is the early termination of a string. Three factors seem to account for the majority of early terminations: Lana's recognition of an error in the string; Lana's depression of an initial word (*question, please, yes, no*), resulting in machine termination of the string; or experimenter interruption of an incorrect or inappropriate response. Many terminated strings contain no errors under the Derivability Criterion, but they are clearly incomplete. Such terminations are illustrated in the following conversation from 6/10/76:

Lana:	*Question you move to.*	15:46:08
Tim:	*Question what name this.*	15:46:15
Tim:	*Question what name this.*	15:46:29
Tim:	*Keyboard name this.*	15:46:44
Lana:	*Question you give.*	15:46:59
Lana:	*Question you put on chow in machine.*	15:47:44
Lana:	*Question you put.*	15:48:13
Lana:	*Question you put.*	15:48:27
Tim:	*No.*	15:48:30
Lana:	*Question you.*	15:48:35
Lana:	*Question you move out room.*	15:48:55
Tim:	*Yes.*	15:48:58

As the timing shows, Tim terminated some of Lana's sentences, but on other occasions the reason for the early termination is not clear. Consequently, we have chosen to list separately those early terminations that otherwise meet the derivability criterion without including them among either the ill-formed strings or the well-formed strings. When percentages or averages are given, they do not include the number of early terminations.

The remaining ill-formed strings are subject to a variety of arbitrary and sometimes non-unique taxonomies. It is possible, for example, to classify some strings as correct until the final lexigram. Such a string as *Chow name-of this to* (5/30/76 11:56:17) is well-formed up to the lexigram for *to*. One could classify separately strings like *Lana want eat milk* (6/16/76 10:53:28) together with all other strings in which the syntax appears correct except that Lana has chosen the wrong lexigram from a substitution set, in this case lexigrams of consumption. One could establish a third category of sentences including all strings from which some lexigram has apparently been omitted, as in *Question you move room* (6/10/76 15:44:15), which seems to lack only the lexigram for *out* or for *into*. Any such taxonomy, however, leads us finally to attempting an interpretation of Lana's intent.

We will classify all strings in Lana's data as well-formed, ill-formed, or terminated. Well-formed strings will include stock sentences, strings derivable from stock sentences, and otherwise well-formed strings containing repetitions.

Table 1. Accuracy rates for 10/11/75 through 11/10/75.

Date	Stock			Conversation				Combined		
	tot	*	%wfs	tot	*	%wfs	T	tot	*	%wfs
10/11	320	19	94.1	111	5	95.5	3	432	25	94.2
10/12	309	29	94.1	18	3	83.3	0	326	21	93.5
10/14	275	8	97	35	2	94.2	2	310	10	96.7
10/16	260	9	96.5	78	2	97.4	7	338	11	96.7
10/17	326	29	90.1	91	22	75.8	7	417	51	87.7
10/18	338	15	95.5	28	1	96.4	4	366	15	95.1
10/19	291	21	92.7	75	4	94.6	4	366	29	92
10/21	199	9	95.4	62	6	90.3	8	261	15	94.2
10/23	224	9	95.1	45	7	84.4	16	269	16	94
10/25	209	11	94.7	43	6	86	5	252	17	93.5
10/26	202	20	90	49	3	93.8	1	251	23	90.8
10/29	249	11	95.5	23	2	91.3	50	272	13	95.2
10/30	202	11	94.5	24	2	91.6	1	226	13	94.2
10/31	288	10	96.5	31	1	96.7	0	319	11	96.5
11/1	226	9	96	32	5	84.3	2	258	14	94.5
11/2	231	10	95.6	20	1	95	3	251	11	95.6
11/3	154	5	96.7	77	3	96.4	5	231	8	96.5
11/4	330	13	96	11	0	100	1	341	13	96.1
11/5	238	5	97.8	65	4	93.8	17	303	9	97
11/6	417	16	96.1	36	2	94.4	12	453	18	96
11/7	270	16	94	85	7	91.7	35	355	23	93.5
11/8	167	10	94	21	5	76.1	2	188	15	92.5
11/9	271	3	98.8	22	5	77.2	6	293	8	97.2
11/10	104	0	100	49	0	100	2	153	0	100
Total	5679	287	94.9	1131	98	91.3	183	6810	385	94.3

Note: tot = total sentences; * = no. of ill-formed sentences; %wfs = percentage of well-formed sentences; and T = terminated strings.

Terminated strings will include all those strings that are well-formed up to and including the last lexigram but that can be derived from stock sentences only by the addition of at least one lexigram. All other strings will be classified as ill-formed.

3. Lana's Performance Before the Hiatus

In the thirty days prior to November 11, 1975, Lana exhibited a generally high level of accuracy in both stock and conversational sentences. In this period, she produced 5,679 stock sentences; 287 were ill-formed by the Derivability Criterion for a well-formedness rate of 94.9%. The daily rates ranged from a low of 90% on 10/26 to a high of 100% on 11/10. During this period she produced 1,131 conversational sentences of which 98 were ill-formed, for a well-formedness rate of 91.3%. Her daily rates ranged from a low of 75.8% on 10/17 to a high of 100% on 11/4 and 11/10. Her well-formedness rate in conversational sentences fell below 90% on six of twenty-four days for which we have data from this period. Those days were 10/12 (83.3%); 10/17 (75.8%); 10/23 (84.4%); 10/25 (86%); 11/1 (84.3%); 11/8 (76.1%); and 11/9 (77.2%). Table 1 reports the complete figures for the thirty-day period.

A closer examination of the conversations during the period before the hiatus shows only four extensive testing sessions. On 10/11, 10/14, 10/21, and 10/26 the experimenters tested Lana on a *same/different* task; only one of the 137 responses during the four periods was incorrect. Naming and color-identification tasks were infrequent and brief, and it is not clear that those short sessions constituted test sessions. Thus 87.8% of the conversational sentences occurred in apparently unstructured exchanges with an experimenter. Errors during these exchanges showed no significant correlation with any single type of sentence.

4. Lana's Return to Language Training

During the month following her return to language training, Lana engaged in language use on twenty-two days. No data are available from days 5/21 and 5/22, and the system broke down on 5/30 at 12:23:56 and remained down until 12:05:59 on 6/8. Lana's performance on stock sentences rose from 78.6% on the first day, 5/13, to 96.1% on 5/16. After 5/16 her accuracy rate on stock sentences fell below 90% on five days: 5/17 (89%); 5/25 (86.8%); 5/26 (88.2%); 5/30 (88.8%); and 6/8 (77.2%). The fall to 77.8% on 6/8 followed an eight-day hiatus. On 6/9 Lana's accuracy rate in stock sentences rose to above 90% and remained there to the end of the period under study. In contrast to her rapid recovery of stock sentence use, Lana's performance in conversation was erratic. During the first four days the accuracy rate rose from 36.1% on 5/13 to 74.3% on 5/16. Thereafter her performance ranged from peaks of 86.7% (5/25); 88.4% (5/27); and 90.5% (6/8) to lows of 15% (5/20); 26.3% (5/26); and 46.1% (6/13). Table 2 reports the complete numerical results of an analysis of the first month following the hiatus.

Three of the lowest scores in conversational sentences can be explained in part by exclusion of a single type of error. Consistently after her return to the language project, Lana omitted the lexigram for *that's* from strings like *Box name-of this that's blue*. On 5/20, for example, thirty strings of this form occur, all of which omit the lexigram for *that's*. These strings occur in a naming task in response to questions of the form *Question what name-of this that's blue* (09:47:28). Several observations must be made in connection with the omission of *that's*. First, this error occurred only rarely before the hiatus. Second, the error was nearly always committed in response to a question containing the correct string. Third, the experimenter always accepted the ill-formed response as correct if the color word was correct. Finally, Lana used *that's* correctly in other types of string after the

Table 2.   Accuracy rates for 5/13/76 through 6/13/76.

Date	Stock			Conversation				Combined		
	tot	*	% wfs	tot	*	% wfs	T	tot	*	% wfs
5/13	366	78	78.6	36	23	36.1	55	438	101	76.9
5/14	185	36	80.5	36	21	41.6	27	221	57	74.2
5/15	280	23	91.7	50	23	54	67	320	46	85.6
5/16	180	7	96.1	39	10	74.3	30	219	17	92.1
5/17	328	36	89	99	32	67.6	26	360	68	81.1
5/18	402	23	94.2	95	37	61	52	497	60	87.9
5/19	119	7	97.1	73	34	54.6	28	192	41	78.6
5/20	166	4	97.5	100	85	15[a]	26	266	89	78.1
5/23	160	8	95	103	44	57.2[b]	17	204	52	74.5
5/24	393	32	91.8	120	56	53.3	47	513	88	82.8
5/25	212	28	86.7	157	26	83.4	20	379	54	85.7
5/26	129	16	88.2	95	70	26.3[c]	12	224	86	61.6
5/27	289	12	95.8	191	33	88.4	22	480	45	90.6
5/28	378	8	97.8	115	19	83.4	32	493	27	94.5
5/29	269	12	95.5	107	21	80.3	26	376	33	91.2
5/30	36	4	88.8	63	9	85.7	13	99	13	86.8
6/8	185	42	77.2	159	15	90.5	26	344	57	83.4
6/9	370	30	91.8	131	30	77	35	501	60	88
6/10	272	26	90.4	49	20	59.1	33	321	46	85.6
6/11	272	8	97	56	19	66	15	328	27	91.7
6/12	255	3	98.8	9	4	55.5	6	264	7	97.3
6/13	324	12	96.2	39	21	46.1	20	363	33	90.9
Total for 6/8–6/13										
	1678	121	92.7	443	103	75.3	135	2121	224	89.4

a. Error figure includes 30 strings omitting *that's* from strings of the form *(object name) name-of this that's (color word)*. If these strings are excluded, the percentage rises to 45%.

b. Error figure includes 12 strings omitting *that's*. If these strings are excluded, the percentage rises to 68.9%.

c. Error figure includes 40 strings omitting *that's*. If these strings are excluded the percentage rises to 68.4%.

hiatus, such as *Question you give this that' orange to Lana* (5/20 16:36:18) and *Question you make this that's shut open* (5/24 12:12:29). This consistent omission appears to represent a new string in Lana's repertory of responses. She omits one of the two lexigrams in her vocabulary that has no physical or situational referent. *That's* has only the syntactic function of linking an object-name or the lexigram *this* with a following color-word or locative string (Stahlke, Rumbaugh, Gill, and Warner 1979). Thirty cases of this error occur on 5/20, twelve on 5/23, and forty on 5/26. If the well-formedness rates in conversational sentences on those days are adjusted accordingly, the percentages become 45%, 68.9%, and 68.4%, respectively.

Table 3.   Lana's use of *that's* six months after the hiatus.

		Number
Well-formed strings		
Question you give M&M	*orange to Lana in room*	1
Question you give M&M	*orange to Lana*	1
Question you give M&M	*yellow to Lana*	1
Question you give apple that's orange		6
Question you give this that's orange		4
Question you give bread that's orange		3
Question you give bread that's read		2
Question you give this that's orange to Lana		1
Shoe name-of this that's red		1
Can name-of this that's yellow		1
Eye name-of this that's shut		2
Feces name-of this that's orange		4
Ill-formed strings		
You make gate	*open shut*	2
You make gate	*shut open*	22
You make door	*shut open*	3
You make window	*shut open*	5
Lana want door	*shut open*	2
Lana want gate	*shut open*	1
Lana want this	*shut open*	3
Gate name-of this	*shut*	4
M&M name-of this	*orange*	1

Lana's anomalous behavior with *that's* reflects a continuing instability in use of that lexigram. An examination of the first six weeks' data from 1977, a period approximately six months later, indicates that her use of *that's* had still not stabilized. Between 1/13/77 and 2/22/77, Lana used seventy-one sentences that should properly have contained the lexigram *that's*. *That's* occurred in its proper position in the string twenty-four times. The strings are listed in Table 3.

The use of *that's* appears most regular in strings containing the substring . . . *give (object-name) that's (color-word)* . . . . Of nineteen such strings, only three omitted *that's*. Of fourteen naming sentences, six, or nearly half, omitted *that's*. All strings containing *shut open* or *open shut* omitted *that's*. We can only conclude that Lana's use of *that's* after the hiatus changed from that described in Stahlke et al. (1979) to a pattern that is much more restricted. That this change began after the hiatus is indicated by the occurrence on 5/24/76 of the well-formed sentence *Question you make this that's shut open* (12:12:29). As the 1977 data indicate, Lana came to use *that's* only in strings containing *give* and strings containing *name-of*. Even in these types of string her use of *that's* did not reach the 85% level of accuracy. The sentences in which she correctly used *that's* are not novel, they are stock sentence types. Thus the accuracy with which she used *that's* was significantly below her post-hiatus stock sentence average of 92.7% and even below her combined average of 89.4% (cf. Table 2). The conclusion seems warranted that a lexigram with no physical or situational reference was more difficult for Lana to retain or regain mastery of than were referential lexigrams, suggesting that lexigrams or words having purely syntactic functions represent a higher level of linguistic behavior than do referential items.

The erratic nature of Lana's accuracy in conversational sentences after the hiatus requires some comment. Tables 4 and 5 show number and duration of conversations and the topics of conversation for each day of the pre- and post-hiatus periods under study. Conversations after the hiatus were demonstrably longer and covered a narrower range of topics than conversations before the hiatus. An examination of the times of day of the pre-hiatus conversations indicates that test conversations, that is, conversations on topics other than the procurement of food and moving in or out of the room for purposes other than eating, did not occur during feeding periods. As indicated on Table 5, three

Table 4.   Distribution of conversations before hiatus.

Topic	10/11	10/12	10/14	10/16	10/17	10/18	10/19	10/21	10/23
food	23,3	13,2	10,2	8,2		32,1	21,1	10,3	
move	5,1			2,1	15,5	8,2	2,1	3,2	36,1
name/color		28,1		2,1	22,3		1,1		
groom/tickle			5,1	9,1	5,1	9,1		5,1	
same/different	18,2		6,1	16,1	13,1		10,1	11,1	
identification					17,1				
put ball									18,1
give ball									36,1
Total	46,6	41,3	11,4	41,7	58,13	17,3	45,4	40,6	82,6

	10/25	10/26	10/29	10/30	10/31	11/1	11/2	11/3	11/4
food	12,4	3,2	1,1	11,2	15,3	17,3	26,2	26,2	3,1
move	19,1	5,1	1,1		4,1	3,1		2,1	6,1
name/color	3,1		1,1						4,1
groom/tickle			5,1		3,1	3,1			
same/different		24,1							
Total	34,6	32,4	8,4	14,3	22,5	20,4	26,2	32,4	9,2

	11/5	11/6	11/7	11/8	11/9	11/10
food	33,3	12,4	21,5	1,1	4,2	2,1
move	3,1	11,2	7,1	4,1		3,1
name/color			8,3	5,1	24,1	19,2
groom/tickle			1,1		3,1	2,1
Total	36,4	23,6	37,10	10,1	31,4	26,5

Note: Read the notation x,y as no. of minutes, no. of conversations.

Table 5.   Distribution of conversations after hiatus.

Topic	5/13	5/14	5/15	5/16	5/17	5/18	5/19	5/20
food	70,1	57,3	67,5	31,2	35,3	23,4	37,3	40,2
move		9,1		3,1	26,1	7,1		
name/color					18,1	109,1[a]	46,1	126,2[b]
name		9,1		3,1	26,1	7,1		
color					49,1	18,1		
Total	70,1	75,5	67,5	37,4	154,7	164,8	83,4	166,4

	5/23	5/24	5/25	5/26	5/27	5/28	5/29	5/30
food	1,1	35,7	63,5	2,2	13,4	15,4	71,3	39,2
move	3,1	12,1	11,2	7,3	13,2	21,3		1,1
name/color	61,1[c]	23,1	28,1	3,1	45,2			
groom/tickle		4,2			3,1	10,1		
name					41,1	6,3		
Total	65,3	74,11	102,8	53,7	76,9	52,11	71,3	40,3

	6/9	6/10	6/11	6/12	6/13			
food	64,8	26,4	30,6	1,1	2,2			
move	9,3				4,1			
name/color					8,1			
groom/tickle	7,1							
name	23,3			6,1	1,1			
Total	103,15	26,4	30,6	7,2	15,5			

a. Lana interrupted this long *name/color* session thirteen times by attempting to request something from the machine with a *please* statement. These statements were all terminated early.

b. A sixty-nine minute *name/color* session occurred between 9:35:06 and 10:44:26, normally a feeding period. Lana interrupted this session 26 times with the statement *Please machine give milk*.

c. This sixty-one minute name/color session occurred between 9:02:11 and 10:03:13, normally a feeding period. Lana interrupted the session 5 times with *Please machine give milk*.

lengthy *name/color* sessions occurred during the morning feeding period. Lana's frequent interruption of these sessions with attempts to request food from the machine coincide with relatively low levels of accuracy. Also, Lana's performance in *color* and *name* tasks appears to have been influenced by the fact that these tasks were often combined into a single longer session. Failure on the part of the experimenter to separate sessions requiring such similar strings as *Color of this box yellow* and *Box name of this that's yellow* appears to have contributed to Lana's erratic use of *that's*. A review of the conversational behavior of the two experimenters who worked with Lana during this period also indicates that each expected somewhat different kinds of behavior from Lana and responded differently to ill-formed strings. The inconsistency of reinforcement and the absence of any discernible program for resuming conversational interaction with Lana must have played a large role in determining the erratic performance levels reflected in

Table 2. Her levels of accuracy in stock sentences produced learning much more like that one would expect from consistent patterns of reinforcement.

During the first three days after the hiatus Lana exhibited several types of behavior that very quickly diminished in frequency. For example, Lana produced twenty strings during conversation that were well-formed except for the rearrangement of two words. A common example of this is *Question you give milk of cup* (5/15/76 9:04:36), where *milk* and *cup* were interchanged. Since Lana received liquids in the morning feeding session and solids in the evening, and since this string and strings like it commonly occurred during food conversations, it is possible that Lana intended to request a cup of milk. This order reversal did not occur with all *of* strings; strings containing *piece of* and *color of* were apparently immune to such rearrangement, but strings containing the names of containers were not. Once again the reference of a lexigram may be a factor in Lana's use of it. The lexigrams *piece* and *color* do not refer to objects that are physically distinct from the item named after *of,* whereas the lexigrams denoting containers do. Furthermore, the software required that Lana use *piece* when requesting certain food items from the computer, and her use of it was consistent in stock sentences. She did not use *piece* consistently in conversation; she frequently produced strings like *Question you give banana* instead of *Question you give piece of banana.* Both strings were reinforced by experimenters. *Piece,* then, seemed to have acquired a sort of situational reference in that it was required when communicating with the computer. This situational reference may have distinguished her use of *piece* from her use of *that's* since the latter was not consistently reinforced in any definable situation, while *piece* quite clearly was. *Color* had no physical referent independent of the object being described, but *color* had to be used in certain test situations and was reinforced much more consistently than *that's.* Thus its reference may have been situational in the same sense as the reference of *piece.*

A second behavior Lana exhibited in the period immediately after the hiatus was a trial-and-error approach to conversation. The following conversation on 5/14/76 illustrates this trial-and-error strategy. Interpretive comments are in parentheses.

Lana: *Question Tim give milk.*   11:27:24
Tim: *No.*   11:27:30
         (It is not clear why Tim refused this request, but the reason may be that he wanted Lana to identify the container as well, as she did successfully at 11:31:24.)
Lana: *Please machine give milk.*   11:27:43
Tim: *Red red red.*   11:27:55
         (The significance of this string is unclear, but several later examples suggest that a malfunction was responsible for the occasional occurrence

of *red* in the printout. It is not known whether this malfunction also caused the lexigram for *red* to appear on a projector. It is apparent, however, that Tim was not allowing this request to be reinforced.)

Lana: *Question Tim give milk of bowl.*   11:28:36

Tim: *No milk of bowl.*   11:28:45

(Tim rejected a string in which Lana had interchanged *milk* and *bowl*. Both experimenters frequently used the strategy of prefixing the ill-formed portion of a string with *no*, as if to indicate to Lana that that portion of the string was incorrect. Lana's response here and elsewhere raises doubts concerning her comprehension of that strategy.)

Lana: *Please machine give bowl.*   11:29:00

Tim: *No machine give bowl.*   11:29:17

(Apparently the same strategy in effect.)

Lana: *Question Tim give feces to milk.*   11:30:01

Tim: *No.*   11:30:06

(Lana's error may have resulted from accidently depressing *feces* instead of *bowl*. Although the string *(container) to milk* is still ill-formed, it is interesting to note that the lexigram classes are correct: *(object-name) (relational term) (object-name)*.

Lana: *Question Tim give cup of milk.*   11:31:24

Tim: *Yes.*   11:31:34

(Tim reinforced the correct string.)

Tim: *Question Lana want more milk.*   11:33:46

Tim: *Question Lana want more milk.*   11:34:08

Tim: *No.*   11:34:21

Tim: *Yes.*   11:34:27

Tim: *Question Lana want more milk.*   11:34:40

Lana: *Yes.*   11:34:50

(Whatever Lana was doing in response to Tim's question was apparently not the behavior Tim sought. Lana's final response suggests that she might have comprehended Tim's question.)

Lana: *Question Tim put red milk of bowl.*   11:35:29

Tim: *No milk of bowl.*   11:35:36

Tim: *Milk in cup.*   11:35:45

(Tim consistently ignored *red* in this conversation. Once again he prefixed the ill-formed portion of Lana's sentence with *no*, but this time he also produced the correct string.)

Lana: *Question Tim put red milk orange.*   11:36:39

(Lana showed no sign of comprehending Tim's strategy.)

Lana: *Question Tim give milk.*   11:37:27

(This well-formed string was not reinforced since it was apparently not the desired string.)

Lana: *Question Tim put red milk.*   11:39:00
Tim: *No put milk.*   11:39:18
         (Unsuccessful identification of error again.)
Lana: *Question Tim put red milk out cup.*   11:40:57
         (Once again Lana produced a string that is ill-formed even though the
         incorrect lexigram *out* is from the correct class of lexigrams.)
Tim: *Milk out cup.*   11:41:11
         (The intent is not clear. It could be that Tim wanted Lana to produce
         something like *Question you put milk in cup,* which he would reinforce
         by pouring milk into Lana's cup. He responded to the situation logically
         by pointing out that the milk, which was not in the cup, was already out
         of the cup. He may have interpreted Lana's ill-formed string a little too
         richly.)
Tim: *Question milk in cup.*   11:41:23
         (Another attempt to follow the logic of the situation?)
Lana: *Question Tim give milk.*   11:41:44
Tim: *No.*   11:41:50
         (Once again Tim rejected a response that is well-formed but not the
         desired response.)
Lana: *Question Tim put red milk cup.*   11:42:57
Tim: *No milk cup.*   11:43:05
Tim: *Milk in cup.*   11:43:13
         (Error identification strategy followed by supplying the correct partial
         string.)
Tim: *Yes.*   11:43:22
         (It is not clear what Tim was responding to.)
Lana: *Question Tim put red milk orange.*   11:44:59
Lana: *Question Time put red milk orange.*   11:45:38
Lana: *Question Tim put red milk in cup.*   11:48:06
Tim: *Yes.*   11:48:09
         (Lana finally produced the desired string, and Tim reinforced it. It is not
         clear whether Lana's well-formed string was the result of chance or of
         'knowledge.' The conversation ended at this point, so the correct behav-
         ior could not be elicited and reinforced again immediately.)

Lana apparently tried a number of partially correct strings before hitting on the
one that worked, a trial-and-error strategy that she employed frequently during
the first few days of conversation. Later on she employed this strategy occasionally when an experimenter for some reason withheld reinforcement from a string
which had been reinforced in the past.

     Also during the first three days after the hiatus, Lana produced thirty-eight
eleven-word strings. The software was designed to terminate a string if a first-
word error occurred, as described earlier, or if the period key was depressed. If

the tenth projector was activated and the next key depressed was not the period key, the eleventh lexigram appeared on the printout and was stored in memory, but the system would then terminate the string. Lana's eleven-word strings are all nonsense strings showing no pattern of lexigrams, and a reasonable guess at a solution is that she was playing with the keyboard. From 5/16/76 through 6/13/76 sixty-five more eleven-word strings occurred, but their frequency fell sharply after the first three days. It is interesting that eleven of these sixty-five strings occurred on 6/8/76, the first day after an eight-day shut-down, suggesting that the novelty of the keyboard after a period of inactivity had something to do with the number of eleven-word strings. An examination of the data from the first seven months of 1977 shows 250 eleven-word strings among approximately 45,000 strings for a rate of 0.5%.

Throughout the post-hiatus period Lana produced novel, apparently unconditioned strings that were well-formed. Whether or not these strings indicate a productive syntax is questionable, but a number of them are worth noting. Three sets of these strings will be dealt with separately. Each new string that she produced during her first five days back was by definition a novel string, whether it was stock or conversational. The well-formed strings from the first five days are listed separately in Appendix 1. Long strings, that is, well-formed strings of eight or more words, will also be listed separately later, in Appendix 2. We first present novel strings of seven words or less.

Lana's first novel string occurred on 5/24/76, when she produced *Question you tickle me out room* (14:49:00). The string meets the Derivability Criterion and occurred during the following exchange:

Tim:	*Question me move into room.*	14:48:21
Lana:	*Yes.*	14:48:23
Lana:	*Question you tickle me out room.*	14:49:00
Tim:	*No.*	14:49:08
Tim:	*Question me move into room.*	14:49:16
Lana:	*Yes.*	14:49:19

The conversation continued to deal with moving in and out of the room and opening and closing the window.

On 5/28/76 a novel exchange occurred as part of a conversation on the topic of grooming and tickling. After several exchanges on grooming and tickling, the following exchange ensued:

Tim:	*Question what name this.*	11:28:43
Lana:	*Question you tickle.*	11:29:42
Tim:	*Question what name this.*	11:30:36
Lana:	*Eye name this.*	11:30:52
Tim:	*Yes eye name this.*	11:31:05

Tim:	*Question what name this.*	11:31:17
Lana:	*Eye name this.*	11:31:23
Lana:	*Yes.*	11:31:28
Tim:	*Question what name this.*	11:31:46
Lana:	*Eye name this.*	11:31:51
Tim:	*Yes.*	11:31:55
Tim:	*Question Lana groom eye.*	11:32:23
Lana:	*Yes.*	11:33:45

This conversation contained the first use of *eye* in the period under study. Because of the face-to-face nature of the grooming activity, it is likely that a certain amount of cueing was involved in Lana's rapid and correct response at 11:30:52, but the conversation is none the less remarkable for the cueing; it represents an unstructured and nearly error-free form of social interaction through a language-like medium. However, caution requires that one not draw important conclusions from a single exchange of this sort.

Lana's first well-formed long sentence was *Question you give this that's orange to Lana* (5/20/76 16:36:18). She repeated it at 16:39:01. At 16:40:39 she produced *Question you give apple that's orange to Lana,* which she repeated at 16:45:54. On 6/8/76 she again produced *Question you give apple that's orange to Lana* (16:54:55) and *Question you give this that's orange to Lana* (16:55:33). On 6/11/76 she produced the sentence containing *apple* twice (16:30:31 and 16:31:25) and the sentence containing *this* once (16:30:56).

Appendix 2 contains a complete list of Lana's long sentences through 6/30/76.

The conversation surrounding Lana's first well-formed long sentences on 5/20/76 is suggestive of how she first came to use them.

Lana:	*Question make.*	16:28:32
Lana:	*Question you make window open.*	16:29:02
Tim:	*No.*	16:29:07
Lana:	*Question you make this open.*	16:30:10
Tim:	*Question make what open.*	16:30:18
Tim:	*Question make what.*	16:30:24
Tim:	*Question make what open.*	16:30:33
Lana:	*Question you make this this that's that's.*	16:30:50
Lana:	*Question you you make.*	16:30:55
Lana:	*Question you make this that's shut open.*	16:31:24
Tim:	*Yes.*	16:31:27
Lana:	*Question you give this that's orange.*	16:33:34
Tim:	*Yes.*	16:33:40
Lana:	*Question you give this that's that's orange to Lana.*	16:34:23
Lana:	*Question you make.*	16:34:32

Lana:	*Question you give this this.*	16:34:43
Lana:	*Question you give this that's orange to Lana.*	16:36:18
Tim:	*Yes.*	16:36:24

Lana's sentences at 16:30:50 and 16:31:24 extended to seven words. 16:30:50 is unfinished at seven words, and the fact that she often terminated sentences that were ill-formed suggests that she might have been aware that this sentence could continue, although she hesitates to make such a judgment. At 16:33:34 she used a sentence which is well-formed even though it lacks the string *to Lana,* a string which usually concludes sentences containing *Question . . . give.* At 16:34:23 she produced the complete sentence, but this time she happened to depress *that's* two times in succession. Finally, at 16:36:18, she produced the well-formed eight-word string *Question you give this that's orange to Lana,* a string that she used once more in this conversation and a few minutes later modified by substituting *apple* for *this.*

During the post-hiatus period under study, Lana produced well-formed long sentences on only seven occasions. However, from 6/16/76 through 6/30/76 she produced sixteen correct long sentences. Nearly all of these were variations on the pattern that developed on 5/20/76; the exceptions included *Question you give Coke in bowl to Lana* (6/22/76 14:04:11); *Question you give juice in bowl of Coke to Lana* (6/22/76 14:10:00); *Question you put Coke in bowl to Lana* (6/22/76 14:14:51); *Question you give cup to juice to Lana* (6/25/76 11:54:37); *Question you give cup of bread to Lana* (6/27/76 11:13:48); and *Question you give piece of bread to machine* (6/27/76 11:14:42). It is impossible to tell from the data whether all of these long sentences correlated with Lana's behavior in such a way as to indicate her intent, nor were they consistently reinforced or stimulated by the experimenters. Thus it is impossible to comment on her use of some of the well-formed long sentences beyond pointing out that they met the Derivability Criterion and therefore shed some light on Lana's developing syntactic capabilities.

5. Conclusions

Not surprisingly, this study of Lana's post-hiatus language behavior leaves many questions unanswered. Certainly such broad questions as the nature of an ape's linguistic abilities and the degree to which these approximate human language abilities are only negligibly closer to resolution now than they have been over the past twenty-five years. Perhaps, however, the effects of six months' language deprivation have enabled us to ask questions of the data with somewhat greater precision. Beyond the results given in the preceding sections, it is possible now to suggest some tentative hypotheses concerning the nature and significance of ape language behavior.

Two of the most firmly established conclusions concern the ape's ability to use symbols and to assign reference to them. These abilities have been discussed extensively in the literature cited at the beginning of this paper and will not be discussed further here. The question of Lana's syntactic capacity, on the other hand, can be explored further. Lana's rapid recovery of stock sentences, her occasional novel strings, and especially her development of well-formed long sentences all suggest considerable syntactic facility. The design of the computer hardware makes it impossible to demonstrate that her syntax is productive, but the mere fact that she was able to construct twenty-three well-formed long sentences over a period of forty-six days with no training in increased sentence length argues that her syntax has a degree of productivity that exceeds what was demonstrable with the pre-hiatus hardware. It is unfortunate that language research with chimpanzees has not continued to pursue studies of syntactic productivity.

Even more important, however, than the evident syntactic productivity is the appropriateness of many of her conversational sentences. For example, her use of *this* in two ways that had not been trained suggests context-dependent language use. She had been trained to use *this* in *color* and *name* sentences, where the referent was before her and her attention was directed to it by the experimenter. Her conversational behavior used *this* both to refer to objects in her environment and to substitute for a name that she did not know (Rumbaugh and Gill 1977). These discourse-governed uses of *this* persisted after the hiatus as well, as did her attempts to restructure strings that were not eliciting some reward. Her use of *this* is an example of her ability to code both semantics and pragmatics into syntactic form, a critical requisite for natural language behavior (Givón 1984).

Lastly, Lana's behavior with *that's* and with *(container) of (substance)* sequences indicates possible limitations on her ability to code information syntactically. *That's* is one of two lexigrams in her repertory that has neither physical nor situational referent. Its use was not well defined semantically, and not unexpectedly it is just such a lexigram that is carried over the hiatus with the least stability. The other word which has no physical referent or situational referent is *of*. *Of* occurs exclusively in the sequences *color of (object-name), piece of (object-name),* and *(container-name) of (substance-name).* Because of its restricted distribution, *of* appears to have caused little difficulty over the hiatus. Apparently linguistic phenomena that are purely syntactic represent a more advanced type of linguistic behavior than phenomena that have semantic or pragmatic relevance.

Lana has demonstrated purposive communicative behavior in her use of Yerkish with humans. While this fact sheds little light on the vexing questions of innateness and of cognitive similarities between chimpanzee and man, it does suggest that the chimpanzee's considerable ability to communicate is enhanced from a human perspective by training in systems that are, if not natural languages, natural language surrogates (Stokoe 1983). It is the ape's capacity for using a natural language surrogate that makes the species a valuable behavioral model for experimentation with techniques for training handicapped humans in communication skills (Parkel, White, and Warner 1977).

Appendix 1: New Well-Formed Strings
Produced from 5/13/76 to 5/17/76

5/13/76:
> Please machine make window open.
> Please machine give M&M.
> Please give M&M.
> Please machine give juice.
> Please machine give apple.
> Please machine give milk.
> Please machine give piece of this.
> Please machine give piece of apple.
> Please machine make slide.
> Please machine make music.
> Please you give apple to Lana.
> Question what name-of this.
> Question Tim give chow.
> Question Tim put chow in room.
> Question Tim put chow in cage.
> Question Tim put chow in bowl.
> Question Tim give bowl of chow.
> Please machine give water.

5/14/76:
> Question you put milk in cup.
> Question Tim give milk.
> Question Tim give cup of milk.
> Please machine give piece of bread.
> Please machine make window shut.
> Question Tim give piece of chow.
> Question Tim put chow into machine.
> Please machine give piece of chow.

5/15/76:
> Question you give milk.
> Please make music.
> Question Tim make slide.
> Question you give apple.
> Question you give apple to Lana.

5/16/76:

Question you give cup of milk.
Question you give milk to Lana.
Question you put chow in machine.

5/17/76:

Question you give chow.
Question you put bread in machine.
Black. (In response to Question what color of this shoe.)
Color of this yellow.

Appendix 2: Well-formed Sentences of Eight Words and Longer, 5/13/76 through 6/30/76

5/20/76:

Question you give this that's orange to Lana.	16:36:18
Question you give apple that's orange to Lana.	16:45:54

6/8/76:

Question you give apple that's orange to Lana.	16:54:55
Question you give this that's orange to Lana.	16:55:33

6/11/76:

Question you give apple that's orange to Lana.	16:30:31
Question you give this that's orange to Lana.	16:30:56
Question you give apple that's orange to Lana.	16:31:25

6/16/76:

Question you give this that's orange to Lana.	16:36:38

6/17/76:

Question you give this that's green to Lana.	16:42:39

6/12/76:

Question you give Coke that's orange to Lana.	13:52:05
Question you give Coke in bowl to Lana.	14:04:11
Question you give juice in bowl of Coke to Lana.	14:10:00
Question you put Coke in bowl to Lana.	14:14:51

6/25/76:

Question you give cup of juice to Lana.	11:54:37

6/26/76:

Question you give apple that's orange to Lana.	14:30:15

6/27/76:

Question you give cup of bread to Lana.	11:13:48
Question you give piece of bread to machine.	11:14:42

6/29/76:

Question you give cup of juice to Lana.	11:11:20
Question you give this that's orange to Lana.	17:02:38
Question you give apple that's orange to Lana.	17:03:04
Question you give apple that's orange to Lana.	17:10:32

6/30/76:

Question you give apple that's orange to Lana.	16:40:03
Question you give this that's orange to Lana.	16:48:17

REFERENCES

Gill, Timothy V. 1977. "Conversations with Lana." In: Rumbaugh, pp. 100–50.

Givón, Talmy 1978. *On Understanding Grammar.* New York: Academic Press.

Givón, Talmy 1984. *Syntax: A Functional Typological Introduction.* New York: John Benjamins.

Parkel, Dorothy A., Royce A. White, and Harold Warner 1977. "Implications of the Yerkes technology for mentally retarded human subjects." In: Rumbaugh, pp. 150–200.

Petitto, Laura A., and M. S. Seidenberg 1979. "On the evidence for linguistic abilities in signing apes." *Brain and Language* 8, pp. 162–83.

Pisani, Pier P. 1977. "Computer programs." In: Rumbaugh, pp. 200–50.

Premack, David 1972. "Language in chimpanzees." *Science* 172: pp. 800–22.

Rumbaugh, Duane M. 1977. *Language Learning by a Chimpanzee: The Lana Project.* New York: Academic Press.

Rumbaugh, Duane M., and Timothy V. Gill 1977. "Lana's acquisition of language skills." In: Rumbaugh, pp. 250–300.

Savage-Rumbaugh, E. Susan, Duane M. Rumbaugh, and Sally Boysen 1980. "Do apes use language?" *American Scientist* 68, pp. 46–61.

Seidenberg, M. S., and Laura A. Petitto 1979. "Signing behavior in apes: A critical review." *Cognition* 7, pp. 177–215.

Stahlke, Herbert F. W. 1980. "On asking the question: Can apes learn language?" In: Keith Nelson (ed.), *Children's Language.* New York: Gardner Press, pp. 100–50.

Stahlke, Herbert F. W., Duane M. Rumbaugh, Timothy V. Gill and Harold Warner. 1979. "The linguistic innateness hypothesis in the light of chimpanzee language." In: Richard L. Schiefelbusch and John H. Hollis (eds.), *Language Intervention from Ape to Child.* Baltimore: University Park Press, pp. 91–105.

Stokoe, William C. 1983. "Apes who sign and critics who don't." In: Judith de Luce and High T. Wilder (eds.), *Language in Primates: Perspectives and Implications.* New York: Springer-Verlag, pp. 100–50.

Terrace, Herbert S., Laura A. Petitto, R. J. Sanders, and Thomas G. Bever 1979. "Can an ape create a sentence?" *Science* 206, pp. 891–902.

von Glasersfeld, Ernst 1977. "The Yerkish language and its automatic paper." In: Rumbaugh, pp. 300–50.

CHAPTER EIGHT

The Interaction of Linguistic Theory and Research on American Sign Language

Ronnie B. Wilbur

1. Introduction

The interaction of linguistic theory and the study of sign language is a two-way street, providing not one, but two applications—that of linguistic theory to the research on sign language structure, and that of the research on sign language to the formulation of an adequate linguistic theory of natural language. Linguistic theory holds among its goals the description of language universals and the characterization of possible human languages. Thus, linguistic theory should predict fundamentals of the structure of American Sign Language (ASL), providing the researchers with some guidelines as to what to look for. However, since linguistic theory has so far been formulated entirely from research on spoken languages, ASL (and other sign languages) constitutes a test case of the claims made by any linguistic theory accounting for universals of language structure.

The history of sign language research reflects differing assumptions about the relationship of sign language and linguistic theory. Prior to 1960, linguistic theory was considered simply irrelevant to sign language, or perhaps one could say that sign language was considered irrelevant to linguistics because sign language was not viewed as being a language. In 1960, sign language research took an enormous leap forward with the publication of William Stokoe's *Sign Language Structure: An Outline of the Visual Communication System of the American Deaf.*

Significant in this study was the application of standard structural phonemic principles to the basic signs in an effort to determine the 'building blocks' of signs. The assumption which Stokoe made was that, parallel to spoken languages which consisted of words composed of minimal units of sound called 'phonemes,' sign language would be found to contain signs which were composed of minimal units of manual/visual structure which he called 'cheremes.' It is something of a confirmation of the structuralist phonemic method that Stokoe *found* the minimal units he was looking for (and it is also a confirmation of generative phonology that the cheremes which Stokoe identified fall prey to exactly the same criticisms that generative phonology aimed at the structural phonemes of spoken languages).

At the same time, in the early stages of sign language research, attempts were made to apply transformational generative grammar to ASL (cf. McCall 1965). The results were not very satisfactory, and the status of ASL as a language was again called into question as a result of the assumptions which were made.

Sign languages differ from spoken languages most obviously in that the modalities of transmission are different. One might expect that the applicability of linguistic theory to sign language might vary, in that one might predict that details of generative phonology would presumably not be relevant to a language which does not involve sound, yet details of transformational syntax might be appropriately applied as the modality of the language should not be relevant to its sentence structure. Yet it is exactly the opposite which is true. Research which has followed generative phonology out of the minimal pair/phoneme paradigm and into distinctive features, redundancy conditions, and predictions based on environmental context and markedness, and, most recently, syllable structure has furthered our understanding of sign language far beyond what was originally predicted. On the other hand, American Sign Language is an inflected language in which word order plays a much smaller role, while complex morphological markings and processes interact with simultaneous use of facial expressions. It has become very clear that a linguistic theory such as transformational grammar, which is heavily based on English and other languages in which word order plays a significant role in syntax, is inadequate to handle languages in which a major portion of the grammar is carried by morphological inflection. ASL and other sign languages rely primarily on modification of the sign movement in order to indicate information concerning subject and object, person, number, temporal aspect and focus, and other morphosyntactic properties (Friedman 1977; Siple 1978; Klima and Bellugi 1979; Wilbur 1979; Wilbur, Klima, and Bellugi 1983). Thus, other theories will need to be developed and tested. This does not mean that a theory should be developed exclusively to handle ASL and other sign languages. Rather, it means that an adequate theory must be able to handle *all* languages, spoken and signed, regardless of the relative importance of word order and inflection.

In the remainder of this chapter, I would like to present linguistic descriptions of selected characteristics of American Sign Language structure, focusing primarily on those which have theoretical implications. Thus, this is not intended to be an introduction to the grammar of ASL (for such a review, see Wilbur 1979).

2. *Phonology*

Stokoe's (1960) initial investigation utilized the phonemic method as outlined in Chao (1934); Hockett (1942, 1948, 1954); Sapir (1925); Swadesh (1934), Swadesh and Vogelin (1939); and Twaddell (1935). This required the determination of minimal pairs, words which differed in meaning as a result of only one phoneme. Using this method, Stokoe identified three 'aspects' of sign structure—what acts, where it acts, and the action. These three aspects he called the designation (DEZ), the tabulation (TAB), and the signation (SIG). These aspects have become known as handshape, location, and motion, respectively. Within these aspects, Stokoe identified the cheremes. Dez or handshape had nineteen cheremes, tab or location had twelve cheremes, and sig or motion had twenty-four cheremes. Each of the cheremes had several allochers. For example, Stokoe, Casterline, and Croneberg (1965; revised 1976:xxix–xxx) note that "the dez chereme symbolized . . . as 'Y' may look like the hand configuration for *y* in the manual alphabet—that is one allocher. It may have the three middle fingers only loosely curled—that is another allocher of 'Y.' It may have the three middle fingers at right angles with the palm—still another. It may have the forefinger and little finger parallel and extended, the thumb either bent or extended—two more allochers. All these allochers are represented by the cheremic symbol 'Y.' Some of them are in free variation; others are selected automatically (are used in complementary distribution). . . ."

Friedman (1976a) departed from Stokoe's description of ASL by providing a different analysis of "phonetic elements of the four articulatory parameters . . . and their distribution in a non-classical phonemic analysis." (The fourth parameter which she, and other researchers, included was orientation of the palm, initially added to the inventory by Battison (1973) and Battison, Markowicz, and Woodward (1975). This shift from three aspects to four parameters destroys Stokoe's original conception of sign structure, but is in keeping with standard phonological analysis. Notice, also, that terminology in the above quote from Friedman has shifted to standard phonological usage, reflecting a general belief among sign language researchers that the system in ASL operates in a manner parallel to spoken language phonology, in spite of the absence of sound.) Friedman presented a different phonemic distribution for handshape, with twenty-nine phonemic handshapes (compared to Stokoe's nineteen). Friedman's analysis included all of Stokoe's handshapes and several others. The number of handshapes included is obviously a function of deciding what has phonemic status and what is allophonic (alternatively, what is basic and what is derived). In addition, Friedman indicated for many variants the environments in which they occurred. Her environments included a wide variety of factors, such as point of contact of the hand, loan signs, iconic signs, morphological plurals, movements such as bending of the fingers or knuckles or opening and closing of the hand, and phonological processes such as reduction, assimilation, and free variation. Friedman did not present the details of how each variant could be predicted from the environments given, but she did provide the first introduction of factors which had been ignored or overlooked, such as point of contact. A current description of the structure of a sign would include not only handshape, location, motion, orientation of the palm, and point of contact, but also orientation of the fingers, speed of production, manner of production (tenseness, evenness), repetitions, facial expression, and others.

Friedman, unlike Stokoe, explicitly allowed for a handshape to be both allophonic and phonemic. (For example, the bent 5 handshape is listed as an allophone of the 5 handshape and also as its own phoneme.) For this reason, her analysis is considered a nonclassical phonemic analysis; that is, it does not adhere to the biuniqueness principle which classical phonemic analyses sought to maintain. (Actually, Stokoe's analysis also violates the biuniqueness principle, but does not appear to do so deliberately as in Friedman's analysis). The biuniqueness principle states that, given any segment (phone), one ought to be able to relate it to one and only one phoneme. This cannot be done if the bent 5 handshape can be related to both the 5 phoneme and the bent 5 phoneme. This problem (also known as phonemic overlapping) plagued the structural linguists. Chomsky (1964) argued for the abandonment of the biuniqueness principle. Thus, in explicitly rejecting biuniqueness, Friedman advanced the state of sign language phonology beyond the structural linguistic level. However, the rejection of biuniqueness in spoken language phonology was accompanied by the development of a generative phonological framework which depended heavily on distinctive features descriptions for segments.

Friedman, however, rejected the possibility of distinctive feature analyses for ASL. She argued that there was little or no motivation for such an analysis and that it was not needed. To the contrary, not only is distinctive feature analysis of ASL sign structures motivated by the same arguments given for spoken languages, but without distinctive features it is not possible to state many of the relevant generalizations about relationships between the various components of a sign. In fact, it is quite clear that the absence of a well-formulated set of distinctive features for each structural component has hindered the discovery of those relationships. Several distinctive feature systems have been offered for ASL handshapes (the other components have received considerably less attention). In an effort to parallel the psycholinguistic research on English distinctive features by Miller and Nicely (1955), Lane, Boyes-Braem, and Bellugi (1976) presented handshapes on videotape masked by visual 'snow,' and analyzed the resultant confusion matrices with clustering and scaling techniques. Thus, they proposed a set of eleven perceptually determined distinctive features for twenty ASL handshapes. Woodward (1973) proposed ten features based on articulatory characteristics but which can account for forty handshapes. Kegl and Wilbur (1976) attempted to determine a set of distinctive features on the basis of articulation, perception, and theoretical descriptive utility. However, it is Woodward's which has provided the greatest utility to date in the statement of generalizations concerning the predictability of various handshape variants from such factors as the point of contact of the articulating hand. Modifications of these handshape features are emerging now from extensive work on the relationship of handshape and point of contact by Mandel (1982) and Boyes-Braem (1981). A final determination of distinctive feature systems for ASL signs will probably not be available until linguistic theory decides how decisions between such competing systems should be made.

A main concern of generative phonology is to provide more than a list of

possible segments and their possible contexts. Instead, the formulation of phonological rules which predict the occurrence of segments as a function of their
environments is desired. (Recent issues of the psychological reality of such
prediction rules are not relevant here, but cf. Wilbur 1981 and Wilbur and Menn
1975). Wilbur (1978) provided a demonstration of the existence of phonological
rules in ASL, at the same time confirming the need for at least two levels of
phonological description, basic or underlying representation and derived or surface representation. The phonological rules relate the underlying form of the
lexical entry to the surface representations in exactly the way that one might
expect in spoken languages (whatever that might be).

The main argument concerns three handshapes, S, A, and Ȧ and the environments in which they occur. Friedman (1976a) gave no indication of an environment for A, which she considered basic. She indicated that A occurred in signs
with contact at the thumb tip and in 'iconic signs,' but gave no further details. S
was considered allophonic with A and occurred in signs with contact on the side
of the hand, loan signs, and "neutral end or initial shape," the latter referring to
signs in which the handshape closed or opened during articulation. Wilbur
(1978) observed the following distribution:

$$S \rightarrow \begin{cases} \text{no contact} \\ \text{hand edge} \\ \text{third joint} \\ \text{wrist} \end{cases}$$

$$A \rightarrow \begin{cases} \text{second joint} \\ \text{thumb face} \end{cases}$$

$$\dot{A} \rightarrow \begin{cases} \text{thumb tip} \\ \text{no contact} \end{cases}$$

Except for the occurrence of Ȧ in no-contact environments, which are primarily
morphologically conditioned (Wilbur 1978, 1979; McDonald 1982), it can be
argued that the occurrences of A and Ȧ are in complementary distribution to S
with S as basic. The following phonological rule can be written to capture this
relationship:

$$\begin{bmatrix} +\text{closed} \\ -\text{thumb} \\ -\text{spread} \end{bmatrix} \rightarrow \begin{bmatrix} +\text{thumb} \\ \langle +\text{spread} \rangle \end{bmatrix} \Bigg/ \begin{bmatrix} \begin{cases} \text{Second joint contact} \\ \text{thumb face contact} \end{cases} \\ \langle \text{thumb tip contact} \rangle \end{bmatrix}$$

The actual statement of this rule will probably change as a result of recent
developments in Mandel (1982) and Boyes-Braem (1981). (The thumb position-

contact relationship is more general than just the handshapes discussed here. Several other handshapes, such as G and its relatives X, H, V, and L, participate in similar modifications of handshape as a function of the contact point.)

Battison (1974) described two constraints on allowable two-handed signs, the Dominance Condition and the Symmetry Condition. Combined, these constraints restrict the handshapes and movements in two-handed signs. For signs in which both hands move, the Symmetry Condition specifies that the handshapes on both hands must be identical and the movement of both hands must be identical or mirror-image opposites. For signs in which only one hand moves, the Dominance Condition restricts the handshape in the nondominant (nonmoving) hand to be either identical to the moving hand or else one of a small set of unmarked handshapes: S, a closed fist; B, a flat palm; 5, the B hand with fingers spread; G, fist with index finger extended; C, hand formed in a semicircle; and O, fingertips meet with thumb, forming a circle. In those signs where both hands move, the handshape of the second hand is predictable from the first hand because they must be identical. Similarly, in those signs where only one hand moves but both have the same handshape, the handshape of the nondominant hand will be specified in the underlying representation as identical to the dominant hand. It is those cases in which only one hand moves and the two hands have different handshapes that are of interest to Mandel (1982). He has identified the Basehand Point of Contact Constraint (BPCC) which holds that:

A point of contact (PC) underlyingly specified in a basehand will produce, in the unmarked case, *that one* hand configuration (HC) in which it is physically most accessible and visually most salient.

This constraint allows Mandel to make a variety of handshape predictions given the point of contact (this is the opposite of what researchers had initially thought, where handshape was considered a major factor and point of contact only a minor factor). Using a small set of handshape features to formulate his predictions, Mandel constructed a number of redundancy rules which specified the unmarked values for the various features, some of which are dependent on the specifications for point of contact. Mandel also was able to relate the orientation of the palm to point of contact. From the redundancy conditions, Mandel was then able to predict most of the handshapes in the nondominant hand, as well as the basic orientation and spatial relationship between the hands. In only a few cases was it necessary to specify the handshape of the nondominant hand in underlying representation, and even in those cases, Mandel was able to show that the handshape specifications were not without rationale.

Another line of research has attempted to determine what the sign language analogue of spoken language syllables might be. Earlier approaches did not prove fruitful (Kegl and Wilbur 1976; Chinchor 1978). Recently, Liddell (1982, 1984) argued that the appropriate parallel to consonants and vowels in ASL would be holds and movements. Although the details of Liddell's suggested analysis must be modified (Wilbur 1982, 1985), the thrust of the proposal seems fundamentally correct. One can formulate questions such as: (1) What are the allowable syllable structures which occur in ASL and other sign languages? (2) What are the other possible segment types and how do they contribute to syllable structure? (3) What are the behaviors associated with various segments and syllables with respect to rhythm, syllable quantity, stress, intonation, and morphophonological rules such as the many types of reduplication? Wilbur and Nolen (1984) reported that the duration of syllables in ASL paralleled that reported for English, roughly a quarter of a second. They also observed that the most frequent syllable types were Movement (M) only and Movement-Hold (MH). Wilbur (1982) argued that there are two different kinds of movement segments—path movement and local movement (elbow rotate, wrist and finger movement). There are essentially 10 categories of movement composed of these two movement types that are used to construct lexical signs in ASL. There are 6 simple categories and 4 complex categories. The simple categories consist of (1) movement from the elbow ("elbow extension," referred to herein as 'path'), (2) elbow rotate, (3) wrist nod, (4) handshape change, (5) finger flutter, and (6) Hold only (no lexical movement, see below). The complex categories consist of 'path' and (7) elbow rotate, (8) wrist nod, (9) handshape change, and (10) finger flutter. The complex categories are possible because of the ability to rotate the elbow or move the wrist and fingers independently of the elbow extension. Wilbur and Schick (1985) report the modifications of movement which result from linguistic stress on signs from each of these categories. Types of modification include elongation of the path movement, the addition of an arc to the path movement, the addition of initial or final movement pieces (resulting in more than one syllable), and changes in the rhythm (e.g., initial restrained movement followed by rapid movement; rapid movement followed by sharp deceleration to a hold).

Of particular interest is the category in which there is no lexical movement, the Hold only category. When these signs are produced in isolation/citation form, there is only transition movement which gets the hand to and away from the location for the sign. There are not many ASL signs like this: MOTHER, FATHER, FINE, NOON, the numbers from 1 to 9 (above 9 there is lexical movement for some numbers), and pointing for various pronominal and deictic functions. How can a sign without movement be stressed?

The sign NOON provided several answers to this question. The sign is usually made with the right hand, open palm, fingertips pointing straight up, with the back of the left hand contacting underneath the elbow. *Three* different stressed versions occurred in their data which treated the contact between the two hands as a 'movement to contact' rather than 'contact as location for sign production.' In one version, the left hand repeatedly bounced up to the right elbow and made contact with it; in a second version, the right arm repeatedly moved downward to make contact with a motionless left hand; in the third version, the left hand moved (fingertips first) repeatedly into the side of the right elbow and made contact with it. In each case, a repeated contact was used; this geminated contact occurs in certain lexical items (SHOE, SICK, HOME) in their citation and unstressed forms. Another version of stressed NOON kept the contact constant and instead introduced a small, repeated bouncing (waving) to the right arm. Bouncing is used as an inserted movement for the citation and unstressed forms of the numbers (Wilbur 1985). In yet another form, the hold of NOON was maintained while the head moved repeatedly left/right. In all cases, there is a need to meet or exceed the minimum movement and duration needed for a syllable (Frishberg 1978; Wilbur and Nolen 1984).

In contrast, a stressed form of the sign FLIRT showed that certain contacts can not be reanalyzed as 'movement to contact.' The unstressed sign FLIRT is made with contact at the thumbtips and with finger fluttering. In one stressed version, the flutter was deleted (as happens in several forms from the finger flutter category); this left *no* lexical movement, creating a derived Hold only form. However, geminated contact between the thumb tips did not occur and is judged unacceptable as a variant for this sign. Instead, contact continued to be treated as a location and was maintained throughout; the stressed form used the small repeated bouncing movement instead.

The differential treatment of contact in these cases is in concord with the notion that there there are two types of contact, (1) contact as place of formation, and (2) contact as part of the movement specification. Signs which allow geminated contact as part of their lexical forms are underlyingly specified for 'movement to contact,' while those that have continuous contact throughout the formation are underlyingly specified for contact as a *location* parameter. The ambiguity of this situation, which has created significant problems for ASL analysis, is demonstrated nicely by the sign MEASURE, which in certain cases treats contact as a location and in others as a movement specification. Thus, one form of MEASURE maintains thumbtip contact and bends one hand at the wrist (parallel to one of the FLIRT forms), but when MEASURE is inflected, as for example in the form meaning 'to measure all over,' the thumbs repeatedly move to contact while a circular path is made. Full specification of phonological processes and rules, their environments and constraints, and what types of crucial ordering (if any) exists, still need further investigation. The role that contact plays as shown by the stress data and the handshape prediction observations of Mandel (1982) illustrate the kinds of generalizations that remain to be uncovered.

Interesting interactions also exist between the phonology of ASL, the lexicon, and the representation of morphological information. ASL exhibits formal structuring at the same two levels as spoken languages (the internal structure of lexical units and the grammatical structure underlying sentences). One difference between ASL and spoken languages is in surface organization: signed languages tend to prefer co-occurring layered (as opposed to linear) organization. There is, however, evidence for sequential affixation as well in ASL (Newkirk, 1979, 1980, 1981; Wilbur, Klima, and Bellugi, 1983), which requires a linguistic analysis similar to those proposed for spoken languages. The simultaneous nature of ASL morphology has been widely discussed (Supalla and Newport 1978; Gee and Kegl 1982; McIntire 1980; Klima and Bellugi 1979; Wilbur 1979, 1982; Supalla 1982; Bellugi 1980; Bellugi and Klima 1982); this simultaneity is amenable to a multi-tiered treatment similar to that which McCarthy (1979, 1981) proposed for Semitic. Several pieces of signs are eligible for phonological or morphological treatment on separate tiers. Local movement carries the root meaning of many signs and may be spread across added path movement when inflections are built or under linguistic stress (however, it does not spread across added path suffixes such as the Continuative inflection). Some handshapes which may function as a separate morphological category for classifiers also probably warrant their own tier (see below), and may be spread across path movement and sequential path suffixes. It probably makes sense to talk about movement-bearing elements and handshape-bearing elements in ASL (and other signed languages). Other characteristics which are spread include contact, location, and orientation. However, it is not clear that these merit their own morphological tiers without falling prey to the criticisms leveled by Fox (1982) against McCarthy's Semitic analysis.

The phonological modifications that accompany inflections in ASL went unrecognized until just recently. A primary reason for this is that these phonological modifications do not always result in a separate, additional segment or syllable added to the beginning or end of a lexical item and thus were not easily identifiable. Signs were viewed as units that could be analyzed into several simultaneous parameters or primes (cf. earlier discussion). This type of analysis continued even after the inflections were identified and catalogued. As a result, inflections have been treated as *simultaneous* modifications. It is important to understand that the notion of *sequential* affixation does not necessarily imply two signs or two syllables, but is rather parallel to what happens in English when the past tense of a monosyllabic verb like 'walk' is produced. Although the past tense suffix is added to the end of 'walk,' the resulting form contains two morphemes but is still only one syllable, one phonological entity, one word. Newkirk (1979, 1980, 1981) in his analysis of the phonological structure of inflections argues for considering inflections such as Continuative, Multiple, Exhaustive, etc. to be, at least in part, sequential; some of these add a syllable to the lexical item, others do not. The Multiple inflection is formed by a smooth, sweeping arc which is added to the path movement of a verb (or after the local movement of a sign that does not have path movement). The last handshape of the verb (if there is more than one) spreads phonetically onto the arc. In BAWL-OUT [Multiple] (meaning 'to bawl out all of them'), the local movement of BAWL-OUT is also spread phonetically onto the suffix (this is *not* repetition of the local movement). Newkirk (1979, 1980, 1981) and Wilbur (1982; Wilbur, Klima, and Bellugi 1983) consider inflections like the Continuative to be two syllables, one primarily the lexical portion, the other the suffix. Inflections like the Continuative (which adds an elliptical path movement to a sign) show spreading of the handshape onto the suffix, but not spreading of the local movement.

This supports the suggestion that handshape spreading is a phonological process in ASL (across morpheme/syllable boundaries) while local movement spreading is merely phonetic. One can also consider the subsequent repetitions of the reduplicated inflections (Continuative, Durative, Iterative, etc.) to be suffixes using the model of sequential affixation proposed by Marantz (1982) for reduplication in spoken languages.

Wilbur, Klima, and Bellugi (1983) argued for phonological layering in ASL. Following the theory of word structure presented in Selkirk (1982), distinctions were made between the root and word levels. The separation of root and word level affixation utilizes the distinction between path movement (word level) and local movement (root level). Another phonological distinction exists between the inflection processes which modify the *rhythmic and dynamic* qualities of the movement (and which serve to modify the meaning of the predicate itself; Wilbur, 1982) and those that modify the *spatial characteristics* of the movement (and which function to modify the arguments of the predicate).

Not all of the phonological separations involve movement. Another separation is for handshapes that serve as classifiers (Kegl and Wilbur 1976; Supalla 1978, 1982; McDonald 1982; Wilbur, Bernstein, and Kantor 1985). These classifiers may function as the Theme (Gee and Kegl 1982) or as the central object (Supalla 1982) of the predicates which allow classifier substitution (those in the productive lexicon), as well as the secondary object or base hand. They form a separate morphological tier and because they occur simultaneously with other root morphemes, they can easily be spread onto handshape-bearing pieces of sign syllables (Wilbur 1982, 1985) and sequential affixes (Newkirk 1979, 1980, 1981).

To say that there is phonological layering is to claim that there are restrictions on basic lexical items, derived forms, and inflected forms. These restrictions may be illustrated as follows:

(1) In the lexicon, basic lexical entries do not make distinctive use of available modifications of *manner* of movement (rhythmic and dynamic qualities). That is, in the lexicon, there are no semantically unrelated minimal pairs which differ only in that one is tense and the other is lax. Similarly, there are no unrelated pairs in the lexicon that differ only in that one of the pair is restrained in manner of production while the other is not. Also, there are no unrelated pairs which differ only that one is reduplicated and the other is not. These phonological characteristics are reserved for morphological purposes.

(2) In the lexicon, basic lexical entries do not make distinctive use of *particular points* in space (as opposed to the body). That is, while two signs, such as APPLE and ONION, may differ only in the location on the face where they are made (ONION near the eye, APPLE on the cheek), there are no minimal pairs of basic lexical entries which differ only in that they are made at two distinct points in space (whether it is starting point, ending point, or location where the entire sign is made).

(3) In the lexicon, basic lexical entries do not make distinctive use of *directions*

in space (as opposed to the body or hands). There are no signs which require a particular direction of movement, except for paired opposites: IN/OUT, JOIN/QUIT, APPEAR/DISAPPEAR, IMPROVE/GET-WORSE, and, of course, UP/DOWN. That is, if a sign has distinct meaningful direction (it would be judged incorrect by a native signer if made without that particular direction), then its opposite should be an existing meaningful sign.

(4) Root level derivational processes affect *local* movement (or add local movement).

(5) Word level derivational and inflectional processes affect the *path* movement (or add one). In addition, they can modify (or add) various *rhythmic* and *spatial* characteristics, such as features of manner of movement, spatial location, orientation, arrangement, and direction (which are apparently excluded from being distinctive in the lexicon).

Thus, much as consonants and vowels appear to be morphologically separated in Semitic, various phonological characteristics (some segments, some features) in ASL are reserved for particular morphological functions. Mechanisms such as separate tiers and spreading of features within and across syllables provide a convenient notation for recording the relationships between the morphological component and the phonological component.

We can see then that for ASL it is possible to apply profitably the basic methods and goals of generative phonology and more recent formulations of autosegmental phonology to the study of sign language structure. We have problems in determining the basic phonemes, arguments over the types of distinctive features to be used, characterization of phonological rules which relate basic and derived forms, redundancy conditions which specify the unmarked values of certain features of handshape and orientation based on the point of contact, suggestions of the nature of the structure of syllables, tier structure, spreading, and, perhaps a unique feature of signed languages, phonological separation for morphological and lexical purposes. This theoretically directed progress in phonology is not matched by similar progress in the area of syntactic structure. Rather, the progress which has been made in describing the sentence patterns of ASL has been obtained in spite of current approaches to syntax, instead of as a result of them.

3. *Morphosyntax*

Looking now at the morphological and syntactic structure of ASL, we see that the nature of ASL sentence structure, to the extent that it has been studied, is not readily amenable to transformational grammar or any related theory in which word order and movement rules play a major role. Transformational rules, as originally separated from phrase structure rules, were context-dependent rules which had the power to add elements to a string, delete elements from a string, modify elements within a string, and move elements around within a string.

Since the advent of Relational Grammar, which focused on the modifications of grammatical relations independent of the surface syntactic manifestation in any language, it has become more apparent that of the four roles of transformational rules, the primary one is that of movement, after which the other functions follow. For example, in going from the active to the passive, the primary change is the movement of direct object into subject position and the demotion of the subject to the *by* phrase (case marked for agent but no longer bearing a major grammatical relation to the verb). After this has happened, a recent version of Chomsky's theory maintains, constraints on allowable surface structures see to it that the correct form of the verb *be* is inserted, the main verb is morphologically marked to the past participle, and the *by* is inserted before the demoted subject. Thus, the revised version of the passive rule serves only to move the noun phrase from direct object into subject position. Everything else, which was formerly handled by the transformational rule itself, now is handled by separate output constraints or filters. When these other functions are removed from the transformations, the central role of transformations as movement rules is revealed, namely to move either noun phrases or wh-words into the appropriate position in the sentence. Thus, by 1976, Chomsky needed only two transformations: 1) move NP, and 2) move WH. These were collapsed the following year into a single rule, move alpha, where alpha was a variable which ranged over movable elements.

There are a few cases in the structure of ASL in which it makes sense to talk about syntax from a transformational perspective. Fischer (1974) notes that Ross's (1967) coordinate structure constraint and complex NP constraint are operative in ASL. (The sentential subject constraint awaits the determination of whether there are sentential subjects.) There also appears to be topicalization in ASL for noun phrases, verb phrases, and possibly whole sentences. In keeping with the suggestion concerning topicalization in most languages made by Creider (1979), Givón (1979), Li and Thompson (1976), Keenan (1976), and others, the topicalization rule in ASL moves the topicalized element to the left, into sentence initial position. Fischer and Gough (1972) postulate a rule of EQUI-NP deletion for ASL, while O'Malley (1975) argues that in fact there are two EQUI rules, one which operates essentially the same as English (and may in fact be a borrowing from English) and the other which is restricted so that it does not apply in sentences with auxiliaries, modals, and negatives. Without using the term 'EQUI,' Padden (1980) discusses constraints on three different types of complement structures. In one type, the relevant constraint of coreferentiality òf the matrix direct object and the arguments of the embedded verb can much more easily be stated in terms of Relational Grammar than in transformational or case grammar.

To look further for other transformational rules is probably a futile exercise. Unlike English which depends very heavily on word order for the expression of grammatical relations, ASL is an inflected language, which uses modification of movement for derivational and inflectional morphology, and for syntactic purposes (Wilbur, Klima, and Bellugi 1983). In addition, the face and head may convey grammatical information simultaneously with the production of the manual sign. Thus, while transformational grammar suggests that we should be looking at the sequence of signs within the sentence for evidence of syntactic transformations, ASL behaves as an inflected language in which word order is relatively (but not completely) unimportant and in which information that may be sequential in some spoken languages is presented simultaneously instead.

The original search for basic word order in ASL cannot be blamed entirely on transformational grammar, because the question of basic word order is relevant to typologies of language and language universals, independent of particular theories. A considerable amount of controversy surrounded the word-order issue, as different researchers used different data (monologues, conversations, metalinguistic judgments) and different analyses to arrive at their conclusions (Fischer 1975; Friedman 1976b; Edge and Herrmann 1977; Lacy 1974; Kegl 1976). What was missing was a complete understanding of the role of positions in space as inflectional markers for verb agreement. Verbs can be started and ended at different points in space (or oriented towards different points in space) to indicate particular grammatical relations. Extensive use of inflection in space eliminates the need to repeat the participants involved, either in noun form or in pronominal form. Thus, a conversation might begin by establishing the participants through the use of explicit noun phrases, locating these participants at specific points in space. Subsequent to this establishment, the antecedents may be referred to through verb agreement, as well as a variety of other pronominal devices which may be simultaneous with the verb sign. In a situation such as this, word order is not a primary strategy for indicating grammatical relations. Instead, the role of word order varies according to a general principle identified by Kegl (1976), which has been termed the Flexibility Condition: The more arguments the verb agrees with, the freer the word order may be.

Although signs do occur in sequence, and the specific sequence may be important in certain circumstances, the simultaneous presentation of grammatical and morphological information must be emphasized again. The verb sign is itself multimorphemic. Klima and Bellugi (1979) have shown that a single predicate may be morphologically inflected to include information on temporal aspect (accomplished through modification of the motion, as discussed earlier); distributional aspect (for *each, certain ones, all over, all around,* and others); number inflections for singular, dual, trial, and plural, temporal focus (*starting to, gradually,* etc.); and reciprocal reference (*each other*). This simultaneous presentation of information involves an ingenious blending of one vs. two hands; modification of speed of signing, path of signing, number of repetitions of the sign, manner of production of the sign (restrained, forceful, etc.); repetitions in horizontal or vertical planes; repetitions in straight line paths, circular paths, or arcing paths; differences in direction of movement or of the repetitions themselves; and other geometrical, dynamic, or qualitative characteristics (Klima and Bellugi 1979; Wilbur, Klima, and Bellugi 1983). (Although we speak of this information as simultaneously presented, it should be pointed out that this is referring to the use of a single sign to carry all the information; within the sign itself, there is sequentiality of presentation as discussed earlier.)

Finally, no discussion of the simultaneous presentation of information in ASL would be complete without at least a brief description of the role of head and facial expression. Certain lexical items have specific facial expressions which accompany them. Certain other facial expressions may serve as adjectives or adverbial phrases, accompanying nouns or verbs respectively. Still other facial expressions and positions of the head may mark specific syntactic structures, such as questions, negatives, topicalizations, gapped constructions, and others which would be interpreted with the copula in English, and some subordinate constructions (Baker-Schenk 1983).

An adequate theory of ASL syntax would have to take into account the extensive system of inflections, verb agreement, classifiers, and concurrent facial expressions and head positions. In addition, Coulter (1979) has argued that ASL is topic prominent in the sense of Li and Thompson (1976). Further, the evidence points in the direction of a discourse-based rather than sentence-based grammar, given tense and aspect marking, and the use of referential devices such as classifiers and verb agreement without mandatory repetition on the antecedent noun phrases after their initial establishment (cf. Friedman 1976b; Kegl 1976, 1978; Kegl, Lentz, and Philip 1976; Kegl and Wilbur 1976; Wilbur and Petitto 1981, 1983). Thus, an adequate theory will have to account for processes which do not depend entirely on word order or necessarily on the sequential presentation of information (which is after all only the surface coding and therefore language specific) and which can handle structures in units larger than sentences, preferably discourse narratives or conversations and paragraphs. Such a theory would have to account for ASL structure, as well as for the structure of spoken languages. The contribution which sign language linguists make to linguistic theory is to identify the problems which have to be solved. Ideally, the contribution which theoretical linguists will make to sign language research (as well as research on other languages) would be to solve the problems.

REFERENCES

Baker-Schenk, C. 1983. *A Microanalysis of the Non-manual Components of Questions in American Sign Language*. Unpublished dissertation, University of California at Berkeley.
Battison, R. 1973. "Phonology in American Sign Language: 3-D and digitvision." Presented at the California Linguistic Association Conference, Stanford, CA.
Battison, R. 1974. "Phonological deletion in American Sign Language." *Sign Language Studies* 5, pp. 1–19.
Battison, R. H., Markowicz, and J. Woodward 1975. "A good rule of thumb: Variable phonology in American Sign Language." In: R. Shuy and R. Fasold (eds.), *New Ways of Analyzing Variation in English II*. Washington, DC: Georgetown University Press, pp. 100–50.

Bellugi, U. 1980. "The structuring of language: Clues from the similarities between signed and spoken language." In U. Bellugi and M. Studdert-Kennedy (eds.) *Signed and Spoken Language: Biological Constraints on Linguistic Form.* Weinheim/Deerfield Beach, FL: Verlag Chemie, 115–140.

Bellugi, U., and E. Klima 1982. "The acquisition of three morphological systems in American Sign Language." *Papers and Reports on Child Language Development* 21, pp. K1–35.

Boyes-Braem, P. 1981. *Significant Features of the Handshape in ASL.* Unpublished dissertation, University of California at Berkeley.

Chao, Y. 1934. "The non-uniqueness of phonemic solutions of phonetic systems." *Bulletin of the Institute of Historical Philology, Academia Sinica* 4, pp. 363–97.

Chinchor, N. 1978. "The syllable in ASL." Presented at the MIT Sign Language Symposium, Cambridge, MA.

Chomsky, N. 1964. "Current issues in linguistics." In J. Fodor and J. Katz (eds.), *The Structure of Language: Readings in the Philosophy of Language.* Englewood Cliffs, NJ: Prentice-Hall, pp. 50–118.

Coulter, G. 1979. *American Sign Language Typology.* Unpublished dissertation, University of California at San Diego.

Creider, C. 1979. "On the explanation of transformations." In: T. Givón (ed.), *Syntax and Semantics,* Vol. 12. *Discourse and Syntax.* New York: Academic Press, pp. 3–21.

Edge, V., and L. Herrmann 1977. "Verbs and the determination of subject in American Sign Language." In: L. Friedman (ed.), *On the Other Hand.* New York: Academic Press, pp. 137–80.

Fischer, S. 1974. "Sign language and linguistic universals." In *Proceedings of the Franco-German Conference on French Transformational Grammar.* Berlin: Athaenium.

Fischer, S. 1975. "Influences on word order change in ASL." In: C. Li (ed), *Word Order and Word Order Change.* Austin, TX: University of Texas Press, pp. 1–25.

Fischer, S., and B. Gough 1972. "Some unfinished thoughts on FINISH." Working paper, Salk Institute for Biological Studies, La Jolla, CA.

Fox, S. 1982. "Autosegmental phonology and Semitic." *CLS* 18, pp. 131–139.

Friedman, L. 1976a. *Phonology of a Soundless Language.* Unpublished dissertation, University of California at Berkeley.

Friedman, L. 1976b. "The manifestation of subject, object, and topic in American Sign Language." In: C. Li (ed.), *Subject and Topic.* New York: Academic Press, pp. 125–48.

Friedman, L. 1977. *On the Other Hand: New Perspectives on American Sign Language.* New York: Academic Press.

Frishberg, N. 1978. "The case of the missing length." *Communication and Cognition* 11, pp. 57–68.

Gee, J., and J. Kegl 1982. "Semantic perspicuity and the locative hypothesis: Implications for acquisition." *Journal of Education* 164, pp. 185–209.

Givón, T. 1979. "From discourse to syntax: Grammar as a processing strategy." In: T. Givón (ed.), *Syntax and Semantics,* Vol. 12. *Discourse and Syntax.* New York: Academic Press, pp. 81–117.

Hockett, C. 1942. "A system of descriptive phonology." *Language* 18, pp. 3–21.

Hockett, C. 1948. "Implications of Bloomfield's Algonquian studies." *Language* 24, pp. 117–31.

Hockett, C. 1954. "Two models of grammatical description." *Word* 10, pp. 210–31.

Keenan, E. 1976. "Towards a universal definition of subject." In C. Li (ed.), *Subject and Topic.* New York: Academic Press, pp. 304–33.

Kegl, J. 1976. "Pronominalization in American Sign Language." Unpublished manuscript, MIT.

Kegl, J. 1978. "Indexing and phononominalization in ASL." Unpublished manuscript, MIT.

Kegl, J., E. Lentz, and M. Philip 1976. "ASL pronouns and conditions on their use." Presented at the Summer Meeting, Linguistic Society of America, Oswego, NY.

Kegl, J., and R. Wilbur 1976. "When does structure stop and style begin? Syntax, morphology, and phonology vs. stylistic variation in American Sign Language." *CLS* 12, pp. 376–96.

Klima, E., and U. Bellugi 1979. *The Signs of Language*. Cambridge, MA: Harvard University Press.

Lacy, R. 1974. "Putting some of the syntax back into semantics." Presented at the Annual Meeting, Linguistic Society of America, New York.

Lane, H., P. Boyes-Braem, and U. Bellugi 1976. "Preliminaries to a distinctive feature analysis of handshapes in ASL." *Cognitive Psychology* 8, pp. 263–89.

Li, C., and S. Thompson 1976. "Subject and topic: A new typology of language." In: C. Li (ed.), *Subject and Topic*. New York: Academic Press, pp. 458–89.

Liddell, S. 1982. "Sequentiality in American Sign Language signs." Presented at the Summer Meeting, Linguistic Society of America, College Park, MD.

Liddell, S. 1984. "THINK and BELIEVE: Sequentiality in American Sign Language." *Language* 60, pp. 372–99.

Mandel, M. 1982. "Prediction of the Base Handshape from Point of Contact." Unpublished manuscript, Northeastern University.

Marantz, A. 1982. "Re reduplication." *Linguistic Inquiry* 13, pp. 435–482.

McCall, E. 1965. *A Generative Grammar of Sign*. Unpublished master's thesis, University of Iowa.

McCarthy, J. 1979. *Formal problems in Semitic phonology and morphology*. Unpublished doctoral dissertation, MIT.

McCarthy, J. 1981. "A prosodic theory of nonconcatenative morphology." *Linguistic Inquiry* 12, pp. 373–418.

McDonald, B. 1982. *Aspects of American Sign Language Predicate System*. Unpublished dissertation, State University of New York at Buffalo.

McIntire, M. 1980. *Locatives in American Sign Language*. Unpublished doctoral dissertation, UCLA.

Miller, G., and P. Nicely 1955. "An analysis of perceptual confusions among some English consonants." *Journal of the Acoustical Society of America* 27, pp. 339–52.

Newkirk, D. 1979. *The form of the continuative aspect on ASL verbs*. Unpublished manuscript, The Salk Institute for Biological Studies.

Newkirk, D. 1980. *Rhythmic features of inflection in American Sign Language*. Unpublished manuscript, The Salk Institute for Biological Studies.

Newkirk, D. 1981. *On the temporal segmentation of movement in American Sign Language*. Unpublished manuscript, The Salk Institute for Biological Studies.

O'Malley, P. 1975. "The grammatical function of indexic reference in American Sign Language." Unpublished manuscript, Research, Development, and Demonstration Center in Education of the Handicapped, University of Minnesota.

Padden, C. 1980. "Complement structures in American Sign Language." Unpublished manuscript, University of California at San Diego.

Ross, J. 1967. *Constraints on Variables in Syntax*. Unpublished dissertation, MIT.

Sapir, E. 1925. "Sound patterns in language." *Language* 1, pp. 37–51.

Selkirk, E. 1982. *The Syntax of Words* (Linguistic Inquiry Monograph No. 7). Cambridge, MA: MIT Press.

Siple, P. 1978. *Understanding Language Through Sign Language Research*. New York: Academic Press.

Stokoe, W. 1960. *Sign Language Structure: An Outline of the Visual Communication System of the American Deaf*. Studies in Linguistics Occasional Papers 8.

Stokoe, W., D. Casterline, and C. Croneberg 1965. *Dictionary of American Sign Language*. Washington, DC: Gallaudet College. Revised ed.: Silver Spring, MD: Linstok Press, 1976.

Supalla, T. 1978. "Morphology of verbs of motion and location in American Sign Language." In F. Caccamise (ed.), *National Symposium on Sign Language Research and Teaching*. Silver Spring, MD: National Association of the Deaf.

Supalla, T., and E. Newport 1978. "How many seats in a chair? The derivation of nouns and verbs in American Sign Language." In P. Siple (ed.), *Understanding Language Through Sign Language Research*. New York: Academic Press.

Swadesh, M. 1934. "The phonemic principle." *Language* 10, pp. 117–29.

Swadesh, M., and C. Vogelin 1939. "A problem of phonological alternation." *Language* 15, pp. 1–10.

Twaddell, W. 1935. *On Defining the Phoneme. Language Monograph* 16.

Wilbur, R. 1978. "On the notion of derived segments in American Sign Language." *Communication and Cognition* 11, pp. 79–104.

Wilbur, R. 1979. *American Sign Language and Sign Systems.* Baltimore, MD: University Park Press.

Wilbur, R. 1981. "The cognitive reality of segmental phonology: Discussant's comments." In: T. Meyers, J. Laver, and J. Anderson (eds.), *The Cognitive Representation of Speech.* Amsterdam: North Holland, pp. 373–4.

Wilbur, R. 1982. "A multi-tiered syllable structure for American Sign Language." Presented at the Annual Meeting, Linguistic Society of America, San Diego.

Wilbur, R. B. 1985. "Towards a theory of "syllable" in signed languages: Evidence from the numbers of Italian Sign Language." In W. Stokoe and V. Volterra (eds.), *Sign Language, 1983.* Silver Spring, MD: Linstok Press.

Wilbur, R. B., M. Bernstein, and R. Kantor 1985. The semantic domain of classifiers in American Sign Language. *Sign Language Studies* 46, pp. 1–38.

Wilbur R., and S. B. Nolen 1984. "The duration of syllables in American Sign Language." Presented to the American Speech-Language-Hearing Association, San Francisco.

Wilbur, R., E. Klima, and U. Bellugi 1983. "Roots: The search for the origins of signs in ASL." CLS 19, pp. 314–36.

Wilbur, R., and L. Menn 1975. "Towards a redefinition of psychological reality: On the internal structure of the lexicon." *San Jose State Occasional Papers* 2, pp. 212–21.

Wilbur, R., and L. Petitto 1981. "How to know a conversation when you see one." *Journal of the National Speech-Language-Hearing Association* 9, pp. 66–81.

Wilbur, R., and L. Pettito 1983. "Discourse structure of American Sign Language conversations." *Discourse Processes* 6, pp. 225–41.

Woodward, J. 1973. *Implicational Lects on the Deaf Diglossic Continuum.* Unpublished dissertation, Georgetown University.

PART THREE
SOCIETAL USAGE

CHAPTER NINE

Folk Natural History: Crossroads of Language, Culture, and Environment

Myrdene Anderson

1. Introduction

I am fortunate to be straddling three disciplines, each plugging into the same real world through data collection in fieldwork settings, sustaining at the same time a body of potentially interlocking theory with implications extending far beyond the ranges of the disciplines themselves. These three disciplines are linguistics, anthropology, and ecology, which key into the three subject matters indexed in the title: language, culture, and environment.

The initial contributions to folk natural history, in its own recent and self-conscious history, concerned the methodology of data collection, the epistemology justifying that methodology frequently not made explicit. I will introduce the issues associated with the development of this hybrid discipline, before analyzing certain of my own data from the Saami language and culture of Norwegian Lapland.

Besides such methodological and theoretical issues, there are two pairs of cross-cutting but complementary foci to such research respecting the holistic character of systems. First, natural history as concentrated, classified knowledge is a tool in the *population's* management of environmental *energy resources*, and as such relates to cultural survival. Secondly, folk classification in general accesses certain principles of the relationships between human language and cognition, while folk natural history or folk natural science, as a specific genre of folk classification, is the basis for the *individual's* management of cultural *information resources*.

2. The Nature of Natural History

Natural history comprises the knowledge about the natural environment held by a set of people sharing a cultural and linguistic tradition. This knowledge grounds folk science for all societies, having a tactical imperative on a par with that of social relations. The degree to which folk natural science is general rather than specialized reflects the division of labor in a society, the extent to which knowledge is consciously systematized and how it is transmitted, and the intimacy of individual transactions with the natural environment. Knowledge transmitted orally may more directly reflect cognitive constraints.

This natural environment is the ultimate source of energy for population survival, and also teems with information for interpreting the past and predicting the future in culturally meaningful ways. The subject matter of folk natural history only starts with resource classification, utilization, and beliefs. The dynamic physical and mental relationships between a human population and its cultural-cum-ecologic setting cannot be meaningfully captured by a catalogue, however comprehensive.

Folk natural science is scarcely a less interesting object of study in a large-scale industrial society where nature is remote or even unnatural, for the attributes of plants and animals which render them convenient handles for linguistic study remain the same. Macroscopic biota in any ecological setting may seem infinite in number but occur in a finite number of groupings made up of discrete organisms reproducing their own kind and moreover sharing bundles of traits. In each language, such discontinuities lend themselves to classification and labeling. The system of Latin binomials in the scientific language of biology is in fact a static nomenclatural convention deriving from the patterns of Indo-European folk science since conformed within a taxonomy to reflect, insofar as possible, the nature of relationships between taxa by virtue of partially shared (and partially reconstructed) evolutionary histories.

Anthropologists and linguists concerned with universal principles of classification of lexical items can best cope with domains having unambiguous boundaries and internal arrangements, such as those characterizing flora, fauna, pronouns, and kinship, or with some combination of the physical properties of the objects of classification and the perceptual abilities of the classifiers, as for color. Other environmental phenomena, such as the meteorologic and geologic, have fewer natural spatial and temporal discontinuities, and both folk and academic classifications appear more arbitrary.

In each case, recurring cross-linguistic structural and developmental patterns underlying classification reflect interesting constraints on human perception and cognition, while varied structures from language to language may relate to discontinuities in the objective universe, to cultural foci, and to the concatenation of language, culture, and cognition.

3. The History of Natural History

3.1. Temporal backdrop

Folk natural history has been pursued—deliberately and incidentally, as an end and as a means—by hunters, farmers, and curers, by naturalists, missionaries, and museum curators, up to the twentieth century, and also by biologists, an-

Table 1.   Some Terms Useful in Discussing Folk Classification

Segregate—an aggregate of objects terminologically distinguished

Lexeme—a lexical label designating a segregate

Domain—the total range of meanings subsumed under a particular folk segregate

Contrast Set—an array of mutually exclusive segregates which occur in the same cultural context and thus share at least one defining feature

Taxonomy—the hierarchical organization of contrast sets by class inclusion

Paradigm—the multidimensional structure of a set of segregates related by feature intersection rather than by hierarchic class inclusion

Component—one of a pair or more of contrasting semantic features serving to differentiate closely related folk taxa

Nomenclature—a terminological system

thropologists, and linguists since then. During the past decades, and particularly in the United States and France, a distinctive specialty has emerged conversant with the issues, methods, and theory in both the natural and social sciences.

As this field established a firm foothold in anthropology two decades ago, major journals commenced organizing whole issues around folk classification (*American Anthropologist* 1964, 1965; *American Ethnologist* 1976, 1981), and some special-interest periodicals have emerged (e.g., *Folk Classification Bulletin* in 1977, becoming *The Journal of Ethnobiology* in 1981). Most published research continues to be embedded in monographs or dispersed through the hundreds of journals addressed to various less focused audiences; this has definite advantages, especially that of inhibiting the fixation of unfortunate jargon.

As it happened, the adaptive radiation into this disparately colonized, interdisciplinary approach spawned a technical vocabulary (Table 1) which has outlived many of the labels describing the approach itself, such as 'folk science,' 'ethnoscience,' 'emics,' 'ethnographic semantics,' 'formal ethnography,' 'formal semantics,' and 'componential analysis,' to mention a few terms specifically or generically coined. The current best cover term is perhaps 'cognitive anthropology,' while the least felicitous may well be 'the new ethnography.'

I will presently survey some of the expansions, contractions, and changing orientations of this discipline; first, some review of the historical antecedents to the study of folk natural history may be useful.

3.2.   Investigational biases

In the West, particularly from the age of discovery onwards, the exposure to new cultures resulted in haphazard and often disparaging notions. Exotic plants and animals, even human beings, were brought to the courts and academic centers of Europe for scrutiny.

As their discipline emerged, anthropologists attempted to be more systematic and less biased, but at the outset they focused on the artifactual products of a culture to the exclusion of ideas. These concrete items could be objectively manipulated, drawn, described, observed in manufacture and use, designated by indigenous terms, and, sometimes, acquired by the ethnographer for museum specimens.

Even such documentation tended to be uneven. The exotic in plant and animal forms and the esoteric in local practices were often emphasized at the expense of the mundane and routine. Comprehensive closure, treating all beliefs and practices and all environmental forms, was rarely a consideration.

Moreover, surveying the products of ethnobiological study, one is struck by the variables not accounted for by historical trends in the discipline, but which instead are patterned as follows. Compared with ethnozoology, ethnobotany has been the more frequent undertaking in any geographical area and is characteristically carried out with greater breadth. This is most noticeably the case in the wet tropics and subtropics. It can be explained by reference to biases of investigators and investigations, regional floras and faunas, and, most of all, to the character of cultural relationships with the different biotic forms.

Biases in investigations and by investigators are only partially predicated upon the styles in ethnobiological research. Naturally, the earliest data were unattested and often ambiguous descriptions of plant and animal utilization. Even later ethnobiological data were often restricted to specimens collected without adequate precision as to their identity, provenience, and sociocultural context.

Botanists and laypersons have exhaustively collected plants as herbarium specimens. Animals do not lead themselves so readily to this type of study and preservation. Consequently, perhaps, over the centuries it has been easier for some botanists to maintain catholic interests in natural history (e.g., Linné), while zoologists have tended to be specialists in at most a few forms or families (e.g., Darwin). This being the case, it follows that botanists more frequently engage in team projects.

Ethnobiological work by persons trained in botany is apt to comprise a comprehensive survey of human-floral relationships. Ethnozoological studies tend to focus on one or more animal types, whether or not they are central in the cultural setting. Anthropologists themselves tend to document culturally important forms at the expense of seemingly peripheral and nonutilized ones, even though all biota play roles in the larger ecological system.

Complementary work by different sorts of specialists, as individuals or in teams, can only partially compensate for uneven ethnobiological documentation, as the dynamic whole will always exceed the sum of its parts. Still, a comprehensive folk botany or folk zoology is, taken singly, itself an enormous research undertaking. The rewards of some balance between detail (often generated by a fine-tuned methodology) and comprehensiveness (dictated by and feeding back

Table 2. Aspects of Field Investigation of Saami Folk Natural History

Ecologic Domain	Linguistic Domain	Socioeconomic Domain
	Data Collection	
biota, terrain, weather . . . collections; photographs; descriptions; identifications spatiotemporal distributions cycles and trends phylogenetic, environmental, and coevolutionary relationships	local common names lexical borrowing contexts and frames of reference segregate relationships encoded: static—type or part; dynamic—stage or food chain	differential knowledge and use by age, sex, occupation . . . circulation of information in space and through time decisions in resource management inventories of economic and other goods recording of recollected uses and techniques photographs of actual natural resources and their preparation recording of related belief systems
	Analysis and Interpretation	
regulatory factors in species diversity and density optimum conditions for resource production reconstruction of introduced and colonizing species impact of radioactivity load	accounting of unnoticed and of unnamed but recognized species and phenomena differentiae in organization of folk ecological concepts stability and change in certain adaptively significant categories	stability and change in documented historic knowledge, use, beliefs, and techniques related to management of energy and information structure, function, and dynamics of ecosystem arising from: conscious decision patterns reflecting short-term and long-term means and ends; other human action, inaction, and premises, including governmental; other species interactions

into a body of theory) encouraged me to envision an ethnoecological study which would not, by fiat, exclude any aspect of a people's environmental experience. It seemed to me that attitudes of environmental apathy and explicit disinterest must complement those of fascination and expertise. My plan for tackling the folk natural history of Saami-speakers in arctic Fennoscandia appears verbatim in the outline in Table 2. In retrospect, this synopsis adequately highlights the actual field research, except that it was in no wise so finite.

3.3. Geographical patterns

In general, macroscopic and utilizable plant forms outnumber faunal types in biomes from pole to pole. Polar faunas, however, include relatively more large forms than are found in temperate and tropical zones, while polar plants are reduced in both number and size. Botanists have been drawn to the tropics by their profuse exotic floras. Numerous tropical plants propagate vegetatively rather than sexually, creating clones of genetically identical plants. Many cases of deliberate plant dispersals have taken place with shoots and tubers rather than with seed crops; these clones can sometimes be traced over great distances. Successive somatic mutations within a clone line offer still more evidence for the ethnobotanist pinning down the direction and order of plant and human migrations. (See Reed 1977; Ucko and Dimbleby 1969; Yen 1974.)

The tropics and subtropics continue to attract the ethnobotanist. Tropical ethnozoology may be neglected, except symbolically, but perhaps this is not so serious considering the tropical cultivator's attention to plants. In temperate regions, as for North American Indian groups, ethnobiology is well represented, much of it arising through salvage anthropology. Arctic ethnobiology is, by comparison, under-studied, botanically and zoologically, and the more general folk ecology is embedded in monograph treatments of whole cultural groups. The not surprising variable explaining much of this mosaic may be the Western investigator's unconsciously equating tropics and comfort, while assuming that an arctic setting harbors discomfort, hardship, and dark-season stress.

The folk science of animal-dominated subsistence systems, particularly those of temperate and arctic hunters and pastoralists, has not attracted the study it deserves. Such ethnoecology may be interestingly balanced between ethnozoology and ethnobotany, inasmuch as the animals exploited are dependent on plant forage.

The feasibility of investigating a comprehensive body of folk scientific knowledge of a pastoral society in the arctic led me to the Saami of Lapland. The reindeer-breeding members of this society manage livestock dependent during the critical winter season on lichens—small cryptogamic plants adversely affected by overgrazing, trampling, fire, and radioactive fallout. I anticipated that the marginal arctic setting, and the socioeconomic pursuits so overwhelmingly shaped by the milieu, would demonstrably channel terminological attention, and that this linguistic system would feed back into the resource management and belief systems.

3.4. Human-environment interactions

Any cultural group will be at least indirectly dependent on plant resources because of their place in the food chain as photosynthetic energy converters. In terms of animal use, as distinguished from animal belief systems, some human groups may have no ethnozoology; but all groups use plants, directly and indirectly, as food and for raw materials.

Plants and animals differentially lend themselves to classification and study, for the folk scientist and for the academic one. Plants are rooted and can be studied in situ or collected for study and use. Growth of individual forms can be observed and tends not to be segmented into unrecognizable stages of dimorphic sexes.

Human interference in the breeding patterns of plants and animals is responsible for numerous morphologically, contextually, and behaviorally distinct new forms, especially in the case of plant crops. Sometimes such varietal forms receive separate or derivative labels marking them off from the more common or original type.

Often biotic forms are discriminated by reference to features other than morphological ones. Context, associations, and, for animals, behavior may be criterial. Thus it appears that species-specific bird calls may make ornithological names unusually comparable at the lower taxonomic levels, both between languages as labels and between any one language's system and Linnean classification. Sometimes a people believes that its names for birds are linguistic renderings of the calls themselves. Any such onomatopoeia operating in several languages is unlikely to result in similar names, but may well produce clusters of bird names with comparable syllabic or iterative patterning, such as for 'cuckoo.' (See Berlin and O'Neill 1981.)

The bilateral symmetry and internal organs shared by humans and other vertebrates foster analogic terminologies for some segregate partitions encoded by a language and provide a basis for comparison between languages. Although the hinges of limbs may bound segregates in a partonomy, it appears that at earlier stages in the development of a lexicon, systematic polysemy may be the rule. Widespread polysemies for hand/arm and foot/leg (Witkowski and Brown 1982) and for eye/face and seed/fruit (Brown and Witkowski 1983) are as pervasive as the wood/tree polysemy in two-thirds of the world's languages (Witkowski, Brown, and Chase 1981). Alongside hypotheses emphasizing cognitive, cultural, and ecological salience underlying such patterning, other part-whole relationships may segment arbitrarily but consistently across a set of forms, aided by metaphor.

Although animal structures for ingestion, digestion, circulation, and respiration are internal, the organs and their functions are generally understood and classified by any human group. Most functioning structures of plants, on the other hand, are microscopic and beyond the purview of the folk scientist.

Ethology shapes human-animal relationships, and especially human-mammal relationships. Overwhelmingly, animals figure in totemic taboo and mythology. Plants tend to be more pragmatically approached; a noteworthy exception is the case of hallucinogenic plants.

As will be discussed in the next section, ethnobiological nomenclatures dealing with small-sized forms may generate more complex labels than those for larger plants and animals. The latter may have lexically unique names not readily derived by etymological methods. At the same time, there is probably more analogic and metaphoric seepage of terminology from the zoological to the botanical domains than in the reverse; hence, a plant may have a foot before an animal has roots.

In general, plants are easier to control then animals, wild or tame, undomesticated or domesticated. However, other features of the environmental system, such as the physiographic and meteorologic, whether predictable or not, do not respond to other than magical interference. This gradation of features—by size, motility, predictability, and importance to subsistence—invites a holistic approach.

4.   The Science of Folk Natural Science

4.1.   Issues of identification, classification, and naming

At some level, all organisms classify, or perceive, significant external elements by similarities and differences as these relate to utility, circadian rhythms, and overall harmony. Classification carried out by humans must be rooted in phylogeny, shaped by natural selection operating on neurological pathways, even though much of human classification concerns the internal and cognitive. The types of classification most amenable to study are those linguistically encoded, but it is a mistake to lose sight of the iceberg for the tip.

Language itself automatically classifies. Individual phenomena may be labeled as unique tokens; but were this the rule, experience would be cumbersome and conditioned learning impossible. Instead, lexical items, or lexemes, label types or segregates sharing certain attributes, thereby streamlining experience into a manageable artifact of the human mind. When segregates (see the list of terms in Table 1) bear relationships to each other by virtue of real or perceived temporal sequence, developmental stages, parts to whole, degrees of intensity, by vertical class inclusion in a hierarachy, or by horizontal differentiation in a coordinate set (Table 3), these relationships may be reflected terminologically as well. The organization of the terminology will follow nomenclatural rules specifying how categories are named.

The processes of perception, classification, and labeling are further linked by cognitive processes. Hunn (1977:41) points out the essential component of identification of tokens belonging to a category, for this may involve either inductive or deductive criteria. General-purpose, descriptive, natural classifications of phenomena close to those that are perceptually distinguishable key into inductive criterial attributes. For the most part, folk and scientific classifications share these features. On the other hand, special-purpose, conceptually based classifications are deductive, relying on a priori defining attributes, as in the case of both folk and scientific theories. (See also Cain 1959; Gregg 1954; Werner and Fenton 1970.)

Table 3. Types of Explicit or Implicit Relationships between Units in a Classification*

Types of Identified or Implicit Relationships
class inclusion (type, kind)
spatial (part, location)
attributive (feature, evaluation)
function (purpose)
operation (object)
comparison (like)
exemplification (illustrated by)
provenience (comes from, made from)
contingency (if . . . , then)
grading (temporal—stage, sequence; spatial—proximity; conceptual—intensity, near salient state)
synonymy (substitutable by)
antonymy (means opposite of)

*Modified from Werner and Fenton (1970:564).

Objects classified by the organism must first be trapped by the neurophysiological sieve of perception. Saliencies are picked by the coarser mesh in the net; these perceptual saliencies are marked with respect to features important to survival, but unmarked with respect to related categories caught by the smaller-gauge mesh.

These patterns include the clearly hard-wired recognition of salient values of color, shape, size, number, location, incidence, and sequence. According to a widely held assumption, the ontogeny of these discriminations in language-learning mirrors their emergence in the phylogeny of a language. The best-documented domains include color perception and orientation in space and time.

The cross-linguistic study of basic color terms of extant and accessible languages by Berlin and Kay (1969) suggested a sequence for the lexical encoding of color terms in any language. Even though the methodology of this study leaves much to be desired, the results were unequivocal, and have since been reinforced by evidence from the neurophysiology of color vision (von Wattenwyl and Zollinger 1979), from other studies of color classification (Kay 1975), and from studies of nomenclatural patterns in general (Witkowski and Brown 1977).

Lexical criteria for color terms exclude all but opaque, nonmotivated forms. There were no languages in the sample with one single color term. A cover term for the domain 'color' was infrequently encountered. Briefly, color rests close to the perception pole of classification and identification, being organized along the dimensions of brightness and hue. Languages having two color terms with the

Figure 1A.   Universal Color Encoding Sequence. Color encoding sequence developed by Berlin and Berlin (1975), Kay (1975), and Kay and McDaniel (1975). Adapted from Witkowski and Brown (1977: 51).

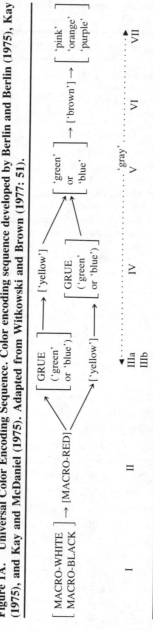

194

Figure 1B.   Universal Color Encoding Sequence. Binary distinctions pertaining to the encoding of (A) macro-black and macro-white, and (B) macro-red and white. Adapted from Witkowski and Brown (1977: 55).

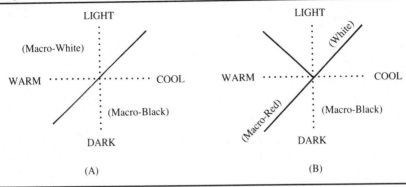

foci of 'black' and 'white' utilize extensions of these terms for all appropriate dark, cool colors and light, warm colors, respectively. Languages having three color terms code for 'black,' 'white,' and 'red.' The next color focus term is for 'yellow' or 'grue' ('green' or 'blue'), followed by the sequence illustrated in Figure 1 (Witkowski and Brown 1981). These researchers have extrapolated from the synchronic pattern a sequence for the development of the color lexicon in any single language; this is also shown in Figure 1. 'Red' is then the first hue to be distinguished in the history of a language.

As a color is based on physical properties of light and the neurophysiology of the receptor, it is a relatively orderly and bounded domain. Brown, Witkowski, and others at the Department of Anthropology of Northern Illinois University have convincingly applied these techniques to the multidimensional categories of folk botany, folk zoology, and folk classifications generally.

The lexical encoding sequences derived from implicational universals from the stock of color lexemes in extant languages have provided a qualitative yardstick for nomenclatural development to check on the reasonableness of reconstructed languages. In at least one such comparison involving the color lexicon formerly established for Proto-Polynesian, Proto-Miwok, and Proto-Mayan (Witkowski and Brown 1981), universal lexical encoding sequences suggest that these proto-languages have been over-reconstructed.

4.2.   Types of classification

Besides being either general purpose or special purpose, classification can be based on any number of relationships between categories, including all those listed in Table 3. A ubiquitous form for the classification of folk ecological, and perhaps other, knowledge is the taxonomy.

A taxonomy organizes taxa by vertical class inclusion in a hierarchy, while

Figure 2A.   Classification of Lexemes by Lexemic Form. Adapted from Conklin (1962: 122).

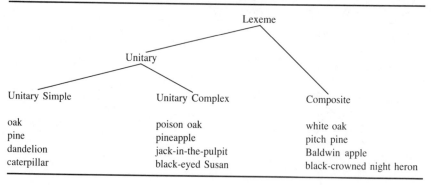

subordinate taxa of any class cluster in a mutually exclusive horizontal contrast set. (Table 1 lists these terms.) Some contrast sets can be analyzed as paradigms if their segregates can be differentiated by distinctive features. For example, in English, herbs, trees, and vines are all plants; they contrast on the dimensions of stem features 'woody'/'not woody' and 'erect'/'not erect.'

While many researchers are comfortable with folk scientific classifications arranged as taxonomies, some find the format procrustean when the categories are ghosts or automobiles (see Durrenberger and Morrison 1979; Van Esterik 1979). Even in folk biological classification, one encounters residual categories and fuzzy sets (e.g., Hunn 1977; Kay and McDaniel 1975).

Taxa in a taxonomy are labeled by lexemes according to nomenclatural rules having some cross-linguistic commonalities. Lexemes carry clues for placing them in appropriate taxonomic rank. Short, opaque, exocentric labels are called

Figure 2B.   Classification of Lexemes by Lexemic Form. Adapted from Berlin, Breedlove, and Raven (1974: 29).

	Lexeme		
	Primary		
	(Analyzable)		
(Unanalyzable)	Productive	Unproductive	Secondary
oak	plane tree	beggar-tick	jack oak
pine	pipe vine	cattail	oriental plane tree
tree	lead tree	poison oak	swamp beggar-tick
maple	crabgrass	jack-in-the-pulpit	blue spruce

'unitary simple' (Conklin 1962:122) or 'unanalyzable primary' (Berlin, Breedlove, and Raven 1974:29) lexemes (Figure 2).

There is virtual consensus that these root lexemes are psychologically salient, will be mentioned most frequently, and are learned first in ontogeny. These terms cluster at the generic rank in a folk taxonomy. The genus category has long fascinated biologists (e.g., Bartlett 1940; Cain 1956; Sokal 1974), even before its significance was properly appreciated.

Environmental, and cultural, genera leap out at us, demand names, and force their relationships on the overall organizations of our cognition. Lower-level taxa, such as species and varieties, often have labels derived through marking of the name for the genus or some other higher-level taxon. Conversely, the genus label may be used for higher-level taxa, such as life forms and unique beginners, by the process of extension. Tables 4 and 5 present a synopsis of these patterns.

The above summary of classificational principles and nomenclatural rules was developed to account for pervasive patterns found in ethnobiology, by Berlin, Breedlove, and Raven (1974), a field team combining expertise in botany, systematics, anthropology, and linguistics. Their investigations of Tzeltal plant classification were initiated some twenty years ago by Berlin. Conceptually, this work built on the principles suggested by earlier ethnobotanists (e.g., Conklin 1954; Bartlett 1940). Certain of these principles and rules have provoked more discussion than others; Hunn (1977), for example, has suggested refinements,

Table 4.   Principles of Folk Biological Classification*

(1)   All languages group organisms into taxa.

(2)   Taxa are further grouped into a small number of classes known as ethnobiological categories.

(3)   The ethnobiological categories are arranged hierarchically:

      unique beginner
      life form
      intermediate (if borne out by further research)
      generic
      specific
      varietal

    Taxa assigned to each rank are mutually exclusive.

(4)   The taxa assigned to each rank characteristically exhibit common linguistic and/or taxonomic features.

(5)   The unique beginner category is often not labeled.

(6)   Life-form taxa are polytypic, number from five to ten, and are labeled by primary lexemes.

(7)   Generic taxa are more numerous, but finite (around 500 classes); are also labeled by primary lexemes; and, being the most frequently mentioned, and the earliest learned, may be cognitively salient building blocks of all folk taxonomies.

(8)   Specific and varietal taxa are apt to be less numerous than generic taxa, and are labeled by secondary lexemes.

(9)   Intermediate taxa, falling in rank between life-form and generic taxa, may exist, but are not linguistically labeled; hence, they have been called covert categories.

*Adapted from Berlin, Breedlove, and Raven (1974:25–27).

Table 5. Patterns of Nomenclature in Folk Biological Classification*

(1) Some taxa marked by primary lexemes are terminal or immediately include taxa designated by secondary lexemes; such taxa are generic and their labels are generic names.

(2) Some taxa marked by primary lexemes are not terminal and and immediately include taxa designated by primary lexemes; such taxa are life-form categories and their labels are life-form names.

(3) Some taxa marked by secondary lexemes are terminal and/or immediately included in taxa designated by primary lexemes; such taxa are specific and their labels are specific names.

(4) Some taxa marked by secondary lexemes are terminal and are immediately included in taxa which are also designated by secondary lexemes; such taxa are varietal names.

*Adapted from Berlin, Breedlove, and Raven (1974:29)

while also establishing some quantitative indices of taxonomic relationships, but these need not be documented here.

4.3. Folk biological hypotheses

The principles of folk biological classification and their interlocking nomenclatural rules presented in Tables 4 and 5 can be stated as hypotheses. These hypotheses may be directed at synchronic cross-language data on ethnobiological categories, or be applied to domains besides ethnobotany and ethnozoology. Moreover, these hypotheses of synchronic structure can be transformed into others focusing on development of individual cognition or diachrony of one or more languages.

Very considerable work has been carried out along all these lines. Recalling the tight analysis now possible with respect to color terms and lexical encoding sequences, corresponding lexical encoding sequence charts for ethnobotanical and ethnozoological life forms are reproduced in Figure 3, with certain helpful definitions in Table 6. The life-form category, as outlined on Table 4, is at the taxonomic rank just above the genus category; for each of the plant and animal domains, there exist a finite number of life forms, usually from five to ten.

The lexical encoding sequence for folk botany posits a stage without any life form, then 'tree' is distinguished, often by a stage of 'wood'/'tree' polysemy (Witkowski, Brown, and Chase 1981). After 'tree' comes either 'grerb' (small

Table 6A. Folk Biological Life Form Category Labels in Folk Zoology

FISH	Creature possessing fins, gills, and a streamlined body, adapted to an aquatic environment
BIRD	Creature possessing feathers, wings, and a bill or beak, adapted to flying
SNAKE	Featherless, furless, elongated creature adapted to crawling, usually lacking appendages
WUG	Small creature usually other than those included in FISH, BIRD, and SNAKE
MAMMAL	Large creature other than those included in FISH, BIRD, and SNAKE

Adapted from Witkowski and Brown (1978: 437).

Table 6B.   Folk Biological Life Form Category Labels in Folk Botany

TREE	Large plant (relative to the plant inventory of a particular environment) whose parts are chiefly ligneous (woody)
GRERB	Small plant (relative to the plant inventory of a particular environment) whose parts are chiefly herbaceous (green, leafy, nonwoody)
BUSH	Plant of intermediate size (relative to TREE and GRERB)
GRASS	Herbaceous plant with narrow, often bladelike or spear-shaped leaves
VINE	Plant exhibiting a creeping or twining or climbing stem habit

Adapted from Brown (1979b: 366–367).

green-herb) or 'grass.' Finally and commonly, 'vine,' 'bush,' and either 'grass' or 'grerb' fill out the life-form inventory.

For folk zoology, there is no documented stage without some labeled life form; this life form or these life forms will be from the roster of 'fish,' 'bird,' and 'snake.' Following these three comes 'wug' (small insect, worm, or 'bug'). Finally, 'mammal' is added (Brown 1979a).

To paraphrase, the most salient categories of 'tree,' 'fish,' 'bird,' and 'snake' are the first to be encoded, while the most marked categories such as 'vine,' 'bush,' and 'mammal' are the last. Or, we could note that large, sessile plants (trees) and small, motile animals other than insects (fish, fowl, and reptiles), are the most salient cognitively, the first to be encoded or learned, the last to be lost or forgotten, and the most frequently referred to by language-speakers.

Figure 3A.   Folk Biological Life Form Lexical Encoding Sequence. Lexical encoding sequence for folk zoological life-forms. Adapted from Witkowski and Brown (1978: 438).

$$\begin{bmatrix} \text{'fish'} \\ \text{'bird'} \\ \text{'snake'} \end{bmatrix} \rightarrow [\text{'wug'}] \rightarrow [\text{'mammal'}]$$

Stages: 1–3   4   5

Figure 3B.   Folk Biological Life Form Lexical Encoding Sequence. Lexical encoding sequence for folk botanical life-forms. Adapted from Witkowski, Brown, and Chase (1981: 2).

$$[\text{no life-forms}] \rightarrow [\text{'tree'}] \nearrow \begin{matrix} [\text{'grerb'}] \rightarrow \begin{bmatrix} \text{'vine'} \\ \text{'grass'} \\ \text{'bush'} \end{bmatrix} \\ \\ [\text{'grass'}] \rightarrow \begin{bmatrix} \text{'grerb'} \\ \text{'vine'} \\ \text{'bush'} \end{bmatrix} \end{matrix}$$

Stages: 1   2   3   4–6

All life forms are abstract and polytypic. Recognition may be facilitated by gross morphology, type of motility, habitat, or behavior, among other attributes. The bibliography samples the extensive literature leading up to the refined hypotheses implicit in Figure 3, as well as those in Tables 4 and 5.

Cross-language investigations suggest that life-form categories may be relatively recent additions to lexical inventories, correlating with societal scale and complexity (Brown 1979a, b). This evidently occurs before any labels for unique beginner categories (such as 'plant' or 'animal') develop. With an increasing division of labor and the isolation of members of a society from primary subsistence activities in the natural environment, the folk biological lexicon contracts at the more specific, lower classes of the taxonomy. The overall evolution of a folk biological domain would then proceed from the encoding of the salient genera and a few of the life-form categories now labeled by opaque, exocentric root lexemes, down to the marking of specific and varietal taxa, and then all the way up to other life-form classes and perhaps a unique beginner.

In the cross-language testing of these hypotheses bearing on universal principles and patterns of classification, the data drawn on may be from banks of published lexical documentation from a hundred or more languages, or it may rely on newly collected information from a familiar or unfamiliar language. Certainly, however, this is not a mechanical process. Information from all the overlapping fields must continually be integrated, and the less sensitive, context-free lexicon materials culled out and replaced by in-depth studies of meaning and behavior.

Of the hypotheses which invite falsification in the ethnosemantic study of folk classification, many would first target ethnobiological domains where there is some sophistication in procedure and purpose. The basic question might be whether or not such classifications are necessarily, or always, or best represented by, taxonomies with an infrastructure of hierarchical class inclusion and horizontal contrast sets of mutually exclusive taxa.

Genera, labeled by opaque lexemes, have been found to be the most numerous taxa, around 500 classes at the upper range and usually close to this number (Berlin, Breedlove, and Raven 1974). Folk botany happens to be the most comprehensively studied domain, however. Fewer animal forms may be lexically distinguished, particularly in cultures devoting much attention to horticulture.

Folk taxonomies and other classifications of general ecological phenomena, and of material and mental culture, call for the same careful study given folk biological classification (Brown et al. 1976). There has been a long-standing assumption that classification of domains beyond the perceptual and ecological will tolerate sloppier edges to classes and more ambiguous relationships between them. All along, while anthropologists, linguists, and psychologists have debated about classification being a grid in the mind of the analyst, the neurologists, physiologists, and ethologists have been discovering that the grid may reside in the genes of the organisms, including those of the species to which the analyst belongs.

5. Saami Folk Science in Spatiotemporal Perspective: Between Winter and a Cold Place

5.1. Ethnosemantics and cultural ecology

When I commenced my Saami field studies—the first sojourn of which was five uninterrupted years—ethnosemantic concerns were only a part of a larger cultural-ecologic approach. Unfortunately, conventional cultural ecology research often studies quantitatively a society's energy relations with the environment without adequate documentation of the qualitative relationships involving information, meaning, and cognition.

Here I will stride through some of the middle-level categories in Saami folk biology, point out the extent of congruencies with the patterns prevailing in the classificatory systems of the other languages thus far studied, and suggest some explanations for the incongruencies. Because of the intent to only start, rather than end, with a linguistic analysis of these domains, these explanations are at another level of abstraction and cannot be used to refine the ethnosemantic approach introduced in the preceding section.

These Saami-speakers in arctic Norway share a cultural lifestyle though not all have the same livelihood. Some 35% of the inhabitants in the focal community of Guov'dageai'dno engages in full-time reindeer management entailing considerable seasonal mobility. Most of the balance raise small stock or dairy cattle, fish, hunt and gather, and/or have wage labor or salaried positions. These occupational groups are not only interdependent in their sparsely settled tundra district, but the nomadic reindeer breeders in particular integrate seasonally with Norwegian-speakers in the coastal areas where reindeer graze during the summer. The overall population of Saami-speakers in this area is about 3,000, for the most part on the tundra of the interior, while Norwegian-speakers in adjacent coastal areas number 50,000. The Saami are bilingual, and, with Finnish, often trilingual, in the case of older persons.

5.2. Vignettes and macro-variables

Already, a number of factors casually anticipated to be of interest (see Table 2), such as arctic setting and bilingualism, skew my investigation on itself. These very factors render my data difficult to analyze in the rote manner outlined in the last section. My first assignment is to express something about the Saami cultural system in terms of itself, rather than translate this understanding into terms which can be compared and contrasted with other languages and cultures.

Four vignettes capturing the essences of real conversations will suffice to set the scene. The first brings up attitudes toward names and naming. Saami respect opaque, unmotivated, exocentric, unsegmentable, simple, primary-unanalyzable root lexemes (see also Figure 2); these are apt to be generic in rank if found in a taxonomy. Even though Saami assume that humans have labeled their universe themselves, and are otherwise thoroughly pragmatic in their relationships of all kinds, a 'good' name captures some magical qualities of the referent and evokes awe.

The second and third vignettes relate episodes which recurred over and over during my first year or two in Saamiland. In these, attitudes toward nature open unexpected windows to folk natural history. The environment is populated by animals, not plants, and these animals are not bosom companions; they are in fact dangerous. Nature is harsh and hazardous.

The fourth vignette confronts us coming and going with issues of bi-lingualism, loan words, calques, folk etymology, and relative competence. A younger bilingual is apt to have a better footing in the national language of Norwegian (''N''), enough so to be able to maintain two separate codes. For the older adult, the imperfectly learned 'high' language interferes with analytical confidence about the first language of Saami.

Saami is sprinkled with Scandinavian and Finnish loan words of various vintages. Some are recognized as such by all, some, or no Saami-speakers—and/or by all, some, or no linguists. Other 'high' language terms can be spon-taneously loan-translated, not always consistently by a single speaker from one time to the next. This problem for the linguist is exacerbated by the high value Saami place on labeling, individuality, and innovation generally.

Despite their emulation of the dominant culture, Saami take a disparaging view of Norwegian natural history, understood to consist of leisurely gathered and carefully pressed mountain flowers, matched by a rigid nomenclature which absolutely guarantees a name, and only one name, for everything. When Saami

Vignette 1: Names and Naming (From Anderson, 1978: 559)

Doluš áigi lávejit boares ol'bmut hui čeappit leat.
Sii dak'ke namaid juokke rássái, juokke spirii.
Dáláš áigi eat leat ain nu čeappit. Eat mátte diŋgaid naw'dit.

In former times the old people used to be very clever.
They made names for every plant, for every animal.
Nowadays we aren't any longer so clever. We don't know how to name things.

In mon dieđe nama dasa, muttu dan goččudit "ruov'di-rássi."

I don't know the name of that, but we call it "iron-plant."

Dat gal lea "ánjelat." Das lea hui buorre namma.

Indeed that's *ánjelat.* It has a really good name.

Vignette 2: Comparative Natural History
(From Anderson 1978: 1)

Ol' bmás:	*Gos don leat eret?*
Dut' kis:	*Ámerikkas.*
Ol' bmás:	*Dobbe orrut vis' sa hir' bmat eadnat spiret, dego elefántat ja leddjunat ja gear' bmašat.*
Dut' kis:	*Elefántat ja leddjunat gáv' dnut Áfrikas, aei Ámerikkas eará go sierra gádi sis' te.*
Ol' bmás:	*Na ba gearbmaš? Leat go ieš dan oai' dnán?*
Dut' kis:	*Gal lean.*
Ol' bmás:	*Don vis' sa bal' láijit.*
Dut' kis:	*Manin?*
Ol' bmás:	*Gear' bmašat leat váralažžat, seammalágáš elefán' tan ja leddjunin. Borret ol' bmuide.*

Companion:	Where are you from?
Ethnographer:	America.
Companion:	I guess a lot of animals live over there, like elephants and lions and snakes.
Ethnographer:	Elephants and lions are found in Africa, not in America except in special enclosures.
Companion:	How about a snake? Have you seen one yourself?
Ethnographer:	Yes, I have.
Companion:	You were no doubt frightened.
Ethnographer:	Why?
Companion:	Snakes are dangerous, just like elephants and lions. They eat/bite people.

Vignette 3: Scenes of Thought and Action
(From Anderson 1978: 277)

Dut' kis	*Gáv' dnut daggár váralaš spiret go Finnmárkos?*
Ol' bmás:	*Máŋgalágán: gumpet, guovžat, geatkit, riebanat, goas' kimat . . .*
Dut' kis:	*Na ba boc' cut, leat go váralažžat?*
Ol' bmás:	*Aei leat.*
Dut' kis:	*Leat go oai' dnán ge gumpe, guovža, geatki, riebana, goas' kima . . . ?*
Ol' bmás:	*Gal lean vuot' tán geatkiid ja riebaniid máŋga hávi meaccis. Lean oai' dnán mearragáddis goas' kimiid.*
Dut' kis:	*It leat gumpe go oaid' nán?*
Ol' bmás:	*In goassege.*
Dut' kis:	*Maid vel lávet deai' vat meaccis?*
Ol' bmás:	*Stalo dieöosge, lea dan oai' dnán ja gul' lán maid.*

Ethnographer: Are there such dangerous animals in Finnmark?
Companion: Many kinds: wolves, bears, wolverines, foxes, eagles . . .
Ethnographer: How about reindeer, are they dangerous?
Companion: No, they're not.
Ethnographer: Have you ever seen a wolf, bear, wolverine, fox, eagle . . . ?
Companion: Certainly, I have followed tracks of wolverine and fox many times in the wilderness. I've seen eagles at the coast.
Ethnographer: Haven't you seen a wolf?
Companion: Never.
Ethnographer: What else are you accustomed to meeting in the wilds?
Companion: *Stallo,* of course, I've seen him and heard him too.

Vignette 4: Bilingualism Refracted (From Anderson 1978: 399)

Dut' kis: *Mii ba dát lea? Gáv' dnu go namma dása? Movt goč' čujuvvu?*
Bárdnis: *Diet gal lea div' ri, mutton lágán divri.*
Áččis: *Vai inseak' ta.*
Bárdnis: *Dát lea namma dárogielas; sámigielas lea "div'ri".*
Áččis: *Muttu divrit leat stuor' rát, dego gusat.*
Bárdnis: *Eai leat. Sámigielas divrit leat unnit, jus' te ná, dego dikkit.*
Áččis: *Nu fal. Na soaite gáv' dnut goabbašagat, stuora divrit ja unna divrit.*
Bárdnis: *Gal soaite, ja unna divrit inseavtaiguin livče ovta lákkái.*

Ethnographer: And what is this? Is there a name for it? How is it referred to?
Son: That is certainly an insect [*div'ri* < N: *dyr* 'animal'], some kind of insect.
Father: Or an insect [*inseak' ta* < N: *insekt* 'insect'].
Son: That's the Norwegian name; in Saami it's *div'ri.*
Father: But *divrit* are big, like cows.
Son: No they're not. In Saami *divrit* are small, like so, such as lice.
Father: Indeed. Perhaps there are both kinds, large *divrit* and small *divrit.*
Son: That must be so, and small *divrit* must be the same thing as insects.

know any Norwegian name for a plant, this will be used in some form even when an indigenous label exists. Remember that in the arctic, the flora is of little direct importance in subsistence, and the plants tend to be small and buried beneath the snow most of the year. This ecological variable certainly has shaped the Saami disinterest in plant classification over the millennia; at the same time, along with

**Figure 4.   Paradigmatic Inspection of Most Frequent Extended Meanings of *eal'li*
'animal' and *šadda* 'plant'. From Anderson (1978: 406).**

Pattern of Extended Meanings
(Most Frequent Underlined)

'LARGE ANIMAL'   'small plant'
'wild animal'   'cultivated plant'
'large wild animal'   'SMALL CULTIVATED PLANT'

Segregate Size

	Large	Small
State		
Wild	cal'li 'large wild animal'	
Cultivated or Domesticated		šadda 'small cultivated plant'

Hays (1982), one recognizes post hoc utilitarian/adaptationist rationales to be
more suggestive than explanatory.

As nomads, Saami are keen on mobility of all sorts. Animals move, behave,
and are altogether more impressive, for their danger or utility, than are plants.
The reindeer, a half-wild, half-domesticated free-ranging herbivore has been a
source for both energy and symbols. A rich vocabulary of opaque terms can be
tapped for everything from description of a single animal to management of a
whole herd. *Boazo* 'reindeer' is indeed an unanalyzable lexeme and a candidate
for generic standing. This term has been in a contrast set with *god'di* 'wild
reindeer' ('the kill,' < *god'dit* 'to kill, to murder').

Another feature of the biota which is significant for Saami is size and cultural

Figure 5.   Focal Meanings of *eal'li* **'animal' and** *šadda* **'plant' together with Coordinate Categories marking Size and Ownership. (Direction of extensions indicated by arrows.) From Anderson (1978: 407).**

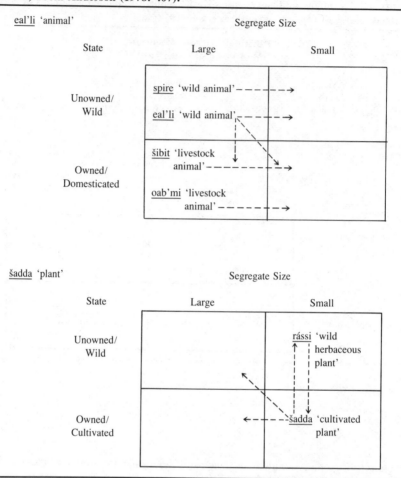

state, that is, whether 'raw' or 'cooked' in Levi-Strauss terms. Although the ethnobiological model presented would not predict any unique beginner cover terms for either 'plant' or 'animal,' two lexemes function as such. Both terms, *šadda* 'plant' and *eal'li* 'animal,' are transparent and polysemous. Figures 4 and 5 display the concatenation of these features, illustrating the dynamics in these sibling semantic domains whereby the essence of 'animal' is both 'large' and 'wild,' while that of 'plant' is both 'small' and 'cultivated.'

Figure 6.   Terms for Domestic Animals by Age and Maturity. From Anderson (1978: 409).

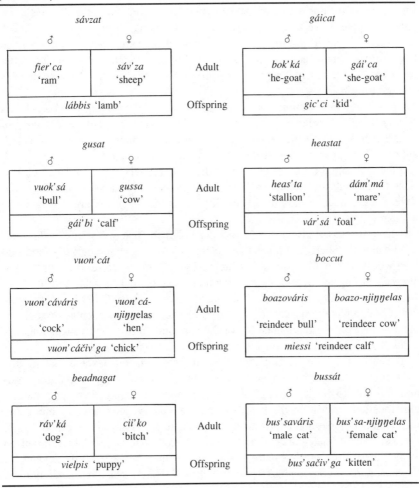

Inasmuch as having pets and holding domesticated livestock are practices borrowed from the contact cultures, labels for these animals consist of fairly obvious borrowed terms. Gender and reproductive maturity may be encoded, and are sometimes obligatorily distinguished. Figure 6 presents these terms. Aside from *boazo/boccut* 'reindeer'/'reindeer' (singular/plural), the only indigenous term is *beana/beadnagat* 'dog'/'dogs.' The dog has been a participant in Saami reindeer management at least since the inception of reindeer herding, which succeeded reindeer hunting about four hundred years ago.

5.3. The organization of taxonomic categories
for fauna and flora

The Saami terms posited as unique beginner cover terms for 'animal' and 'plant' only infrequently are used in this sense. *Eal'li* 'animal' is an extension of *eal'li* 'alloanimal,' which is in turn only one of dozens of terms derived from *eallit* 'to live.' *Šadda* 'plant' is a nominal derived from *šad'dat* 'to grow,' which better describes the incremental aspect of maturing than *eallit* 'to live,' which denotes the enduring living state.

However, *eal'li* 'animal' in a still more extended meaning can be used as 'living thing,' to refer to biota generally. This extension into the category of what I'll have to call the 'superordinate unique beginner' is quite unexpected, although it does mean, most literally, 'living thing' in the first place.

Figures 7 and 8 organize the taxa at the higher levels in the Saami classifications for animals and plants, showing how the salient features of 'size,' 'appendages,' and 'mode of mobility or sessility' work through the entire 'living thing' domain.

I have discussed elsewhere (Anderson 1978) the lexemic status of the mid-level category labels for animals and plants. Some are phonologically modified loan words, especially from the Scandinavian. At this juncture, the fourth vignette concerning the Saami *div'ri* 'crawling creature, bug, insect' and the Norwegian *dyr* 'animal, large animal' comes into better focus. Other loan words are virtually completely masked to the native speaker of Saami, such as *rassi* 'leafy plant'—also expressing something of the connotation of 'weed'—which apparently is an older acquisition from Scandinavian, from *gress* 'grass.'

Because of this difficulty in dealing with heterogeneous lexemes having distinct linguistic histories, I have bypassed the analytical stage of assigning taxonomic rank to Saami biological terms, instead arranging them in a natural classification strictly on the basis of native speakers' judgments of hierarchic inclusion and horizontal contrast sets. These natural classes I have called 'major classes,' 'subordinate classes,' and 'terminal taxa.' The major classes organized as hypothetical genera in Figure 7—in spite of their being lexically deviant for the most part—come together again in Figure 9. Here I tabulate separately three types of labels: opaque, transparent, and what could be called translucent (the loaned or calqued labels).

Any impression of the cognitive and practical salience of arctic fauna relative to flora seems to be borne out, there being over twice as many labeled terminal folk taxa for animals (202) as for plants (94). Half of the zoological segregates at this lowest, most specific level are labeled by simple, opaque Saami terms, as opposed to one-third in the case of plants. The proportion of transparent labels was reversed between the two major classes of biota.

The remaining terminal taxa labels have lexemic or back-translated cognates in the Fennoscandian contact languages. Scandinavian loans and calques, from

Figure 7.   Taxonomic Structure of the Domains of *eal'li* 'animal' and *šadda* 'plant'. From Anderson (1978: 420–421).

Taxonomic Structure of the Domain of *eal'li* 'animal'

eal'li₂ 'animal'							
olmuš 'human'	*eal'li₁* 'animal'						
	spire₂ 'large wild animal'		*guolli* 'fish'	*div'ri₂* 'small creature'			
	lod'di₁ 'flying vertebrate'	*spire₁* 'mammal, other land vertebrate'		*lod'di₂* 'flying invertebrate'	*div'ri₁* 'crawling elongate invertebrate'	*gobbá* 'beetle, globular invertebrate'	*skálčo* 'shelled invertebrate'

Taxonomic Structure of the Domain of *šadda* 'plant'

šadda 'plant'						
muorra₂ 'tree'		*guobbar* 'fungus'	*rássi₁* 'small wild plant'			
(las'ta-) muorra₁ '(deciduous-) tree'	*goac'ci-muorra* 'conifer tree'		*rássi₂* 'foliage plant'	*suoi'dni* 'bladed plant'	*jeagil* 'lichen'	*sammal* 'moss'

different historic and prehistoric periods, for example, constitute 17% of the terminal taxa labels for animals and less than 5% for plants.

These three sorts of labels correspond in a broad way with the evaluations which Saami make of names and naming, illustrated in the first vignette. High-

Figure 8. Paradigmatic Substruction of the Domains of *eal'li* 'animal' and *šadda* 'plant'. From Anderson (1978: 416–417).

Paradigmatic Substruction of the Domain of *šadda* 'plant' Showing Membership of Each Class

		lastat 'leaves' +	–	–
	ruottas 'root'	+	+	–
maða miel'de 'according to size' +	+	*(las'ta-) muorra* '(deciduous) tree' **10**	*goac'ci-muorra* 'conifer tree' **3**	*guobbar* 'fungus' **5**
máðdagat 'stems' (prominent)	–	*rássi* 'leafy plant' **48**	*suoi'dni* 'bladed plant' **14**	*jeagil* 'lichen' **11**
				sámmál 'moss' **3**

Paradigmatic Substruction of the Domain of *eal'li* 'animal' Showing Membership of Each Class

		soajit 'wings' +	–	–
	juolgit 'feet'	+	+	–
maða miel'de 'according to size'	+	*lod'di₁* 'bird' **74**	*spire* 'mammal, other land vertebrate' **44**	*guolli* 'fish' **29**
stuoris 'large size'	–	*lod'di₂* 'flying invertebrate' **19**	*div'ri* 'elongate crawling invertebrate' **19**	*gob'bá* 'beetles, globular invertebrate' **6**
				skál'žo 'shelled invertebrate' **11**

LEGEND
xxx Number of taxa; fauna classed in 202 terminal taxa.

LEGEND
xxx Number of taxa; fauna classed in 94 terminal taxa.

Figure 9. Taxonomic Categories for Fauna and Flora showing Nomenclatural Patterns and Membership. From Anderson (1978: 565).

FAUNA

MAJOR CLASSES—7: ○3 □2 △2

		Subordinate Classes				Terminal Taxa		
		○	□	△		○	□	△
lod'di₁ 'bird'	6:	1	5	0	74:	49	21	4
spire 'animal'	2:	0	2	0	44:	20	19	5
guol'li 'fish'	2:	0	2	0	29:	16	5	8
lod'di₂ 'flying creature'	2:	0	2	0	19:	6	11	2
div'ri 'crawling creature'	1:	0	0	1	19:	9	6	4
gob'bá 'floating creature'	1:	0	1	0	6:	0	6	0
skál'žo 'shelled creature'	1:	0	0	1	11:	0	0	11
Total	15:	1	12	2	202:	100	68	34

FLORA

MAJOR CLASSES—7: ○5 □1 △1

		Subordinate Classes				Terminal Taxa		
		○	□	△		○	□	△
muorra 'deciduous tree'	1:	1	0	0	10:	7	2	1
goac'ci-muorra 'conifer tree'	1:	0	1	0	3:	3	0	0
guobbar 'fungus'	1:	1	0	0	5:	2	3	0
rássi 'leafy plant'	4:	2	1	1	48:	13	32	3
suoi'dni 'bladed plant'	1:	1	0	0	14:	4	10	0
jeagil 'lichen'	1:	1	0	0	11:	2	9	0
sámmál 'moss'	1:	1	0	0	3:	1	1	1
Total	10:	7	2	1	94:	32	57	5

LEGEND:
○ opaque labels
□ transparent labels
△ loaned or calqued labels

Grand Total for All Biota
Terminal Folk Taxa— 296
○ 132
□ 125
△ 39

level general terms are not judged as frequently as lower-level specific terms; among these, opaque labels are thought to be primary, unique, mysterious, beautiful, appropriate, and unequivocal.

The transparent and translucent names are less exotic, for persons believe that these can be constructed by anyone at any time. Names are created and discovered daily, for individuals as well as segregates, and it is a mark of distinction to be known as a person clever at naming and innovating generally.

The loan and calqued terms, when recognized as such in folk etymology, tend to enter Saami usage with the booster accompanying much borrowed from the majority culture, from terminology to technology. Foreign labels often enter Saami at the higher levels in the folk taxonomy, while calques are concentrated at the level of terminal taxa labels. This appears reasonable to expect, since the former general terms are most apt to be in the foreign-language vocabularies of the bilinguals and trilinguals, and since the latter are often Saami translations of school-learned Norwegian terms. The loan words—characteristically semantically broad to start with—become even more diffuse and general than in the donor language; again, *div'ri* 'insect' from *dyr* 'animal' exemplifies this. In fact, *rassi* 'leafy plant' from *gress* 'grass,' is sometimes extended to be a 'plant' cover term, as shown in Figure 5.

Another problem with sorting just the indigenous Saami labels by lexical type has to do with the near-infinite productivity of all Saami nouns, verbs, and even prepositions. In the case of *eal'li* 'animal' and *eallit* 'to live,' for example, the semantic space may be inextricably involuted.

For these and numerous other reasons (Anderson 1978), I found that determining lexemic status was in some instances difficult, impossible, or arbitrary. Hence, the Saami classifications cannot be compared uniformly with those for other folk biological systems. However, even though I cannot tabulate the number of generic-rank labels for either plants or animals which would be meaningful for the Saami case or defensible for comparative purposes, it is clear that *all* taxa at *all* ranks from *both* biotic domains do not total anywhere near 500. The actual figure, probably of little real significance, is approximately 350—including synonyms.

I should explain that the gathering of all data, ethnosemantic and other, was almost exclusively in natural contexts. When terms for plants and animals were employed, I might be able to divert some conversation to the term, its referent, or the relationships between terms, between referents, between segregates, or between term and referent. Controlled elicitation frames were neither possible nor desirable to use, and in general I eschew techniques which place the investigator in high profile.

The Saami orthography employed here approximates the phonemic, and differs in various ways from the several orthographies presently or recently in use for the North Saami dialect spoken in the northernmost regions of Norway, Sweden, and Finland (consult Anderson 1978 for details).

6. Issues of Significance

Numerous issues, classic as well as unique, have been mentioned in the course of the foregoing sections. Many of the recurring ones have inspired tomes. Perhaps purely linguistic issues can more easily be pushed to resolution than those which are philosophical or physiological; Hunn (1977) discusses polysemy, synonymy, and homonymy, among other things, in a manner which can enlighten these relationships in domains besides the ethnobiological.

Hunn (1977:41–75) is equally lucid in distinguishing inductive and deductive emphases in classification. Folk biological classification and scientific systematics both focus on discontinuities, similarities, and differences in the real world, and build inductively from this level where perception itself plays a crucial role. When folk biological classifications and even terminological regularities compare so readily with those of the Latin system of binomials, there should be no surprise. It is the higher-rank categories, the last to be labeled, which are the product of deductive theories about the basic order in the universe. I wish to explore this point with respect to the Saami data.

Although terminal taxa labels are not included in this paper (see Anderson 1978:400–558), an inspection of their organization within the subordinate classes, which in turn are included in the major classes listed in Figures 4, 5, 7, 8, and 9, shows that the lower-level taxa are in fact highly deductive. This is not simply a consequence of the transparency of many of the major classes which may correspond to life forms. The most pervasive deductive bias enters the classification through the nomenclature associated with the subordinate classes. These key into the relationship which a set of segregates bears to the overall ecological system.

The consequence of this is a coarse-grained, context-sensitive, relative, deductive bias in Saami classification having to do with biome phenomena. The concept of ecological niche is commonplace and honored in the nomenclature and in expectations derived from personal experience in nature. A contributing factor may be that in an arctic setting, biological resources are not as directly crucial as access to them, this access predicated on information and mobility rather than identification.

Here sociocultural patterns fraction along economic lines. Much ethnobiological clumping at the rank of the terminal taxa arises by virtue of mobile persons being familiar with the effect of habitat and altitude on plant and animal growth. Reindeer-holding families typically have a minimum of two living sites each year: one in the winter on the tundra, with a dry inland climate and snow cover extending well over seven months of the year; and another residence in the summer at the coast, with much more variable climate and ecology. This very experiential range which permits clumping of certain biotic taxa produces attention to detail in other ecological domains, such as the meteorologic and physiographic.

Because some of the Saami nomads seldom witness their winter rangelands in summer or their coastal summer pastures in winter, this, too, promotes a coarse-grained classification. The sedentary Saami, living year-round in the tundra region, attend noticeably more to fine-grain differentiations of terminal taxa.

I have stressed that, while handling variation between speakers and variability of single speakers in different contexts and at different times has been a ubiquitous concern in all genres of research and especially in ethnosemantics, this becomes particularly challenging with respect to Saami or any other group placing a high premium on creativity in language and culture. I have no solutions for analyzing synergy, and if I thought such solutions existed, field work would be robbed of its texture. One of my more optimistic hypotheses is that the human scientist requires some critical mass of paradox in order to function at all.

REFERENCES

Anderson, Myrdene 1978. *Saami Ethnoecology: Resource Management in Norwegian Lapland.* Unpublished dissertation, Yale University. (Available from: University Microfilms, Ann Arbor, MI, 1978. No. 79-15912.)

Bartlett, Harley Harris 1940. "History of the generic concept in botany." *Bulletin of the Torrey Botanical Club* 67:5, pp. 349–62.

Bateson, Gregory 1970. "Form, substance, and difference" (19th Alfred Korzybski Memorial Lecture). *General Semantics Bulletin. Yearbook of the Institute of General Semantics* 37, pp. 5–13.

Berlin, Brent 1970. "A universalist-evolutionary approach in ethnographic semantics." In: A. Fischer (ed.), *Current Directions in Anthropology. Bulletin of the American Anthropological Association* 3, Pt. 2, pp. 3–18.

Berlin, Brent, and Elois Ann Berlin 1975. "Aguaruna color categories." *American Ethnologist* 2:1, pp. 61–87.

Berlin, Brent, Dennis E. Breedlove, and Peter H. Raven 1968. "Covert categories and folk taxonomies." *American Anthropologist* 70:2, pp. 290–9.

Berlin, Brent, Dennis E. Breedlove, and Peter H. Raven 1973. "General principles of classification and nomenclature in folk biology." *American Anthropologist* 75:2, pp. 214–42.

Berlin, Brent, Dennis E. Breedlove, and Peter H. Raven 1974. *Principles of Tzeltal Plant Classification: An Introduction to the Botanical Ethnography of a Mayan-Speaking People of Highland Chiapas.* New York and London: Academic Press.

Berlin, Brent, and Paul Kay 1969. *Basic Color Terms: Their Universality and Evolution.* Berkeley, CA: University of California Press.

Berlin, Brent, and John P. O'Neill 1981. "The pervasiveness of onomatopoeia in Aguaruna and Huambisa bird names." *Journal of Ethnobiology* 1:2, pp. 238–61.

Brown, Cecil H. 1974. "Unique beginners and covert categories in folk biological taxonomies." *American Anthropologist* 76:2, pp. 325–7.

Brown, Cecil H. 1979a. "Folk zoological life-forms: their universality and growth." *American Anthropologist* 81:4, pp. 791–817.

Brown, Cecil H. 1979b. "Growth and development of folk botanical life-forms in the Mayan language family." *American Ethnologist* 6:2, pp. 366–85.

Brown, Cecil H. 1979c. "A theory of lexical change (with examples from folk biology, human anatomical partonomy and other domains)." *Anthropological Linguistics* 21:6, pp. 257–76.

Brown, Cecil H. 1980. "Nonbiological classification reconsidered: a response to Durrenberger and Morrison." *American Ethnologist* 7:1, pp. 184–7.

Brown, Cecil H. 1981. "More on folk zoological life-forms." *American Anthropologist* 83:2, pp. 398–401.

Brown, Cecil H. 1984. *Language and Living Things: Uniformities in Folk Classification and Naming.* New Brunswick, NJ: Rutgers University Press.

Brown, Cecil H., John Kolar, Barbara J. Torrey, Ti pawan Truong-Quang, and Philip Volkman 1976. "Some general principles of biological and non-biological folk classification." *American Ethnologist* 3:1, pp. 73–85.

Brown, Cecil H., and Stanley R. Witkowski 1980. "Language universals. Appendix." In: David Levinson and Martin J. Malone, *Toward Explaining Human Culture: A Critical Review of the Finds of Worldwide Cross-Cultural Research.* New Haven, CT: HRAF Press, pp. 359–84.

Brown, Cecil H., and Stanley R. Witkowski 1981. "Figurative language in a universalist perspective." *American Ethnologist* 8:3, pp. 596–615.

Brown, Cecil H., and Stanley R. Witkowski 1983. "Polysemy, lexical change, and cultural importance." *Man,* 18, pp. 72–89.

Brown, Roger W., and Eric H. Lenneberg 1954. "A study in language and cognition." *Journal of Abnormal and Social Psychology* 49, pp. 454–62.

Bruner, J. S., J. J. Goodnow, and G. A. Austin 1954. *A Study of Thinking.* New York: Wiley.

Bulmer, R. N. H. 1967. "Why is the cassowary not a bird? A problem of zoological taxonomy among the Karam of the New Guinea Highlands." *Man* 2, pp. 1–25.

Bulmer, R. N. H. 1970. "Which came first, the chicken or the egg-head?" In: J. Pouillon and P. Maranda (eds.), *Échanges et communications, Mélanges offerts à Claude Lévi-Strauss à occasion de son 60-ème anniversaire.* The Hague: Mouton, pp. 1069–91.

Bulmer, R. N. H., and M. J. Tyler 1968. "Karam classification of frogs." *Journal of the Polynesian Society* 77, pp. 333–85.

Cain, Arthur James 1956. "The genus in evolutionary taxonomy." *Systematic Zoology* 5:3, pp. 97–109.

Cain, Arthur James 1958. "Logic and memory in Linnaeus's system of taxonomy."

Cain, Arthur James 1959. "Deductive and inductive methods in post-Linnaean taxonomy." *Proceedings of the Linnaean Society of London* 170:2, pp. 185–217.

Chase, Paul K. 1980. "Acquisition of folk zoological life-forms by American children." *The Journal of Anthropology* 2:2, pp. 104–21.

Clark, Eve V., and Herbert H. Clark 1978. "Universals, relativity, and language processing." In: Joseph H. Greenberg, Charles A. Ferguson, and Edith A. Moravcsik (eds.), *Universals of Human Language,* Vol. 1. *Method and Theory,* Stanford, CA: Stanford University Press, pp. 225–77.

Conklin, Harold C. 1954. *The Relation of Hanunóo Culture to the Plant World.* Unpublished dissertation, Yale University. (Available from: University Microfilms, Ann Arbor, MI, 1967. No. 67-4119.)

Conklin, Harold C. 1962 "Lexicographical treatment of folk taxonomies." In: F. W. Householder and S. Saporta (eds.), *Problems in Lexicography: Report of the Conference on Lexicography, Indiana University, 11–12 November 1960. International Journal of American Linguistics* 28:2(4), pp. 119–41.

Conklin, Harold C. 1964. "Ethnogenealogical method." In: W. H. Goodenough (ed.), *Explorations in Cultural Anthropology: Essays in Honor of George Peter Murdock.* New York: McGraw-Hill, pp. 25–55.

Dougherty, J. W. D. 1978. "Salience and relativity in classification." *American Ethnologist* 5:1, pp. 66–80.

Durrenberger, E. Paul, and John W. Morrison 1979. "Response to Comment of Penny Van Esterik to Cecil H. Brown." *American Ethnologist* 6:2, pp. 408–9.

Ellen, Roy F., Andrew Stimson, and James Menzies 1976. "Structure and inconsistency in Nuaulu categories for amphibians." *Journal d'agriculture tropicale et de botanique appliquée* 23:7–12, pp. 125–38.

Frake, Charles O. 1962. "The ethnographic study of cognitive systems." In: Thomas Gladwin and

W. C. Sturtevant (eds.), *Anthropology and Human Behavior*. Washington, DC: Anthropological Society of Washington, pp. 72–85.

Frake, Charles O. 1964. "Notes on queries in ethnography." In: A. Kimball Romney and Roy Goodwin D'Andrade (eds.), *Transcultural Studies in Cognition*. *American Anthropologist* 66:3(2), pp. 132–45.

Friedrich, Paul 1970. *Proto–Indo-European Trees*. Chicago: University of Chicago Press.

Gal, Susan 1973. "Inter-informant variability in an ethnozoological taxonomy." *Anthropological Linguistics* 15:4, pp. 203–19.

Gardner, Peter M. 1976. "Birds, words, and a requiem for the omniscient informant." *American Ethnologist* 3:3, pp. 446–68.

Geoghegan, William H. 1976. "Polytypy in folk biological taxonomies." *American Ethnologist* 3:3, pp. 469–80.

Goodenough, Ward H. 1956. "Componential analysis and the study of meaning." *Language* 32, pp. 195–216.

Greenberg, Joseph H. 1975. "Research on language universals." In: Bernard J. Siegal (ed.), *Annual Review of Anthropology* 4. Palo Alto, CA: Annual Reviews, pp. 75–94.

Greene, Edward L. 1909. *Landmarks of Botanical History* (Smithsonian Miscellaneous Collections 54). Washington, DC: Smithsonian Institution.

Gregg, John R. 1954. *The Language of Taxonomy: An Application of Symbolic Logic to the Study of Classificatory Systems*. New York: Columbia University Press.

Hage, Per, and Wick R. Miller 1976. " 'Eagle' = 'bird': A note on the structure and evolution of Shoshoni ethnoornithological nomenclature." *American Ethnologist* 3:3, pp. 481–8.

Haugen, Einar 1957. "The semantics of Icelandic orientation." *Word* 13:3, pp. 447–59.

Hays, Terence E. 1976. "An empirical method for the identification of covert categories in ethnobiology." *American Ethnologist* 3:3, pp. 489–507.

Hays, Terence E. 1982. "Utilitarian/adaptationist explanations of folk biological classification: some cautionary notes." *Journal of Ethnobiology* 2:1, pp. 89–94.

Hunn, Eugene S. 1977. *Tzeltal Folk Zoology: The Classification of Discontinuities in Nature*. New York: Academic Press.

Kay, Paul 1971. "Taxonomy and semantic contrast." *Language* 47:4, pp. 866–87.

Kay, Paul 1975. "Synchronic variability and diachronic change in basic color terms." *Language in Society* 4, pp. 257–70.

Kay, Paul, and Chad K. McDaniel 1975. "Color categories as fuzzy sets." Working Paper 44, Language Behavior Research Laboratory, University of California at Berkeley.

Kay, Paul, and Chad K. McDaniel 1978. "The linguistic significance of the meanings of basic color terms." *Language* 54, pp. 610–46.

Lévi-Strauss, Claude 1966. *The Savage Mind*. Chicago: Chicago University Press.

Lounsbury, Floyd G. 1955. "The varieties of meaning." *Georgetown University Monograph Series on Languages and Linguistics* 8, pp. 158–64.

Mathiot, Madeleine 1970. "The semantic and cognitive domains of language." In: Paul L. Garvin (ed.), *Cognition: A Multiple View*. New York: Spartan Books, pp. 249–76.

Miller, George A. 1956. "The magical number seven, plus or minus two: some limits on our capacity for processing information." *The Psychological Review* 63:2, pp. 81–97.

Randall, Robert A. 1976. "How tall is a taxonomic tree? Some evidence for dwarfism." *American Ethnologist* 3:3, pp. 543–53.

Raven, Peter H., Brent Berlin, and Dennis E. Breedlove 1971. "The origins of taxonomy." *Science* 174, pp. 1210–3.

Reed, Charles A. (ed.) 1977. *Origins of Agriculture*. The Hague and Paris: Mouton.

Scheffler, Harold W., and Floyd G. Lounsbury 1971. *A Study in Structural Semantics: The Siriono Kinship System*. Englewood Cliffs, NJ: Prentice-Hall.

Sokal, Robert R. 1974. "Classifications: purposes, principles, progress, prospects." *Science* 185, pp. 1115–23.

Spradley, James P. 1970. *You Owe Yourself a Drunk*. Boston: Little, Brown.

Stross, Brian 1973. "Acquisition of botanical terminology by Tzeltal children." In: M. S. Edmonson (ed.), *Meaning in Mayan Languages*. The Hague: Mouton, pp. 107–41.

Sturtevant, W. C. 1964. "Studies in ethnoscience." *American Anthropologist* 66:1(2), pp. 99–131.

Trager, George L. 1939. " 'Cottonwood = tree,' a South-Western linguistic trait." *International Journal of American Linguistics* 9, pp. 117–18.

Tyler, Stephen A. (ed.) 1969. *Cognitive Anthropology*. New York: Holt, Rinehart and Winston.

Ucko, Peter J., and G. W. Dimbleby (eds.) 1969. *The Domestication and Exploitation of Plants and Animals. Proceedings of a Meeting of the Research Seminar in Archaeology and Related Subjects Held at the Institute of Archaeology, London University*. Chicago and New York: Aldine Atherton.

Van Esterik, Penny 1979. "Reply to Comment by Cecil H. Brown." *American Ethnologist* 6:2, pp. 408.

von Wattenwyl, André, and Heinrich Zollinger 1979. "Color-term salience and neurophysiology of color vision." *American Anthropologist* 81:2, pp. 279–88.

Werner, Oswald, and Joann Fenton 1970. "Method and theory in ethnoscience of ethnoepistemology." In: Raoul Naroll and Ronald Cohen (eds.), *A Handbook of Method in Cultural Anthropology*. New York and London: Columbia University Press, pp. 537–78.

Witkowski, Stanley R., and Cecil H. Brown 1977. "An explanation of color nomenclature universals." *American Anthropologist* 79,1: pp. 50–57.

Witkowski, Stanley R., and Cecil H. Brown 1978. "Lexical universals." *Annual Review of Anthropology* 7, pp. 427–451.

Witkowski, Stanley R., and Cecil H. Brown 1981. "Lexical encoding sequences and language change: color terminology systems." *American Anthropologist* 83:1, pp. 13–27.

Witkowski, Stanley R., and Cecil H. Brown 1982. "Culture, environment, and polysemy." Unpublished manuscript.

Witkowski, Stanley R., Cecil H. Brown, and Paul K. Chase 1981. "Where do tree terms come from?" *Man* 16:1, pp. 1–14.

Yen, D. E. 1974. *The Sweet Potato and Oceania: An Essay in Ethnobotany* (Bernice P. Bishop Museum Bulletin 236). Honolulu: Bishop Museum Press.

CHAPTER TEN

Linguists and Reading in the 1980s

Georgia M. Green

1. Introduction

I am going to depart a little from my announced title and instead of discussing linguistics and reading, I'm going to talk about linguists and reading, interpreting *linguistics* as 'what linguists do.' I have two reasons for this. First, it will facilitate dealing with this subject in human rather than abstract terms: "How might/do/should linguists affect individuals responsible for reading education?" is a topic more concretely dealt with than "What is the outlook for the relationship between linguistic theory and educational psychology or educational policy for the 1980s?" Second, even when the more abstract question is made concrete by defining, usually in an arbitrary fashion, what 'linguistic theory' 'is'—as if there were some such complete, consistent, and universally accepted monolithic object—the answers tend to be irrelevant to linguistics and ultimately a waste of time for educational theory. Much sound and fury was generated in educational research by the *Syntactic Structures* (Chomsky 1957) model of language (more accurately, by a misinterpretation of the *Syntactic Structures* theory), and perhaps as much by Fillmore's (1968) theory of 'case grammar,' long after the theories had been abandoned by their inventors and most mainstream linguists, and thousands of federal dollars had been spent on studies designed to show how (or if) they could contribute to increasing literacy levels. None of this research has been incorporated into any reading curriculum that I am aware of, so I imagine that there have not been any overwhelmingly positive results. Even now the theories represented as being linguistic that are attracting the most attention are European Text Linguistics and Halliday and Hasan's theory of cohesion. It is not difficult for *linguists* to recognize how these theories distort and mistake the relation between message and text (Morgan and Sellner 1980), but it is apparently not so obvious to the rest of the world that the 'message' 'of' a text is not 'in' the text, but must be *guessed at* by the reader, who must make inferences about the intentions and beliefs of the creator of the text, based on what *is* in the text (Green 1982; Green and Morgan 1980).

2. Educational Materials

The traditional province of linguists in reading education has been in the design of teaching materials. Linguists have applied their understanding of language in more or less 'official' capacities to reading education and the resolution of reading difficulties since the days of the American structuralists, when Bloomfield (1942) proposed that the first texts children read contain only words whose letters stand in a one-to-one relationship with the sounds they represent. This meant that no words with silent letters could be used, nor any words with double letters, nor any words with digraphs, where a sequence of letters represents a single sound. This allows the principle of decoding to be taught independently of the vagaries of the English spelling system, but it makes for a rather strained text, as it eliminates all of the thousands of common words with 'silent *e*,' as well as such useful words as *the, she, they, this, thing, little,* and *small.*

Later, Fries' reading curriculum (1963, 1966) attempted to teach grapheme-allophone correspondences inductively, via minimal pairs, and warned strongly against pronouncing sounds separately from the words they must be part of. Since that time, various other more or less coherently articulated theories about language have been advertised as being the basis for a 'linguistic' approach to the teaching of reading. As Durkin (1974:241), writing in a reading education text, comments, "The term linguistic has sufficient market value that just about everything available to teach reading is referred to as being linguistic. As a result, the description has lost any specific meaning it might once have had."

There is now a (more or less token) bona fide linguist on the consultant list of practically every publishing house that markets a basal reader series. (Basal readers are the books children use in their reading groups in learning to read. They have workbooks of all sorts to go with them.) Thus, there is a long-established tradition of applications of linguistics to reading. But the connections I have mentioned barely scratch the surface of the opportunities potentially available for linguists to put to use what hard-won understanding of language they have.

What I would like to do here is to describe in more detail the actual and potential opportunities in the field of reading for individuals who are trained in linguistics and have an enthusiasm for improving the success rate of programs intended to enable the ability to read to be acquired. This long circumlocution for 'teaching reading' is a function of the fact that the more I observe and read about beginning reading, the more mysterious to me the process becomes by which a child who in September cannot read at all, in January can read unfamiliar materials, providing the syntax and vocabulary would be comprehensible orally. Nonetheless, I believe that the linguist's training and experience provide expertise which can contribute to the solution of various problems in literacy. This expertise includes not only knowledge of universals of language, and of phonological, grammatical, and discourse theory. It also includes knowledge of the nature of nonstandard dialects of English, and the background to evaluate research on language acquisition as significant and relevant, and equally, a skeptical attitude and a sensitivity to linguistic phenomena at a variety of levels, ranging from distinctive features to discourse organization.

Let us begin with the traditional opportunity for linguists in reading, that of consulting or editing a basal reader series. This is what Roger Shuy did for Ginn, and Eric Hamp does for Harper & Row. Ordinarily this sort of job is not available to the enthusiastic linguist with a brand new Ph.D.—there is not much turnover among consultants, and it's a pretty closed market. But there is not much work to do either, and even if it is a lucrative position (I have no idea how much, if any, financial compensation is involved), there is not much challenge to it. I have been told that the linguistic consultant's contribution is more or less limited to occasional consulting about high-level decisions concerning what skills the program should stress, and approving the order in which grapheme-phoneme correspondences are 'taught.' According to the schedules in the basal reader systems, this takes about two and a half years—until the middle of third grade. Never mind that the child who is functioning normally in the school system has had to cope with almost all such correspondences by the end of first grade—perhaps by luck or design 'silent p' (*pneumonia*) has been avoided; *ph* as /f/ and various pronunciations of *ough* certainly cannot have been.

But it doesn't have to be this way. There are all sorts of things a well-trained linguist could do for a basal reader publisher to greatly improve the product. For instance, a linguist with an interest in discourse could, without making any waves, prove invaluable as an editor and writer.

Before I explain how, let me first explain a little about the making of basal readers. The books themselves, the hardbound readers that children read from in class, in what are called 'directed reading lessons,' consist of short passages, 150 to 800 words or so each in grades one and two, perhaps topically arranged. Some of them are written by the staff of the publisher or by writers specifically commissioned to write basal reader stories, but many of them are adapted from copyrighted published material, both fiction and nonfiction. These passages are almost always selected or (more often) edited to fit one or more readability formulae. These formulae supposedly measure primarily gross linguistic properties like word length, word frequency, and sentence length. The reason behind the widespread use of reading formulae is more one of politics than one of educational policy, but that's another story. The fact that the formulae are interpreted in diverse ways does not make things any less complicated, since some potential purchasers (and thus some publishers) feel that EVERY selection (or even every sentence in every selection) must meet the criteria for a certain level; this despite the fact that the authors of the formulae intended them to be applied to some small number of randomly chosen 100-word passages per text, to give an index of readability of the text as a whole.

In addition, publishers offer, often free of charge with the basal readers, a teacher's manual which details for the teacher such things as how to teach new words introduced in each lesson, and questions to ask to see if students understand what they read.

Now, what could a linguist bring to the preparation of these materials? Well, it is easily demonstrated that blind adherence to such readability formulae can actually contribute to making a text more difficult to understand, instead of easier, as Davison et al. (1981) have argued. For example, a passage that went originally like this:

> In 1851, Gail Borden . . . discovered a way of preserving milk by condensing it.

was adapted, and supposedly made easier, by replacing long and 'difficult' words, and eliminating subordination, to read like this:

> In 1851, Gail Borden . . . found a way to take some of the water out of milk. This made it keep much longer.

The adaptation doesn't make it clear that the *purpose* of removing the water was to keep the milk from spoiling; in the adaptation, this resultant effect could be interpreted as an unintended consequence, an accident. In another text, a passage that reads as follows:

> Every morning the big hippos waited for him to wake up so they could take care of him.

is broken up into shorter sentences to read:

> All the big hippos would wait for him to get up. They wanted to take care of him.

The adaptation removes the (difficult?) words *every* and *morning,* and replaces them with *all* and a rather literary use of *would* to indicate habitual action. Again, the adaptation does not make it clear that the big hippos waited for *him* to get up BECAUSE they wanted to take care of him. Shortening the sentences and 'simplifying' the vocabulary like this thus makes texts less explicit, and consequently makes it HARDER to infer correctly the message intended by the author, as it removes clues that indicate correct inferences. After looking at adaptations for three years, I am convinced that it's what gets left out, not what gets left in, that makes a text harder to understand.

But a linguist with some sensitivity to discourse, to how a text encodes a message, given responsibility for actually editing text selections, could exercise enough control over the adaptation process to prevent adaptation from making the reading task unnecessarily and unproductively difficult.

Anaphoric relations may get lost in the shuffle along with subordinating conjunctions and specific vocabulary when readability formulae govern the production of texts for basal readers, as in this excerpt from a second-grade reader:

> The teddy bear was named for a famous man. His name was Theodore Roosevelt, but everyone called him Teddy. He was President of the United States.

This is the first paragraph of a section titled "The Teddy Bear Story," and the facing page is a full-page, full-color photograph of a teddy bear. Apparently it takes a linguist to notice that *The teddy bear* in this context (both in the title and in the first sentence) is easily interpreted as definite and specific, perhaps as referring to the pictured toy, rather than as generic and referring to the genus of such toys. If it is, then *His* and *He* in the following sentences are also most easily understood as also referring to some toy, and the reader gets a markedly different understanding of the text from what was (presumably) intended.

Another contribution a linguist could make to the production of a better basal reader involves the editing or construction of the questions that accompany reading selections for teachers to use to gauge students' comprehension of the passages. For example, in order to assist teachers in informally assessing a student's reading ability, one teacher's manual would have the student read the following passage aloud:

> Mike saw a frog in the park.
> He wanted Mother to see it too.
>
> Mike ran home with the frog.
> He said, "Look, Mother.
> I got this frog in the park.
> I'll name it Bozo the Frog."
>
> Mother said,
> "Let's not have a frog in the house, Mike."

and answer these questions:

1. Where was Mike?
2. What did Mike find?
3. How did Mike go home?
4. How did Mother feel about Bozo?

If a child answers three or more correctly s/he reads at 'Level 5,' which is the latter part of first grade. Apparently I'm not that good a reader because I couldn't answer questions 1 or 3. But (I hope you will believe) *I am* a good reader. Then why couldn't I answer these questions after reading the story aloud with the amount of attention I ordinarily devote to reading aloud to my children, which is enough to ensure normally expressive intonation? I would say it is because the questions are not well designed to assess comprehension: Question 3 is entirely too vague, because *how* is a very vague interrogative. Question 3 could be asking what route Mike took, how he felt, what means of transportation he used, as well as what is intended here: at what rate did he go home? I know this is what is intended, because the teacher's guide tells us what the answers are, and the answer to (3) is: He *ran* or *fast* or *He ran fast.* (The answers to 1, 2, and 4 are

1. In the park
2. A frog
4. She did not want him/Bozo/a frog in the house. She did not like him.

Question 1 is not a very good question for several reasons. For one thing, Mike is in two different places, as well as en route between them in the span of this 48-word 'story.' There is no single correct answer to the question as phrased.

In addition, the question asks about (and therefore treats as important) something that is really incidental to the story; it doesn't really matter in this story where the frog came from, and truly competent readers realize this and don't retain such irrelevant details.[1] Any linguist who has studied discourse properties of texts knows that this is not a good question to ask someone to see if she or he has understood this text.

Linguists are also involved in the standardized assessment of reading ability. Cecilia Freeman has just finished a report for the Ford Foundation with the help of Arnold Zwicky and G. Richard Tucker on the standardized reading comprehension test used in the state of New York as part of the Regents Competency Testing program. Charles Fillmore was involved in a similar analysis of a different test a few years ago. Analyses like these (and many more could still be done) can be used to evaluate test instruments, to discover whether the tests do in fact test the abilities they are supposed to be testing.

Many of the tasks I have described as suitable for a linguist probably do not actually require a Ph.D. in linguistics. A lot of them could be done by any sensible person who is articulate about language. Unfortunately, most sensible people aren't very articulate about language, and I think that a lot of people who are articulate about language aren't very sensible.

Another thing such a person could do—if the publisher could be persuaded of the marketability of it—is select materials that would be suitable for inclusion in a reader without being adapted, that is, already existing stories with acknowledged literary merit that managed to meet the sentence length and word length or frequency criteria of the readability formulae used by the publisher. It wouldn't be easy, but I think it could be done, and it could only help in making reading a more attractive activity and in enhancing the ability to appreciate literary styles (an ability that is required later on, but is not much cultivated in elementary reading curricula).

So far I have not said anything about what a 'pure' phonologist or syntactician could do for a basal reader publisher. This is mainly because I haven't been able to think of very much. Possibly linguists could provide valuable consultation in the construction of workbook pages for practicing letter-sound correspondences. I have seen supplementary materials where such help could have been used. In one, for example, children are supposed to put numbered tiles in lettered frames so that a picture corresponding to the number matches a lettered answer box indicating the letter that represents the initial sound or the word that names the picture. (This sounds more complicated than it is; my four-year-old can do it.) It doesn't seem like a bad way to help kids practice using the code of sound-letter correspondences. And it has a payoff—if the tiles are all placed correctly, shapes on their reverses form a specified design. But there are flaws in the choice of words represented in the 'games'; there is no sensible rationale guiding the choice of words whose beginnings (or endings) the children are supposed to find the letters for. In the same puzzle where children are asked to practice such regular correspondences as m - /m/, n - /n/, f - /f/, r - /r/, p /p/, and t - /t/, they are expected to be able to match e with a word beginning with [ə] ~ [iy] (depending on how one chooses to pronounce it), and a with [ɛ] ~ [ey], and c and k differentially with /k/. In the next puzzle, where the objective again is "to supply the beginning sounds of words with the help of pictures," children are expected to match a picture of a female head with a crown on it with the letter ('sound'?) q, along with matching a kite with k and a cup with c, and nine other, regular consonant initials. Practicing the regular correspondences provides help for kids who really need help to understand the *principle* of decoding. But practicing the less regular ones isn't likely to help at all, and the children who need to learn irregular spellings don't get to practice them much when most of the correspondences are regular.

3. Research Opportunities

Despite a history of strained (in both senses) interaction between educational research and theoretical linguistics, there is a place in educational research for individuals trained in linguistics and interested in problems of literacy. To give an idea of the variety of issues linguists have gotten involved in, let me just indicate some of the projects linguists have been involved in at the Center for the Study of Reading since 1976. Among those that can be characterized as basic research there are the following:

Marilyn Adams: Models of word recognition. TR 107.
John Barnitz: Interrelationship of orthography and phonological structure in learning to read. TR 57.
Alice Davison: Linguistics and the measurement of syntactic complexity: The case of Raising. TR 173.
G. M. Green: Discourse functions of inversion constructions. TR 98.
G. M. Green: Organization, goals, and comprehensibility of narratives; Newswriting, a case study. TR 132.
G. M. Green. Linguistics and the pragmatics of language use. TR 179.
G. M. Green, R. Kantor, J. Morgan et al.: Problems and techniques of text analysis. TR 168.
G. M. Green and M. Laff: Five-year-olds' recognition of authorship by literary style. TR 181.
William Hall and L. Guthrie: Cultural and situational variation in language function and use: Methodology and procedures for research. TR 148.

William Hall and W. Nagy: Theoretical issues in the investigation of words of internal report. TR 146.

Gabriella Hermon: On the discourse structure of direct quotation. TR 143.

Jerry Morgan: Two types of convention in indirect speech acts. TR 52.

Jerry Morgan and M. Sellner: Discourse and linguistic theory. In: R. C. Spiro et al. (eds.), *Theoretical Issues in the Study of Reading*. Hillsdale, NJ: Erlbaum.

Bonnie Nash-Webber: Inferences in an approach to discourse anaphora. TR 77.

Bonnie Nash-Webber and R. Reiter: Anaphora and logical form. TR 36.

Some of the more applied research includes:

Marilyn Adams: What good is orthographic redundancy? TR 192.

Tom Anderson, Bonnie Armbruster, and Robert Kantor: How clearly written are children's textbooks? RER 16.

John Barnitz: Reading comprehension of pronoun-referent structures by children in grades 2, 4, and 6. TR 117.

Alice Davison, Robert Kantor et al.: Limitations of readability formulae in guiding adaptation of texts. TR 162.

G. M. Green: On the appropriateness of adaptations in primary-level basal readers. Learning to read in American schools. Center for the Study of Reading.

G. M. Green, R. Kantor, J. Morgan et al.: Text analysis of two texts. TR 169, 170.

William Hall and L. Guthrie: On the dialect question and reading. TR 121.

Margaret Steffensen, R. Reynolds, Erica McClure, and L. Guthrie: Black English vernacular and reading comprehension: A close study of 3rd, 6th, and 9th graders. TR 199.

Some research still in progress that was initiated when Kantor was at the Center involves attempts to teach children to understand connected text better (especially not very well connected text) by teaching them to ask themselves why the authors said what they said in the order they said it, to reconstruct the connections that adherence to readability formulae induced the authors to leave out.

I'm not sure how to characterize my recent research. Strictly speaking, it is two projects designed to test empirically some assumptions involved in the design of basal readers that my observations as a linguist have led me to question. One project questions two assumptions about the use of readability formulae in designing readers.

The first assumption that I am questioning is the idea that children cannot read material that has longer sentences and less common vocabulary than readability formulae for their grade allow, with at least as much understanding as when they read material adapted to meet the criteria of formulae. The second assumption I am questioning is the notion that even if they could read unadapted material as well, they would prefer to read the shorter, adapted material, despite the fact that the adapted material has less detail, less characterization, less motivation for actions narrated, and in general, less style than the original.

I asked second graders to read two retyped versions of a story (one, the original, as it appeared in a regular children's book; the other an adaptation of it that was published in a popular basal reader). Then the children were interviewed about which one they liked reading better, and why. They were also asked to read one version of a different story (either the original or the adapted version), and a measure of their ability to understand it was taken. In general, children preferred the original version to the basal by about two to one, saying they found it more interesting and more exciting, though harder, and criticizing the basal version for being babyish and unrealistic ("[In the one I like] things happen more like real. Lions don't live in houses; a lion would live in a cave.") The comprehension differences between versions were insignificant.

My other project examines whether providing connected text with either redundant or crucial illustrations actually hinders some children in learning to decode print, by unwittingly teaching them to depend primarily on the illustration to understand text, rather than on the printed words. If so, it probably affects mainly those children who come to first grade without much internal motivation to learn to read, and who quickly lose what motivation they might have had when they find out what kind of sappy stories they're going to be expected to read. I chose two stories that only make sense when accompanied by their illustrations, and two whose illustrations tell almost as much of the story as the text does. Both kinds are very common in first-grade readers. Children read the stories either as published, or without the illustrations, or with the illustrations only and no text; and answered questions about the content of the story. If poor readers are depending on the illustrations to understand stories, they should do better answering questions on illustrated texts, regardless of whether the illustrations are crucial or redundant, and relatively poorly on unillustrated texts. Good readers, who will not have learned to depend on illustrations, should find texts with crucial illustrations relatively hard, regardless of whether the illustrations are present or not, as they will not be accustomed to looking to the illustrations to make sense of the text. They should find texts with redundant illustrations relatively easy, with or without the illustrations present, for the same reason. In fact, the poor readers averaged 41% better on illustrated text, and good readers averaged 25% better on text where illustrations were redundant, whether provided or not.

Readability research is another area where the talents and training of a linguist can be put to practical use, and not just in developing better means for grading instructional materials, although this remains important. A number of linguists have pinpointed many of the faults of extant formulae even when used as intended (which is not all that often) (cf. articles by Griffin, Selden, etc., in

Davison, Lutz, and Roalef 1981). Nonetheless, the reality is that pressure for 'plain language,' not just in elementary education but in commercial and official documents as well is now being mandated by legislation, and if linguists are involved in the implementation of criteria, perhaps it will help to avoid the potential disaster that would ensue if formulae are naively constructed and blindly applied. Imagine, for instance, trying to write instructions for filing tax returns that accurately represented the tax laws in sentences less than eighteen words long and words of less than three syllables.

4. Teacher Education

Finally, it is possible, and surely worthwhile, for linguists—or at least for relevant results of empirical linguistic research—to be directly involved in the training of individuals who will teach reading, although the logistics of how best to do this are still unclear to me. Some years ago (I don't know if it's still the case), Northeastern Illinois University, which concentrated on teacher training, required a course in linguistics for *all* its undergraduates. This seems like an ideal solution to the problem of teachers and aides who conclude that a child has a reading problem when he reads:

Ned asked, "Have you been sleeping?"

as:

8. /ned akst yu bin sliypin/

or who conclude that a child has a 'language' problem because her answers to questions like "Where did Charlie hide the money?" are just phrases and not full sentences. Somehow many teachers seem to lose sight of the fact that the normal way to answer questions like that, even for them, is with phrases that give just the requested information, and not with sentences like *Charlie hid the money under a stone*, which include that information along with a lot of redundant material (i.e., *Charlie hid the money*). But of course, a linguistics course for elementary and secondary education students has to be the right course, and taught by someone who has not only a solid understanding of the theoretical and empirical issues treated, but also an appreciation of students' concerns about classroom practice. A course that concentrates on acoustic phonetics, alternative theories of syntax, and internal vs. external reconstruction is likely to do more harm than good in that it makes linguistics look abstruse and irrelevant to teaching practices, and so predisposes the student not to pay attention to any of it.

I have examined some of the textbooks and supplementary materials used in training teachers, and couldn't find much to complain about in the discussions relating language to reading; they looked pretty sensible. I have sat in on some classes, and some of the lectures on linguistic topics were positively brilliant—I wanted to applaud. So this is not a blanket indictment of all current materials in teacher education. Still, I have seen people in elementary school classrooms trying to get second graders to induce the correct spelling of *baked* by having them 'sound out' *bake* plus *-e-d* and trying to get them to correct *a apple* to *an apple* by asking, "Is that how you say it?" when in fact that is how the children say it. A problem exists despite the availability of good materials in teacher education, and I don't know what the answer is.

This concludes the (undoubtedly incomplete) catalog I have to offer of opportunities for linguists in the field of reading. But I am not finished until I make two things very clear. First, the opportunities I have been talking about do not, for the most part, take the form of established positions with codified job descriptions. The publishers and test makers don't know they need linguists as badly as I think they do. Linguists who want to do the kind of work I have described will have to persuade the appropriate executives of their usefulness, and create the positions. Second, and it is impossible to stress this too much: In spite of the reputation that applied linguistics has in some quarters as a haven for students who can't make it in theoretical courses, the opportunities I have described are not for the faint of heart or the feeble of mind. Only the best, most alert, most broadly educated, most critically analytical are fit for the tasks I have described. They are not tasks that can be done adequately by the second-rate. Anyone can hack out a grammar of Gwambo-Mambo in this theory or that, and propose modifications of grammatical theory on the basis of that experience. If they're wrong, someone will be sure to let them know, and no lasting harm will be done.

But not just anyone can edit texts and questions and otherwise design instructional materials in accordance with both the results of relevant empirical research and common (and cultivated) sense. Not just anyone can teach prospective teachers things they didn't think they wanted to know about the nature of language. These jobs bear a lot of responsibility, and are not likely to be bestowed lightly on a linguist by a discipline which has been too often burned by premature espousal of linguists' ideas. And of course, the responsibility isn't one to be borne lightly either, for it is a responsibility for decisions potentially affecting the lives of millions of children.

NOTES

1. Actually, the supposedly correct answer is only an inference, and an invalid one at that, from what the text says. As anyone who has taken an elementary syntax course knows, *Mike saw a frog in the park* is structurally ambiguous, and Mike could well have seen a frog that was in the park without being in the park himself. However, connecting the assertion that Mike ran home with the frog and his claim that he got the frog in the park with the first sentence would enable the reader who can do that sort of thing to disregard the relative-clause reading of the ambiguous sentence with a fairly high degree of certainty.

REFERENCES

Bloomfield, Leonard 1942. "Linguistics and reading." *Elementary English Review* 19:125–130, 183–186.

Chomsky, Noam 1957. *Syntactic Structures*. The Hague: Mouton.

Davison, Alice et al. 1981. "Limitations of readability formulas in guiding adaptations of texts." Technical Report 162. Champaign, IL: Center for the Study of Reading, University of Illinois.

Davison, Alice, R. Lutz, and A. Roalef (eds.) 1981. "Text readability: proceedings of the March 1980 Conference." Technical Report 213, Champaign, IL: Center for the Study of Reading, University of Illinois.

Durkin, Dolores 1974. *Teaching Them to Read*. Boston: Allyn and Bacon.

Fillmore, Charles 1968. "The case for case." In: E. Bach and T. A. Harms (eds.), *Universals in Linguistic Theory*. New York: Holt.

Fries, Charles 1963. *Linguistics and Reading*. New York: Holt, Rinehart and Winston.

Fries, Charles, R. G. Wilson, and M. K. Rudolph 1966. *Merrill Linguistic Readers*. Columbus, OH: Charles E. Merrill Books.

Green, Georgia M. 1982. "Linguistics and the pragmatics of language use." *Poetics* 11:45–76.

Green, Georgia M., and Jerry Morgan 1980. "Pragmatics, grammar, and discourse." In: P. Cole (ed.), *Radical Pragmatics*. New York: Academic Press.

Morgan, Jerry, and M. Sellner 1980. "Discourse and linguistic theory." In: R. C. Spiro et al. (eds.), *Theoretical Issues in the Study of Reading*. Hillsdale, NJ: Lawrence Erlbaum Associates, pp. 165–200.

CHAPTER ELEVEN

Applications of Linguistics to the Language of Legal Interactions

Judith N. Levi

1. Introduction

If one reflects for a while on the nature of the two professions of linguistics and the law, one is likely to recognize that they share an important characteristic: that of being essentially grounded in language. And although the linguist uses that language as primary data for analysis and reflection, while the lawyer generally has much more practical concerns in focusing on language, nevertheless it remains true that both linguist and lawyer are continually engaged in studying, analyzing, and struggling to understand those aspects of language that constitute their principal professional preoccupation.

It may therefore be somewhat surprising to recognize that linguists have virtually ignored the language of the law until quite recently. Indeed, it is just in the last decade or so that linguists, and other social scientists concerned with language, have discovered the tremendous resources of natural data that await discovery within the world of law. Perhaps to make up for lost time, more and more linguists are now turning to the language of the law as a subject for primary research. At the same time, more and more legal professionals have begun to hire linguists as consultants whose training and expertise are being recognized as invaluable to the lawyer in analyzing a wide variety of cases. In order to examine some of these newly developing points of intersection between the two professions, I will review in the pages below some examples of the ways in which the major subfields of linguistic inquiry are proving applicable to particular problems and processes in the world of law.

Let us first consider a few of the reasons that have helped to bring the language of the law into focus for contemporary linguistic analysis; these reasons have primarily to do with the inner development of the linguistic profession itself. As the field of intense and exciting linguistic exploration gradually expanded over the last two decades from a profitable but nevertheless narrow focus on syntax, on out to the mistier land of semantics and thence to the vast uncharted regions of pragmatics, linguists began to recover from their collective amnesia of the 1960s and to remember that language was not just strings of symbols on paper, but rather a living, changing, vastly subtle medium for communication between human beings in real-life situations. And so linguists, still hungry for regularities and patterns but with a commendably developing appetite for empirical variety as well, began to get curious about some of these less tractable aspects of linguistic systematicity that were coming to light as they studied such subjects as meaning, socially determined variables in natural language, and the construction of understandings not only from the formal nature of what was actually said, but also from the who, what, where, and when of that particular utterance and even from what wasn't said. This gradual expansion of research interests within linguistics has led in recent years to the development of such research areas as pragmatics, speech act theory, conversational analysis, and communicative competence, and to a closer integration of theoretical linguistics with the 'hyphenated' disciplines of psycholinguistics and sociolinguistics, which of course had been paying attention to many of these other context-dependent variables all along.

One result of this broadening of intellectual horizons in linguistics was the recognition that language in 'special contexts' (such as the language of professions like law, medicine, politics, or science) should not be treated as some embarrassing deviation from a set of purportedly normal rules of grammar but rather could be regarded as an especially rich source of *relevant* data not only in terms of its own specialness (e.g., the terms and constructions peculiar to legal language) but even more importantly as a test of the generalizations about all natural language that linguists are committed to discovering. And of all 'special contexts,' the language of the law is particularly intriguing, since the consequences of one's use of language in a legal setting can be, literally, a matter of life or death. But even if we consider legal settings of far less consequence than a murder trial, for example, we must recognize that the legal system itself has one of the most highly elaborated systems of interrelationships between language use on the one hand, and social, economic, political, and even moral forces on the other. In this regard it is ideally suited to contemporary linguistics which seeks to look beyond the formal structure of language itself to the human significance of the message the language was meant to impart. The sociologist Brenda Danet (1980b:448) has emphasized an additional affinity between linguistic and legal systems that is pertinent here, in noting that both law and language "are rule-governed symbolic systems that are uniquely human and essential to the fabric of society." Thus we see that it is both natural and exciting for linguists to bring the language of the law into the scope of their investigations.

Interestingly enough, just as linguists were beginning to discover the fascination of legal language, a number of simultaneous developments were taking place in (other) social sciences that would also provide the impetus for new research into language and the law. The historical background here was slightly different from that in linguistics, in that the social sciences (especially sociology, anthropology, and of course political science) had long been interested in the study of legal systems as social, cultural, and political phenomena of tremendous significance and complexity. Nevertheless, the role of *language* in these legal systems had been almost totally neglected. Until rather recently, it appears, most social scientists, like the average layperson not trained in linguistics, took language too much for granted; a natural resource like air and water, it was perhaps too familiar and too ubiquitous to be recognized as an essential and remarkably influential component of just the social interactions that social scientists are interested in studying. As a result, an enormous amount of sociology, political science, psychology, and even anthropology was done without regard to the fact that the language of the investigators, as well as the language of the people and phenomena investigated, were variables that ought to be recognized and analyzed in their own right. Fortunately, this intellectual blind spot and methodological weakness is gradually being corrected (albeit very slowly and unevenly throughout the social sciences), as a result of a number of developments internal to the social sciences that parallel somewhat the changes just discussed in regard to linguistics.

To begin with, there appears to be growing understanding of a point made recently by the British sociologist Robert Dunstan concerning the naturalness of taking language as an object of study in the social sciences. Dunstan writes:

> That language is socially organized makes it a proper object for sociological study. When one further considers that language is itself the vehicle for social action then language use becomes *the* object of sociological inquiry. (1980:61)

But just as linguists have been slow to recognize the potential of legal language as an object of study, so social scientists did not appear to appreciate the significance of language as an inherently *social* phenomenon until a number of concurrent but originally unrelated developments had transpired in Western scholarship. These include:

a. a growing interest in *interdisciplinary* studies of social phenomena, including language behavior;
b. the development of empirical research in conversational analysis and communicative competence in both sociology and sociolinguistics;
c. increasing understanding of the potential of modern recording technology for communications research;
d. the spreading, albeit nonuniversal, influence of post-Wittgensteinian ordinary language philosophy;
e. the elaboration of 'interpretivist' or 'constructionist' alternatives to 'positivist' epistemology in the social sciences, with the concomitant growth of ethnomethodology;
f. responses by at least some researchers to public criticism of the sociology of

the professions, including their allegedly elitist, exclusionary, and/or mystifying language practices.

(See Dunstan 1980 and Danet 1980b, for further comment on these developments.)

So we see that the growth of interest in the language of legal interactions is the result of a variety of intellectual and social developments that have, so to speak, 'conspired' to bring linguists and other social scientists into this developing area of scholarship. We should also note at this point that both of these groups of researchers have a commitment to taking spoken language, rather than written language, as their primary data, since it is the speech of individuals that is the most natural manifestation of their linguistic abilities. Here the linguist and social scientist's perspective differs significantly from that of the lawyer, the legal scholar, and the layperson, who tend to think of 'legal language' much more as the written language of laws, statutes, judicial opinions, and legal documents of various sorts than as the ephemeral and less prestigious speech that is generated every day in legal contexts. It is undeniable that the written language of legal documents and legal professionals also provides a challenging subject of study for the intrepid researcher from any discipline, and some very interesting results are already available. (See, for example, Mellinkoff 1963; Redish 1979; Danet 1980b; and Charrow et al. 1982.) Nevertheless, the primary emphasis of this chapter will be on applications of linguistics to the *spoken* language of legal interactions, since that is the area of liveliest research activity in recent years and may well be the area that will offer us the most surprises—and the most significant research applications—in the end.

The range of linguistic subfields that have potentially fruitful applications to particular domains of legal interactions is impressively, and somewhat surprisingly, extensive; these applications are indicated somewhat schematically, and certainly not exhaustively, in Table 1. Psycholinguistics and sociolinguistics lead the list because they constitute the areas of linguistics in which more empirical studies of legal language have been published than any other. Semantics and pragmatics follow because these appear to be areas especially rich in potential applications, even though to date very little has been published to bear this prediction out; most of the work in these areas has been carried out by individual linguists hired as consultants or expert witnesses to work with lawyers and litigants in actual legal cases. Finally, the traditional core subjects of morphology and syntax, phonetics and phonology are indicated, although these last subjects will not be discussed in the present paper. In the sections to follow, I will select one area of research for each of the four subfields of linguistics just cited (psycholinguistics, sociolinguistics, semantics, and pragmatics) and use it to suggest some of the ways that research in that particular subfield has been applied to language analysis in legal domains. (For a more extensive discussion of applications, see Levi in preparation.)

Table 1. Applications of Linguistics to Legal Domains

I. Psycholinguistics
  A. Psychology of memory: eyewitness testimony
  B. Social psychology: language variation in courtroom
  C. Psychology of comprehension
    1. Oral jury instructions
    2. Written forms, regulations, laws, contracts

II. Sociolinguistics
  A. Language variation and social evaluation
  B. Linguistic minorities and the law
    1. Problems in judicial system
    2. Problems in education
    3. Cross-dialectal problems for native speakers too

III. Semantics
  A. Lexical semantics
    1. Denotations (or, whence crucial definitions?)
    2. Connotations (in courtroom and advertising)
    3. Lexical presupposition
    4. Problems in synonymity
    5. Variation (individual and chronological)
    6. Ambiguity and vagueness
  B. Sentential semantics
    1. Comprehensibility in speech and writing
    2. Devious language: presuppositions and syntactic deception
    3. Some problems in advertising
    4. The legal approach to interpretation

IV. Pragmatics and Discourse Analysis
  A. Speech act theory applied to legal discourse
    1. Analysis of courtroom 'questioning'
    2. Verbal offenses
    3. FTC and truth in advertising
  B. Conversational analysis
    1. Taped conversations as evidence
    2. Plea bargaining
  C. Communicative competence
    1. Parties in courtroom proceedings
    2. Consumers as targets of advertising
    3. Consumers in adhesion contracts

V. Morphology and Syntax
  A. Courtroom questioning: forms and functions
  B. Comprehensibility of jury instructions
  C. Plain English and readability requirements
  D. Descriptions of legal morphology and syntax

VI. Phonetics and Phonology
  A. Forensic technology: voice identification and voice lie detection
  B. Speech differences (phonological) and social evaluation
  C. Which similarities (phonological) constitute brand name/copyright infringement?

2. Applications of Psycholinguistics

There are three major areas of psychology and psycholinguistics that are currently being applied to the language of legal processes and interactions. These are:

1. the psychology of memory, as applied to the reliability of eyewitness testimony;
2. social psychology, as applied to social judgments based on courtroom speech and affecting legal outcomes;
3. the psychology of language comprehension, applied both to the oral language of judge-to-jury instructions and to the written language of legal and bureaucratic documents.

In this section, I will discuss only the first of these three areas, using it to illustrate how scholarly investigations in psychology and psycholinguistics can help us to understand the real-world processes that take place in courtroom settings. The second major area will be discussed in some detail below under the heading of sociolinguistic applications, while the third will not be treated in this paper for reasons of space. (Readers interested in this third topic may consult such representative studies as Charrow and Charrow 1979 and Elwork, Sales, and Alfini 1982, on jury instructions; and Campbell and Holland 1982, Charrow, Crandall, and Charrow 1982, Felker 1980, and Holland and Redish 1981, on the written language of legal documents.)

In the area of memory and eyewitness testimony, one leading researcher is Elizabeth Loftus, of the University of Washington Department of Psychology. Integrating the very extensive psychological literature on memory, which dates back over the last hundred years, with her own recent experimental studies, Loftus has identified a wide range of psychological and psycholinguistic factors that can alter the memory of an eyewitness between the time an event is observed and the time that testimony about that event is produced. The significance of this research is particularly telling when viewed in the light of the fact that juries tend to give tremendous weight to an eyewitness account, weight that is in many cases far out of proportion to any chance of the testimony being actually reliable (Loftus 1979:8ff).

In her 1979 book *Eyewitness Testimony,* Loftus first documents the fact that "the testimony of one or more eyewitnesses can be overwhelmingly influential" (op. cit.:9), not only when there is no evidence of any other kind but even when all the other available evidence tends to point in the opposite direction. The implications or the administration of justice are obvious—and serious.

Loftus's work on eyewitness testimony in particular recognizes that the phenomenon of memory must be analyzed as a three-stage process, involving (1) the acquisition and initial storage of information concerning an event, (2) the retention of this information over a period of time, and (3) the retrieval of information for verbal reporting. At each of these three stages, the mental processes of an individual may produce memories that vary in smaller or larger ways from the event that was the original stimulus. In Stage 1, the stage of actual observation and initial storage of the memory, both 'event factors' (having to do with the situation) and 'witness factors' (having to do with the personality and expectations of the person involved) have been identified that can change the content of the stored memory from what was actually seen. During Stage 2, the retention phase, the stored memory may be subtly altered either as a result of the witness's subsequent thought processes, or as a result of different kinds of 'postevent information' acquired by the witness, consciously or unconsciously, through conversations, reading, interrogations, or other kinds of intervening experiences. In Stage 3, the stage of retrieval for reporting, the content and thus the accuracy of a witness's recall is subject to further modification as a result of a number of psychological, social, and linguistic variables in the recall environment. Table 2 presents a graphic summary of some of the factors affecting memory that are discussed in Loftus 1979; for present purposes, we will of course concentrate on just the linguistic factors.

As Table 2 reveals, the factors influencing one's memory during Stage 1 are virtually all nonlinguistic (e.g., degree of stress experienced, stereotypes about event participants, and exposure time). However, language does play a significant role in affecting the memories of witnesses to events during the stage of memory retention and the stage of memory retrieval. In regard to the stage of memory retention, the research of Loftus and others suggests strongly that both the acquisition of 'postevent information' from the outside and one's own internal thought processes can subtly change what we remember of an earlier incident; both of these experiences are, of course, transmitted and hence directly influenced by language.

In one of the most intriguing and frequently cited experiments (Loftus and Palmer 1974), Loftus and a colleague showed subjects a film of an automobile accident and then asked them questions about pertinent details, varying the wording to see the effect of lexical presuppositions on both content and accuracy of subjects' recall. The first linguistically important discovery was that subjects who were asked, "About how fast were the cars going when they smashed into each other?" tended to report a significantly higher speed than those subjects who were asked, "About how fast were the cars going when they hit each other?" The second linguistically significant discovery was that the lexical presupposition of violent collision carried by the verb *smashed* much more strongly than by *hit* influenced other areas of the subjects' memory in addition to the obvious one of vehicular speed. For example, when the same subjects were questioned one week later, without any additional viewing of the film, and were asked, as one of a series of questions, "Did you see any broken glass?" subjects who had earlier heard the word *smashed* answered "Yes" more than twice as frequently as those who had heard the same question with the word *hit* instead— even though in fact the film had shown no broken glass at all (Loftus 1979:78).

Table 2.   Factors Affecting Reliability of Memory*

Stage of Memory	Linguistic Factors	Nonlinguistic Factors
1. Acquisition (and initial storage)		*"Event factors"* such as: exposure time, frequency of exposure, degree of violence *"Witness factors"* such as: personal stress, expectations, contextual biases
2. Retention	*Acquisition of postevent info* through linguistic input such as conversations, interrogations, media reports *Internal thought processes* especially labeling, guessing, repeated retrievals (causing "freezing effect")	Whether details were central or peripheral Timing of postevent info Creation of compromise memories Postevent info acquired through nonlinguistic sources (e.g., photographs)
3. Retrieval	Style of interrogation (open or controlled questions) and its effect on style of reporting Question wording	Status of interrogator Retrieval environment Motivation(s) of recaller

*This table is based on information provided in Elizabeth F. Loftus, *Eyewitness Testimony* (Harvard University Press, 1979), especially Chapters 3, 4, and 5.

While the first discovery concerns the effect of question wording on recall of an event (i.e., during Stage 3), the second discovery indicates that questions asked (*or* accounts read, *or* conversations heard) while a memory is stored can change the form of that memory so that information recalled *at a later date* will emerge significantly different from that originally entered into memory.

Definite descriptions that occur in the language with which postevent information is communicated can also influence one's memory during Stage 2, since these descriptions presuppose the existence of an object that may in fact not have been part of the original experience or of the initially stored memory. In another experiment, Loftus (1975) showed subjects a film of an automobile accident and later questioned them about the speed of one of the cars; one group of subjects was asked about the speed of the car "while traveling along the country road" while the second was asked about the car's speed "when it passed the barn while traveling along the country road.'' Although no barn had appeared in the film, 17% of subjects who had heard the misleading question mentioning the nonexistent barn reported *later on* that they had seen a barn, while only 3% of those whose question had not included the misleading definite description did the same. As Loftus remarks, ''Thus, casually mentioning a nonexistent object during the course of questioning can increase the likelihood that a person will later report having seen that nonexistent object'' (1979:60).

These findings are, of course, significant not only for psychological research into the permanence or mutability of stored information but also for the administration of justice; in particular, these findings suggest that attorneys engaged in courtroom questioning of eyewitnesses need to know much more about very fine details of linguistic interactions that have transpired outside of court than, in fact, they are ever likely to have available. This follows from the fact that the kinds of suggestions that are carried by certain lexical choices (such as *smashed* vs. *hit* vs. *contacted*) and definite descriptions can be conveyed not only in the course of formal courtroom questioning (during which attorneys may have the right to object to the opposing counsel's question as inappropriately 'leading') but also in the course of informal questioning many days, weeks, or months prior to a trial by such varied individuals as one's friends, insurance agents, reporters, and other individuals discussing a significant event with an eyewitness.

Not only can the content of our stored memories be changed by information derived from *external* sources, but linguistically coded information created by our own thoughts can have the same effect. A number of experiments reported by Loftus (1979:80–6) suggest that our stored memories can be altered by (1) *labeling* a particular object or situation with one word or phrase rather than another and subsequently recalling it more clearly (Carmichael et al. 1932; Bornstein 1974, 1976); (2) *guessing* with less than full confidence about part of a memory and later merging the content of that guess into what was until then a hazy or incomplete memory (Hastie et al. 1978); and (3) the *'freezing effect'* of repeating an earlier recollection until what was recalled only tentatively and incompletely at first becomes so familiar that one is convinced that the oft-repeated recollection is fully identical to what was actually seen originally (Kay 1955). In all these cases, it is the linguistic expression that we choose in our own minds after an event is witnessed but before it must be recalled that manifests a transforming power on the information first entered there. As Loftus sums up, ''it appears that a subject's *linguistic* responses to an object can cause distortions similar to those that have been observed when others provide the information externally'' (Loftus 1979:82, emphasis added).

During the third and final phase assigned to memory by psychological investigators, linguistic form and content continue to exert a significant influence. Two of the areas which have been studied are (1) the linguistic mode or style of answering used by the witness when asked to recall stored information, and (2) the actual wording of the questions used. In the first case, experiments have been

designed to test the effects of two major types of interrogation on the completeness and the accuracy of witness recollection. When a witness is asked
something open-ended like, "Tell us everything you can remember," the response is likely to be in a narrative form whose internal sequencing is a function
of the witness's own memory and style. On the other hand, if the witness is asked
a series of very specific questions by the interrogator (whether this is a police
officer, an insurance agent, a reporter, or a relative), the sequence of information
recalled will be controlled not by the witness but by the person asking the
questions, and the responses elicited will then not be in narrative form. Loftus
reports on a series of experiments by others (Cady 1924; Marquis et al. 1972;
Snee and Lush 1941) that show that the linguistic style of a witness's testimony—that is, free narrative versus answers to more or less directive questions—influences both the accuracy and the completeness of a witness' recollec-
tions. Specifically, the narrative form of response tends to produce the most
accurate but not the most complete reporting, while a series of well-chosen
questions has the opposite effect: coverage tends to be more complete, but
responses are less accurate (partly because, as already observed, the wording of a
question can introduce false and misleading information). This psycholinguistic
research implies that the optimal mode of questioning a witness (assuming that
both accuracy and completeness are desired) is to permit the witness to deliver a
narrative-style report first, and then to fill in the gaps by means of a series of
more specific questions. Any other procedure will contribute to error in witness
recall.

When we look at the specific wording of questions asked a witness during
Stage 3, we see once again that lexical presupposition can influence the content
of a stored memory in such a way that the recalled information is significantly
altered. Just as the definite descriptions discussed earlier that may occur in the
language a witness hears during the storage phase of memory can suggest the
existence of an object not present in the event originally observed, so too the use
of the definite article in a question about a crucial object can cause the witness to
recall something he or she had never actually observed. In yet another auto-
mobile-accident film experiment (Loftus and Zanni 1975), Loftus and a colleague tested 100 subjects after they had viewed a film, using paired questions
such as these: "Did you see a broken headlight?" vs. "Did you see the broken
headlight?" Loftus reports,

> Witnesses who received the questions using "the" were much more likely to report
> having seen something that had not really appeared in the film. In the first experi-
> ment 15 percent in the "the" group said "yes" when asked about a nonexistent
> item, while only 7 percent in the "a" group made that error. In the second study
> the difference is even more striking: 20 percent versus 6 percent. On the other
> hand, witnesses who received the question with "a" were much more likely to
> respond "I don't know" both when the object had been present and when it had
> not. (1979:96)

This finding is particularly important because although linguists are likely to recognize the crucial role played by 'little words' like articles and conjunctions in semantic interpretation, nonlinguists—whether they are highly educated judges and attorneys or less educated jurors and witnesses—are much less likely to be sensitive to these matters, and thus will not always observe when the presence of a definite article has changed an otherwise unobjectionable courtroom question into one which may well be ruled inadmissible on the grounds of being a 'leading' question. Even outside of the courtroom, the effect of this existential presupposition can alter the testimony or deposition of a witness in a way that might critically affect the outcome of a case.

Loftus reports on two other experiments showing how lexical presupposition embedded in the wording of a question can influence the content, and hence the accuracy, of witness recall (Loftus 1979:94–5). The first experiment, done by Richard J. Harris (1973), involves marked and unmarked adjective pairs like *tall* and *short, deep* and *shallow, old* and *young.* Harris found that using the marked form of the adjective (i.e., *short, shallow,* or *young* in the preceding pairs) caused the subjects' estimates to move in the marked direction in comparison with estimates of subjects who had heard the unmarked adjective. For example, the two questions, "How tall was the basketball player?" and "How short was the basketball player?" asked of two different groups elicited responses that averaged 79 and 69 inches, respectively; thus, those who heard the marked adjective, carrying a presupposition (in this case) of shortness, revised their estimates downwards by accepting the speaker's presupposition. A somewhat similar experiment was done by Loftus as part of a market research interview series; she found that shoppers who were asked, "Do you get headaches *frequently* and, if so, how often?" produced estimates three times as great on the average as the estimates given by shoppers asked instead, "Do you get headaches *occasionally* and, if so, how often?"

The work by Loftus and others on the psychology of eyewitness memory has important potential application to legal practitioners and to psycholinguists alike. On the one hand, it shows some of the intriguing ways that language form and language content interact with other nonlinguistic mental processes, such as memory for shapes, colors, and situational gestalts. On the other, it suggests that lawyers and litigants need to understand more about the syntax, semantics, and pragmatics of courtroom questioning not only in order to win their own cases but in order to suggest possible changes in the rules of evidence that will strengthen the system of justice and make it less subject to the distorting effects of both linguistic and extralinguistic factors on the accuracy of courtroom testimony.

3. Applications of Sociolinguistics

The domain of sociolinguistics is the interaction of language and society; the purpose of sociolinguistics is to discover the nature and complexities of this multidimensional interaction. It is therefore natural that the language of legal processes and legal interactions should attract the attention of sociolinguists, especially in view of the fact that our legal system is not only a highly significant institution within our social organization but one whose functioning is unusually dependent on both oral and written language. The relevance of legal language to sociolinguistic scholarship is further heightened by the remarkable parallelism noted by sociologist Brenda Danet and cited earlier, namely, that ''both [law and language] are rule-governed symbolic systems that are uniquely human and essential to the fabric of society'' (Danet 1980b:448). Although a full appreciation of this relevance has been somewhat slow in coming within sociolinguistics, research activity has been increasing significantly in the last few years.

Sociolinguistic studies of the language of legal interactions thus far fall into two major categories. The first is the study of the relationship between language variation and social evaluation in the courtroom, while the second concerns the problems encountered in the legal system by members of linguistic minorities (including limited- and non-English-speaking people, as well as the hearing-impaired and the deaf). Since the second of these categories includes many articles which, while focusing on language-related problems, do not represent direct applications of linguistics per se, it will not be treated in any detail in this review; readers interested in specific references may find them in Levi (1982), especially Section A7 on Communicative Competence and Section B1 on Rights of Linguistic Minorities).

One of the major research efforts in the study of language variation in legal settings has been carried out by an interdisciplinary research team based at Duke University. In 1974, with funding from the Law and Social Science Program of the National Science Foundation, this group began its study of spoken language in American trial courtrooms; the investigators, led by the anthropologist William M. O'Barr, also included three lawyers, two social psychologists, a linguist, and another anthropologist. The central hypothesis of the Duke research team was suggested in part by a substantial body of empirical research in social psychology and sociolinguistics, carried out earlier and independently in *non*-legal settings. These studies suggested that our judgments of whether a person is telling the truth are heavily influenced by our *social* and *psychological* evaluation of the speaker, and that these judgments are in turn heavily influenced by the way that person speaks. Thus, whether other people will believe what we say depends not merely on what we say, but also on how we say it and on the others' overall evaluation of us as people. The relevance of this research for studies of court-room language and behavior should be clear; the outcome of a trial may hinge crucially on the testimony of a witness, yet that witness's credibility may be a function not so much of the *content* of the testimony, but more of a bundle of linguistic, social, and psychological factors, which rules of evidence and trial lawyers' practical experience may not yet recognize as having any significance. It is these factors that the Duke team set out to investigate.[1]

The research group began by observing and tape recording over 150 hours of criminal trial proceedings in a North Carolina Superior Court. Both the observers' detailed notes and the audio recordings were then analyzed, first to identify the significant dimensions of language variation among the lawyers and witnesses in these trials, and then to correlate the *linguistic* variables with different *social* variables observable in the courtroom. The hypotheses suggested by these observational analyses were then tested empirically in a series of simulated-jury experiments, using both undergraduate and law school students as subjects.

Significant stretches of actual courtroom dialogue between lawyers and witnesses were re-recorded by actors in several different versions, each of which illustrated one of the important linguistic variables identified by the research team; different groups of subjects were then asked questions based on the particular version of the reenacted testimony that they had heard. Subjects were asked to rate witnesses for such personal qualities as competence, trustworthiness, and attractiveness; they were also asked to rate lawyers for such professional qualities as intelligence, fairness, skillfulness, and being in control. These social judgments were then analyzed to see how they correlated with the three major dimensions of linguistic variation set up deliberately by the experimenters. These dimensions, all subsumable under the broad heading of *speaking style,* are (1) power vs. powerless speech, (2) narrative vs. fragmented testimony, and (3) perseverance vs. acquiescence in simultaneous speech. Let us consider each one briefly in turn.

The study of what O'Barr and his colleagues came to call 'power speech' vs. 'powerless speech' grew out of an interest in investigating the influence of some proposed sex differences in American speech on witness credibility in American trial courtrooms. In the early 1970s, the linguist Robin Lakoff, along with some other researchers, proposed that women's speech in this country is characterized by a set of lexical, semantic, syntactic, and phonological features which systematically differentiate that speech from the speech more typically heard from men (Lakoff 1973, 1975). The features proposed by Lakoff as typical of women's speech include a higher frequency of intensifiers (e.g., *very, so, awfully, terribly*), so-called empty adjectives, polite rather than direct locutions, qualifying expressions known as 'hedges,' more formal or even overcorrected grammatical constructions, question intonation on declarative sentences, and a broader range of intonation patterns (particularly for expressive purposes) than is encountered in typical men's speech. Together, these features comprise a more tentative, deferential, polite, exaggerated, indirect, and/or emotional style of speaking than the speech style customarily heard in, or at least stereotypically associated with, American men's speech; moreover, the former style is one we would expect to be taken less seriously and to be less persuasive (in a courtroom or elsewhere) than the latter style, which is considered to be more direct, assertive, and 'rational'.

The Duke research team included the set of features proposed as characterizing women's speech among the variables to be examined in their study. Not too surprisingly, perhaps, they found that although many female witnesses did use the mode of speech identified by Lakoff, many female witnesses did not use it, while some male witnesses did. Instead of a direct correlation between these features and the sex of the witnesses, they found instead that "the mode of speech we are considering seemed to depend on the social position of the witness vis-à-vis the court" (Lind and O'Barr 1978:71). Witnesses with higher status (such as physicians, parole officers, and other professionals of either sex) tended to exhibit the features in question less frequently than did witnesses with less prestige or lower status (for example, the unemployed or unskilled of either sex). As a result, the researchers decided to use the term 'powerless speech (mode)' to refer to the more deferential and tentative style of speech, and to use the term 'power speech (mode)' to refer to a more assertive and direct mode of speech in which the features in question show up less frequently.

The major research question at issue then became one of determining how the use of these two styles of speech by witnesses would correlate with simulated jurors' social evaluations of the witnesses, since those social evaluations in turn would affect the jurors' judgments of the witnesses' credibility. In order to examine this question, tapes were prepared on which substantially the same testimony was recorded in four different ways: a female witness using the power mode, a female witness using the powerless mode, a male witness using the power mode, and a male witness using the powerless mode. Subjects in the experiment were provided with some background information about the case of which the testimony was a part, and then were told to imagine themselves as jurors hearing the testimony in court. After hearing the recorded material, they were asked to rate the witnesses along such social dimensions as competence, social attractiveness, trustworthiness, and convincingness. The researchers report that

> there are striking differences in the social evaluations produced by the power and powerless testimony. For both the male and female witnesses, the power speech testimony produced perceptions that the witness was more competent, attractive, trustworthy, dynamic, and convincing than did the powerless testimony. . . . These findings confirm that variation in the manner chosen by a witness for verbal expression may have strong effects on how those hearing the testimony evaluate the witness. (1978:72)

Lind and O'Barr note further that

> since witnesses using power and powerless speech were perceived differently on a number of social evaluation dimensions which have been found in other social psychological studies to influence acceptance of a communication, we suggest that this speech variable could affect the outcome of trials in which a crucial witness used the power or powerless mode of speech. (1978:73)

The second linguistic dimension that the researchers sought to analyze was the difference between *narrative* and *fragmented* testimony. Witnesses are compelled to answer the questions that lawyers on both sides put to them, but the lawyers have a great deal of freedom in deciding whether to permit the witness to answer at some length and in his or her own fashion, or whether to restrain the witness's response by requiring relatively brief or restricted answers. The researchers suspected that the linguistic variable of long vs. short answers might therefore correlate highly with such social psychological questions as control and respect. Thus, they comment,

> We noted . . . the principle in Anglo-American legal procedure that most of the control over the substance and form of testimony is delegated to the interrogating attorney. Since this principle of attorney control is widely known, it seemed likely that narrative testimony would be seen by jurors as an instance of voluntary, partial transfer from the attorney to the witness of control over evidence presentation. . . . A group of social psychological models—termed attribution theory—suggests that the type of testimony heard would be interpreted as carrying information about the attorney's perception of the witness. (1978:75)

Once again, we have an instance of a linguistic variable that seems to influence social evaluation of a speaker, which evaluation in turn will influence how much the testimony of that speaker will be believed.

The results of this part of the study are somewhat complex, since the variables analyzed include not only the narrative/fragmented style difference, but also the sex of the witness and the degree of legal training of the experimental subjects (since both undergraduates and law students were used). The general conclusion, however, is clear: jurors tend to respond more favorably to witnesses delivering narrative testimony than to witnesses forced into a more fragmented mode of speech; presumably, this is in part because the jurors infer that the attorney would cede partial control of the linguistic interaction only to witnesses who command a certain measure of respect in the attorney's eyes. The implication once again is that the higher social evaluations accorded to these witnesses will correlate strongly with their credibility for the jurors; thus, all other elements held constant, testimony delivered in a narrative style has a better chance of being believed than testimony heard through a series of restricted questions.

In addition to the general conclusion reported just above, the researchers discovered some very interesting correlations relating to the very same sex differences originally proposed by Lakoff to distinguish men's and women's speech. Of the four possible combinations of testimony style and sex of witness, the undergraduates rated *lowest* a male witness delivering testimony in a fragmented style, while the law students rated *highest* a female witness delivering testimony in a narrative style (1978:78). Note that these two categories both involved witnesses who are speaking in a mode that might be considered to be atypical for their sex in a sociolinguistic context like a courtroom; drawing on social attribution theory, Lind and O'Barr speculate that only such clearly atypical speech behavior (that is, speech patterns contrary to sex stereotypes for assertiveness) might be interpreted by jurors as particularly strong evidence of the attorney's attitude toward the witness, which in turn would influence their own evaluations of the witness's personal characteristics. A male witness not permitted by the attorney to speak freely would thus be downgraded in reliability or competence, while a female witness unexpectedly ceded control would be upgraded in terms of just such variables. Although this particular explanation is offered as a 'highly speculative' part of the analysis, the overall evidence concerning this particular linguistic dimension of testimony style strongly supports the following conclusion:

> when differences do occur in reactions to narrative and fragmented testimony they are in the direction of more favorable evaluations of witnesses giving narrative answers. Further, that the testimony type affected not only evaluations of the witness but also perceptions of the attorney-witness relationship shows that listeners use court conversations to arrive at rather complex beliefs about what they hear. (1978:79–80)

The third linguistic dimension examined in the Duke studies is called 'perseverance and acquiescence in simultaneous speech,' in other words, who wins the linguistic tug of war when an attorney and a witness end up speaking at the same time. As in the area of narrative vs. fragmented testimony, linguistic behavior here seems likely to be a good measure of social control in the courtroom dialogue.

Once again, actors recorded testimony that was similar to actual occurrences of simultaneous speech recorded during hostile cross-examination in the North Carolina criminal courtrooms; in this case, only male actors were used. Four different versions of the testimony were recorded, including one control tape with no simultaneous speech at all and three other tapes in which the degree of 'attorney perseverance' (and, concomitantly, the degree of 'witness acquiescence') varied. Subjects received some background information about the case, listened to the tapes, and then were asked to respond as if they were jurors to questions about the witness, the attorney, and the defendant against whom the witness testified.

The results showed that *any* occurrence of simultaneous speech caused the subjects to see the attorney as having less control than in the case where there was no simultaneous speech. Second, subjects tended to rate the attorney as less intelligent and less fair to the witness when he persisted in simultaneous speech than when he acquiesced. Once again, however, significant differences were observed between male and female subjects when asked about the attorneys showing the most and least perseverance. One of these differences is that female subjects tended to rank the attorney as less skillful and the witness as less competent and less likeable when the attorney persevered the most, in sharp contrast to male subjects who tended to rank the attorney as more skillful and the witness as more competent and more likeable under the same conditions (1978:82–3). In discussing these ratings, the authors suggest (again quite tentatively in the absence of more extensive supporting evidence) that the women downgraded the attorney's performance when he persevered because they thought he was being unfair to the witness in cutting him off, while the men upgraded the attorney's performance in the same circumstances in the belief that the attorney ought to reassert his control in a hostile verbal interaction with a witness. Interestingly, the authors point out that these sex-correlated differences in attorney ratings

> are congruent with research on the behavior of women and men when they are themselves involved in interpersonal conflict. Previous research suggests that, where sex differences in conflict behavior do occur, females seem more oriented to interpersonal relations and males seem more preoccupied with the outcome of the conflict. (1978:84)

In any case, the results of this particular study did confirm that (1) the linguistic variable of perseveration vs. acquiescence in simultaneous speech influenced the subjects' social evaluation of the witness, and (2) the social evaluation of the witness in turn influenced judgments about the witness's credibility (as shown by subjects' ratings of the defendant's aggressiveness, which was the subject of the witness's testimony).

To summarize the findings of the Duke University research, it appears that for all three linguistic dimensions examined, judgments of witness credibility were made as a function of social psychological judgments about the witness, which in turn were significantly affected by the linguistic style in which the witness's testimony was delivered. These findings are of relevance to scholarship in linguistics and social psychology, as well as law. In regard to the significance of language in social psychological behavior, the studies demonstrate that social psychological theories of social control, credibility of communication, and attributions of power and status relations must look closely at *linguistic* variables in order to provide a more complete account of these aspects of human behavior. In the domain of sociolinguistics, the empirical findings extend our knowledge of sex differences in language behavior and language attitudes, since significant differences were observed both as a function of the sex of the experimental subject and as a function of the sex of the witness. Thus, we saw on the one hand that subjects of different sexes reacted differently to the same language behavior (such as attorney perseverance), while on the other hand, all subjects manifested different reactions to the same linguistic style when used by witnesses of different sexes, reactions which were further influenced by the degree to which the witness (whether male or female) deviated from sex-stereotypical patterns of linguistic interaction. These courtroom studies both confirm earlier research concerning the interaction of language and social behavior, and suggest fruitful directions for future research to see whether and to what extent the patterns observed in the courtroom may be generalizable to a broader range of sociolinguistic contexts. (For further discussion of the implications of this research for social science in general, see O'Barr 1982:118–23.)

The discoveries made by the Duke team are also important for the study and the practice of law. Current rules of evidence for admissible courtroom testimony focus primarily, if not exclusively, on the content and sources of the evidence provided by witnesses, and do not take into account at all the variation in style of presentation that was the subject of the Duke research. Yet if, as these studies strongly suggest, the credibility of witnesses is directly influenced by just such linguistic variables, it is possible that the judicial system should begin to consider revising its rules of evidence and/or its instructions to jurors in such a way that legally irrelevant but psychologically salient biasing factors might be at least identified, and taken into account, in courtroom proceedings. (For some specific suggestions on how the law might be modified, in both theory and practice, see O'Barr 1982:113–8). Needless to say, this task must await both further empirical studies by social scientists and careful communication between those scientists and legal practitioners in order to discover just what response can be, and should be, taken by the law in response to pertinent research.

4. Applications of Semantics

The application of semantics to the study of the language of the law must necessarily follow paths that are different from those for the application of more empirical branches of linguistics, such as psycholinguistics and sociolinguistics. Indeed, any teacher or student of semantics who has struggled to understand just what we really *know* about meaning may wonder how such a relatively inchoate and foggy part of linguistics could possibly be of relevance to any legal proceedings where presumably precision and certainty are striven for. The recognition that semantics is indeed a rather difficult and hard-to-apply branch of linguistics is certainly an apt one here. Yet the experience of linguists working in this area has been that their semantic knowledge and expertise can be put to challenging and productive uses in a surprisingly wide variety of legal situations.

Semantics comprises both lexical and sentential semantics, and shades with seemingly intractable subtlety into the area of pragmatics. In this section, however, I will focus on just one aspect of lexical semantics to illustrate how the central notion of *denotation* in lexical semantics has been applied in a number of different legal situations. (For reasons of space, I will have to leave for another time a discussion of how other basic concepts of lexical semantics play their respective roles in legal analyses of disputed language; some of these other concepts, which have demonstrable applicability to legal language, include connotation, lexical presupposition, style or register of a lexical item, individual variation in lexical meaning, and vagueness and ambiguity of lexical items. For discussion of at least some of these variables, see Bryant 1962; Danet 1980a; and Probert 1966.)

It would be hard to estimate the large number of legal cases arising every year in which the (or at least one) central issue is to determine the *denotation* of a particular word or phrase. Indeed, there is a standard reference work available in any major legal library entitled *Words and Phrases* (St. Paul, MN: West Publishing Company), whose sole function is to index those cases in American law in which a word or phrase of significance to the legal outcome has been defined by the court. The work thus far comprises forty-six volumes of citations and definitions (going back to cases in the seventeenth century), and is of course subject to continual updating as more definitions are added every year. Determining the denotation of a word or phrase may be central in a contracts case (e.g., a lease agreement, a labor contract, or an insurance policy), or in a number of other kinds of civil or even criminal suits (e.g., in a class action suit charging false and misleading advertising, or in a criminal case alleging wire fraud for deceptive sales pitches delivered over the telephone).

In cases involving the interpretation of disputed language, it is standard policy in the American legal system to consider such interpretation to be the province of the court, which is to say that the judge is the person who will have the final say in a legal case. The assumption behind this legal tradition seems to be that as long as the language at issue is the same as the language of the court, namely, English, the judge (or, in certain cases, the jury) is as competent as anyone else to arrive at the meaning in question. Partly as a result of this long-standing assumption (and partly as a result of the generally prevalent ignorance of what linguistics is and how it can be useful), the American legal system lacks a tradition of consulting 'language experts' such as the professional linguist in order to resolve disputes concerning language.

Nevertheless, the picture is brightening for linguists in this regard, since a growing number of lawyers are turning to linguists to provide expert testimony (or, at the very least, pretrial advice and expertise) concerning what a word (or any stretch of disputed language) may or must mean. When such testimony becomes part of the court record, it can influence the judge's decision even though the linguist in no way replaces the judge as final arbiter. Even in the (probably more numerous) cases where the linguist's testimony is excluded by the judge, the linguist's analyses can be incorporated by the trial lawyers in ways that can still affect the outcome of the case; for example, the lawyers may manage to include parts of the analysis in their own summary statements to the judge or jury, they may enter it into the record as a written 'offer of proof,' or they may make use of it to frame their questions differently when examining witnesses whose testimony *is* admitted by the court. (For example, in my first legal consulting case, my testimony was excluded by the judge; nevertheless, the lawyer with whom I was working managed to get not only some of my linguistic arguments but also some crucial diagrams I had prepared into the court record as a part of the testimony of the defendant, who had hired me. This maneuver turned out to be crucial to the outcome of the case, for when the judge eventually ruled in favor of the defendant, he cited four arguments he had found particularly convincing, two of which were originally mine.)

With this background in mind, let us now consider just a few of the instances in which linguists have been hired to apply their semantic expertise to specific legal cases whose outcomes depended crucially on the denotation of a word or phrase.

The distinguished linguist Dwight Bolinger was hired as a consultant in a class action suit brought in a California court against General Foods Corporation for "unfair business practices, false and misleading advertising, fraud, damages, and injunctive relief" (Bolinger 1981). The subject of the complaint was the set of products General Foods had begun to market under the rubric "International Coffees," which the plaintiffs alleged were not true coffee at all but rather products consisting primarily of sugar and chemicals, and containing less than one-third and in some cases less than one-fourth actual coffee. Bolinger wrote the lawyers for the plaintiff a letter in which he used both dictionary definitions and his own intuitions to support the plaintiffs' claim that, among other things, the use of the words *International Coffees* would lead the average consumer to believe that the products were in fact pure (100%) coffee, and that the phrase *instant coffee beverage* which appeared (not accidentally) in smaller type both in advertisements and on the packaged product would in no way counter this message. (I do not know the outcome of the suit, by the way.) Here the question on which linguistic expertise was sought was what the average consumer of the product in question would understand by the wording of the advertisement and on the product itself.

A somewhat different case involving what the "average" person would understand from particular wording was brought to Professor Andrew Schiller of the University of Illinois at Chicago by a legal firm. This case (as described in Schiller 1979) concerned a person who held an "accidental death and dismemberment" insurance policy, and who, while swimming in the Dead Sea, had suffered a heart attack and drowned. The linguistic question put to Schiller was whether the average person holding such an insurance policy would interpret the words *accidental death* in such a way as to believe that the cause of death just described would be covered by that policy. Note that in this case, as in many other contract cases, the legal approach is not to seek a dictionary definition, nor the definition that might be provided by a lawyer or a linguist or some other professional; instead, the court adopts a context-sensitive approach to meaning and thus asks what would the *average member of the intended audience* of the written document understand by the term in question. (In this connection, Bryant 1962 is particularly illuminating in making explicit the wide range of legal approaches that lawyers and judges may take to interpret disputed language; the tack taken in the Schiller case is only one of many with extensive legal precedents.) In this instance, the legal profession is asking a commendably sensible and pragmatically appropriate question; whether or not its procedures for obtaining a comparably sensible answer are valid ones is another issue.

Schiller's approach in providing his opinion was to explain that many words can be analyzed in terms of semantic features whose positive or negative values can be used to compare related and/or contrasting terms. In this particular case, the insurance policy explicitly included coverage of deaths due to "accidents" but explicitly excluded coverage of deaths due to "disease or bodily or mental infirmity." As a result, Schiller addressed the issue of just which semantic features might be said to underlie the two crucial terms *accident* and *disease*. Although I disagree with Schiller's approach to semantic analysis, as well as with the specific features he proposed for the two crucial terms in question, it is nevertheless instructive to observe the way in which one linguist attacked the very difficult problem of testifying as to what a word or phrase must mean to some specific audience.

Basically, he argued that both *accident* and *disease* share the features of [+ injurious] and [+ contingent] (where the latter feature means the event must have a cause), but differ on a number of other features. Specifically, he argued that

1. *accident* is [− intentional] and [− foreseeable] while *disease* is sometimes [+ intentional] and/or [+ foreseeable] and sometimes not;
2. *accident* has the feature [− duration] while *disease* has the feature [+ duration]; and
3. only *disease* has the feature [+ essential nature].

The feature of [+ essential nature] is intended to indicate that diseases, unlike accidents, have recognizable and systematic properties in their own right, permitting us to recognize, label, and classify recurring instances of the 'same' disease—a process Schiller claims we do not engage in with respect to accidents. On the basis of these features, and particularly on the grounds that a heart attack is not normally construed as having an 'essential nature,' Schiller concluded that the cause of death would be judged by the average policyholder to have been an accident, and that the policyholder's heirs should therefore collect. (He never heard from the legal firm again, and therefore concluded that they had represented the insurer rather than the insured.)

Schiller's analysis is an interesting one, for it points up one of the very serious problems faced by linguists in performing semantic analysis for a fee, namely, to what extent and with what degree of certitude can we answer the very difficult question, "What does this word mean?" The fact that legal precedent refines the question in such a way as to ask, in essence, "What does this word mean to the target audience of the document?" makes it a better question but does not necessarily make the task of the linguist significantly easier. For example, as a linguist I would take issue on theoretical grounds with Schiller's claim that word meaning can be insightfully analyzed in terms of componential analysis using binary features, but I would also take issue on 'intuitional' grounds with the specific analysis he proposed. In this particular case, *my* internal lexicon requires me to distinguish between accidents and diseases in part by means of whether the cause is external or internal to the injured party; for me, an accident always has an external cause (e.g., a roof tile falling on your head) and thus I could never say that a heart attack (not brought on by any external stimulus) was an example of an accident. The moral of the story here is that absolute answers about the denotation of a word are impossible to provide, that widespread individual variation in mental definitions must be recognized and taken into account, and that the most satisfactory answer to a question like the one put to Schiller may have to include the proviso that linguistics has not yet developed any systematic means for answering denotational inquiries of this sort.

Much to his credit, lexical semantics specialist Charles J. Fillmore of the University of California at Berkeley made just such a qualified assertion of linguistic indeterminacy when he provided testimony to the Federal Trade Commission concerning proposed changes in advertising wording for over-the-counter (OTC) drugs (Fillmore 1975). The document he produced is a splendid discussion of the complexities, intricacies, and indeterminacies that must be recognized and understood by anyone seeking simple or direct answers to lexical semantic questions. Fillmore was asked to testify in regard to

> the possibility of there being in the English language expressions which, when used in advertisements for given OTC drug products, could communicate to consumers exactly the same information as the terms which the Food and Drug Administration has approved . . . for the labeling of that category of drug products. (Fillmore 1975:1)

In other words, the FDA had already approved a certain set of terms that advertisers of OTC drugs were permitted to use in selling purported remedies for health conditions referred to, in familiar advertising, by such terms as 'heartburn' or 'acid indigestion,' 'occasional irregularity,' and 'insomnia.' The manufacturers and advertisers were seeking to have the set of approved terms extended to include a wider variety of terms for each condition. Fillmore was asked to testify on the feasibility and, presumably, the advisability of thus widening the set of lexical items that would appear in advertisements to the public. In his fifty-eight-page testimony, Fillmore painstakingly explained the semantic issues raised by such a request, and demonstrated how a number of principles of lexical semantic theory could be applied directly to the specific context of drug advertising to the American consumer. The particular issues addressed in his analysis include the following:

1. the fundamental fact that to ask what a word *means* is, according to Fillmore, to use a verb "whose interpretation can only be fully specified in a propositional frame with four variables," which Fillmore expresses (1975:25) as:

    "E" means (= has meaning) "M" to "I" in "C"

    > where "E" is an Expression
    > "M" is its Meaning
    > "I" is its Interpreter
    > "C" is its Context

2. linguistic and social reasons for the near to total absence of full synonyms in a language;
3. the dimensions along which related words may differ (including register, range, aspect, transparency, and degree along a continuum);

4. the effects of semantic change over time, especially in sets of near-synonyms, such as the ones now used in OTC drug advertising to designate health conditions;

5. the implications of widespread individual and cultural variation in interpreting apparently common terms like 'heartburn,' 'occasional irregularity,' and 'insomnia' (all of which are FDA-approved for OTC drug advertising);

6. the fact that the semantic field of health conditions is one in which miscommunication is particularly likely to occur given the preponderance of words in this area whose meanings are vague, subjective, technical, and/or obscure (and hence not likely to be clearly or uniformly understood by any audience);

7. the absence of relevant empirical testing of representative consumer samples, and the reasons why such testing would be difficult if not impossible to conduct;

8. the pragmatics of advertising language and communication (including why Gricean principles of cooperativity do not apply straightforwardly in an ad);

9. the inherent obstacles to clear communication in the context of commercial advertising.

Thus, Fillmore responded to what might have appeared to be a simple question in lexical semantics with a lucid discourse on the many reasons why no comparably simple answer can easily be provided. As one consequence of his reasoning, he recommended that the language of drug advertising be especially carefully supervised and regulated, because of the implications of poor communication for the public health.

One of the most pertinent ramifications of Fillmore's testimony for the present discussion of applications of linguistics to legal issues is the fact that even when a linguist *cannot* provide a simple and clearcut answer to a semantic question, an intelligent and reasoned discussion of just why such an answer cannot be *responsibly* produced may be at least as valuable a contribution to the public good (or to private understanding) as a simpler response might have been. For if it is true, according to our best understanding of semantics, that a simple answer to a certain semantic question is unavailable to linguists in our present state of knowledge (or that a 'simple' answer proposed by one or another interested party is unjustifiable), then it is essential that an informed acknowledgment of the limits of such semantic inquiry be made. In fact, this explicit recognition of the complexities of the subject matter and the consequent boundaries of accepted understanding should then prove to be the very best, and the most responsible, answer that we can give as 'language experts' in such situations. If we fail to meet naive expectations about the ascertainability of meaning, we should not (or at least not necessarily!) misinterpret *that* failure as a failure of our own skills. Rather, it may need to be understood as an opportunity to educate our collaborators about the real nature of language and of semantic knowledge—and that, it seems to me, is precisely where our responsibility and our talents lie. (What to do when our 'collaborators' decline to be educated and continue to push for The Simple Answer is another story. For one linguist's remarks on this problem, see Johnson 1982, an account and analysis of the author's experience as an expert witness in a murder trial.)

The preceding examples are intended to suggest just a few of the ways in which a linguist's understanding of fundamental semantic principles may be applied to help resolve legal disputes concerning the denotation of a word or phrase. From my own experience and discussions with colleagues, it is my impression that linguists are being hired more and more frequently for semantic questions of different sorts, involving both lexical semantic and sentential semantic issues. Unfortunately, however, very little has been published to date by linguists about their extra-academic experience in these matters, so that information is hard to come by except by word of mouth. (The cases cited are thus typical; my information was drawn from a personal communication with Dwight Bolinger, and from the two unpublished sources of Fillmore 1975 and Schiller 1979.) Nevertheless, the reader interested in exploring some additional discussions of how semantics may be applied to legal disputes will find some relevant discussion within the pages of Atkinson and Drew (1979), Blunk and Sales (1977), Danet (1980a, b), Garfinkel (1975), Kasprzyk et al. (1975), and Langendoen (1970); in addition, the works of Bryant (1962), Mellinkoff (1963), Philbrick (1949), and Probert (1966) will suggest many more dimensions of semantic analysis as seen by members of the legal profession themselves. Finally, spending some time with the *Words and Phrases* reference set mentioned earlier (p. 247) will certainly reward the curious by demonstrating the enormous range of semantic challenges that have been addressed over the last three centuries by the American legal system. Examining this work, or the cases selected from it and analyzed in Bryant (1962), will also give the legally naive linguist a better sense of what some of the numerous non-linguistic factors are that necessarily affect every semantic decision taken in a legal context.

5. Applications of Pragmatics

Since research by linguists in the area of pragmatics is a relatively recent phenomenon, it should not be too surprising to note that the number of publications devoted to the application of pragmatic principles specifically to the understanding of language used in legal domains is still quite small. As a result, in this section I will restrict myself to sketching out some of the topics that have already been addressed in this area, and to indicating a number of others that might profitably be taken up in the future. I will organize the discussion around the not entirely discrete topics of speech act theory, conversational analysis, and communicative competence.

Speech act theory (based on the seminal set of lectures published as Austin 1965 and elaborated in such works as Cole and Morgan 1975; Ross 1970; Sadock

1974; and Searle 1969) may be viewed as an attempt to understand how what we hope to accomplish *by* saying something (i.e., speaker intention communicated through language) affects the way we actually say it (i.e., the form of a specific context-bound utterance), and vice versa. Its value to the analysis of language used in legal contexts, and especially in the very consequential forum of the courtroom, lies in the fact that it permits us to go beyond the relative super-ficialities of language form to the social and psychological functions of our language, and thus to gain a deeper understanding of that language by embedding its study securely in the context of specific utterances or *acts* of speaking. In addition, Hancher (1980:254) argues that speech act theory is particularly well suited to analyses of legal language, on the following grounds:

> Speech-act theory and the law are made of much the same stuff. Pragmatic con-cepts such as authority, verifiability, and obligation are basic to both. Each elabo-rates and refines ordinary language behavior, the one descriptively and the other prescriptively. Such compatibility argues for a lasting marriage. . . .

This comment by Hancher concludes an intriguing article in which the author argues that members of both the linguistic and the legal professions stand to gain much through an application of speech act theory to the language and practice of the law. To illustrate his claim that there exist important natural links between principles of the law and principles of speech act theory, Hancher demonstrates how the Austinian concept of *uptake* plays a central role in the definition of such legal concepts as the proper serving of a writ, defamation, and constructive and judicial notice. As far as I know, Hancher (1980) is the only article available in the literature to date which directly addresses the issue of how (and why) to apply speech act theory to the language of the law. (Although the title of Kevelson 1982 suggests an equal degree of relevance to this subject, the article in fact fits more into a framework of philosophical and semiotic analyses than into the more specifically linguistic discussions of such works as Cole and Morgan 1975, Sadock 1974, and Ross 1970; as such, I found it less pertinent to this general area than the contribution by Hancher.)

One other set of writings which does take into account the applicability of speech act theory to the analysis of language in legal settings is the work pro-duced by researchers at the Centre for Socio-Legal Research at Oxford. Studies such as Atkinson and Drew (1979) and Dunstan (1980) draw heavily upon speech act theory as a source of insight in distinguishing between the somewhat misleading formal aspects of the question-and-answer pattern of courtroom inter-rogation and the wide range of underlying social and psychological processes that are carried out within the constraints of that superficial pattern. That is to say, the fact that much of what happens linguistically in a courtroom is through the *form* of questions and answers should not mislead the language researcher into believing that the *functions* of these questions and answers correspond in any direct way to their formal properties; nor should the student of courtroom language confuse the highly constrained and very specialized organization of questions and answers in a courtroom with that observable in the more informal settings of natural conversations, since the pragmatics of the two types of settings are dramatically distinct. Rather, principles of speech act theory (inter alia) must be applied to identify the kinds of speech *acts* being performed by each actor at each point in the interchange; only a linguistic analysis informed by this sort of functional perspective will provide an adequate and accurate picture of the true nature of this kind of language behavior. (A methodologically quite different approach to the analysis of courtroom questions, which seeks to measure attorney 'coerciveness' and 'combativeness' as a direct function of question form, may be found in the work of sociologist Brenda Danet and her colleagues; see Danet and Bogoch 1980; Danet and Kermish 1978; and Danet et al. 1980.)

The very thorough microanalyses of courtroom speech reported in Atkinson and Drew (1979) rely not only on speech act theory but also on the comparably recent and comparably blossoming research area of *conversational analysis;* this work thus seeks to extend the pioneering work of Grice (1975), Sacks et al. (1974), and Schenkein (1978) to the analysis of speech in legal settings. Here too the methodological claim is that we must go well beyond the *form* of a particular question-answer sequence in courtroom interrogations to consider how that question-answer pair fits within the whole linguistic (and paralinguistic) context in which it is situated.

Dunstan (1980) provides a good example of the fruitfulness of this approach in analyzing one particular courtroom sequence, during which the examining attorney in essence asks for the same information five times. By the fifth time, the witness' "No" answer carries a very different message (and presumably intonation) than the first, even though the (written) form is identical; similarly, the very fact that the examining attorney repeats his question numerous times with only minor variations in form makes the last occurrence of what is essentially a request for the same information functionally very distinct from the first. In his analysis of this courtroom interaction, Dunstan emphasizes that no single utterance by a trial participant can be properly understood without reference to its 'sequential environment' (thus seriously calling into question the more purely formal and sequence-independent analyses provided by Danet and her colleagues in their analyses of courtroom questioning). In addition, Dunstan, like Atkinson and Drew in their longer study, argues strenuously that no analysis of courtroom interaction can ignore the seemingly 'minute' details of courtroom language behavior (some suprasegmental, some suprasentential), many of which go well beyond the written form appearing in a standard transcript of courtroom proceedings; the kinds of details used in such a microanalysis to understand the discourse include pauses, interruptions, repetitions, pitch, tempo, and intonation, as well as a host of discourse-level rhetorical strategies employed by skillful attorneys to further their own ends, whether to discredit a hostile witness by, say, badgering rapid-fire repetitions or to enhance the image of a friendly witness by, say, choosing respectful modes of address and permitting the witness to testify freely without undue interruption. Each of these linguistic devices can color the message intended by the speaker, or can influence the interpretation assigned to that message by the hearer. Because of this, Dunstan cautions (1980:75):

> The efficacy of any "device" is inextricably linked to the detail and contingency of the task at hand. For that reason, any research procedure which removes utterances from their context of occurrence, and which considers them without reference to the specific tasks for which they are produced, cannot help but fail to reveal the resources and methods used by participants in organizing their interaction. An analogous procedure would be to blindly cross a road, not on the basis of having looked to see what is coming, its speed, and so on; but on the basis of statistical probability.

In addition to the analysis of courtroom speech in studies like those just considered, there are two other areas of language and the law in which speech act theory might be productively applied, although very little published work has yet appeared in either. These two areas are (1) verbal offenses and (2) laws pertaining to language in advertising.

When I speak of a category of 'verbal offenses,' I mean those instances in which what one says or writes (often in combination with a particular set of pragmatic, or contextual, conditions) can get one in trouble with the law; for the present, I will not attempt a more technical definition of the category than that. Some of the verbal offenses that I have in mind (and I am sure that the legal system defines many more) are: perjury, libel and slander, plagiarism, verbal assault, and (in America) threats to the life of the President. I shudder to think of the number of pages written on each of these topics in the legal literature, but despite what strikes me as the intrinsic research appeal of this category for a linguist, I know of only a handful of publications *by linguists* on this topic. Thus, the only listings in Levi (1982) that appear to address the subject of one or more verbal offenses directly are Epstein (1982) for perjury; Bosmajian (1978), Hancher (1980) (for the section on defamation), and Jones (1971) for libel and slander; Danet, Hoffman, and Kermish (1980) on threats to the life of the President; and Swett (1969) for verbal assault (although this is rather indirect—Swett reports on a murder trial in which jurors did not understand the defendant's remark about how the man he *admitted* having killed had "put him . . . in the dozens" and so they could not properly recognize the possibility of mitigating factors in reaching their verdict). (See also Shuy 1981, to be discussed below, for the role of linguistic analysis in regard to what constitutes solicitation to murder; and possibly Williams 1976.)

It appears at first glance that the language of advertising should provide another good testing ground for the applicability of speech act theory, for certainly it is true that the functions of advertising language are more complex and far less obvious than their surface forms. And, in recent years, the language of advertising, like the language of law and of medicine, has been attracting increasing attention on the part of linguists (see, for example, Garfinkel 1978; Geis 1982; O'Barr 1979; and Smith 1982). However, the number of studies written by linguists specifically on *legal* aspects of the language of advertising remains very small. (In making this assertion, I must stipulate that it is based solely on the linguist-oriented sources that I have had available. If articles by linguists on legal aspects of advertising language have appeared in the presumably vast literature produced in and for journals of advertising, marketing, communication studies, speech, and rhetoric, then it is only my own ignorance and lack of time that have caused their omission here.)

The only published works that I know of that might be relevant here are Geis (1979 and 1982). On the other hand, the unpublished category includes three excellent essays relating, at least in part, to the work of the Federal Trade Commission in regulating the language of advertising: Garfinkel (1975), Langendoen (1970), and the testimony discussed earlier in Fillmore (1975). Each of these at least touches on the usefulness of applying speech act theory, Gricean principles of cooperativity (Grice 1975), and other pragmatic concepts in analyzing legally significant dimensions of the language of advertising. The linguistic questions faced by the Federal Trade Commission, only a few of which are brought out in these essays, would surely be a fascinating subject of study for linguists interested in applying their theoretical expertise to problems in the real world. Yet it is clear that any in-depth studies of such questions have yet to appear in print. (In 1981, the National Science Foundation awarded funding to Professor Jack Bilmes of the University of Hawaii at Manoa's Department of Anthropology for a research project entitled "Discourse and Decision-Making in the Federal Trade Commission." We can therefore hope for a published report of his results in the near future.)

Turning now to *conversational analysis,* the reader will recall that studies such as Atkinson and Drew (1979) have applied principles concerning the structure and organization of conversational interaction to the study of courtroom language. In addition, a few linguists have been called upon to apply their knowledge of conversational analysis as expert witnesses in both criminal and civil law cases. Roger Shuy of Georgetown University, for example, has served as an expert witness in a number of criminal trials in which surreptitiously recorded conversations have been entered as evidence. In one of the trials (reported in Shuy 1981), Shuy was hired to analyze the structure of two conversations between a businessman and a former employee of his, tape recorded surreptitiously by the latter at the request of the FBI. These conversations formed the basis of a state indictment against the businessman, called Jones in Shuy's account, for soliciting the murder of his wife as well as of the judge in Jones's divorce trial.

In Shuy's report of this case, he discusses how he used principles of conversational analysis first to arrive at his own understanding of the structure of the two conversations, and later to explain his findings to the jury in the case. His procedure, in brief, was to identify topics in each conversation, to analyze who introduced and/or recycled which topic, and finally to analyze the responses by each speaker to topics introduced by the other. Deviations from the organizational patterns of 'normal' conversations could then be used to suggest possible deviations from normal *intentions* by at least one of the speakers. In the case at hand, such a deviation occurred when the employee was found to have introduced eighteen out of the twenty-two topics in the conversations; the fact that he dominated the conversation far more than is common in 'normal' conversations strongly suggested the presence of a hidden agenda on the employee's part.

In explaining the relevance of this kind of structural analysis to the proceedings of a criminal trial, Shuy comments (Shuy 1981:19–20):

> The problem was to determine what the structure of the conversations could tell us about the meaning of the event. It was up to the jury, of course, to decide for themselves exactly what had taken place from what was said on the tapes. It was not appropriate for me to tell them what the intentions of the speakers were or what their words actually meant. The court agreed that this was the sole province of the jury to determine. My role, quite differently, was to help the jury understand the structure of the conversation as a clue to the possible intentions of the speakers and to help them distinguish exactly what was said by whom. . . .
>
> Topic analysis helped the jury understand who controlled the conversation and who produced minimal and often evasive responses to these topics. It helped them understand the separate agendas of Foster and Jones by noting their topic recycling patterns. It helped them obtain a holistic or macro-picture of the entire conversation to use as a reference point into which micro elements of the conversation could be appropriately placed. . . .

Shuy's experience thus illustrates the fact that the contribution that a linguist can make to a legal case is often primarily one of teaching and explanation in regard to his or her particular area of expertise. The analyses that a linguist provides must still be interpreted by the trier of fact, whether this is a jury or a judge, in accordance with the relevant principles of law and the specific circumstances surrounding the case at hand. Still, Shuy's experience, as well as my own and that of other linguists who have served as expert witnesses, demonstrates that linguistic testimony can play a valuable, and at times decisive, role in the outcome of both civil and criminal cases.

The subject of 'communicative competence' is another rich source of ideas for linguistic research concerning the language used in legal settings, although here too linguists have published relatively little of direct relevance to this subject. (It is, however, likely that linguists have been applying their understanding of this subject as consultants and expert witnesses without necessarily writing up their experiences for a broader scholarly audience.) Probably the best introduction to the research potential of this subject is provided in Johnson (1976), in which the author relates Hymes's sixteen 'components of speaking' (Hymes 1972) to the rather unusual setting of the American trial courtroom.

The relevance of the notion of 'communicative competence' to our understanding of language in legal settings lies in the fact that even native speakers of English generally lack the 'communicative competence' required to participate as productively and successfully as possible in a variety of legal settings, not the least important of which is a courtroom; most of us simply do not have the opportunity to learn the very different set of rules for speaking (or not speaking!) that are required of, say, participants in a trial. As a result, whether we end up as plaintiffs, defendants, jurors, or witnesses, our ignorance will render us less effective in carrying out our roles than we might otherwise be. That this is the case was most effectively illustrated for me by an anecdote reported in Fillmore (1978), concerning the examination of prospective jurors by lawyers in a criminal court in Berkeley, California. Fillmore reports (1978:166–7):

> The examining attorney asked the prospective juror the following question:
> Do you accept without question the American legal doctrine that a man is innocent until proven guilty?
> The prospective juror responded:
> I think a man should be *treated* as innocent until proven guilty, but it would be funny to say that he *is* innocent until proven guilty.
> The interrogator:
> The doctrine I am speaking of is precisely that a man *is* innocent until proven guilty. Do you or do you not accept that doctrine?
> The prospective juror:
> But if he *is* innocent, then it would be *wrong* to prove him guilty. So why have the trial?
> The prospective juror was challenged for cause and excused from jury service.

If we assume that both participants in the above dialogue were sincere and straightforward, then we can readily see how a citizen's normal ignorance of the rules of language and language use in a courtroom (such as formulaic statements of principles of law, as in the above example) could lead to innumerable misunderstandings, many of which might have far more serious consequences for individuals and for the administration of justice than those resulting from the incident described above. And if native speakers of English face this kind of problem, imagine the difficulties faced by non-native speakers of English whose competence in even non-legal settings is limited at best (and nonexistent at worst).

Studies pertaining to communicative competence of the native speaker of English in American (or British) courtrooms include Atkinson and Drew (1979), O'Barr (1981), Philips (1980), and Platt (1978). The special cross-linguistic and cross-cultural problems faced by speakers of other languages with limited knowledge of English who must appear as participants in American courtrooms are addressed in Bresnahan (1979), Brière (1978), Gumperz (1982), and Segalowitz (1976). (Note also that the more general studies of interethnic communication problems exemplified by Gumperz 1978 and Gumperz and Cook-Gumperz 1981, while not specifically on communication in legal settings, nevertheless are extremely relevant in this connection.) The problems of interpreting for speakers of other languages without competence in English are taken up in Abarca (1970), Cronheim and Schwartz (1976), and Pousada (1979), while the legal problems of the deaf are reviewed in Myers (1970). Finally, the difficulties faced by native English speakers whose level of education inadequately prepares them for the communicative style of courtroom discourse are at least suggested in the non-linguistic but partly relevant studies of Fears (1977), Mileski (1971), and Swett (1969).

6. Conclusions

We began this report by considering the reasons that linguists should be interested in examining the language of the law for their own professional purposes, that is, to further their understanding of the structure, organization, and use of natural language. It should now be clear not only that the language of the legal domain has great intrinsic interest as a source of relevant data for testing hypotheses in linguistics and related social sciences, but also that linguistics can be applied to solve real-world problems and to assist individuals who must deal with the legal system to work more successfully towards their own objectives.

In regard to the testing of linguistic hypotheses, we have seen that empirical research already carried out on language and the law has contributed to a deeper understanding of such phenomena as the interaction of language and memory, social evaluation of people as a function of the way they speak, gender-related differences in interpreting language behavior, and the intricate interrelationships between linguistic form and social function in the organization of courtroom 'conversation.'

We have also observed that linguistics can be applied for a variety of significant purposes within the legal system. For example, it can be used to help produce fairer trails by demonstrating the tremendous fallibility of a witness' memory (so that a jury will not give it the automatic credence that it usually commands) or indicating the effect of language style on witness credibility (so that litigants can take whatever steps are possible to avoid being discredited for reasons extraneous to the accuracy of their testimony). More generally, linguistics can be used to improve the functioning of the legal system by uncovering and then testing some of the unquestioned assumptions about how language works in courtroom and other legal settings. In fact, O'Barr has argued cogently (1981, 1982) that this is probably the most important contribution that linguistic and social science research can make in this area:

> All of these studies, whether about witness behavior or juror comprehension, can contribute information about the validity of assumptions which the courts now make about the degree to which effective communication actually occurs through the language currently used in trial courtrooms. Demonstrating the degree to which legal assumptions about communication are indeed valid is a first step toward

eventually reforming the legal process to make it more comprehensible to those who use it. (O'Barr 1981:403)

Finally, individual linguists, working as consultants with litigants and lawyers, can contribute their knowledge of language structure and language use in individual cases, helping to ensure that no legal penalties are unjustly assigned, and no legal remedies unjustly withheld, because of a lawyer's or a judge's or a jury's ignorance of the way language really works. To a reader who might object that, in fact, even we specialized scholars don't know how language *really* works, I can only respond that we cannot fail to improve even our limited understanding by the challenge of working outside our profession with people to whom language matters as much as it does to us. In this respect, the courtroom may turn out to be the best classroom for us all.

NOTES

1. The discussion here draws primarily on Lind and O'Barr 1978; for a fuller discussion of these issues, see the more comprehensive work of O'Barr 1982.

REFERENCES

Abarca, Tony 1970. "Equal administration of justice: Reflections of a Spanish-speaking interpreter." *Civil Rights Digest*, pp. 8–11.
Atkinson, J. Maxwell, and Paul Drew 1979. *Order in Court: The Organization of Verbal Behavior in Judicial Settings*. London: Macmillan.
Austin, J. L. 1965. *How to Do Things with Words*. New York: Oxford University Press.
Blunk, R. A., and B. D. Sales 1977. "Persuasion during the voir dire." In: B. D. Sales (ed.), *Psychology in the Legal Process*. New York: Spectrum Publications, pp. 39–58.
Bolinger, Dwight 1981. Personal communication.
Bornstein, M. H. 1974. "Perceptual generalization: A note on the peak shift." *Psychological Bulletin* 81, pp. 802–8.
Bornstein, M. H. 1976. "Name codes and color memory." *American Journal of Psychology* 89, pp. 269–79.
Bosmajian, Haig A. 1978. "Freedom of speech and the language of oppression." *Western Journal of Speech Communication* 42, pp. 209–21.
Bresnahan, Mary I. 1979. "Linguistic limbo: The case of the non-native English-speaking defendant in the American courtroom." Paper read at the Eighth Annual Colloquium on New Ways of Analyzing Variation in English (NWAVE-VIII). Montreal.
Brière, Eugène 1978. "Limited English speakers and the Miranda rights." *TESOL Quarterly* 12:3, pp. 235–45.
Bryant, Margaret M. 1962. *English in the Law Courts*. New York: Frederick Ungar Publishing Company. (Originally published: New York: Columbia University Press, 1930.)
Cady, H. M. 1924. "On the psychology of testimony." *American Journal of Psychology* 35, pp. 110–2.
Campbell, L., and V. Melissa Holland 1982. "Understanding the language of documents because readability formulas don't." In: Robert J. DiPietro (ed.), *Linguistics and the Professions*. Norwood, NJ: Ablex, pp. 157–172.
Carmichael, L. C., H. P. Hogan, and A. A. Walter 1932. "Experimental study of the effect of

language on the reproduction of visually perceived form." *Journal of Experimental Psychology* 15, pp. 73–86.

Charrow, Robert P., and Veda R. Charrow 1979. "Making legal language understandable: A psycholinguistic study of jury instructions." *Columbia Law Review* 79:7, pp. 1306–74.

Charrow, Veda R., J. A. Crandall, and Robert P. Charrow 1982. "Characteristics and functions of legal language." In: R. Kittredge and J. Lehrberger (eds.), *Sublanguage: Studies of Language in Restricted Semantic Domains*. Berlin: Walter de Gruyter, pp. 175–90.

Cole, Peter, and Jerry L. Morgan (eds.) 1975. *Syntax and Semantics*, Vol. 3. *Speech Acts*. London and New York: Academic Press.

Cronheim, Alan J., and Andrew H. Schwartz 1976. "Non-English speaking persons in the criminal justice system: Current state of the law." *Cornell Law Review* 61, pp. 289–311.

Danet, Brenda 1980a. "'Baby' or 'fetus'? Language and the construction of reality in a manslaughter trial." *Semiotica* 32:3–4, pp. 187–219.

Danet, Brenda 1980b. "Language in the legal process." *Law and Society Review* 14:3, pp. 445–564.

Danet, Brenda, and Byrna Bogoch 1980. "Fixed fight or free-for-all? An empirical study of combativeness in the adversary system of justice." *British Journal of Law and Society* 7, pp. 36–60.

Danet, Brenda, Kenneth B. Hoffman, and Nicole C. Kermish 1980. "Threats to the life of the President: An analysis of the linguistic issues." *Journal of Media Law and Practice* 1:2, pp. 180–90.

Danet, Brenda, and Nicole C. Kermish 1978. "Courtroom questioning: A sociolinguistic perspective." In: Louis N. Massery II (ed.), *Psychology and Persuasion in Advocacy*. Washington, DC: Association of Trial Lawyers of America, National College of Advocacy, pp. 100–50.

Danet, Brenda, et al. 1980. "An ethnography of questioning in the courtroom." In: Roger Shuy and Anna Shnukal (eds.), *Language Use and the Uses of Language: Papers from the Fifth Annual Colloquium on New Ways of Analyzing Variation*. Washington, DC: Georgetown University Press, pp. 222–34.

Dunstan, Robert 1980. "Contexts for coercion: Analyzing properties of courtroom 'questions.'" *British Journal of Law and Society* 7, pp. 61–77.

Elwork, A., B. D. Sales, and J. J. Alfini 1982. *Making Jury Instructions Understandable*. Charlottesville, VA: Michie.

Epstein, Judith H. 1982. "The grammar of a lie: Its legal implications." In: Robert J. DiPietro (ed.), *Linguistics and the Professions*. Norwood, NJ: Ablex, pp. 133–42.

Fears, Denise 1977. "Communication in English Juvenile Courts." *The Sociological Review* 25, pp. 131–45.

Felker, Daniel 1980. *Document Design: A Review of the Relevant Research*. Washington, DC: Document Design Center.

Fillmore, Charles J. 1975. "Prepared testimony—OTC [over-the-counter] drug advertising rule." Testimony submitted to the Federal Trade Commission. Unpublished manuscript, University of California at Berkeley.

Fillmore, Charles J. 1978. "On the organization of semantic information in the lexicon." In: Donka Farkas, Wesley M. Jacobsen, and Karol W. Todrys (eds.), *Papers from the Parasession on the Lexicon*. Chicago: Chicago Linguistic Society, pp. 148–73.

Garfinkel, Andrew 1975. "Linguistic aspects of truth in advertising." Paper read at the Fourth Annual Conference on New Ways of Analyzing Variation in English (NWAVE-IV). Washington, DC, Georgetown University.

Garfinkel, Andrew 1978. *A Sociolinguistic Analysis of the Language of Advertising*. Unpublished dissertation, Georgetown University.

Geis, Michael L. 1979. "Linguistic deception in television advertising." In: Robert K. Herbert (ed.), *Conference on Linguistic Metatheory: Applications of Linguistic Theory to the Human Sciences*. East Lansing, MI: Michigan State University, pp. 76–102.

Geis, Michael L. 1982. *The Language of Television Advertising.* New York: Academic Press.

Grice, H. P. 1975. "Logic and conversation." In: Peter Cole and Jerry L. Morgan (eds.), *Syntax and Semantics,* Vol. 3: *Speech Acts.* London and New York: Academic Press, pp. 41–58.

Gumperz, John J. 1978. "The conversational analysis of interethnic communication." In: E. L. Ross (ed.), *Interethnic Communication.* Athens, GA: University of Georgia Press.

Gumperz, John J. 1982. "Fact and inference in courtroom testimony." In: John J. Gumperz (ed.), *Language and Social Identity.* Cambridge: Cambridge University Press, pp. 163–95.

Gumperz, John J., and Jenny Cook-Gumperz 1981. "Ethnic differences in communicative style." In: Charles A. Ferguson and Shirley Brice Heath (eds.), *Language in the USA:* Cambridge: Cambridge University Press, pp. 430–45.

Hancher, Michael 1980. "Speech acts and the law." In: Roger W. Shuy and Anna Shnukal (eds.), *Language Use and the Uses of Language.* Washington, DC: Georgetown University Press, pp. 245–56.

Harris, Richard J. 1973. "Answering questions containing marked and unmarked adjectives and adverbs." *Journal of Experimental Psychology* 97, pp. 399–401.

Hastie, R., R. Landsman, and Elizabeth F. Loftus 1978. "Eyewitness testimony: The dangers of guessing." *Jurimetrics Journal* 19, pp. 1–8.

Holland, V. Melissa, and Janice C. Redish 1981. "Strategies for understanding forms—and other public documents." In: D. Tannen (ed.), *Proceedings of the Thirty-second Annual Georgetown University Roundtable.* Washington, DC: Georgetown University Press, pp. 205–18.

Hymes, Dell 1972. "Models of the interaction of language and social life." In: John J. Gumperz and Dell Hymes (eds.), *Directions in Sociolinguistics: The Ethnography of Communication.* New York: Holt, Rinehart and Winston., pp. 35–71.

Johnson, Bruce C. 1976. "Communicative competence in American trail courtrooms." *Centrum: Working Papers of the Minnesota Center for Advanced Studies in Language, Style, and Literary Theory* 4:2, pp. 139–50.

Johnson, Robert E. 1982. "Courtroom interaction and the application of linguistic arguments." Unpublished manuscript, Gallaudet College.

Jones, W. R. 1971. "Actions for slander—Defamation in English law, language, and history." *Quarterly Journal of Speech* 57:3, pp. 274–83.

Kasprzyk, D., D. E. Montano, and Elizabeth F. Loftus 1975. "Effects of leading questions on jurors' verdicts." *Jurimetrics Journal* 16, pp. 48–51.

Kay, H. 1955. "Learning and retaining verbal material." *British Journal of Psychology* 46, pp. 81–100.

Kevelson, Roberta 1982. "Language and legal speech acts: Decisions." In: Robert J. DiPietro (ed.), *Linguistics and the Professions.* Norwood, NJ: Ablex, pp. 121–32.

Lakoff, Robin 1973. "Language and woman's place." *Language in Society* 2, pp. 45–79.

Lakoff, Robin 1975. *Language and Woman's Place.* New York: Harper and Row.

Langendoen, D. Terence 1970. "A study of the linguistic practices of the Federal Trade Commission." Paper read at the Annual Meeting of the Linguistic Society of America, Washington, DC.

Levi, Judith N. 1982. *Linguistics, Language, and Law: A Topical Bibliography.* Bloomington, IN: Indiana University Linguistics Club.

Levi, Judith N. In preparation. *Language and the Law in the U.S.A.*

Lind, E. Allan, and William M. O'Barr 1978. "The social significance of speech in the courtroom." In: Howard Giles and Robert N. St. Clair (eds.), *Language and Social Psychology.* Baltimore, MD: University Park Press, pp. 66–87. (Also published: Oxford: Basil Blackwell, 1979.)

Loftus, Elizabeth F. 1975. "Leading questions and the eyewitness report." *Cognitive Psychology* 77, pp. 560–72.

Loftus, Elizabeth F. 1979. *Eyewitness Testimony.* Cambridge, MA: Harvard University Press.

Loftus, Elizabeth F., and J. C. Palmer 1974. "Reconstruction of automobile destruction: An example of the interaction between language and memory." *Journal of Verbal Learning and Verbal Behavior* 13, pp. 585–9.

Loftus, Elizabeth F., and G. Zanni 1975. "Eyewitness testimony: The influence of the wording of a question." *Bulletin of the Psychonomic Society* 5, pp. 86–8.

Marquis, K. H., J. Marshall, and S. Oskamp 1972. "Testimony validity as a function of question form, atmosphere, and item difficulty." *Journal of Applied Social Psychology* 2, pp. 167–86.

Mellinkoff, David 1963. *The Language of the Law*. Boston and Toronto: Little, Brown.

Mileski, Maureen 1971. "Courtroom encounters: An observation study of a lower criminal court." *Law and Society Review* 5:4, pp. 473–538.

Myers, Lowell J. 1970. "Legal problems of the deaf." *Journal of Rehabilitation of the Deaf* 3:4, pp. 36–41.

O'Barr, William M. 1979. "Language and advertising." In: J. A. Alatis and G. R. Tucker (eds.), *Georgetown University Round Table on Languages and Linguistics 1979*. Washington, DC: Georgetown University Press, pp. 272–86.

O'Barr, William M. 1981. "The language of the law." In: Charles A. Ferguson and Shirley Brice Heath (eds.), *Language in the USA*. Cambridge: Cambridge University Press, pp. 386–406.

O'Barr, William M. 1982. *Linguistic Evidence: Language, Power, and Strategy in the Courtroom*. New York: Academic Press.

Philbrick, Frederick A. 1949. *Language and the Law: The Semantics of Forensic English*. New York: Macmillan.

Philips, Susan U. 1980. "Discourse agreement in courtroom question-answer sequences." Paper read at the Summer Meeting of Linguistic Society of America, University of New Mexico, Albuquerque.

Platt, Martha 1978. "Language and speakers in the courtroom." In Jeri J. Jaeger et al. (eds.), *Proceedings of the Fourth Annual Meeting of the Berkeley Linguistics Society*. Berkeley, CA: Berkeley Linguistics Society, pp. 617–27.

Pousada, Alicia 1979. "Interpreting for language minorities in the courts." In: James Alatis and Richard Tucker (eds.), *Language in Public Life*. Washington, DC: Georgetown University Press, pp. 186–208.

Probert, Walter 1966. "Courtroom semantics." *American Jurisprudence: Trials* 5, pp. 695–805.

Redish, Janice C. 1979. *Readability*. Washington, DC: American Institutes for Research.

Ross, John Robert 1970. "On declarative sentences." In: Roderick A. Jacobs and Peter S. Rosenbaum (eds.), *Readings in English Transformational Grammar*. Waltham, MA: Ginn and Company, pp. 222–72.

Sacks, H., E. A. Schegloff, and G. A. Jefferson 1974. "A simplest semantics for the organization of turn-taking for conversation." *Language* 50, pp. 696–735.

Sadock, Jerrold M. 1974. *Toward a Linguistic Theory of Speech Acts*. London and New York: Academic Press.

Schenkein, J. (ed.) 1978. *Studies in the Organization of Conversational Interaction*. London and New York: Academic Press.

Schiller, Andrew 1979. "The language of accidental death and dismemberment: A case of forensic linguistics." Paper read at American Association for Applied Linguistics, Los Angeles.

Searle, John R. 1969. *Speech Acts: An Essay in the Philosophy of Language*. Cambridge: Cambridge University Press.

Segalowitz, N. 1976. "Communicative incompetence and nonfluent bilingualism." *Canadian Journal of Behavioral Science* 8 pp. 122–31.

Shuy, Roger W. 1981. "Topic as the unit of analysis in a criminal law case." Paper read at Georgetown University Roundtable on Languages and Linguistics, Washington, DC. Published in: Deborah Tannen (ed.), *Analyzing Discourse: Text and Talk (GURT 1981)*. Washington, DC: Georgetown University Press, 1981, pp. 113–26.

Smith, Raoul 1982. ''A functional view of the linguistics of advertising.'' In: Robert J. DiPietro (ed.), *Linguistics and the Professions*. Norwood, NJ: Ablex., pp. 189–99.

Snee, T. J., and D. E. Lush 1941. ''Interaction of the narrative and interrogatory methods of obtaining testimony.'' *The Journal of Psychology* 11, pp. 229–336.

Swett, Daniel H. 1969. ''Cultural bias in the American legal system.'' *Law and Society Review* 4:1, pp. 79–110.

Wang, William S.-Y. 1980. ''Assessing language incompetence.'' *The Linguistic Reporter* 22:8.

Williams, George M., Jr. 1976. ''The opacity of real conspiracies.'' In: Henry Thompson et al. (eds.), *Proceedings of the Second Annual Meeting of the Berkeley Linguistics Society*. Berkeley, CA: Berkeley Linguistics Society, pp. 406–12.

Words and Phrases (Permanent Edition) 1970. St. Paul, MN: West Publishing Company.

CHAPTER TWELVE

Interpretive Competence and Theories of Human Communication

Robert E. Sanders

1. Introduction

The principal objective of communication research is to account for the role of communication (coding, transmitting, and conversely, acquiring information) in preserving or changing social practices, institutions, and relationships. This obviously requires a concern with the interplay among cognitions, predispositions, social relations, acculturation, and goals that determines the effect(s) that communicated information has, and the effect(s) that result from varying the ways in which it is coded and transmitted. However, communication research does not necessarily have to be concerned with the properties of language or conventions of use that make the social functions of human communication possible. If the properties of language or conventions of use are not limiting, and if the determinants and effects of communicated information are extralinguistic, then communication research can take it for granted that the principles of language production and interpretation enable the expression of an infinitely large and unbounded corpus of information.

Much research attention has been given to the effects of communicated information on large populations rather than individuals, and it stands to reason (though it turns out not to be entirely correct) that the determinants and effects of communicated information on an aggregate are extralinguistic. On the other hand, a considerable amount of ordinary communication involves individuals, not aggregates. The prototypical instance is conversation, and the predominant effect of communicated information in conversations is linguistic: the effect of a message or message sequence in a conversation consists of the subsequent conversation. The effect thus depends heavily on the principles of interpretation, production, and conventions of use that constrain what can meaningfully be said (communicated) next.

The program in this paper is to contribute to an account of the effects of communicated information on individuals in conversation, and to indicate how this generalizes to other genres of communication. The specific undertaking this involves is a specification of constraints on what can meaningfully be said next in a sequence of messages (e.g., utterances). An indication emerges from this of the interrelationship and respective boundaries of communication research and language studies—something which has been (more or less) recognized as problematic in studies of language, but which has been taken as a self-evident matter of distinct but complementary interests in communication research.

2. *Determinants and Constraints in Conversation*

There are four substantial motivations for hypothesizing that over and above psychological and sociological determinants of response, there are constraints on what can meaningfully be said next in a conversation. The first, though not the most compelling, is that some such constraints have been indicated in one way or another by several independent sources. Grice's (1967, 1975) notion of the Cooperative Principle, especially its constituent Maxim of Relation, presupposes constraints on what can be said next, and indicates that it matters to the assignment of interpretations whether those constraints are satisfied or breached. Halliday and Hasan's (1976) concern with text cohesion begins with the premise that there are ties that bind the parts of a discourse into a whole, and such principles of cohesion would of course entail that constraints on what can (coherently) be said next emerge as the text progresses. Van Dijk's (1977) effort to display formal constraints on sequencing the constituents of a text represents a fully explicit, though narrow, treatment of the general idea. Schank's (1977) contention that responses are anomalous if they supply or request information that has already been stated, implied, or presupposed leads naturally to the formulation of constraints on what can be said next. And Reichman's (1978) evidence that speakers often jump back and forth between topics, but in doing so utilize various devices to mark such shifts and identify the present topic, indicates that there are constraints on what can be said next which can be breached as long as transition markers are provided to compensate.

A second, and more powerful, motivation for positing constraints on what can meaningfully be said next is that it is not obvious how certain facts about conversation can be accounted for otherwise. Intuitively, there is something odd about X's responses in (1)–(3) below, not because their content is irrelevant—at least in the case of (1) and arguably (2) as well—but because *as responses* they are irrelevant, not meaningful, unresponsive.

(1)   A: Here's the cup of coffee you ordered.
       ?B: This is the cup of coffee I ordered.

(2)   K: I have no idea where I put the car keys.
       ?X: Creative ideas won't likely pan out if some effort isn't put into
             them.

(3)   P: Isn't that a pretty bouquet of flowers in the window?
       ??X: No, I don't think I'll do laundry tonight

First, note that the very notion of a response being odd is difficult to explain solely with reference, for instance, to the atypicality of the determinant or the low probability of that response. Attributing the oddness of X's responses to atypical determinants fails because the oddness of the responses has to be evident before it can be surmised that the determinants are atypical. And, for reasons akin to the ones Chomsky (1957:14–17) gave for rejecting empirical accounts of grammaticality, the oddness of those responses cannot be attributed to their being improbable: responses can be made which are wholly improbable without thereby being odd, e.g., whenever the response is about an innovation or is linguistically innovative. Second, it is similarly problematic to explain the special status of 'odd' responses, as marked by the warrants they provide for making a transition to meta-talk. Third, the oddness of a response is not directly a function of its determinants, but instead depends on what its antecedents in the conversation (and the situation) are: accordingly, the oddness of X's response in (1) vanishes if antecedently a requested cup of coffee had been so delayed that its arrival could foster mock awe; similarly, if K's dilemma in (2) had been preceded by an effort to innovate a way of not misplacing the keys, X's response follows; and X's response in (3) stops being odd if P had been soliciting X to do the laundry, and had been offering the indicated flowers as a bribe of some kind. Thus, the oddness of X's responses (or their aptness) must be a function of constraints on what can meaningfully be said next, given the sequence that occurred beforehand.

A third motivation is that there is empirical support for the claim that the interpretation of an utterance, and the response to it, are contingent on what the antecedent sequence consists of—on which way a message 'fits into' the antecedent sequence (Potoker 1982). The converse of this, of course, is that there are constraints on what can meaningfully be said next.

A fourth motivation, perhaps the most powerful for positing such constraints, is provided by the cumulative results of work on both semantic and pragmatic theories of interpretation. Three distinct classes of interpretation have emerged from those efforts (propositional content, or truth conditions; conventional and conversational implicatures; and illocutionary acts). Regardless of how explicit the assignment functions are for each class of interpretation, it will remain undecided which type of interpretation to actually assign in a given instance. For example, suppose two acquaintances are talking casually while they stand at a street corner waiting to go across, and one says, *Here comes a maniac—speeding and running lights*. The hearer could interpret that utterance as reporting or describing a state of affairs and could thus respond with further information about it (e.g., *Doesn't look drunk—probably some kid*). But the hearer could just as well interpret the utterance as conversationally implicating that the indicated transgression strikes the speaker as a particularly serious one, and thus respond with an indication of agreement or dissent from that assessment (e.g., *I don't think it'd get a rise from a cop*). And of course the hearer could instead interpret the utterance as the performance of an illocutionary act such as 'warning,' and aptly respond with an overt acknowledgment of the act, or by commenting on warrants in the situation for performing the act (e.g., *Thanks—I didn't see it*). Excepting extrasensory perceptions of the speaker's intent, the only evident basis for deciding among such interpretive options is the way an utterance fits into the antecedent sequence (whether the sequence in question is simply the conversation, or is some more extended sequence known to the interpreter, up to the entire history of interactions between the speaker and the interpreter). And if an uttered expression cannot have an interpretation assigned to it in a principled way unless it has some requisite connection to the antecedent sequence, then conversely, there are constraints on what can meaningfully be said next.

3. Principles of Relevance

I have attempted elsewhere to make explicit the different ways in which uttered expressions fit into (relevantly respond to) the antecedent sequence (Sanders 1980, 1981), and to indicate the practical and theoretical consequences of the resulting constraints on response (Sanders 1982). While I consider these efforts to be on the right track, and to point to the pertinent issues, they include defective formulations because of an incorrect starting assumption, and they largely gloss over a number of related issues in semantics and pragmatics. My intention here is to summarize that analysis, indicate some of its particular weaknesses, and then reformulate the pertinent relationships.

As I have defined the problem, the question is whether there are distinct ways in which utterances can be relevant to their antecedent(s), such that preferences for an interpretation from a given class in specific instances are warranted by the type of relevance involved. This way of accounting for interpretive choices in conversation is not as novel or as unmotivated as it might seem on the surface. Searle (1969:e.g., 141–146) and Green and Morgan (1981:177ff.), among others, have posited that the types of interpretations an utterance receives are entirely a matter of what illocutionary act the speaker is understood to perform (e.g., asserting, requesting, advising, or a social action of some other kind). That is, the way in which an utterance's content is used in a given instance is assumed to depend on what the speaker's intentions in speaking are. However, this brings us back to essentially the same problem we began with; namely, how does one know what the speaker's intentions are. Green and Morgan are ready to say that it is basically a mystery: "the link between intentional acts . . . and their interpretation is so underdetermined by the objective data . . . that there will be many a slip twixt cup and lip" (op. cit.:177). However, their mistake is to equate intentions with the actor's actual reasons for acting. Rather, an actor's intentions are constructions, the (conventionally specified) motivation that the actor would have to have to deliberately exhibit the observed pattern of actions and reactions. This is essentially Burke's (1945) analysis and the working presumption of most psychotherapists. Hence, intentions are readily inferred—and perhaps only knowable—from the antecedent sequence of acts and utterances. My effort to base the interpretation of utterances on their relationship to the antecedent sequence is thus not a departure from others' appeal to intentions, except for the greater explicitness of the analysis.

The interpreter does have pertinent objective data to work with, then, in deciding between classes of interpretation: what has happened, and been said and done, antecedently; and the linguistic features, especially the semantics, of the uttered expression in question. (A distinction is necessary here between the *semantic value* or truth conditions an expression of language has across different speakers and circumstances of utterance, and its *communicative value*, the interpretation it actually receives in specific circumstances of utterance; however, it can be the case, and often is, that the communicative value is the same as the semantic value.) It is thus appealing to suppose that each class of interpretation is preferred on the basis of a distinct type of relevance between the semantics of the uttered expression and features of its antecedent(s). The types of relevance between an uttered expression and its antecedent can be expressed in set-theoretic terms as a general relationship, $REL_{ue,a}$, that holds when any of three conditions are satisfied: when there is a non-empty intersection between the set of features of the uttered expression's semantic value, SV_{ue}, and (i) the set of features of the antecedent's semantic value, SV_a; or (ii) the set of features of the universe of discourse attached to the antecedently indicated state of affairs, UD_a; or (iii) the set of features of the felicity conditions of an illocutionary act the antecedent could be counted as, FC_a.

(4) $REL_{ue,a} = {}_{dfn}[SV_{ue} \cap (SV_a \vee UD_a \vee FC_a) \neq \emptyset]$

These three alternative warranting relationships are illustrated in (5)–(7) respectively; X's replies have the respective communicative values of propositional content, an implicature, and an act:

(5) B: I'll be finished with this project by Tuesday.
     X: I think you're going to be among the first to be done.

(6) J: I'll meet you down at the Bear's Claw Pub.
     X: I'm under age.

(7) P: Your glasses are all smudged—how can you see?
     X: Mind your own business.

This account entails that interpreters must search back through the prior sequence to locate a given utterance's specific antecedent. It is likely an empirical question how this is done: perhaps depending on culture, personality, or situation, interpreters could designate as the antecedent the first constituent to have any one of the three types of relevance to the utterance's semantics; or there could be preferences for one class of interpretation over the next, so that the prior sequence is searched for antecedents with the requisite relationship before it is searched again on some other basis; or discourse markers of various kinds are utilized to identify the antecedents of utterances.

Despite the problems I will enumerate below, this general approach has several merits. First, it motivates a useful meta-theoretical distinction between the possible interpretations that follow from rules of language, conventions of use, etc.—and warrants for focusing on specific interpretations by emerging properties of the interaction. Second, it makes a number of correct predictions. It predicts that when interactants are unacquainted, misinterpretations are most likely at the beginning of a conversation when there are few antecedents of utterances known to both interactants; interactants will therefore tend to manufacture such antecedents by asking for background information to stereotype the other, or will utilize antecedents in the immediate sensory field by talking about, e.g., the weather. The approach here also predicts that speakers' assertions about the intended meaning of an utterance will be disbelieved if the alleged meaning is not warranted by the utterance's basis of relevance in the antecedent sequence. It further predicts that speakers and hearers can disagree about the interpretation of an utterance, and that the content of such disagreements is what warrants were provided in the antecedent sequence for one interpretation or the other. And it predicts that when speakers anticipate saying something that could have costly or beneficial results depending on how it is interpreted, they will manipulate the sequence to 'set the stage' or lead up to it. Finally, the notion that interpreters search backwards to locate the antecedent of the utterance in question is suggestive about there being interpretive strategies, and about the requirements of speaking so as to produce a certain effect by constraining what the other(s) can meaningfully say next.

On the other hand, there are a number of unresolved problems in the original analysis. Most of them result from a mistake in the starting premise that preferences for interpretations from one class or another can be warranted entirely in terms of relationships between the utterance's semantics and features of antecedent interpretations. This results not only in relationships that are too broad or too restrictive, as detailed below, but in the dubious contention that the warranted interpretation cannot in principle be self-evident, and that interpreters are bound to search out each utterance's antecedent before its interpretation is decided. At best, these principles of relevance are necessary but not sufficient.

With regard to warrants for preferring that the communicative value of an uttered expression be its propositional content I specified that there had to be features of the state of affairs indicated by the uttered expression in common with features of states of affairs indicated antecedently. I have further specified that such overlaps are generally marked by overlaps in the lexical material comprised by underlying semantic representations. However, an utterance with that relationship to its antecedent can nonetheless be odd if it supplies wholly superfluous information, asks a question in response to the answer being given, asks permission to act after being ordered to do so, etc. Moreover, when utterances have commonalities in their lexical material, there may nonetheless be some other type of relationship involved between the uttered expression and its antecedent(s) so that a communicative value from some other class is preferred.

With respect to the basis of relevance that warrants a preference for communicative values from the class of implicatures, I specified that the relationship must consist of common features between the semantics of the uttered expression and the universe of discourse (e.g., associated scripts) surrounding the state of affairs antecedently specified. This disregards that the same interpretive warrants are provided when this relationship is reversed, when the universe of discourse attached to the uttered expression has features in common with the semantics of the antecedent(s), or when the commonalities are entirely within the universes of discourse attached to the uttered expression and its antecedent(s) respectively. However, if this warranting relationship is broadened that way it becomes wholly inclusive: such a relationship could probably be worked out between any two utterances if the analysis were pushed far enough.

The problem with the way I have specified warrants for preferring communicative values from the class of illocutionary acts is similar. I have specified the relationship so that the interpretation of an utterance as an act is contingent on its including some semantic indicator of an antecedent illocutionary act. But it is not only dubious that illocutionary acts are inherently 'retaliatory'; it raises the question of how it is possible for there to be an initial illocutionary act in the sequence. It would have to be the case either that initial acts are understood as responses to some antecedent act outside of or prior to the specific conversation in progress, or that the initial act is given that interpretation on a post hoc basis because it was responded to as an act subsequently. All of that is cumbersome, and in addition it disregards two other relationships which utterances-as-acts can have to their antecedents. First, it disregards instances when the utterance can be counted as some act because the felicity conditions of that act were (in part or wholly) talked about antecedently (e.g., if the other person expresses a desire for something and the speaker states an intention to bring that thing about, then it would be warranted to focus on that stated intention as a promise because a felicity condition for promising had been created antecedently). Second, saying that utterances only count as illocutionary acts if their semantics indicate that an antecedent act was performed disregards that insofar as an utterance reciprocates an antecedent act (compliment for compliment, insult for insult), or is the reciprocal of an antecedent act, it is warranted to prefer interpreting the utterance as an illocutionary act even if its semantics do not indicate the antecedent was an act.

It should be emphasized here that the problems with the way I have treated illocutionary acts (and other classes of interpretation) do not stem from disregarding the insistence of speech act theorists that all utterances have the intentional aspect of actions. Although Austin (1962) did show that the formal properties of utterances do not distinguish between performatives and constatives, the claim here is that they are distinguished in context by the relationships of utterances to their antecedent(s). Moreover, Searle's (e.g., 1969, 1975) effort to view the distinct classes of interpretation I have indicated as simply different (types of?) illocutionary acts ultimately fails: for example, granted that providing information is an illocutionary act, it is one thing to focus on the information that was provided and to make a response to that; it is something else entirely to focus on the utterance as being an informative *act* and to make a response to *the speaker's having done that*.

4. Improving the General Analysis

If the problem is that principles of relevance are necessary but not sufficient conditions for preferring that an utterance's interpretation be from one class or another, then the need is for additional criteria. The specified relationship between the utterance's semantics and the antecedent's semantics that warrants a focus on propositional content is too broad. If the relationships that warrant preferences for the class of implicatures and the class of illocutionary acts respectively were revised as indicated above, they would also be too broad. In that case, the principles of relevance would not uniquely identify the warranted interpretation of an utterance. The problem then remains to explain how it can be determined which of those candidates fits best into the antecedent sequence of interpreted utterances, behaviors, and events.

There seem to be just two principal ways in which to specify that one among several possible interpretations of an utterance best fits into the antecedent sequence. One is an essentially quantitative approach: the interpretation that fits best has the greatest number of constituent features in common with the composite set of semantic features, features of the universe of discourse, and features of the circumstances of utterance comprised respectively by antecedent interpretations. The other approach presumes that conversations are conducted within some kind of conceptual framework or schema of the transaction (e.g., a script or plan): the interpretation which fits best is the one which is generically or specifically called for in the schema, or is at least admissible at that juncture in the transaction.

But a decisive weakness of the quantitative approach is that the interpretations it specifies as fitting just as well as or better than others into the antecedent sequence will not necessarily be the preferred ones. For example, a seemingly gratuitous response as in (1) or (8) has virtually all of its semantic features in common with the antecedent's, yet (at least in those two cases, in the absence of additional context) the preferred interpretations are not from the class of semantic references and assertions as the quantitative approach would predict—they are from the class of implicatures:

(8)   A: Mr. Smith is out of the office just now.
       B: Mr. Smith is *always* out of the office just now.

A second weakness of the quantitative approach is that it cannot handle a basic fact about ordinary communication, namely that the interpretation of an utterance can be altered subsequently by the way in which the sequence proceeds from it. This is essentially Lewis's (1979) conception of language games: if the presuppositions of uttered expressions can be changed after the fact then the assignment of interpretations must be equally fluid. This is evident when someone takes bantering a little too far, and tries to undo the damage by saying something like *I was only joking*. Thus, given that X's response in (6) would be interpreted as an implicature on the basis of its relationship to its antecedent, and accordingly answered by J as in (9), X's response would be reinterpreted after the fact if J responded as in (10) or (11):

(9)   J: I'll meet you down at the Bear's Claw Pub.
       X: I'm under age.
       J: Then we'd better meet at the Farmer's Diner.

(10) J: I'll meet you down at the Bear's Claw Pub.
       X: I'm under age.
       J: Amazing. I'd never guess it from the way you act.

(11) J: I'll meet you down at the Bear's Claw Pub.
       X: I'm under age.
       J: Don't think you can avoid me with an excuse like that.

The alternative approach is far more productive. There are numerous precedents (e.g., Wittgenstein 1953; Schank and Abelson 1977) for saying that actors make predictions about each other's conduct in social transactions, and organize their own actions, on the basis of cognitive schemata. Such schemata can specify role relationships and role requirements, achievable goals, sufficient means, etc. in a situation: among other things, this would result in expectations of what can be talked about, what it would be better to indicate implicitly, what interpersonal attitudes can be expressed and thus what actions can be performed. On that basis, alternative interpretations of an utterance can be matched against expectations. If a man tells a woman whom he knows casually and is not courting that he thinks her dress is sexy, then (a) if they are at a cocktail party, the utterance will likely be interpreted at face value (propositional content); (b) if he is being interviewed by her for a job and the interview is just beginning, then the utterance will likely be interpreted as implicating resistance to her being in a superior position; but (c) if he is being interviewed by her for a job and the interview is coming to a conceivable negative conclusion, the utterance will likely be interpreted as an act, perhaps a hostile one such as an insult, or a manipulative one such as flattery.

It is unacceptably vague, however, to attribute interpretive decisions entirely to finding a match between schema-based expectations and one of the alternative possible interpretations of an utterance: it is doubtful that such schemata can be formalized in any general way, or in a way that is not ad hoc; and there are problems (to be detailed below) in each class of interpretation with efforts to specify the derivation of interpretations prior to and independent of a concern with the utterance's place in the ongoing transaction. Rather, principles of relevance along the lines of the earlier analysis still apply: it is just that as noted, those principles cannot uniquely specify the preferred (class of) interpretation without reference to and underlying conception of the transaction.

The upshot is that each of the original principles of relevance has to be revised to include, among other things, the additional requirements for an utterance to be relevant that are imposed by the cognitive schema overlaid on the transaction. These requirements are: first, the candidate interpretation (that follows if the utterance is relevant on a given basis) must be called for, or at least admissible, in the schema; second, adding the candidate interpretation to the antecedent sequence must advance the transaction towards a resolution as that is defined by the schema. These conditions will be labeled α and β, respectively, and are more precisely stated as follows:

(12) $\alpha =\ _{dfn}[\gamma \in CS]$
      where γ is a candidate interpretation from the pertinent class, and CS is the set of constituents of the cognitive schema.

(13) $\beta =\ _{dfn}[CS|T_i + \gamma = T_{i+1}]$
      where CS is the cognitive schema, γ is the candidate interpretation, and T_i is the i_{th} juncture of the transaction as specified by the schema.

The warranting relationship for interpretations from the class of propositional content was originally said to be an overlap in the semantics of the utterance and the semantics of the antecedent: the defect in this is that interpretations from other classes may be preferred even though that relationship holds, and the relationship fails to mark as anomalous certain gratuitous utterances. These defects are removed by α and β. α specifies that such semantic commonalities must not only hold, but that there is a place in the schema for entering that content; and β specifies that in addition, adding the utterance on that interpretation to the sequence advances the transaction towards a resolution. The revised principle of relevance can be stated as a complex condition for preferring that an utterance's interpretation be its propositional content

(14) $([SV_{ue} \cap SV_a \neq \emptyset] \cdot \alpha \cdot \beta) \rightarrow (CV_{ue} = PC)$
where SV_{ue} and SV_a are the sets of features of the semantic values of the uttered expression and those incorporated into the antecedent sequence; CV_{ue} is the communicative value of the uttered expression; and PC is propositional content

The warranting relationship for interpretations from the class of implicatures was originally said to be an overlap between the semantics of the utterance and the universe of discourse attached to the antecedent: the defect in this is that it is too limiting, and overlooks equivalent relationships between the universe of discourse attached to the utterance and the antecedent's semantics, and between the universes of discourse attached to the utterance and the antecedent respectively. However, to broaden the warranting relationship that way makes it all-inclusive—except with reference to α and β. Even though implicatures are always possible on the basis of that expanded set of relationships, they would not be the preferred interpretation unless it was specified or admissible in the transaction to make the implicated statement in question, and unless doing so at that juncture advanced the transaction. Hence, the warranting condition for preferring that an interpretation be in the class of implicatures is the following:

(15) $([((SV_{ue} \cap UD_a) \vee (UD_{ue} \cap SV_a) \vee (UD_{ue} \cap UD_a)) \neq \emptyset] \cdot \alpha \cdot \beta) \rightarrow (CV_{ue} = Imp)$
where SV_{ue} and SV_a are as above; UD_{ue} and UD_a are the sets of features of the universes of discourse attached to the states of affairs indicated by the uttered expression and the antecedent sequence respectively; CV_{ue} is as above; and Imp is an implicature.

Finally, the warranting relationship for interpretations from the class of illocutionary acts was originally said to be an overlap between the semantics of the utterance and features of the state of affairs specified by an antecedent act's felicity conditions: the defect in this is that it is too limiting. It treats illocutionary acts as being invariably retaliatory, and disregards such warranting relationships as when the felicity conditions of the act the utterance in question could count as overlap an antecedent's propositional content or when the utterance in question includes a mention of an antecedent act. Expanding the warranting relationship in that way does not result in too broad a net because of the limiting conditions provided by α and β:

(16) $([((SV_{ue} \cap FC_{aA}) \vee (FC_{ueA} \cap SV_a)) \neq \emptyset] \vee [aA \in SV_{ue}] \vee [ueA = aA] \cdot \alpha \cdot \beta) \rightarrow (CV_{ue} = IA)$

where SV_{ue} and SV_a are as above; FC_{ueA} and FC_{aA} are respectively the felicity conditions of illocutionary acts which the uttered expression and its antecedent could be counted as; ueA and aA are putative occurrences of those acts; CV_{ue} is as above; and IA is an illocutionary act.

Although there is undeniably something unsatisfying about this revised approach (it circumvents problems in making explicit the warrants for interpretive preferences by appealing to something as inexplicit as conceptualizations of the transaction), it is difficult to explain the disambiguating influence of 'background information' in any other way.

Consider, for example, that in terms of principles of relevance alone, B's response in (17) could equally be intended as propositional content, an implicature, or an act:

(17)   A: How come you're always lounging around here after lunch?
       B: I can work so efficiently in the morning that I'm usually done by
            noon.

Assuming overlaps in the lexical material in *work efficiently* and *lounging,* and in *noon* and *after lunch,* B's response is relevant on semantic grounds; assuming that A's question is about both the fact of B's lounging *and* the place, B's response breaches the maxim of quantity; given that a question about the motives or causes of the hearer's conduct could be counted as a challenge, B's response is relevant to the felicity conditions of the challenge. However, if the role-relationship between A and B is specified so as to call into play certain conceptualizations of the sort of transaction that A's question would be part of, there are grounds for preferring one class of interpretation ahead of the others. Thus, if A is B's employer or supervisor, and they are not close friends, and they are at work, then A's question would most likely count as a challenge (depending on the history of past transactions between them), and B's response is intuitively an illocutionary act (e.g., justification). If A and B are potential sexual partners, and the place where B habitually lounges is where A is routinely located, then in scripts concerned with courting rituals it would be significant that B hangs out around A and that would be the force of A's question; B's response in that case would breach the maxim of quantity and implicate, for instance, a disinterest in or inhibition about a liaison with A. However, if A and B were close friends, then no significance obviously attaches to the question beyond its face value, and B's response intuitively reads as an assertion about his/her patterns of work and relaxation.

This revised set of formulations is obviously a retreat from the presumption in the original analysis that interpretive preferences within and among classes of interpretation are entirely a function of formal relationships among utterances and their antecedent(s) in a sequence. Although principles of relevance are likely sufficient as representations of the constraints on what can meaningfully be said next, they are generally too weak to correctly predict the preferred (class of) interpretation of the utterances in anonymous overheard conversations. On the other hand, bolstering the analysis by invoking cognitive schemata does not represent an abandonment of the central idea that the preferred interpretation is decided on a nonidiosyncratic and systematic judgment of the utterance's fit in the antecedent sequence: the cognitive schema which an interpreter overlays on a conversation represents a hypothesis about the nature of the transaction in progress. Such hypotheses are usually based on what is said and done at the outset, and always confirmed or not by whether the transaction unfolds as the schema predicts.

It is another matter whether an individual will actually prefer the interpretation that is warranted by the utterance's fit in the antecedent sequence. There could be biases fostered by idiosyncratic beliefs and attitudes, goals, acculturation, or special factors in the interpersonal relationship. Accordingly, there is a three-part distinction required in theory between: (a) the meaning of an (uttered, even contextualized) expression, with respect to a class of interpretation; (b) the meaning of an utterance as a response to a precursor of a sequence of other utterances, behaviors, and events; (c) the meaning of an utterance to the individuals participating in the transaction in which it occurred, given their interpersonal relationship, acculturation, beliefs, attitudes, and goals. The first and second of those are components of a theory of interpretive competence. The third involves interpretive performance.

5. Issues in Semantic and Pragmatic Theories of Interpretation

On the surface, the major issue in semantics and pragmatics for some time now is what contributions to the meaning of an expression are made, respectively, by the expression's linguistic properties and by conventions or circumstances of use, and by what principles they are made. However, the real controversy has been about the degree to which the different classes of interpretation, which surfaced in efforts to work out that interrelationship, can be folded together and reduced to just one class or another. Searle (1969, 1972) has actively opposed the idea that propositional content can be specified in any but a trivial sense without reference to the class of speech acts, and he has in addition subsumed the class of implicatures under the rubric of indirect speech acts (Searle 1975). Conversely, there have been efforts to expand lexical material so that information pertaining to illocutionary acts or conversational implicatures is made part of an expression's semantics (e.g., Ross 1970; Gordon and Lakoff 1975). And most recently, the increasingly narrow scope of semantics in philosophical logic fosters the idea that actual meanings are usually implicated, with 'best interpretations' selected on pragmatic grounds along the lines of Grice's (1967) Cooperative Principle (e.g., Gazdar 1979; Atlas and Levinson 1981).

However, these diverse efforts have the same objective: to account for the meaning(s) uttered expressions *actually* have (as opposed to the semantic representations of sentences *in vacuo* that Katz and Fodor 1963, are routinely vilified for). From the foregoing analysis, it should be clear that this is a muddled objective. Work within all of the classes of interpretation, no matter how sensitive it is to contextual factors like the identity of the speaker, or the time and location of the utterance, is insensitive to the warrants for interpretive choices based on the utterance's fit in the antecedent sequence, and also to the interpretive biases fostered by interpreters' cognitions, acculturation, goals, etc. Hence, none of the work on interpretations *within* a class can in principle account for the meaning(s) expressions actually have. Rather, to put the objective more precisely, such work has to aim at accounting for the meaning(s) expressions *can* have across members of a speech community, depending on how their utterance fits the antecedent sequence. Work on the assignment of interpretations within a class is inadequate to fully account for 'interpretive competence'—how people go about the job of deciding what in particular the uttered expression means at that juncture, given the rather large number of things it *could* mean. The warrants for interpretive choices I have posited represent a concern with that problem, based on the presumption that interpretive choices are not typically a simple function of mental sets and other idiosyncrasies, but are heavily dependent on a systematic basis for deciding on the meaning which the utterance most likely has at that juncture in the sequence.

All of this indicates that semantic and pragmatic theories have to be conceived of more conservatively. In fact, there is reason to suppose that such theories cannot even be fully autonomous, specifying for any uttered expression of the language the array of interpretations which interpreters have to choose among. Rather, semantic and pragmatic theories may in general specify only skeletal interpretations and accompanying constraints on how they can be fleshed out by interpreters engaged in a transaction. This is more evident from an analysis of specific efforts in the respective classes of interpretation.

For example, under the heading 'script-based semantics' Raskin (1982) proposes an enriched conception of lexical material, and uses it to account for (a) what the interpreter knows about the indicated state of affairs from knowing what the expression (semantically) means, and (b) the fact that interpreters are usually cognizant of only one of an expression's alternative semantic values at any given juncture. It should be noted, but it is not problematic here, that Raskin's lexicon collapses the distinction in pragmatics between an uttered expression's truth-conditions and its conventional implicatures; in fact, from the point of view of the behavior of propositional content in a theory of interpretive performance, voiding that distinction is all to the good (its importance in philosophical logic notwithstanding). But it is problematic that Raskin attempts to build an account of the one interpretation on which interpreters focus into the framework of a self-contained set of combinatorial rules that mark alternative lexical scripts as 'most likely' on the basis of the interpreter's knowledge of the world. This leaves it vague what contextual factors, and under what circumstances, would alter such conceptions of 'most likely' readings. The same objective as Raskin's could be achieved more parsimoniously if the 'most likely' lexical scripts were marked according to extra-lexical criteria, in particular (a) which scripts intersect other such lexical material brought forward in the interpreted antecedent sequence, and (b) whether it is admissible according to the cognitive schema involved to talk about what is indicated by one or another lexical script.

The work done on implicatures following Grice has, of course, been dominated by concerns in philosophical logic with precisely what distinguishes conventional meanings (semantic values) from implicatures, and conventional implicatures from conversational ones; there has also been a concern with identifying the basis for inferring the specific implicatum of an uttered expression in context (e.g., Gazdar 1979; Atlas and Levinson 1981). Given an identification of semantic values with truth-conditions, implicatures are viewed as what in addition is known about the indicated state of affairs by virtue of the speaker's saying less or more than is minimally needed. While work along these lines is generally well motivated, solves a number of problems, and is making explicit some bases for pragmatic inferences much of the richness of Grice's (especially, 1967) original notion of conversational implicatures is lost. From Grice's examples, conversational implicatures only sometimes and only incidentally are about additional features of the indicated state of affairs than what is specified by the expression's truth conditions. Rather, *conversational implicatures involve the conditions that warrant the particular breach of the maxims which has occurred* (relative to the universe of discourse attached to the indicated state of affairs). Thus, when two people are gossiping about a third and one suddenly makes a radical topic shift, that may implicate that the third person has come into earshot (rather than implicating more about the person than was actually said); and when a letter of recommendation for a job applicant deals with his/her personality and omits all mention of ability, that only implicates a negative judgment of the applicant (making further claims than were actually stated) because it implicates some reluctance on the writer's part to comment. The reduction of conversational implicatures that has occurred in recent work thus obscures precisely what distinguishes them (in a communicatively interesting sense) from propositional content, but to do otherwise leaves open how implicatures are inferred. Of course, a substantial basis for accounting for such specific inferences is provided by the work here on interpretive competence. The specific implicatum inferred is that feature of the attached universe of discourse which intersects features of the antecedently indicated state of affairs or attached universe of discourse, given a breach of one or more of the maxims in particular.

Work on speech acts, particularly illocutionary acts, has not much advanced Searle's (1969) treatment. I think that the reason does not involve a particular defect in the central idea as much as it involves an indeterminacy in the relationship between utterances with certain features and interpretations of that class (e.g., Stampe 1975; Green and Morgan 1981). The problem with Searle's assumption that constitutive rules (felicity conditions) warrant assigning a specific illocutionary force to utterances made in specific situations is that the felicity conditions of a number of acts which an utterance could count as often hold in the same situation. However, if the problem is treated as an aspect of interpretive competence, then the features of the utterance and the felicity conditions that matter in a given circumstance are the ones that intersect specific features of the antecedent sequence, as in (16).

6. Issues in Communication Research

It cannot be the case that the effects of utterances (messages) in conversation are simple functions of the information communicated by them, or even that there is a determinate relationship between an utterance and its effect (that being, a subsequent utterance, or closure). The requirements for speaking meaningfully in a conversation, and for speaking so as to (most likely) be understood in a particular way, greatly constrain what can be said next but do not in any sense compel it. Yet given those constraints, what can be meaningfully said next may well not be what one feels compelled to say on the grounds of psychological or sociological pressure. It is an empirical question how often, and in what circumstances, one's felt predispositions are in conflict with interpretive constraints, and how often such conflicts are resolved in the direction of uninterpretability. But the fact that there are not typically very many instances in which transactions break down in that way suggests that interpretive constraints usually dominate. In that case, speakers have available to them strategic tools for producing certain effects, though not tools which guarantee that a specific effect will occur. Insofar as the antecedent sequence is shaped so as to delimit what can meaningfully be said next, and particularly so as to further delimit which of the things the other would (in the speaker's estimation) want to say next, the other is left with the choices of either saying what the speaker is pushing for, saying something he/she does not want to say, or being incoherent.

This is not the way in which the effects of utterances (messages) are investigated in communication research. Rather, research has persistently sought to establish what (fixed, predictable, or typical) effect along some dimension a message with certain features has. On the face of it, this seems to ignore the fact that effects must depend on how the message is understood, and that the interpretation of messages is problematic. However, as noted at the beginning, the rationale for doing this is that the focus is on the response of aggregates to messages, not individuals: the reasoning is that interpretive variations among individuals will cancel out in favor of a dominant interpretation in the aggregate, and that constraints on next utterances do not apply because the effects measured are extralinguistic. Even if so, the analysis of interpretive competence here

282 ROBERT E. SANDERS

entails that on an interpersonal level, the meanings of messages (per individuals or aggregates alike) are not constant, they are functions of the message's fit into an antecedent sequence. Accordingly, Jackson and Jacobs (1983), Bradac (1983), and Hewes (1983) to the contrary, at least some of the inconsistencies that plague research on message effects are probably not a simple result of using inadequately varied, or biased, stimulus materials.

There end up being two morals to this tale. First, it is obviously a serious mistake for communication research to take for granted the principles of composition, use, and interpretation that are the core of semantic and pragmatic theories, and to assume that the effects of messages are a function of some entirely separate body of principles and relationships.

On the other hand, such a narrow view is not likely to dissipate with any useful result as long as semantic and pragmatic theories rest on false assumptions that they are self-contained and carry within them the basis for explaining facts about human communication:

> It is sometimes argued that pragmatic phenomena of the type I shall be talking about are indeed out of the purview of linguistics, since they are not, strictly speaking, grammatical phenomena, but rather reflect all sorts of non-linguistic facts about the speaker, his environment, and the real world. My position is that this is, technically speaking, balderdash. If two sentences are apparently synonymous, and if an addressee reacts one way to one and another way to the other, he is discriminating between them on linguistic grounds. If, conversely, I find that I may utter a particular sentence in one sort of social environment, but cannot appropriately utter the same words in another, although I have the same message to convey, I must suspect that this is part of my linguistic knowledge just as much as it is part of my cultural heritage, or whatever I bring to the interpretation of the sentence from my real-world experience. If the effectiveness of communication is at issue, I maintain that the problem is one for linguists to work on. . . . (R. Lakoff, (1977:79–80)

There is in short a mistaken idea shared by communication research and language studies—namely, that human communication is simply a result of having information to convey, and (rules of) a language to say it in. The concern here with interpretive performance may, among other things, contribute to disposing of that assumption and fostering more productive and cooperative work in communication research and language studies.

REFERENCES

Atlas, J. D., and S. C. Levinson 1981. "It-clefts, informativeness, and logical form: Radical pragmatics (revised standard version)." In: P. Cole (ed.), *Radical Pragmatics*. New York: Academic Press, pp. 1–61.

Austin, J. 1962. *How to Do Things with Words*. Oxford: Oxford University Press.

Bradac, J. 1983. "On generalizing cabbages, messages, kings, and several other things: The virtues of multiplicity." *Human Communication Research* 9, pp. 181–7.

Burke, K. 1945. *A Grammar of Motives*. Reprinted: Berkeley, CA: University of California Press, 1969.

Chomsky, N. 1957. *Syntactic Structures*. The Hague: Mouton.

Gazdar, G. (1979). *Pragmatics: Implicature, Presupposition, and Logical Form*. New York: Academic Press.

Gordon, D., and G. Lakoff 1975. "Conversational postulates." In: P. Cole and J. L. Morgan (eds.), *Syntax and Semantics*, Vol. 3. *Speech Acts*. New York: Academic Press, pp. 83–106.

Green, G. M., and J. L. Morgan 1981. "Pragmatics, grammar, and discourse." In: P. Cole (ed.), *Radical Pragmatics*. New York: Academic Press, pp. 167–81.

Grice, H. P. 1967. "Logic and conversation." Harvard: The William James Lectures.

Grice, H. P. 1975. "Logic and conversation." In P. Cole and J. L. Morgan (eds.), *Syntax and semantics*, Vol. 3. *Speech Acts*. New York: Academic Press, pp. 41–58.

Halliday, M. A. K., and R. Hasan 1976. *Cohesion in English*. London: Longman.

Hewes, D. E. 1983. "Confessions of a methodological puritan: A response to Jackson and Jacobs." *Human Communication Research* 9, pp. 187–91.

Jackson, S., and S. Jacobs 1983. "Generalizing about messages: Suggestions for design and analysis of experiments." *Human Communication Research* 9, pp. 169–81.

Katz, J. J., and J. Fodor 1963. "The structure of a semantic theory." *Language* 39, pp. 170–210.

Lakoff, R. 1977. "What you can do with words: Politeness, pragmatics, and performatives." In: A. Rogers, B. Wall, and J. P. Murphy (eds.), *Proceedings of the Texas Conference on Performatives, Presuppositions and Implicatures*. Arlington, Virginia: Center for Applied Linguistics, pp. 79–105.

Lewis, D. 1979. "Scorekeeping in a language game." *Journal of Philosophical Logic* 8, pp. 339–59.

Potoker, S. 1982. *The Interpretation of Discourse*. Unpublished master's thesis, State University of New York at Albany.

Raskin, V. 1982. "Script-based semantic theory." Paper given at the Summer Conference on Language and Discourse Processes. East Lansing, MI: Michigan State University. Published in: W. A. Donohue and D. G. Ellis (eds.), *Current Issues in Language and Discourse Processes*. Hillsdale, NJ: Lawrence Erlbaum Associates, to appear.

Reichman, R. 1978. "Conversational coherency." *Cognitive Science* 2, pp. 283–327.

Ross, J. R. 1970. "On declarative sentences." In: R. A. Jacobs and P. S. Rosenbaum (eds.), *Readings in English Transformational Grammar*. Waltham, MA: Ginn and Company, pp. 222–72.

Sanders, R. E. 1980. "Principles of relevance: A theory of the relationship between language and communication." *Communication and Cognition* 13, pp. 77–95.

Sanders, R. E. 1981. "The interpretation of discourse." *Communication Quarterly* 29, pp. 209–17.

Sanders, R. E. 1982. "The role of meaning in producing an effect." Paper given at the Summer Conference on Language and Discourse Processes. East Lansing, MI: Michigan State University.

Schank, R. C. 1977. "Rules and topics in conversation." *Cognitive Science* 1, pp. 421–41.

Schank, R., and R. Abelson 1977. *Scripts, Plans, Goals and Understanding: An Inquiry into Human Knowledge Structures*. Hillsdale, NJ: Lawrence Erlbaum Associates.

Searle, J. R. 1969. *Speech Acts: An Essay in the Philosophy of Language*. Cambridge: Cambridge University Press.

Searle, J. R. 1972. "Chomsky's revolution in linguistics." *New York Review of Books* June 29, pp. 16–24.

Searle, J. R. 1975. "Indirect speech acts." In: P. Cole and J. L. Morgan (eds.), *Syntax and Semantics*, Vol. 3. *Speech Acts*. New York: Academic Press, pp. 59–82.

Stampe, D. W. 1975. "Meaning and truth in the theory of speech acts." In: P. Cole and J. L. Morgan (eds.), *Syntax and Semantics*, Vol. 3. *Speech Acts*. New York: Academic Press, pp. 1–40.

Van Dijk, T. A. 1977. *Text and context: Explorations in the Semantics and Pragmatics of Discourse*. London: Longman.

Wittgenstein, L. 1953. *Philosophical Investigations*. Oxford: Blackwell.

PART FOUR
HISTORICAL
PERSPECTIVES

CHAPTER THIRTEEN

Linguistics, Nationalism, and Literary Languages: A Balkan Perspective

Victor A. Friedman

1. Introduction

The processes which led to and continue to affect the formations of the modern literary languages of the Balkan peninsula have their parallels in Western Europe and elsewhere in the world, and yet the Balkans constitute a unique 'living laboratory,' because of both the great diversity of languages and ethnic groups and the fact that these processes are well documented, relatively recent, and ongoing. The relationship of linguistics to the developments in these languages has undergone a number of changes. In this article, I wish to document some of these and comment on their significance.

2. Historical Background

I will begin with a few remarks on the historical background of the linguistic composition of the Balkans. The Albanians speak a language which is often claimed to be descended from Illyrian, which may have been the language spoken on the territory of present-day Albania (and western Yugoslavia) in ancient times. Recent studies of the evidence of toponymy and vocabulary, however, indicate that Albanian may be descended from a Dacian or Thracian dialect which was being spoken in what is now eastern Serbia up to the time the Slavs crossed the Danube and invaded the Balkans (ca. A.D. 550–630). At that time, the linguistic ancestors of the Albanians would have been pushed southwest into present-day Albania (cf., e.g., Fine 1983:10–11).

The Greeks came to the Balkans some time around the second millenium B.C., displacing or absorbing other Indo-European and/or non-Indo-European peoples (cf. Gindin 1967, Neroznak 1978).

From the third or second century B.C. through the first century A.D., the Romans gradually annexed most of what is now the Balkans south of the Danube, and the second century A.D. saw their relatively brief (107–271) occupation of Dacia (roughly, modern Transylvania and western Wallachia). Studies of the language of inscriptions indicate that Roman linguistic influence extended to the so-called Jireček line, running from the coast of central Albania, across Macedonia south of Skopje to Sofia and across the Balkan mountains in central Bulgaria (cf. Rosetti 1938). South of this line, the dominant language was Greek. Romanian in its various forms (e.g., Daco-Romanian and Aromanian, see below) is descended from the language of Roman colonists and Romanized peoples north of the Jireček line and east of Dalmatia. A hotly contested issue between the Romanians and Hungarians, however, is the question of whether the Romanian of present-day Romania, especially Transylvania, is descended from the language of Romanized Dacians (and hence 'autochthonous'), or whether it is descended from the language of Romans and Romanized peoples living south of the Danube who did not cross over the Danube (or at least into Transylvania) until after the arrival of the Magyars in the late ninth century (cf. Fine 1983:10).

As was mentioned earlier, the Slavs came to the Balkans south of the Danube during the sixth and seventh centuries A.D. They did so in two main groups. One group—the East South Slavs—settled in what is now Bulgaria and Macedonia and penetrated all the way to the tips of the Peloponnesian peninsula. Those Slavs on the territory of modern Greece have been gradually Hellenized, a process which continues into the present day. The second group (leaving to one side the Slovenes) consisted of a single tribe, probably the *Slaveni,* who were divided and ruled by two Iranian military aristocracies, the *Serbs* and the *Croats,* who were Slavicized but whose names have remained as ethnonyms to this day (cf. Fine 1983:53,56–57). These West South Slavs eventually occupied the rest of what is now Yugoslavia (Croatia, Serbia, Bosnia-Hercegovina, Montenegro).

The Ottoman Turks spent the second half of the fourteenth century conquering the Balkans, a process which continued into the fifteenth century and reached its peak during the sixteenth.[1] It can be argued that it was the Turkish conquest which created the Balkans as the geopolitical and sociocultural entity we know today. From the Turkish conquest to the nineteenth century, the region was generally known as *Turkey in Europe.* As the Ottoman Empire disintegrated during the nineteenth century, this term became increasingly inapplicable to the area and distasteful for much of the rest of it, and ultimately the term *Balkan,* based on the Turkish name of the mountain chain running through central Bulgaria (Slavic *Stara Planina,* Greek *Haimos,* Latin *Haemus*) came to replace it.[2] Nonetheless, it is the common heritage of the so-called 'Turkish Yoke' which gives a background to the various Balkan national consciousness.[3]

There are many other peoples living in the Balkans, e.g., Armenians, who were first brought there by the Byzantines in the ninth century, Ladino-speaking Jews who fled the Spanish Inquisition for the relative tolerance of the Ottoman Empire in the fifteenth century, Circassians transplanted by the Turks, Hungarians, Saxon Germans, Ruthenians, etc. The literary languages of these groups, however, are based outside of the Balkans, and they have not, for the most part, participated in the intense multilingualism which resulted in the formation of the Balkan *Sprachbund,* i.e., the linguistic league comprising the Albanian, Greek, Balkan Slavic, and Balkan Romance languages, which show significant structural similarities and lexical borrowings from various sources, as well as a common background of Turkish influence (cf. Sandfeld 1930). These other languages will therefore not be discussed here.[4] One other ethnic group which is relevant to the present discussion, however, is the Roms (Gypsies), i.e., the Indic speakers who entered the Balkans at the beginning of the second millenium A.D. (Ventcel' and Čerenkov 1976:283). Many Roms have remained in the Balkans to this day, their dialects show significant Balkan features resulting from linguistic contact, and the process of Romani literary linguistic formation—while also taking place elsewhere in Europe—has a very strong center in the Balkans.

3. Literary Language and Ethnicity

I will thus be considering six language groups in the Balkans: Greek, Turkic, Romance, Albanian, Slavic, and Indic. Each of these groups is represented by one or more literary languages ranging from well established to nascent. Some of these languages have claims to older written traditions, e.g., that of ancient Greek, Old Church Slavonic, etc., but as the International Commission of Inquiry into the causes of the Balkan Wars wrote (d'Estournelles de Constant et al. 1914:29), ". . . the Turkish conquest came, leveling all the nationalities and preserving them all alike in a condition of torpor, in a manner comparable to the action of a vast refrigerator." In terms of the study of the formation of literary languages, this leveling resulted in a break of continuous development, so that as the nationalities came out of their 'torpor' during the course of the nineteenth and twentieth centuries, they found that their literary languages had likewise been 'refrigerated.' It is the process of 'thawing' which resulted in the diverse developments I am about to discuss.

Before doing so, however, I should note here that the additional extra-linguistic factor of *ethnicity* must be taken into account. According to present-day thinking, language, i.e., mother tongue, is one of the most important determinants of ethnicity. An important factor in the leveling alluded to above, however, was the use of religion as the definer of *millet* 'nationality' in the Ottoman Empire. Under this system, all adherents of the Orthodox Christian church headed by the Patriarch of Constantinople (i.e., Greek Orthodox) were 'Greek,' while all adherents of the State religion of the Turkish Empire, i.e., Islam, were 'Turks.' The Greek Orthodox church gradually took advantage of its privileged position in Constantinople to eliminate the autocephalous Bulgarian and Serbian churches (in 1765 and 1767, respectively). Thus Bulgarians, Serbs, and all other orthodox peoples in European Turkey were treated as ethnic 'Greeks' who happened to speak some other language, e.g., Slavophone Greeks, Albanophone Greeks, as opposed to Hellenophone Greeks. Likewise, the Moslem Albanians, Bosnians, Pomaks, Torbeš, etc. were all 'Turks.'[5] From this it can be seen that while mother tongue is generally taken as the primary determiner of ethnicity, e.g., in modern multinational states such as Yugoslavia or the USSR, such was not always the case. These facts of the identification of religion and ethnicity bear not only upon the developments of the previous century, but also upon certain current trends and facts.

The definition of the term 'literary language' is complicated by two factors: the meaning of the term 'literary' and that of 'language.' Although both these phenomena are linguistic, their definitions are largely extra-linguistic, i.e., mainly political, e.g., it has been said that a language is a dialect with an army of its own. Thus, for example, the Germanic-speaking peoples of Scandinavia have no less than three mutually comprehensible languages, while people in Italy, China, and the Arab world speak mutually incomprehensible dialects of the same language. In the Balkans, as elsewhere, the situation is further complicated by the fact that linguistic claims and the associated ethnic claims are intimately connected with territorial and other political claims. For the purposes of this chapter, I will accept the definition of literary language as one which is codified and used in all spheres of a given political or ethnic unit's national life (cf. Close 1974:31).[6] I will define the following Balkan languages as literary: Greek, Turkish, Romanian, Albanian, Macedonian, Bulgarian, and Serbo-Croatian. In addition, I will be commenting on Romani, Aromanian, Moldavian, Croatian, and Bosnian, insofar as these languages, dialects, variants, or standards shed valuable light on various processes of development. Since the study of the literary development of any one of these languages—or even one stage of development—has proven sufficient for monographic works, I will attempt here only a survey of the most basic processes and conflicts and enter into greater detail only for selected languages.

4. The Literary Language in the Balkans

Beginning with Greek, it can be said that the standardization of modern Greek has suffered considerably at the hands of linguists due to the diglossia which their disagreements encouraged. Greek diglossia goes back to the first centuries before and after the beginning of the Christian era when, in the face of Roman conquest and general decline, teachers and writers began to attempt to imitate the classical Attic of antiquity, thinking of it as the language of a Golden Age. At the same time, they actively discouraged the speaking and writing of the Hellenistic koine, which was the common language of the Greek-speaking world (cf. Browning 1983:44–45). This artificial Atticizing Greek was the ancestor of Byzantine Greek, the official language of the Byzantine Empire, and it began a tendency which culminated in the current diglossia. By the end of the eighteenth and beginning of the nineteenth centuries, as Greek independence became a real possibility, several opposing linguistic camps emerged: one wished to continue the tradition of Byzantine Greek, another wished to return to classical Greek, a third wished to 'purify' the spoken language of its postclassical elements, and a fourth wished to use the actual spoken language as the basis of the literary language. In the years immediately after independence (1821), the Peloponnesian dialects came to form the basis of a demotic koine (*dhimotikí*). When Athens became the official capital in 1833, the Athenian dialect was overwhelmed by the flood of newcomers, so that at the present time, the demotic standard is based on the speech of the capital, which in its turn has its origins in the Peloponnese. During the years which followed the establishment of independence, however, a period of political reactionism set in as the old Phanariot nobility from Constantinople moved in and took over. With this political reaction came linguistic reaction: the rise of puristic Greek (*katharévousa*). Katharévousa is not the descendant of Byzantine Greek, but is rather Atticized demotic. As such, it is a mishmash of archaic, pseudo-archaic, and contemporary forms. The end of the nineteenth century saw the rise of a new bourgeoisie and the decline of the old Phanariot power, and with this came the rise of literary demotic lead by the writer and philologist Jean Psichari. During the twentieth century, the opposition between katharévousa and demotic has come to embody the political opposition between the right and the left. Under liberal governments, demotic was used in elementary school instruction and there was hesitation and variation in the use of katharévousa elsewhere. Under right-wing governments, such as the military junta which ruled Greece from 1967 to 1974, demotic was banned from all spheres of public life. Since the overthrow of the junta in 1974, demotic has more or less replaced katharévousa in both public and private life, although katharévousa must still be studied in higher classes because of the literature which has been written in it. The differentiation of katharévousa and demotic occurred at all linguistic levels. Thus, for example, in phonology, katharévousa has clusters /kt, pt/ where demotic has /xt, ft/; in morphology katharévousa uses declined participles where demotic uses gerunds in -*ontas;* in lexicon, katharévousa *ixthýs* vs. demotic *psári* 'fish;' *ophthalmós* vs. *máti* 'eye;' etc. (cf. Browning 1983:100–118). The orthography of demotic, however, has remained relatively conservative and is generally perceived as a valuable link with the past. There are those who would reform the spelling to conform with pronunciation, but they can be compared to those who would radically reform English spelling.

The development of literary Turkish provides an interesting contrast with that of Modern Greek. In the course of its use as the official language of the Ottoman Empire and the political center of the Islamic world, Osmanli, i.e., Ottoman Turkish, incorporated so much Arabic and Persian vocabulary, syntax, and even morphology and phonology, that by the nineteenth century this language was incomprehensible to the ordinary speaker of what was called *kaba türkçe* 'vulgar Turkish.' Lewis (1967:xx) provides an excellent example of how Osmanli sounded in comparison to *kaba türkçe:* ". . . it was as if we said, . . . 'What is the conditio of your progenitor reverendus?' instead of 'How's your father' " In Turkey, as elsewhere, the nineteenth century brought in a period of reform, the Tanzimat of 1839, which stemmed the tide of Arabic and Persian borrowing.

Thus, for example, there were attempts to teach a simplified or purified Osmanli (*en sade osmanlıca*), writers experimented with Western influences, especially French, and in 1918 Enver Paşa proposed an orthographic reform whereby the Arabic letters would be written separately and with vowel signs. Atatürk's comment on this last idea, however, sums up the early attempts at reform: *İyi bir niyet, fakat yarım iş; hem de zamansız* 'A good intention, but it only goes halfway, and it is not timely,' i.e., too little, too soon (cf. Korkmaz 1973:43–50). In 1923, Turkey became a republic headed by Mustafa Kemal Atatürk. In 1928, Atatürk caused the entire country to switch to the Latin alphabet—an orthography which he devised in consultation with linguists—virtually overnight. The change of alphabet greatly facilitated the process of eliminating or naturalizing Arabic and Persian vocabulary, not only by cutting off the link with those languages but also by rendering phonological irregularities predictable from the Arabic orthography opaque (cf. Perry 1982:16). In 1932, Atatürk founded the Turkish Language Society (originally the Türk Dili Tetkik Cemiyeti, later the Türk Dil Kurumu) and held the first Turkish Language Conference. Atatürk's intention was to create a literary Turkish based on the common spoken language and purged of that part of its Arabic and Persian component—lexical, syntactic, morphological, and phonological—which had not entered common usage. The Turkish Language Society was charged with creating new vocabulary based on dialect words, borrowing from other Turkic languages, and—most important—new derivations based on roots already present in the language. The extremist purism of the Turkish Language Society during the thirties, however, gave rise to one of the most bizarre linguistic theories ever to emerge from a standardization movement, viz., the so-called Sun Language Theory (*Güneş Dil Teorisi*). According to this theory, all human language originated from man's utterance of the primal syllable *A(ğ)*, and all words of all languages can be derived by a series of formulae from this primal syllable. An additional feature of this theory was that it claimed that Turkish was the mother of all languages (cf. Tankut 1936). While this theory rendered most Turkish theoretical linguistic work of the period invalid, it did have the positive effect of tempering radical purism, for if Turkish was the mother language, then the Arabic and Persian words in it were, ultimately, of Turkish origin and could thus be claimed as native Turkish. In a period when radical purism threatened to create a new kind of diglossia, this admittedly ludicrous theory did serve a useful function. It is even suspected that Atatürk himself launched this theory for the purpose of controlling the radical purists (Heyd 1954:34). It is in the role of purism that Greek and Turkish provide an instructive contrast. The purism of Greek is archaizing and politically conservative, that of Turkish is innovating and politically liberal or radical. During the most recent period of military rule in Turkey, when public discussion of politics was forbidden, right-wing and left-wing papers began to editorialize on linguistic usage. The former, led by *Tercüman*, attacked the Turkish Language Society as too radical, the latter, led by *Cumhuri-*

yet, defended it. Both sides did so in the name of Atatürk—the former claiming that the Turkish Language Society had gone too far, the latter claiming that it was carrying on his mission.

The case of Romanian is considerably different from both Greek and Turkish. Although there is no question regarding Romanian's ancestry, there is considerable debate over its provenance, as was mentioned earlier. Be that as it may, by the fourteenth century, Church Slavonic was the official language of the Romanian kingdom(s) whose dominant religion was Orthodox Christianity; the earliest document is from 1352 (Rosetti 1966:187). The earliest document in Romanian is a letter from 1521. With the Turkish conquest, Greek gradually became the dominant language in Wallachia and Moldavia because of the *millet* system and the power of the Phanariot nobility. The situation in Transylvania was considerably more complicated. After the reformation, Transylvania had four official religions: Catholicism, Calvinism, Lutheranism, and Unitarianism. The ruling classes had two languages: Hungarian and German. The majority of the population consisted of disenfranchised Romanian-speaking Eastern Orthodox serfs. As education was tied to class and religion, there were no Romanian schools. During the eighteenth century, the Hapsburgs introduced the Uniate church into Transylvania, which they had acquired from Turkey at the end of the preceding century, in an attempt to Catholicize the Romanian-speaking majority and thus promote centralization and the integration of Transylvania into their empire. The result was that Romanians were exposed to education, learned that their language was descended from Latin—the language of the 'noble Romans' who had ruled a vast empire—and thus acquired a new sense of dignity before their Magyar and German masters. The resultant movement, called 'Latinism,' served as the basis of Romanian nationalism and the development of the Romanian literary language (cf. Verdery 1983:84–121). The movement spread from Transylvania to Wallachia and Moldavia, where it took hold.

The subsequent rise of literary activity was particularly concerned with lexicographic considerations and the relationship of Romanian to Latin and the living Romance languages that already had literary traditions, especially French and to a lesser extent Italian, in the coining of neologisms and devising an orthography. The former was more important for the lexicon, the latter for orthography. The dialectal base of the literary language which emerged was that of Wallachia, particularly Bucharest.[7] In 1859 Moldavia and Wallachia were, for all practical purposes, united into an independent country, and the Cyrillic alphabet which had been used for Romanian since the sixteenth century was officially replaced by a Latin orthography. Transylvania became part of Romania between 1918 and 1920.

Unlike Greek and Turkish, where divisions have been language-internal, the divisions affecting Romanian have been external, viz., Moldavian on the one hand and Aromanian on the other. As a result of the annexation of Bessarabia by the Russian Empire in 1812, the principality of Moldavia was divided in half.

The half that remained dependent on Turkey—Moldavia proper—formed part of the independent Romanian state in 1859. Bessarabia became part of Romania in 1919 and was re-annexed by Russia in 1940. During the interwar period, Russian claims to Bessarabia were historico-political: the 'people' of Bessarabia wanted to live in a communist state. After World War II, however, the Russians could no longer use this argument, since Romania was also a socialist country, and so the concept of a separate Moldavian nationality with its own Moldavian literary language was pursued in earnest (cf. King 1973:100–105). Although it would appear that Moldavian is a Russified dialect of Romanian which differs from literary Romanian primarily in its use of Cyrillic orthography, the differences are difficult to determine from secondary sources, because the Romanians cannot include Soviet Moldavian in their dialect studies (although, interestingly enough, they do include the Istro-Romanian, Aromanian, and Meglenoromanian dialects of Yugoslavia, Albania, and Greece), while Soviet linguists devote most of their efforts to demonstrating Moldavian's links with East Slavic. Neither Balkanists nor Romance linguists treat Moldavian as a language coming into their purview.

Aromanian—the Romance language of scattered groups living in Albania, Greece, and Macedonia—had separated from Daco-Romanian (the language of Romania proper) by the tenth century. While it could not be integrated with literary Daco-Romanian for a variety of reasons (see Close 1974:67), the fact that it does *not* constitute a separate Balkan literary language is worthy of comment in the context of the pluralistic policies of Yugoslavia, particularly Macedonia. It would appear that religion is still an important defining ethnic factor insofar as all the non-Slavic Moslem minorities of Macedonia have or are obtaining a certain degree of legal linguistic autonomy, whereas the Aromanians, who constitute the most significant non-Slavic (Orthodox) Christian minority (5% of the population) do not have such rights.

Like Romanian, Albanian did not have an ancient continuous literary tradition. The earliest document is a baptismal formula embedded in a Latin text from 1462. While Albania was under Ottoman rule, an Albanian literature did develop among the Albanians who had fled to Italy, the Arbëresh, but they did not have much effect upon events in Albania. The Albanians were divided among three religions: Catholic in the north (10%), Orthodox in the south (20%), and Moslem all over (70%) (Byron 1979a:17). The Ottoman *millet* system worked especially to the disadvantage of the Albanians. The Orthodox were subject to helleniza-tion, the Moslems were considered 'Turks' and were therefore denied linguistic rights even after various Christian peoples had begun to gain theirs, while the Catholics were few in number and largely isolated in the mountains of the north (although there was a significant community in the city of Shkodër [Scutari]) (see Skendi 1980:187–204). The *millet* system also put the Albanians in danger of being completely partitioned by their Greek and Slavic Christian neighbors as the Ottoman Empire was disintegrating, and so in 1878, in the wake of the Congress of Berlin, a group of Albanians formed the League of Prizren to promote Albanian nationalism and to defend Albanian territorial integrity. An important part of the League's program was the promotion of the Albanian language, since this was the one national characteristic which cut across religious boundaries. A key issue at the time was the choice of an alphabet. Each of the possibilities had religious implications: Arabic implied Moslem, Greek implied Orthodox, and Latin implied Catholic.[8] In the case of the Latin alphabet, the choice of symbols and digraphs was of interest to the European powers, because they were sponsoring schools and seeking to extend their influence in the area. Thus, for example, Austria-Hungary and Italy, which were publishing textbooks and supporting schools especially in the Catholic north, purposefully supported different orthographies (Skendi 1980:218–220). In 1908, the Young Turks came to power, and the Albanians were briefly permitted linguistic freedom. That same year an Albanian Alphabet Congress was held in Bitola (Monastir), and it was a key step leading ultimately to the current Latin orthography. Realizing the implications of an Albanian literary language, viz., an independent Albanian state, the Young Turks quickly suppressed the Latin alphabet, but their efforts were in vain. Independence was declared in 1912, and from then until World War II the main focus of linguistic efforts was the dialect question. Albanian has two very different dialect groups: Geg (north) and Tosk (south), e.g., Geg has phonemic length and nasality, Tosk does not; Geg preserves intervocalic /n/ and drops /ə/, Tosk rhotacizes the /n/ and keeps the /ə/ (e.g., the name of Albania: Geg = *Shqipnia*, Tosk - *Shqipëria*); Geg has an infinitive and shortened participle lacking in Tosk; there are also many lexical differences. In the early years people wrote more or less in their own dialects and attempts at dialect integration were threatened by a high degree of artificiality, e.g., Faik Konitza's suggestion that the Geg indefinite article *nji* and the Tosk indefinite article *një* both be used in literary Albanian, but that the former be used for feminine nouns and the latter for masculine (Byron 1976:50)—whereas in fact no Albanian dialect ever makes a gender distinction in the indefinite article. Under King Zog (1925–1939), efforts were made to base a literary standard on the southern Geg dialect of Elbasan, but serious standardization did not progress until after World War II.

At this point it should be noted that for a variety of historical and political reasons the region of Kosovo, which is predominantly Albanian, was awarded to the kingdom of Serbia in 1913 and subsequently became part of Yugoslavia. In Albania, the number of Gegs is only slightly greater than the number of Tosks, but Gegs are the only Albanian group in Kosovo and they are the overwhelming majority in Macedonia, in which the Albanians constitute 13% of the population. After World War II, the Tosk dialect of Korçë gradually emerged as the basis of the standard of Albania, while Albanians in Yugoslavia continued to pursue standard Geg. The Yugoslav government tried to encourage the idea of two separate nationalities and languages, *Albanski* for Albania vs. *Šiptarski* (from Albanian *Shqiptar* 'Albanian') for Yugoslavia, but this failed. In 1968 the Albanians of Kosovo officially accepted the Tosk-based literary standard of Albania, thus producing *gjuha unifikuar* 'the unified language' (see Byron 1979b). Kosovo intellectuals keep length and nasality, and efforts have been made to integrate certain Geg features, e.g., the reflexive possessive pronoun *i vetë* (Tosk dialects lack such a pronoun altogether), but the standard is still Tosk in the vast majority of its features.

Unlike the other language groups considered thus far, the South Slavs have been considerably more fragmented. The territory of modern-day Yugoslavia was divided between Austria-Hungary and Turkey at the beginning of the nineteenth century. Autonomy, independence, and unification were achieved in bits and pieces during the course of the next hundred years, so that by the end of World War I the boundaries of Yugoslavia were more or less what they are today. Of concern to us here are the West South Slavs other than the Slovenians (cf. note 4), i.e., the Serbs and Croats (and to a lesser extent the Bosnian Moslems).

During the nineteenth century, the literary languages of the West South Slavs were characterized by a tendency toward increasing unity while those of the East South Slavs were characterized by a tendency toward division. The differences among the West South Slavs are considerable. Serbs are Orthodox and use Cyrillic; Croats are Catholic and use the Latin alphabet. Croatian dialects are much more divergent from one another than Serbian.[9] Croatian tends to borrow from Latin and German and tends to create neologisms whereas Serbian is more likely to borrow from Greek and Turkish and accept loanwords from other Slavic languages, e.g., Croation *kolodvor* Serbian *stanica* 'station.' A major dialectal division cutting across these lines is the reflex of Common Slavic *$\bar{e}$ (æ, orthographic ě, Cyrillic ѣ, named *jat*'); there are three main possibilities: /i/, /e/, and /je/~/ije/ (the last choice being dependent on length). The reflex /e/ occurs in Serbia and adjacent parts of Croatia, /i/ occurs along the coast and /je/~/ije/ elsewhere. In 1850, Serbian and Croatian linguists and intellectuals signed the *književni dogovor* in Vienna, agreeing to adopt a Hercegovina-based /ije/*što* (ijekavian-štokavian) standard developed by the Serb Vuk Karadžić as a common literary language. This was a compromise for both sides brought about by the political necessity of the need for a common language. Croatian was too fragmented dialectically, e.g., the cultural center, Zagreb, was in the middle of the Kajkavian area, the medieval-renaissance Croatian literary tradition was in Čakavian, and Štokavian speakers constituted the numerical majority. Vuk's language met stiff resistance in Serbia, where it was not officially adopted until 1868. The Serbs had been using a form of Church Slavonic called *Slavenoserbian,* which had an established literary tradition and orthography, albeit no connection with the spoken language. Vuk not only rejected the grammar and vocabulary of this language, advocating instead use of the vernacular, but he also reformed its Cyrillic orthography, eliminating obsolete letters ⟨ъ, ь, Ж, Ѧ, ѣ⟩ and, following the principle of one letter per sound he introduced the grapheme ⟨j⟩ from the Latin alphabet and thus rewrote ⟨я⟩ as ⟨ja⟩, ⟨ю⟩ as ⟨jy⟩, and ⟨й⟩ as ⟨j⟩. This last move outraged many Serbs because of its Roman Catholic implications. The majority of Serbs never accepted the ijekavian pronunciation, however, and, ironically enough, Vuk's ijekavian standard came to be identified as Croatian while Serbian has remained ekavian. In 1954 a new agreement was signed in Novi Sad in which the various Serbo-Croatian-speaking peoples of Yugoslavia reaffirmed their commitment to a unified literary language. In March 1967, however, a group of Croatian intellectuals issued a manifesto proclaiming Croatian as a separate language, and the problems continue to this day. In recent years, the Serbo-Croatian-speaking Moslems who constitute the majority in Bosnia-Hercegovina and are recognized as a separate ethnic group, viz., *muslimani*, have also been agitating for a separate codified standard distinct from both Serbian and Croatian. Further conflict is created by the competition between the prestige dialects of the Serbian and Croatian capitals (Belgrade and Zagreb) which both differ from Vuk's standard, among other things, in their loss of phonemic tone (see Magner 1981). Thus, the centripetal forces of the nineteenth century have been replaced by centrifugal ones in the twentieth (see Naylor 1980).

The situation of the East South Slavs, i.e., the Bulgarians and Macedonians, has been quite different. As a group, they were severely threatened by hellenization during the first half of the nineteenth century due to the *millet* system, but with the establishment of an independent Bulgarian church (the Exarchate), different tensions began to manifest themselves. Two centers of Slavic literacy had arisen on East South Slavic territory during this period: one in southwestern Macedonia and one in northeastern Bulgaria. The people of the southwest had a distinct regional identification as Macedonians, and with the uncompromising attitude of the users of the northeast Bulgarian standard—especially after the establishment of the Exarchate—came the development of a separate ethnic and linguistic consciousness among many Macedonians. In dialectal terms, there is a relatively thick bundle of isoglosses coinciding roughly with the Serbian-Bulgarian political border which fans out when it reaches Macedonia, so that the dialects of Macedonia are transitional between Serbian and Bulgarian. Serbia and Bulgaria also had conflicting territorial claims to Macedonia (as did Greece), and in part they tried to support these claims by linguistic arguments (as well as force of arms, e.g., the Second Balkan War of 1912). Thus, for example, the Serbian linguist Aleksandar Belić claimed that the northern and central Macedonian dialects were Serbian on the basis of a single isogloss, viz., the reflex of common Slavic */tj, dj/ as dorso-palatal stops /k̑, g̑/, like the Serbian palatal stops /ć, ʒ́/, vs. the Bulgarian reflexes /št, žd/ (Belić 1919:250, but see Vaillant 1938:119). The official Bulgarian attitude to this day is that Macedonian is a 'regional variant' of Bulgarian, based on other isoglosses (see B.A.N. 1978).

A comparison is sometimes made between Macedonian and Moldavian (e.g., King 1973:100–102). The claim is that just as the Russians have fostered a Moldavian language in order to justify the annexation of Bessarabia from Romania, so the Yugoslavs have created a Macedonian language to justify their territorial claims against Bulgaria. There are, however, considerable differences between the two situations. Macedonian linguistic separatism is attested in print since 1875, and the first definitive outline of the bases for a Macedonian literary language date from 1903, i.e., while Macedonia was still a part of Turkey (see Friedman 1975). Thus, while the official recognition of a separate Macedonian language and nationality may well be in Yugoslav interests, the fact remains that this language and ethnic identification arose among Macedonians themselves as a result of historical and linguistic circumstances quite independent of Yugoslav interests and before such interests even existed. The same cannot be said of Moldavian, since Bessarabia was already annexed to Russia in 1812.

After the Second Balkan War, Macedonia was divided among Serbia (later, Yugoslavia), Greece, and Bulgaria. In Greece, Macedonians have been subject to gradual but unrelenting hellenization. In Bulgaria, only the Bulgarian language has been permitted, except during the period from 1946 to 1948 (i.e., from the end of World War II up to the Tito–Stalin break), when Macedonian was officially recognized in Bulgaria as a minority language. In Yugoslavia, Macedonian was treated as a Serbian dialect between the two world wars, but literature was published and plays were performed as 'dialect' literature. On August 2, 1944—in keeping with Tito's pluralist nationalist policy—Macedonian was officially recognized as a separate literary language in Yugoslavia. The basis was the West Central dialect region (bounded roughly by the towns of Titov Veles, Kičevo, Bitola, and Prilep), and a generation of young linguists set about establishing norms. There was a brief period when some people proposed waiting until a team of Russian experts could be brought in, but their proposal was not accepted (see Friedman 1985:40). The orthography follows the principles of Serbian as opposed to Bulgarian, e.g., in its use of ⟨j⟩ and the single graphemes ⟨љ, њ⟩ for /l, ń/ as opposed to Bulgarian Cyrillic, which is like Russian. Macedonian presents one of the few examples where linguists participated in a more rational arrangement of dictionary entries. Following the classical tradition, the codifiers of the literary language at first listed verbs by the first singular (present). In literary Macedonian and the West Central dialects on which it is based, a verb can have one of three stem-vowels in the present tense: /a/, /e/, /i/, e.g., 3 sg gleda 'look,' piše 'write,' nosi 'carry.' Whereas the third singular constitutes the bare present stem, however, the first singular ending, /-am/, completely neutralizes the opposition, e.g., 1 sg gledam, pišam, nosam. An American linguist, Horace Lunt, convinced the codifiers of the literary language to use the third singular rather than the first as the standard citation form (see Lunt 1951). This not only gave the dictionary entry more predictive power but also helped spread the standard use of stem vowels, as this is an area of considerable dialectal variation (see Friedman 1985:38–40). At present, a major problem for literary Macedonian is the fact that Skopje—the capital and principal cultural and population center—is outside the West Central dialect area and is subject to considerable Serbo-Croatian influence. Nonetheless, an entire generation of speakers educated in the literary language has grown up, and they can and do use it consistently.

Literary Bulgarian, like Serbo-Croatian and Greek, had to face threats from archaizers who wanted Church Slavonic to become the official language of the emerging Bulgarian state. Having overcome these (although the Bulgarian orthography was not completely modernized until 1944) as well as the hellenizers, the creators of literary Bulgarian were faced with the task of integrating a number of divergent dialects. Among the many issues which had to be resolved were the pronunciation of *jat* (Cyrillic ⟨ѣ⟩) and the form of the masculine definite article. A major isogloss, the so-called *jat*-line, separates the eastern two-thirds of Bulgaria from the western third. West of the line *jat* is consistently pronounced /e/, east of the line the rules are more complicated. During the early years of the formation of literary Bulgarian, the political and cultural center was Tŭrnovo in the northeast, but later it shifted to Sofia in the west. The ultimate result was an attempt to blend the two sets of systems. Thus, e.g., the literary language has a basically eastern vocalism, including the pronunciation of *jat,* but the consonantism is that of the west. Similarly, in the case of the masculine definite article, the Bulgarian dialects have two forms: /-ə/ and /-ət/. The language planners (arbitrarily) assigned the value 'oblique' to the form /-ə/ and 'nominative' to the form /-ət/, e.g., *ezikŭt* 'the language' *na ezikŭ* 'of/in/to the language.' A similar type of solution was reached for the presence vs. the absence of the auxiliary in the third person of the past indefinite (see Friedman 1982). At the present time, the fact that Sofia is the major population and cultural center of Bulgaria is having a significant impact on the literary language, e.g., the consistent use of /e/ for etymological *jat* is becoming increasingly acceptable. On the whole, however, having experienced increasing centrifugal tendencies in the nineteenth century and definitive split in the twentieth, the two East South Slavic literary languages are currently characterized by tendencies to unify around their respective standards as opposed to the increasing fragmentation in West South Slavic.

This brings us to Romani. Although literary activity in Romani dates only from the early years of this century, a number of attempts have been made to use it in at least some of the functions of a literary language, e.g., in literature, education, etc., in the USSR, Scandinavia, France, England, Eastern Europe, and elsewhere. The past decade or so has seen a significant upsurge in Romani nationalism, e.g., the formation of the World Romani Congress, and concomitant with these activities there have been renewed attempts to create a Romani literary language. Activities outside the Balkans are beyond the scope of this paper, and activities outside of southern Yugoslavia, which has the largest settled Romani population in the world, are not taking place on such a large and public scale. I will comment here on a specific event which may prove to be of considerable significance, viz., the publication of a bilingual Romani grammar

(Romani and Macedonian) in Skopje in 1980 (Jusuf and Kepeski 1980). This grammar is a significant signal of the efforts to create a Romani literary language for use in the schools, and can be compared with certain Macedonian works by Ǵorǵi Pulevski from the end of the nineteenth century (see Friedman 1975). Both reflect the rising national consciousness of their respective peoples, both are polyglot as a reflection of the linguistic situations of their respective users, and both reflect that lack of consistency and standardization characteristic of the pre-codified stage of a nascent literary language. In the case of Macedonian, Pulevski's work, like other manifestations of Macedonian nationalism at that time, was lost or suppressed, although the results achieved after 1944 were consistent with the beginnings signaled by it. In the case of Romani, Jusuf and Kepeski's grammar may be able to serve as the starting point for a Romani literary standard, at least in Macedonia and adjacent parts of Serbia and Kosovo.

The chief problems facing all attempts at a Romani literary standard are the integration of or selection among divergent dialects and the expansion of vocabulary. Jusuf and Kepeski's grammar draws on the three main dialects of Skopje: Arlija, Džambaz, and Burgudži. The Arlija dialect is Jusuf's native one and is also the oldest one in Skopje. It is thus the basic dialect used in the grammar, but the authors' main approach to dialect selection is to avoid selection, i.e., they randomly use different dialect forms throughout the text, including some of the paradigms. For the expansion of vocabulary, Jusuf and Kepeski have followed the practice endorsed by the World Romani Congress of borrowing words from Hindi. Unfortunately, they have not adapted these borrowings to Romani phonology, e.g., they spell words with voiced aspirates, which are utterly foreign to the Romani sound system, e.g., *bhavi* 'consciousness.' The situation is reminiscent of the problems faced by Romanian in the last century, when it turned to other Romance languages with which it had had no contact for centuries. In the field of orthography, Jusuf and Kepeski have chosen the Latin alphabet, although they supply a conversion table for a Macedonian-based Cyrillic and use it when citing Romani forms in their Macedonian text. The bialphabetical linguistic practice which is already well established in Yugoslavia made this obviously internationally aimed option easier.[10]

We should also mention here a more recent work by Marcel Cortiade (1984) in which he proposes to overcome certain dialect differences by means of the use of morphophonemic symbols in the spelling system, e.g., orthographic ⟨Romeça⟩ for phonetic [romesa]/[romeja]/[romeha]/[romea] 'Rom' (instrumental case), where the various realizations of what was originally intervocalic [s] are readily predictable. In other environments, however, there is considerable variation in the treatment of [s], and so, ultimately, a choice will have to be made. Cortiade has argued that one of the more conservative Balkan dialects should serve as the basis of literary Romani, since various innovations are predictable in terms of the original base, but not vice versa. When we look at the factors that have led to the selection of dialect bases for the various Balkan literary languages, we see a combination of political, cultural, and numerical considerations. Thus, for example, in the case of literary Macedonian, the choice of the West Central dialect base was motivated by three major factors: it was the most distinct from both Bulgarian and Serbian, it was the single largest relatively homogeneous regional dialect, and it was most readily comprehensible by the largest number of speakers from other regions. In the case of Serbo-Croatian, Vuk Karadžić chose his native dialect. The victory of literary Tosk over literary Geg as the basis of the Albanian standard is due at least in part to the fact that the majority of the leaders of postwar Albania are Tosks, which in its turn resulted from various historical and cultural factors (see Byron 1979a). In Bulgaria and Greece, the dialect in the first area to become independent of Turkish domination ended up as the basis of literary language, although other factors (shift of the capital in Bulgaria, diglossia in Greece) have significantly complicated the picture. Similarly, in Turkey and Romania, it is the dialects of the capitals which have had the prestige to serve as the basis of the literary languages, although in the case of Romania, the original impetus came from outside the literary region. In this context, it can be said that the considerable Romani literary activity outside of the Balkans will also have to be taken into account, but the precise outcome of interaction and integration remains to be seen.

5. Linguistics and Nationalism

As can be seen from the foregoing, the use of linguistics in the formation of literary languages and the affirmation of nationalism has had a wide variety of effects. Historical linguistics has been used by archaizers and purifiers especially in the cases of Greek and Turkish. On the other hand, dialectology has been the key to efforts of separatism and unity among the Slavic, Romance, and Albanian languages. To these latter can now be added Romani. In the fixing of orthographies, phonology has played a role in all but Greek, which has retained its historical spelling. All of the other languages claim 'phonetic' spelling, although in fact *phonemic* would generally be a better term. Of these languages, Romanian has the least consistent orthographic system, i.e., most influenced by historical spelling, e.g., two signs for [ɨ], viz., ⟨â⟩ and ⟨î⟩. Of the Slavic languages, Bulgarian is distinguished from Serbo-Croatian and Macedonian by a greater tendency toward morphophonemic spelling, e.g., prefixes ending in underlying voiced consonants are subject to regressive assimilation of voicing when added to stems beginning with voiceless consonants. This change is indicated in Serbo-Croatian and Macedonian spelling but not in Bulgarian, e.g., *raspraviti* (SC), *raspravi* (M), *razpravja* (B) 'tell, relate;' *Razoružiti* (SC), *razoruži* (M), *razoръža* (B) 'disarm.' As a result of the 1944 spelling reform, Bulgarian also has a few morphologically conditioned pronunciation rules of a type not found in Serbo-Croatian and Macedonian.[11] Another example of a phonological phenomenon affected by standardization is the automatic devoicing of underlying voiced consonants in final position. This phenomenon is absent in Greek, Romanian, and Serbo-Croatian; it is uniformly present in Macedonian, Bulgarian, and Turkish; and it also occurs in some dialects of Romani and Albanian.[12] The approach in the Slavic languages has been to portray the underlying phoneme orthographically, e.g., *narod-narodi* [narot-narodi] 'people-peoples.' In Turkish, after considerable vacillation, the current orthographic practice favors phonetic representation, e.g., *kitap-kitabım* 'book-my book.' In the case of Albanian, the central dialects are characterized by final devoicing, while this feature is absent further north and further south. In this instance, after some vacillation, language planners have opted definitively for spelling final voiced consonants, e.g., *zog-zogu* 'bird-the-bird,' despite the fact that this does not represent the pronunciation of the Tosk region whose dialects form the basis of the standard language. The spelling of final voiced consonants is helping to spread the literary pronunciation to areas where it is not native. In the Romani of Jusuf and Kepeski, as elsewhere, alternatives are used but not selected, e.g., the spellings ⟨dad⟩ and ⟨dat⟩ 'father.' The situation and potential are the same as in Albanian but the result remains to be seen. It is worthy of note that Cortiade (1984) has suggested a morphophonemic orthography for Romani which could significantly minimize problems created by the representation of dialectal differentiation.

In the realm of morphology, we have seen how the alternatives offered by different dialect forms can be used to enrich the literary language, as in the standard Albanian use of the Geg reflexive pronoun *i vetë;* or they can be used to create artificial distinctions as in the case of the two Bulgarian definite articles. In the case of syntax and lexicon, the dialects can be used to enrich the literary language and earlier stages of the language can likewise be drawn upon, but a key issue which is less significant for phonology and morphology is the extent and source of foreign borrowing (lexical) and imitation of foreign models (syntactic). This latter has been an especially important issue for Macedonian, where the tremendous influence of Serbo-Croatian during the years immediately after World War II threatened to alter its syntactic patterns significantly. Concerted efforts on the parts of both codifiers and users of the literary language have succeeded in reversing this trend, however.

This brings us to a consideration of the sources of authority in language codification in modern times. Each of the socialist countries, viz., Albania, Bulgaria, Romania, and Yugoslavia, has an Academy of Sciences and an Institute of Language, either as a branch of the Academy or as a separate institution closely associated with it.[13] These institutes are responsible not only for linguistic research but also for developing and defining literary norms and publishing grammars, dictionaries, and other authoritative works. Each institute has its journal in which both theoretical and practical linguistic questions are addressed. The institutes are not the only sources of normativization, however. There are also teachers' unions and other language organizations which publish linguistic or language journals on a more popular level and which are more devoted to practical considerations of usage and codification. Similar linguistic topics are also discussed in the daily press, and there are many popular books on 'language culture,' i.e., normative usage. As a result, the codification of the literary languages has developed in part through dialogue between codifiers and users. In Greece and Turkey, language codification has been more closely tied to political parties, as has been seen, and linguistic tendencies are associated with political tendencies. Although the Turkish Language Society functions in a manner similar to an institute of language, neither Greece nor Turkey has quite the same type of institution, because of differences in sociopolitical structure, and the Ministry of Education frequently plays a more active role in decision making.

In future language planning and language standardization in the Balkans, linguistics can be used to advance compromise solutions to specific problems—choices or interpretations—or it can be used to justify divisive tendencies which are always present in potential. In Greek and Turkish, special problems are created by the strength of archaizing or puristic tendencies, while the Slavic and Albanian literary languages' main source of difficulty is that their cultural and political capitals are not identical with the sources of the literary language. Linguistics has the greatest potential in aiding rational solutions to problems such as dialectal compromise and enrichment of vocabulary in the case of Romani, where these processes are still in their early stages.

NOTES

1. The Ottomans first entered Europe in 1345. They first settled there, in Gallipoli, in 1354. The battles of Maritsa (1371) and Kosovo (1389) were decisive in their conquest of Slavic territory. Constantinople fell in 1453, and the Albanian hero Skanderbeg died in 1467, signaling the final conquest of Albania. The first siege of Vienna was 1529; the second, in 1683, marked the beginning of Ottoman territorial losses in Europe.

2. In recent years, the term *Southeastern Europe* has become increasingly common. This is due in part to pejorative connotations which have become attached to the term *Balkan* and in part due to arguments over whether *Balkan* can include Hungary, on the one hand, or exclude Romania, Greece, and/or European Turkey, on the other. In this chapter, I take the most widely accepted definition of the term, viz., the peninsula comprising the modern nations of Yugoslavia, Romania, Albania, Greece, Bulgaria, as well as European Turkey (Turkish Thrace).

3. It is an interesting but little-known fact that while popular belief in the Balkans attributes many social ills to the Turkish occupation, popular belief in Turkey attributes these same ills in Turkey to Turkey's having spent so much time ruling the Balkans.

4. I will be including Turkish because of its influence on all the members of the Balkan *Sprachbund*, but I will exclude Slovenian because, despite the fact that its literary form is based in a Balkan country (Yugoslavia), it is not a Balkan language, i.e., it is not a member of the linguistic league.

5. The Catholics of Northern Albania, Bosnia-Hercegovina, Croatia, etc. were not subject to the same denationalizing pressures through the *millet* system, but various

sovereign Catholic states, e.g., Austria-Hungary and Italy, exerted similar denationalizing pressures when they had the opportunity.

6. I should note here that I will be using *literary* as a cover term for 'literary,'
   'standard,' and 'national.' These admittedly important distinctions do not affect the
   considerations of this article and will therefore not be discussed, for the sake of
   greater conciseness.

7. There were early attempts to create a literary Romanian which combined Daco-
   Romanian and Aromanian dialects, but these were abandoned as impractical (Close
   1974:67). Within Daco-Romanian, dialectal differentiation is not as great as, for
   example, in other Romance languages (Du Nay 1977:111).

8. Cyrillic was also used to write Albanian, especially in Macedonia, but it was never a
   serious contender as a possible national alphabet.

9. The names of the principal Croatian dialects are based on their words for 'what,'
   viz., *ča, kaj,* and *što*. The Serbian dialects are virtually all *što* dialects.

10. The Soviet Union provides an instructive contrast. There, Romani, like all other
    national or literary languages except Estonian, Latvian, Lithuanian, Georgian, Ar-
    menian, and Yiddish, must use a Russian-based Cyrillic alphabet.

11. For example, the graphemes ⟨a⟩ and ⟨я⟩ will be pronounced [ə], [jə], even under
    stress, in certain word-final endings.

12. The details for Turkish are actually more complicated, but they need not concern us
    here.

13. In Yugoslavia, each republic and the autonomous region of Kosovo has its own
    academy.

REFERENCES

B.A.N. 1978. "Edinstvoto na bŭlgarskija ezik v minaloto i dnes" ["The Unity of the Bulgarian
    Language in the Past and Today"]. *Bŭlgarski ezik [Bulgarian Language]* 28:1, pp. 3–43.
Belić, Aleksandar 1919. *La Macédoine.* Paris: Bloud and Gay.
Browning, Robert 1983. *Medieval and Modern Greek.* Cambridge: Cambridge University Press.
Byron, Janet L. 1976. "Faik Konitza dhe gjuha letrare shqipe" ["Faik Konitza and the Albanian
    Literary Language"]. In: Edward Licho (ed.), *Faik Konitza 1876–1976.* New York: Vatra,
    pp. 49–51.
Byron, Janet L. 1979a. *Selection Among Alternates in Language Standardization: The Case of
    Albanian.* The Hague: Mouton.
Byron, Janet L. 1979b. "Language planning in Albania and in Albanian-speaking Yugoslavia."
    Word 30:1–2, pp. 15–44.
Close, Elizabeth 1974. *The Development of Modern Rumanian.* London: Oxford University Press.
Cortiade, Marcel 1984. *Romani fonetika thaj lekhipa [Romani Phonetics and Spelling].* Place of
    publication given as Filån Than 'some place or other': no publisher.
Du Nay, André 1977. *The Early History of the Rumanian Language.* Lake Bluff, IL: Jupiter Press.
d'Estournelles de Constant, Baron, et al. 1914. *Report of the International Commission to Inquire
    into the Causes and Conduct of the Balkan Wars.* Division of Intercourse and Education,
    Publication No. 4. Washington, DC: Carnegie Endowment for International Peace.
Fine, John V. A. 1983. *The Early Medieval Balkans.* Ann Arbor, MI: University of Michigan Press.
Friedman, Victor A. 1975. "Macedonian language and nationalism in the nineteenth and early
    twentieth centuries." *Balkanistica* 2, pp. 83–98.
Friedman, Victor A. 1982. "Reportedness in Bulgarian: Category or stylistic variant?" *International
    Journal of Slavic Linguistics and Poetics* 25–26, pp. 149–63.

Friedman, Victor A. 1985. "The sociolinguistics of literary Macedonian." *International Journal of the Sociology of Language* 52, pp. 31–57.

Gindin, L. A. 1967. *Jazyk drevnejšego naselenija juga balkanskogo poluostrova* [*The Language of the Earliest Population of the South of the Southern Balkan Peninsula*]. Moscow: Nauka.

Heyd, Uriel 1954. *Language Reform in Modern Turkey*. Jerusalem: Israel Oriental Society.

Jusuf, Šaip, and Krume Kepeski. 1980. *Romani gramatika—Romska gramatika* [*Romani Grammar*]. Skopje, Yugoslavia: Naša Kniga.

King, Robert R. 1973. *Minorities Under Communism: Nationalities as a Source of Tension Among Balkan Communist States*. Cambridge, MA: Harvard University Press.

Korkmaz, Zeynep 1973. *Cumhuriyet döneminde türk dili* [*The Turkish Language in the Republican Period*]. Ankara: Ankara University Press.

Lewis, G. L. 1967. *Turkish Grammar*. Oxford: Oxford University Press.

Lunt, Horace 1951. "Morfologijata na makedonskiot glagol" ["Morphology of the Macedonian Verb"]. *Makedonski jazik* [*Macedonian Language*] 2:6, pp. 123–31.

Magner, Thomas F. 1981. "The Emperor's new clothes or a modest peek at the Serbo-Croatian accentual system." *General Linguistics* 21:4, pp. 248–58.

Naylor, Kenneth E. 1980. "Serbo-Croatian." In: A. M. Schenker and E. Stankiewicz (eds.), *The Slavic Literary Languages*. New Haven, CT: Yale Concilium on International and Area Studies, pp. 65–83.

Neroznak, V. P. 1978. *Paleobalkanskie jazyki* [*The Ancient Balkan Languages*]. Moscow: Nauka.

Perry, John R. 1982. "Language Reform in Turkey and Iran." Paper presented at the Atatürk Centennial Symposium, University of Chicago. To be published by Arizona University Press.

Rosetti, Al. 1938. *Istoria limbii române II. Limbile balkanice* [*History of the Romanian Language II. The Balkan Languages*]. Bucharest: Fundatia Pentru Literatură și Arta "Regele Carol II."

Rosetti, Al. 1966. *Istoria limbii române, IV, V, VI* [*History of the Romanian Language IV, V, VI*].

Sandfeld, Kr. 1930. *Linguistique balkanique*. Paris: Klincksieck.

Skendi, Stavro 1980. *Balkan Cultural Studies*. Boulder, CO: East European Monographs, No. 72.

Tankut, H. R. 1936. *Güneş-Dil Teorisine göre Dil Tetkikleri* [*Linguistic Investigations According to the Sun-Language Theory*]. Istanbul: State Publishing House.

Vaillant, A. 1938. "Le problème du slave macédonien." *Bulletin de la Société Linguistique de Paris* 39:2:116, pp. 194–210.

Ventcel', T. V., and L. N. Čerenkov 1976. "Dialekty cyganskogo jazyka" ["The Dialects of the Gypsy Language"]. In: *Jazyki Azii i Afriki*, Vol. I. *Indoevropejskie jazyki* [*Languages of Asia and Africa: Indo-European Languages*]. pp. 283–339. Moscow: Nauka.

Verdery, Katherine 1983. *Transylvanian Villagers: Three Centuries of Political, Economic, and Ethnic Change*. Berkeley, CA: University of California Press.

CHAPTER FOURTEEN

Salutary Lessons from the History of Linguistics

Shaun F. D. Hughes

1. Chomsky and 'Cartesian Linguistics'

Chomsky (1966) made a claim for a particular attitude towards language which he called 'Cartesian Linguistics' which was distinguished by

> the observation that human language, in its normal use, is free from the control of independently identifiable external stimuli or internal states and is not restricted to any practical communicative function, in contrast, for example, to the pseudo language of animals. It is thus free to serve as an instrument of free thought and self expression. (op.cit.:29)

In particular, Chomsky identified the so-called Port-Royal grammar (GGR) as having made a crucial breakthrough in linguistic thought with its diligent application of a Cartesian approach to language (see Arnaud and Lancelot 1660). [1] Even though this approach to grammar was to be swamped by the empiricist linguistics of the nineteenth century, Chomsky feels it is necessary to call attention to this 'Cartesian linguistics,' because he finds that he himself has now become a champion of its cause.

> The creative aspect of language use is once again a central concern of linguistics, and the theories of universal grammar that were outlined in the seventeenth and eighteenth centuries have been revived and elaborated in the theory of transformational generative grammar. With this renewal of the study of universal formal conditions on the system of linguistic rules, it becomes possible to take up once again the search for deeper explanations for the phenomena found in particular languages and observed in actual performance. (op.cit.:72–3)

Chomsky (1966) really tells us more about Chomsky and his attitudes towards language than providing any substantial contribution to the history of linguistic theorizing (metalinguistics). Certainly the book caused something of a stir when it first appeared, but has now, I suspect, been largely forgotten. But it was an interesting and important book in its time even if, as has subsequently turned out, the main premises upon which his book is based (that rationalist, i.e., mentalist, linguistics and such notions as deep or surface structure began with the 'Cartesian' linguists) have been shown to be erroneous (see especially Salmon 1969 and Aarslef 1970).[2] It was an interesting study because it showed the leading figure of the linguistic avant-garde, an avant-garde in which some of the more militant members had made a fetish of their break with the past, i.e., with all previous and erroneous views of language, making an appeal to history in order to foster an intellectual ancestor on a theoretical approach which many considered to be completely innovative and fresh. Therefore, transformational-generative grammar, instead of being just a fad, could be shown to have a distinguished intellectual lineage. While the empiricists and the historians of linguistics castigated Chomsky for the inadequacies of *Cartesian Linguistics*, the book, as so often with any of Chomsky's enterprises, stimulated others to investigate more closely aspects of the history of linguistic thought. A few years later, a volume of such metalinguistic studies followed (Parret 1976) in which a sympathetic Robin Lakoff (1976) looks at the claims made by Chomsky for the GGR. Those aspects of the work which Chomsky had found so appealing originated neither with the GGR nor with Descartes. They had already been expounded in a new Latin grammar published as Lancelot (1644). In the third edition of Lancelot (1644), which appeared in 1654, he indicates in his preface his indebtedness to the work of the Spanish scholar Sanctius (1587) and his followers Scoppius (1659) and Vossius (1635)[3] (Lakoff 1976:362–3). Lakoff identifies four main themes in Sanctius (1587):

(1) Language is a product of the human mind. Since the mind is a rational thing, so is language. (2) It is necessary to look for explanations for grammatical phenomena. These may not always be immediately evident, but that doesn't mean they don't exist. (3) Nothing in language is accidental. (4) Prescriptivism is worthless: a grammarian's authority is only as valid as the logic behind his analyses. (1976:367; see also Padley 1976:97–110)

These positions can be seen underlying the premises of the GGR and are not at all incompatible with Chomsky's own positions.

Now the point of going over this familiar territory is not to demonstrate that historical aspects of linguistic thought are not at all Chomsky's forté. That is really an irrelevant issue, for whether or not the GGR is 'Cartesian' or not is beside the point. What was important in Chomsky's study is that it was making a claim for the application of rationalist and mentalist methodologies to language, a position which had not been taken seriously until his time in English-speaking linguistic circles. Chomsky was mounting a frontal attack on the current linguistic ideology which was thoroughly imbued with the principle of logical empiricism. Chomsky's quarrel with the prescriptivists and American structuralists had not even really been over their methods of analyzing grammar. At one point, after reviewing a traditional analysis of a sentence he states:

It seems to me that the information presented . . . is, without question , substantially correct and is essential to any account of how the language is used or acquired. The main topic I should like to consider is how information of this sort can be formally presented in a structural description, and how such structural descriptions can be generated by a system of explicit rules. (Chomsky 1965:64)

The quarrel, then, is not over details of analysis, but rather how this analysis works within a larger framework, that is, on a metascientific level, on the level of how one goes about 'doing' linguistics. In his two-volume study of meta-science, Gerard Radnitzky (1968) traces the fortunes and influences of the two major approaches available to Western science. Volume one, entitled *Anglo-Saxon Schools of Metascience,* surveys contributions to human science of those whose philosophical tradition is logical empiricism, while Volume two, *Continental Schools of Metascience,* surveys the rationalist or 'hermeneutic-dialectic' approach, one for much of this century associated with continental thinkers. It is this latter tradition with which Chomsky so clearly identifies himself and for so long as linguists continue to identify with the premises of logical empiricism, they will continue to be hostile to Chomsky's work (as, for example, Sampson 1980). Not only has Chomsky championed rationalism, but he has also created a renewed awareness and interest in the methodology of linguistics in relation to the other sciences.[4]

From the benefit of hindsight, it is now possible to see that Chomsky's own approaches to linguistics are both more traditional and less innovative than they once seemed. Nevertheless, they were different in approach and methodology to linguistics up to that time, especially linguistics as practiced in North America.[5]

2. The Demise of the Paradigm

It has been fashionable for some time when discussing the recent history of linguistics to see the major events, and in particular Chomsky's theoretical innovations and his rapid rise to prominence, in terms of a theory of the structure and nature of scientific knowledge together with a theory of the nature of the advancement of knowledge as defined in Thomas S. Kuhn (1970).[6] It was Ludwig Wittgenstein who made the observation that science contains not only formulae (theories) and the rules for the application of these formulae but also an entire tradition surrounding that science (Kuhn 1970:44–5).[7] Kuhn refined this idea and called this tradition a 'paradigm' (a word with a nice 'grammatical' ring about it). As set out in Kuhn (1970), the paradigm contains within it not only the traditions of a science which define it but even, though they might not be immediately recognizable, the traditions which destroy the paradigm and create a new one, thus causing the science to 'advance.'

This definition of Kuhn's, and indeed, this study as a whole, has been enormously important—and enormously controversial. Unfortunately, even though Kuhn himself has modified his concept of the paradigm, this modification has not been incorporated into subsequent printings of Kuhn (1970), so that some of the least satisfactory of Kuhn's ideas continue to be extremely influential and productive.

In a collection of essays, one of which by Kuhn himself (1974) is a response to his critics, Margaret Masterman (1974) shows the terminological inadequacy of the term 'paradigm' as it was used in the first edition of *The Structure of Scientific Revolutions* published in 1962. In this article Masterman catalogues twenty-one different and identifiable usages of the term (Masterman, 1974:61–5). It is in response to this particular criticism that Kuhn (1977) sought to refine and reassess this key concept.

Kuhn now defines 'paradigm' in two ways. First, the paradigm is defined as a particular 'scientific community' or 'disciplinary matrix' (Kuhn 1977:294–7). The constituents of this matrix are seen to be the 'objects of group commitment,' singularly or collectively described in Kuhn (1970) as paradigms (Kuhn 1977:297). In particular, these constituents are symbolic generalizations, models, and exemplars (ibid.). The term 'exemplar' provides the second definition of 'paradigm,' and the rest of the paper is devoted to a discussion of the paradigm as exemplar. Kuhn is also at pains to deny, albeit only in a footnote, as a "vicious consequence" (of his lack of an adequate definition of paradigm in Kuhn 1970) the most common meaning of the term 'paradigm' as it is used in linguistic circles.

> The most damaging of these consequences grows out of my use of the term "paradigm" when distinguishing an earlier from a later period in the development of an individual science. During what is called, in *Structure of Scientific Revolutions,* the "preparadigm period," the practitioners of a science are split into a number of competing schools, each claiming competence for the same subject matter but approaching it in quite different ways. This developmental stage is followed by a relatively rapid transition, usually in the aftermath of some notable scientific achievement, to a so-called postparadigm period characterized by the disappearance of all or most schools, a change which permits far more powerful professional behavior to the members of the remaining community. I still think that pattern both typical and important, *but it can be discussed without reference to the first achievement of a paradigm* [emphasis added]. Whatever paradigms may be, they are possessed by any scientific community, including the schools of the so-called preparadigm period. My failure to see this point clearly has helped make a paradigm seem a quasi-mystical entity or property, which, like charisma, transforms those infected by it. *There is a transformation, but it is not induced by the acquisition of a paradigm* [emphasis added]. (Kuhn 1977:295)

Kuhn's theory of scientific revolution was originally developed with reference to the natural sciences, but it is perhaps only natural that it should have been eagerly adopted by the social sciences. While Kuhn does not specifically take up the issue of the applicability of his theories to the social sciences, there are a few hints that he is wary of the adoption of his methodologies by these disciplines (Kuhn 1977:221–2, 231–2) because a social science, '*Geisteswissenschaft,*' differs from the natural science, '*Naturwissenschaft,*' for a social science tends not to have a single consensus in its scientific community, but rather works with several often contradicting models.[8] Nevertheless, some linguists have taken up

Kuhn's (now rejected) theory of 'paradigm shift' and applied it to their own discipline to isolate a 'Chomskyan paradigm.'

> It is no accident that many linguists of the Chomskyan school have enthusiastically embraced Thomas Kuhn's doctrine of the history of science as a series of 'Gestalt switches' or 'conversion experiences,' in each of which no reasoned grounds can be assigned for the adoption of the new intellectual 'paradigm' and the old 'paradigm' has disappeared ultimately only because its remaining adherents died out. (Sampson 1980:158–9, summarizing Percival 1976)[9]

One of the ironies of this situation is that those who take up this notion of a 'Chomskyan paradigm' superseding a 'Bloomfieldian structuralist paradigm,' is that the Bloomfieldians tried very hard to make linguistics into a *Naturwissenschaft*, whereas the 'Chomskyan paradigm' is very much concerned with the philosophical issues which characterize a *Geisteswissenschaft*. Yet despite the widespread acceptance of the existence of such a Chomskyan paradigm, and its corollary that there was a radical discontinuity between the linguistics of Chomsky and his predecessors,[10] some historians of linguistics have been attacking both concepts (see Sampson 1980:130–65; Hymes and Fought 1981:2–6, 244–7). As has been shown, Kuhn himself has rejected this particular use of the concept 'paradigm,' and Hymes and Fought, after observing that linguistics (in common with the other social sciences as noted by Kuhn) does not have a single core of theory as is typical for the pure sciences, remark:

> Kuhn's model, often in a deceptively simplified second-hand version, nevertheless continues to appeal to enough writers to keep it in the current literature, despite the generally unfavorable view of it taken by most commentators. (Hymes and Fought 1981:246)[11]

Even a sympathetic commentator such as Frederick J. Newmeyer who, as we noted, tacitly accepts the notion of a 'Chomskyan paradigm,' is aware that this paradigm itself is in a state of crisis, although he does not investigate the issue further:

> In recent years there has been an undeniable fragmentation of the once monolithic theory. Many alternative models of linguistic description have been proposed, some heralded as making as much a break from mainstream transformational grammar as this theory made from structural linguistics. But with marginal exceptions, the debate has taken place well within the general framework of theoretical assumptions first articulated in *Syntactic Structures*. A truly alternative theory with any credibility has yet to emerge. (Newmeyer 1980:20)

But what those scholars who adhere uncritically to a Kuhnian model (without realizing that the model itself has been modified by its author and granted only limited application) seem to fail to realize is that 'metascience' is a *Geisteswissenschaft*, and that there are indeed several competing models within the 'disciplinary matrix' of metascience.[12] Since these competing models have not been as popular as that of Kuhn in attempting to interpret the history of linguistics, this is not the place for a detailed analysis of their theoretical frameworks, although two such writers deserve to be mentioned.

Paul Feyerabend provides the most radical alternative to Kuhn. He argues that continuity and diversity are more important to the advancement of science than the consensus of a scientific community (1975, 1978). Feyerabend argues that scientific breakthroughs often occur on the fringes or even outside the scientific community (or 'paradigm' in the first of Kuhn's revised definitions). Furthermore, Feyerabend (1978) argues that the very notions of 'scientific community' and 'paradigm,' while they may be a convenience to the bureaucrats and funders in the advanced nations, may in fact serve to hinder the advancement of science rather than promote it.

Michel Foucault, on the other hand, has turned his attention to what he calls the 'human sciences,' which include linguistics (see, for instance, 1971, 1972). In particular, he has investigated the systems of knowledge as practiced in the sixteenth and seventeenth centuries (i.e., at the early stages of the rise of modern science), in order to show the multivalenced nature of human knowledge and its progression. He also draws attention to interactions between continuities and discontinuities of systems of knowledge, while at the same time focusing his attention on the methodologies of writing history.

3. A Battle of Grammars

Among the consequences of the application of an inaccurate Kuhnian model of scientific progress to contemporary linguistics is that such a model obscures the strong ties to the previous 'paradigm(s)' inherent in the current model(s). At the same time, the recognition and acceptance of such a model by academic departments, funding agencies, and the scholarly community at large, may in fact act as an inhibiting factor in the continuing advancement of linguistics. After a period of intellectual ferment, linguistic innovation becomes stifled and openly discouraged, and the opportunities to develop new approaches are severely restricted because they are at odds with what now passes for orthodoxy. Such a situation has already occurred before in the history of English grammar and therein lies the salutary lesson from the history of linguistics which, it seems to me, should remind us that the current linguistic orthodoxy is just that, and that, moreover, it is an orthodoxy marking time and without much sense of direction and leadership.

For the purpose of this chapter, let us assume that the modern history of linguistics in English begins with the Latin–English grammars of the early sixteenth centuries. Although the grammatical model used in England was that established in the main by Donatus and Priscian, not all vernacular traditions interpreted this grammar in the same way when it came to applying it to their own languages (see Padley 1976 and related studies such as Rowe 1974, Michael

1970, and Vorlat 1975). Probably the most interesting period so far as this early history is concerned is the seventeenth century. This was a time of immense activity and interest in all kinds of language study, and even though the main lines of investigation are clear, there is a considerable amount of variation in direction and emphasis in the varying traditions, English, French, German, and so on. Some of these lines of investigation may be seen to parallel twentieth-century concerns. Using a terminology that is really out of context, but still useful in an attempt to understand in general terms what was going on, there were, for example, those who were distressed to find the study of language a *Geisteswissenschaft* and who made various attempts to turn that study into a *Naturwissenschaft*. Such efforts foundered on the same rock on which American structuralists came to grief. Distressed by the vicissitudes of semantic variance in natural languages, these seventeenth-century linguists devoted a great deal of time and effort in an attempt to develop a universal, philosophical, and accurate language which would appeal to all members of '*homo loquens.*' This would be a language in which every word would have a precise, accurate, and invariable meaning. Words would become as logical as are numbers. The most notable English attempt to develop such a grammar is found in Wilkins (1668). The twentieth-century heard this:

> Thereafter, at any time or place, we can decide whether any set of objects has the same number as this first set, by merely repeating the counting process with the new set. Mathematics, the ideal use of language, consists merely of elaborations of this process. The use of numbers is the simplest and clearest case of the usefulness of talking to oneself, but there are many others. We think before we act. (Bloomfield 1933:29)

Implicit in this statement is a concealed disappointment that the rest of language is not as perfectly analyzable and useful as numbers. The American structuralists tried to study language without recourse to semantics and the seventeenth-century writers tried to study semantics without recourse to language. As a consequence both enterprises failed to achieve their stated goals. The history, development, and influence of these seventeenth- and eighteenth-century attempts to devise a universal grammar have been admirably chronicled in specialized studies such as those by James Knowlson (1975) and Murray Cohen (1977).

In England the writing of grammars continued apace during the seventeenth century, with works appearing in both English and Latin (see Alston 1974, especially Volume I, *English Grammars Written in English and English Grammars Written in Latin by Native Speakers*). Grammars were first written in English during the sixteenth century in order to help students learn Latin as, for example, Linacre (?1512/?1515) and its later revision, Linacre (?1525). The most famous of these grammars was the one attributed to William Lily (1549), a text which was still being used in one of its many subsequent revisions until the middle of this century. Lily's grammar achieved its prominence by being the only grammar to be officially licensed for use in the public schools. As a consequence, Latin grammars in English during the following century tend to be derivative, basing their authority for a large part on their amplification or exposition of the material found in Lily (Padley 1976:119–20). The same is also true of grammars in English, which to a large extent also adhere to the methodology and presentation found in Lily. It was not until the middle of the seventeenth century that a grammar was published which represented a break with this tradition. John Wallis published the first edition of his *Grammatica Linguae Anglicanae* in 1653[13] and lived to supervise a fifth edition in 1699 (Wallis 1653, 1699).

Wallis's claim is that he is describing English on its own terms, not imposing upon it the structure of Latin as too many of his predecessors had done (Kemp 1972:108–15), even though he retains a Latin terminology. As a result, he excludes case and gender in his discussion of the nominal system (cf. Greaves 1594), omits the moods,[14] and recognizes only two tenses in his discussion of the English verbal system. It is quite clear, therefore, that there are several traditions at work in English grammar during the seventeenth century, and even though Wallis's work qualifies as a breakthrough which might trigger a 'Gestalt switch,' nothing happens. Nevertheless, Wallis's work is not without its influence and there are constant references to his work in the contemporary literature. Yet if this new approach were to have triggered a 'paradigm shift,' this would have occurred during the 'grammar wars' of 1711–1712. During this period no fewer than three substantial grammars of English appeared, each vying with the others for recognition as a model grammar, and each based upon differing methodological principals (Gildon and Brightland 1711; Greenwood 1711; Maittaire 1712). Gildon and Brightland base their grammar on Wallis and GGR, Greenwood is presented within a Latin-based framework, while Maittaire is very much influenced by Greek in his terminology and presentation. A contemporary pamphlet, *Bellum Grammaticale* (1712) indicates that in some circles these books caused quite a stir.[15]

The most innovative of the three gammars is Gildon and Brightland (1711), even though it is largely derivative of the work of Wallis and GGR.[16] Nevertheless it presents a synthesis of these works and in doing so introduces a clear alternative to the way in which English grammar had been customarily taught.

> What we propos'd to our selves first, was to make our selves perfect Masters of what he [Brightland] design'd, which we found was to have a *Grammar* of our own Mother Tongue, by which Children and Women, and others, who were ignorant of those call'd the Learned Tongues, might learn to Read and Write *English* with as great Justness and Exactness as the Learned may be suppos'd to do. Hence these two Particulars arose first, That we are not to forge a New *Language,* nor to alter the *Orthography* now in Use and Settled by Custom. . . . On the contrary we ought to lay down the certain *Rules* of Reading and Writing this *Language,* as it is establish'd by the general Use of the Learned themselves, and the Nature of the Tongue. . . .

Hence I believe it is pretty plain, that the *Rules* of our Tongue are only to be drawn from our Tongue it self, and as it is already in Use. (Gildon and Brightland 1711:A5r–v)

This has a modern ring to it because it echoes the principle articulated more formally by Ferdinand de Saussure:

> Static linguistics or the description of a language-state is *grammar* in the very precise, and moreover usual, sense that the word has in the expressions "grammar of the Stock Exchange," etc., where it is a question of a complex and systematic object governing the interplay of coexisting values.
> Grammar studies language as a system of means of expression. Grammatical means synchronic and significant. . . . (Saussure 1959:134)

Even though Greenwood (1711:A4v) makes a nod in the direction of Wallis, and indeed translates large sections of Wallis (1653, 1699), he ends up only mouthing Wallis's principles, not taking them seriously. For example, Greenwood reintroduces the case system with his discussion of the genitive case (Greenwood 1711:51–5) and while he states that English has no gender, he spends several pages discussing it with its rules (op.cit.:55–8). By a similar sleight of hand, he introduces all the Latin moods into his grammar in some detail, while still making the claim that there are no moods in English (op.cit.:118–23). And while he admits that English has only two formal tenses, he belies this statement by having all the Latin terminology of tense prominently set out as he insists that the periphrastic tenses be counted as contributing to the category 'tense.' Therefore, he is able to discuss the tenses of the active and passive verbs (142–8) and the moods of verbs (149–52) as if Wallis had never existed. It is for this and similar inconsistencies that *Bellum Grammaticale* (1712) takes Greenwood to task. The number and distribution of the parts of speech in English grammar is a complicated issue. Michael (1970:210–80) identifies fifty separate systems in the period from 1500 to 1800. The most Latinate (and most popular) systems list eight parts of speech, and a version of it can be found in Lily (1549) (Michael 1970:214–6). Greenwood (1711) has seven parts of speech (system 7 in Michael 1970:220–1), Mattaire (1712) has eight (system 8 in Michael 1970:222). Wallis, on the other hand, never really pinned down the parts of speech, even though he discusses words under nine headings (system 25 in Michael 1970:203–5, 241). Gildon and Brightland (1711) admit only four parts of speech (system 33 in Michael 1970:255–6), drawing upon Arnaud and Lancelot (1660). *Bellum Grammaticale* (1712) criticizes Greenwood (1711) for not keeping up with current theory.

> In the *second* Chapter you stand to your *Pan-Puddings, Lily's eight* Parts of Speech, and describe them much in as easy Words; tho' Mr. *Johnson* in his *Grammatical Commentaries,* has confuted this Division [Johnson 1706:5; also quoted in *Bellum Grammaticale* 1712:53], and your *Antagonist* had done the same [Gildon and Brightland 1711:69], yet you keep the old exploded Track, without giving any one Reason for it; nor could you indeed produce any other, than what

the *Wild Irish* did for their Horses drawing with their Tails, *viz.* Their Grand-fathers did so. Mr. *Lane* in his *Key to the Art of Letters*, reduces the Parts of Speech to four [Lane 1700:19ff.—system 31 in Michael 1970:254–5, drawing upon Arnaud and Lancelot 1676:30ff.] and the *Messieurs* of *Port-Royal* have made it out beyond Controversy, that there are no more in Nature of Language in *general*, than four Parts. (*Bellum Grammaticale* 1712:24)

For most of the pamphlet, the author of *Bellum Grammaticale* (1712) keeps up a continuous attack on Greenwood (1711), whom he calls *Scindaptus*, for his conservatism, his disorganization, and his obscurantism, particularly since it appears that Greenwood had access to Gildon and Brightland (1711) some time before it was written, yet failed to take advantage of it:

For tho' you found such irrefragable Arguments in his [Brightland's] Notes for many Things, and had the Advantage of having his Work before you the best Part of a Year, you have notwithstanding chosen to persist in your own erroneous Opinion, tho' founded on no Manner of Reason, or for which at least you have not vouchsaf'd to afford us any *one*. (*Bellum Grammaticale* 1712:58)

Furthermore, Greenwood is out of line with the desire for reform in the teaching of grammar that appears to be favored by some of the more prominent public school masters of the day,[17] as can be seen by the commendatory letters in Johnson (1706:c2v–crv).

When the author of *Bellum Grammaticale* (1712) turns to Maittaire (1712) in a postscript, he finds a target much easier to dispose of. Maittaire is a classicist, and even though he is writing a vernacular grammar, his classical interests are never far away. As he says in his preface:

The Dependence, which the English has in the Derivation of Words upon Greek and Latin, made it necessary for me to intermix many things relating to those two Languages, and even to Hebrew; wherefore i have inserted in the beginning an Hebrew and Greek Alphabet, and towards the end . . . a Saxon one, from which Tongue the English drew its Original. (Mattaire 1712:viii–ix)

For this Maittaire (here called *Heterologus*) is rightly chastised by the author of *Bellum Grammaticale* (1712:62):

'Tis a sure Way indeed to make the Study of *Greek* and *Latin* necessary to the Understanding of *English!* A most worthy Author of the *English Grammar!* We have indeed a Story of a Person that lov'd the Sound of *Greek,* tho' he did not understand it. . . .

It is not necessary to look further at Maittaire's grammar except to say that it forces English into much more of a classical mold than Greenwood's grammar— or for that matter even Lily's grammar of two centuries earlier. It is perhaps significant that Maittaire's grammar was never reprinted.

The period 1711–1712 provided a clear choice for the future development of English grammar. The author of *Bellum Grammaticale* (1712) is in no doubt about which way grammatical studies should go. Even though he does criticize Gildon and Brightland (1711), he notes that some improvements have already been made in the second edition of 1712 (*Bellum Grammaticale* 1712:23), and he quite clearly thinks that the grammars of Greenwood and Maittaire are more than inadequate.

> To conclude, I must say of these two latter *Grammarians,* as a Master of Music did to two who appeal'd to him to decide who sung best: Truly said he to one, you sing the worst that ever I heard any one in my Life; and you (to the other) don't sing at all. *Scindaptus* has given us the worst grammar in the *English* Tongue that ever I saw, but *Heterologus* has given us no Grammar at all, I mean peculiar to our Language. (*Bellum Grammaticale* 1712:68)

Once again from hindsight, it is quite clear that this opinion is correct. If ever the time were opportune for a 'Gestalt switch' it was then. There was dissatisfaction with the current 'paradigm' in the teaching and presentation of grammar, and various alternatives were explored, especially by those who were influenced by Wallis and GGR. A new grammar (Gildon and Brightland) appeared in 1711, went through two impressions of the second edition in 1712, and a third edition in 1714. It synthesized the innovations of Wallis and GGR and presented a truly synchronic grammar. But Gildon and Brightland (1711) was not to serve as the focal point for a new 'paradigm.' While it is clear that the alternative presented by Maittaire is rejected, Greenwood's grammar, despite all its methodological inadequacies, remained the most influential of these works and signaled the tenacity and ultimate victory of the status quo. Even though it did not go into a second edition until 1722 or a third one until 1729, Greenwood's concise grammar of 1737 had three editions in ten years. When Samuel Johnson published his dictionary in 1755, he included in it a grammar with which Greenwood would have been happy and in which the parts of speech are increased to nine (system 10 in Michael 1970:255–8) and the accidence is in line with that of Latin (Johnson 1755). There is not even a nod in the direction of Wallis or GGR. Their influence will continue for some decades yet before it will peter out completely. In step with Johnson will be the conservative and influential grammars that will guide the teaching of English for nearly two centuries, viz., those of Priestly (1761), Lowth (1762), and Murray (1795).

The lesson to be drawn from this is that the history of linguistics does not work as those who use an outdated and uncritical Kuhnian model claim that it should. Merely being correct in one's analysis of language will not guarantee that one will be in a position to overthrow a current orthodoxy. The rapid rise to prominence of Chomsky was not a reflection of the correctness of his theory, but also a response to some much broader and deeper feelings of dissatisfaction with the logical-empirical view. Had that philosophical orthodoxy remained intact, then it is likely that Chomsky's influence would have been severely restricted. In the eighteenth century there was no overwhelming dissatisfaction with the prevailing philosophical orthodoxy, so despite an interest in the alternative rationalist methodologies early in the century, by the 1750s grammatical orthodoxy was firmly reestablished within a logical-empirical framework. The traditional school grammars of English once again began to resemble the early sixteenth-century models of Linacre and Lily. It was not until the influence of Saussure began to be felt in the middle of the twentieth century that a school grammar could once again make the claims and espouse a position with which Gildon and Brightland, two hundred and fifty years earlier, would have felt comfortable.[18]

NOTES

1. Many later editions—see, for instance, Arnaud and Lancelot 1664, 1676. The former was translated into English as *A General and Rational Grammar, . . .* (London: J. Nourse, 1753), reprinted in facsimile in: R. C. Alston (ed.), *English Linguistics 1500–1800* 73, Menston, England: Scolar Press, 1968. A modern annotated edition is J. Rieux et al. (eds. and trans.), *General and Rational Grammar: The Port-Royal Grammar. . . .* Janua Linguarum, Series Minor 208. The Hague: Mouton, 1975.

2. Among some of the more recent studies which deal with aspects of what Chomsky termed 'Cartesian Linguistics,' the following are useful: Droixhe (1978), especially Part Two, "Langage et raison," pp. 227–326; Padley (1976), especially pp. 154–259; Knowlson (1970); and Slaughter (1982).

3. After the second edition (Amsterdam: ex officina I. Blaeu, 1662), Vossius's book is also known as *Aristarchus, sive de arte grammatica.*

4. See in particular Itkonen (1978) for a study of the theory of grammar within a hermeneutic-dialectic philosophy of metascience which is critical of some of Chomsky's positions (up to 1976); and Botha (1981) for a straightforward exploration of grammatical theory within a hermeneutic-dialectic approach avoiding areas of controversy.

5. Sampson writes within an empirical framework and is basically hostile to Chomsky's rationalism and mentalism, as well as his achievements.

6. An example of the application of the concept of paradigm to linguistic history is Hymes (1974b), especially the opening essay by Hymes (1974a), which argues that tradition in linguistics is more important than 'paradigm shifts': the same approach is found in Wells (1979).

7. For a background survey of the theories of metascience see Suppe (1977a and b).

8. Despite Kuhn's reservations (as in Kuhn 1977), scholars have, with varying success, tried to apply his theories to social science, as for example, Gutting (1980) and Barnes (1982).

9. Cohen (1977:xvi–xviii) draws upon Kuhn (1970) and Foucault (1971, 1972) for a framework within which to organize his study.

10. Newmeyer (1980), without mentioning Kuhn (1970) or paradigms, assumes a 'Chomskyan paradigm' in his second chapter, "The Chomskyan Revolution," pp. 19–59.

11. Radnitzky (1968) surveys these traditions up through the 1960s.

12. A similar deceptively simplified secondhand version of Kuhn's earlier uncritical notion of 'paradigm' (Kuhn 1970) has also crept into rhetoric and composition

theory. Berlin and Inkster (1980:13) see a 'paradigm' as a discrete entity standing in the way of progress in their field.

> It is our contention that the current-traditional paradigm is even more powerfully and profoundly entrenched than has been supposed. And if we are correct in our analysis of the metaphysical and epistemological assumptions informing the paradigm and the implications of those assumptions, then the current-traditional paradigm represents a danger to the teachers, students, the wider purposes of our educational enterprise, and even our social and human fabric.

A similar position has been taken in an influential article by Hairston (1982) and challenged (rightly, I think) by Blom (1984). Hairston (1984) remains unrepentant and apparently unaware of Kuhn's later work.

13. For a detailed bibliography see Kemp 1972:71–3, an edited reprint of the sixth edition of Wallis (London: Guil. Bowyer, 1765).
14. Even though Michael (1970:426) attributes the first repudiation of moods in English to James Greenwood (1711:119), Wallis (see Kemp 1972:346–9) also dispenses with the Latin moods and tenses so far as English is concerned. But it was Ramus (Pierre de La Ramée) (1569) who first dismissed the mood as a grammatical category (see Padley 1976:89–90). Ramus wrote two school grammars (1559a and b), translated into English in 1585. This grammatical approach influenced the grammars of Greaves (1594), Ben Jonson (1640) and is also found in Wallis.
15. Cohen (1977:47) attributes this tract to Gildon without comment.
16. Gildon and Brightland (1711:A6v) list their sources: GGR, 1660 and thereafter, and Wallis, 1653 and thereafter; Lane (1700) and Jonson (1640).
17. Those mentioned are Knipe (1686); Baxter (1679); Samuel Mountfort, Master of Christ's Hospital; and Johnson (1706).
18. It may be a coincidence, but in discussing sentences Gildon and Brightland (1711:141) (taken from Arnaud and Lancelot 1676:153) say:

> The Construction of Words, is generally distinguish'd into *Concord* [Convenance], and *Government* [Regime]; the first, by which the Words ought to agree among themselves, and the second, when *one* causes any Alteration in the other.

The most recent version of transformational generative grammar is outlined in Chomsky (1982a). The terms 'government' and 'binding' are succinctly defined in Chomsky (1982b:6–7).

> The theory of *binding* is concerned with the relations of anaphors and pronominals to their antecedents, if any. . . . The theory of *government* contains such principles as the *Empty Category Principle*. . . . The concept of government plays a central unifying role throughout the system.

Even though the interpretation and application of these terms are worlds apart, concord and government as outlined in GGR (1660) seem to do much the same in that theory of grammar as Chomsky wants binding and government to fulfill in a universal grammar.

REFERENCES

Aarsleff, Hans 1970. "The History of Linguistics and Professor Chomsky." *Language* 46, pp. 575–85. Reprinted in: Hans Aarsleff, *From Locke to Saussure: Essays on the Study of Language and Intellectual History*. Minneapolis: University of Minnesota Press, 1982, pp. 101–19.

Alston, R. C. 1974. *A Bibliography of the English Language from the Invention of Printing to the Year 1800.* Corrected reprint of vols. 1–10. Ilkley, England: Janus Press.

Arnaud, Antoine, and Claude Lancelot 1660. *Grammaire générale et raisonnée.* Paris: Pierre le Petit.

Arnaud, Antoine, and Claude Lancelot 1664. *Grammaire générale et raisonée,* 2nd ed. Paris: Pierre le Petit.

Arnaud, Antoine, and Claude Lancelot 1676. *Grammaire générale et raisonnée.* 3rd ed. Paris: Pierre le Petit. Reprinted in facsimile in: H. E. Brekle (ed.), *Grammatica Universalis,* Vols. 1–2. Stuttgart–Bad Cannstatt: Friedrich Frommann Verlag, 1966.

Barnes, Barry 1982. *T. S. Kuhn and the Social Sciences.* New York: Columbia University Press.

Baxter, William 1679. *De analogia, sive arte linguae latinae commentariolus. . . .* London: R. Everingham.

Bellum Grammaticale: or, the Grammatical Battel Royal In Reflections On the Three English Grammars. Publish'd in about a Year last past . . . 1712. London: J. and M. Jerund. Reprinted in facsimile in: R. C. Alston (ed.), *English Linguistics 1500–1800* 204. Menston, England: Scolar Press, 1969.

Berlin, James A., and Robert P. Inkster 1980. "Current-Traditional Rhetoric: Paradigm and practice." *Freshman English News* 8:2, pp. 1–4, 13–4.

Blom, Thomas E. 1984. "Response to Maxine Hairston. . . ." *College Composition and Communication* 35, pp. 489–93.

Bloomfield, Leonard 1933. *Language.* New York: Holt, Rinehart and Winston.

Botha, Rudolf P. 1981. *The Conduct of Linguistic Inquiry: A Systematic Introduction to the Methodology of Generative Grammar,* Janua Linguarum, Series Practica 157. The Hague: Mouton.

Chomsky, Noam 1965. *Aspects of the Theory of Syntax.* Cambridge, MA: MIT Press.

Chomsky, Noam 1966. *Cartesian Linguistics: A Chapter in the History of Rationalist Thought. Studies in Language* 1. New York: Harper and Row.

Chomsky, Noam 1982a. *Lectures on Government and Binding: The Pisa Lectures,* 2nd rev. ed. *Studies in Generative Grammar* 9. Dordrecht, Holland, and Cinnaminson, NJ: Foris.

Chomsky, Noam 1982b. *Some Concepts and Consequences of the Theory of Government and Binding. Linguistic Inquiry Monograph* 6. Cambridge, MA: MIT Press.

Cohen, Murray 1977. *Sensible Words: Linguistic Practice in England 1640–1755.* Baltimore and London: Johns Hopkins University Press.

Droixhe, Daniel 1978. *La Linguistique et l'appel de l'histoire (1600–1800): Rationalisme et révolutions positivistes.* Geneva and Paris: Librairie Droz.

Feyerabend, Paul 1975. *Against Method: Outline of an Anarchistic Theory of Knowledge.* London: NLB.

Feyerabend, Paul 1978. *Science in a Free Society.* London: NLB.

Foucault, Michel 1971. *The Order of Things: An Archeology of the Human Sciences. World of Man.* New York: Pantheon.

Foucault, Michel 1972. *The Archeology of Knowledge. World of Man.* New York: Pantheon.

Gildon, Charles, and John Brightland 1711. *A Grammar of the English Tongue, With Notes, Giving the Grounds and Reason of Grammar in General. . . .* London: John Brightland. [2nd ed., 1712; 8th ed., 1759.] Reprinted in facsimile in: R. C. Alston (ed.), *English Linguistics 1500–1800* 25. Menston, England: Scolar Press, 1967.

Greaves, Paul 1594. *Grammatica Anglicana, praecipuè quatenus à Latina differt, ad unicam P. Rami methodum concinnata.* Cambridge: Iohannis Legatt. Reprinted in facsimile in: R. C. Alston (ed.), *English Linguistics 1500–1800* 169. Menston, England: Scolar Press, 1969.

Greenwood, James 1711. *An Essay Towards a Practical English Grammar. . . .* London: R. Tookey. [2nd ed. 1722; 5th ed., 1753; abridged as *The Royal English Grammar. . . .* London: J. Nourse, 1737; 9th ed. 1780.] Reprinted in facsimile in: R. C. Alston (ed.), *English Linguistics 1500–1800* 128. Menston, England: Scolar Press, 1968.

Gutting, Gary (ed.) 1980. *Paradigms and Revolutions: Applications and Appraisals of Thomas*

Kuhn's Philosophy of Science. Notre Dame, IN, and London: University of Notre Dame Press.

Hairston, Maxine 1982. "The winds of change: Thomas Kuhn and the revolution in the teaching of writing." *College Composition and Communication* 33, pp. 76–88.

Hairston, Maxine 1984. "Reply." *College Composition and Communication* 35, pp. 493–4.

Hoenigswald, Henry M. (ed.) 1979. *The European Background of American Linguistics: Papers of the Third Golden Anniversary Symposium of the Linguistic Society of America.* Dordrecht, Holland: Foris.

Hymes, Dell, and John Fought 1981. *American Structuralism,* Janua Linguarum, Series Maior 102. The Hague: Mouton.

Hymes, Dell 1974a. "Introduction: traditions and paradigms." In: Hymes (ed.), pp. 1–38.

Hymes, Dell (ed.) 1974b. *Studies in the History of Linguistics: Traditions and Paradigms. Indiana University Studies in the History and Theory of Linguistics.* Bloomington, IN: Indiana University Press.

Itkonen, Esa 1978. *Grammatical Theory and Metascience: A Critical Investigation into the Methodological and Philosophical Foundations of 'Autonomous' Linguistics. Amsterdam Studies in the Theory and History of Linguistic Science,* Series IV. *Current Issues in Linguistic Theory* 5. Amsterdam: John Benjamins.

Johnson, Richard 1706. *Grammatical Commentaries: Being an Apparatus To a New National Grammar: By way of Animadversion Upon the Falsities, Obscurities, Redundancies, and Defects of Lily's System Now in Use.* . . . London: Author. Reprinted in facsimile in: R. C. Alston (ed.), *English Linguistics 1500–1800* 187. Menston, England: Scolar Press, 1969.

Johnson, Samuel 1755. *A Dictionary of the English language.* . . . London: W. Straham. Numerous facsimile eds., such as: New York: AMS, 1967.

Jonson, Ben 1640. "The English Grammar." In: *The Works of Benjamin Jonson,* 2 vols. London: Richard Bishop, Vol. 2, pp. 31–84. Reprinted in facsimile in: R. C. Alston (ed.), *English Linguistics 1500–1800* 349. Menston, England: Scolar Press, 1972.

Kemp, J. A. (ed. and trans.) 1972. *John Wallis: Grammar of the English Language.* . . . *The classics of Linguistics.* London: Longman. Edited reprint of 6th ed. London: Guil. Bowyer, 1765.

Knipe, Thomas 1686. Ἀπολλοδώρου τοῦ Ἀθηναίου Γραμματικοῦ Βιβλίο ἤκη ἤ περὶ Θεῶν Βιβλίον. . . . London: Typis E. Redmayne.

Knowlson, James 1975. *Universal Language Schemes in England and France 1600–1800.* Toronto and Buffalo: University of Toronto Press.

Kuhn, Thomas S. 1970. *The Structure of Scientific Revolutions,* 2nd ed., enlarged. In: *International Encyclopedia of Unified Science,* Vols. 1 and 2: *Foundations of the Unity of Science,* Vol. 2, No. 2. Chicago: University of Chicago Press.

Kuhn, Thomas S. 1974. "Reflections on my critics." In: Lakatos and Musgrave, pp. 231–78.

Kuhn, Thomas S. 1977. "Some second thoughts on paradigms." In: Thomas S. Kuhn, *The Essential Tension: Selected Studies in Science Tradition and Change.* Chicago and London: University of Chicago Press, 1977, pp. 293–319. First published in: Suppe (ed.) pp. 459–82.

Lakatos, Imre, and Alan Musgrave (eds.) 1974. *Criticism and the Growth of Knowledge. Proceedings of the International Colloquium in the Philosophy of Science,* 1965, Vol. 4. 2nd corrected reprint. Cambridge: Cambridge University Press.

Lakoff, Robin 1976. " 'La Grammaire générale et raisonnée, ou la grammaire de Port-Royal.' " In: Parret, pp. 348–73.

Lancelot, Claude 1644. *Nouvelle méthode pour apprendre facilement et en peu de temps la langue latine.* Paris: A. Vitré.

Lane A. 1700. *A Key to the Art of Letters: or, English a Learned Language.* . . . London: A. and J. Churchil. Reprinted in facsimile in: R. C. Alston (ed.), *English Linguistics 1500–1800* 171. Menston, England: Scolar Press, 1969.

Lily, William 1549. *Brevissima institutio sev ratio grammatices.* . . . London: Reginald Wolfe.

English translation: *A Short Introdvction of Grammar, generally to be vsed in the Kynges Maiesties dominions.* . . . London: Reginald Wolf, 1549. This latter published in facsimile in: R. C. Alston (ed.), *English Linguistics 1500–1800*, 262. Menston, England: Scolar Press, 1970.

Linacre, Thomas ?1512/?1515. *Linacri progymnasmata grammatices vulgaria.* London: Richard Pynson.

Linacre, Thomas ?1525. *Rvdimenta Grammatices.* London: Richard Pynson. Reprinted in facsimile in: R. C. Alston (ed.), *English Linguists 1500–1800* 312. Menston, England: Scolar Press, 1971.

Lowth, Robert 1762. *A Short Introduction to English Grammar.* . . . London: J. Hughs. Reprinted in facsimile in: R. C. Alston (ed.), *English Linguistics 1500–1800* 18. Menston, England: Scolar Press, 1967.

Maittaire, Michael 1712. *The English Grammar: or, an Essay on the Art of Grammar.* . . . London: W. B. for H. Clements. Reprinted in facsimile in: R. C. Alston (ed.), *English Linguistics 1500–1800* 6. Menston, England: Scolar Press, 1967.

Masterman, Margaret 1974. "The Nature of a paradigm." In: Lakatos and Musgrave, pp. 59–89.

Michael, Ian 1970. *English Grammatical Categories and the Tradition to 1800.* Cambridge: Cambridge University Press.

Murray, Lindley 1795. *English grammar, adapted to the different classes of learners.* . . . York: Wilson, Spence and Mawman. Reprinted in facsimile in: R. C. Alston (ed.), *English Linguistics 1500–1800* 106. Menston, England: Scolar Press, 1968.

Newmeyer, Frederick J. 1980. *Linguistic Theory in America: The First Quarter-Century of Transformational Generative Grammar.* New York: Academic Press.

Padley, G. A. 1976. *Grammatical Theory in Western Europe, 1500–1700.* Cambridge: Cambridge University Press.

Parret, Herman (ed.) 1976. *History of Linguistic Thought and Contemporary Linguistics. Foundations of Communications* (Library Editions). Berlin and New York: Walter de Gruyter.

Percival, W. K. 1976. "The applicability of Kuhn's paradigms to the history of linguistics." *Language* 52, pp. 285–94.

Priestly, Joseph 1761. *The Rudiments of English Grammar.* . . . London: R. Griffiths. Reprinted in facsimile in: R. C. Alston (ed.), *English Linguistics 1500–1800* 210. Menston, England: Scolar Press, 1969.

Radnitzky, Gerard 1968. *Contemporary Schools of Metascience,* 2 vols. *Studies in the Theory of Science,* I and II. Gothenburg, Sweden: Akademiförlaget.

Ramus (Pierre de La Ramée) 1559a. *Grammaticae libri quattuor.* Paris: A. Wechelus. English translation: *The Latine grammar of P. Ramus.* . . . London: Robert Waldegrave, 1585. Reprinted in facsimile in: R. C. Alston (ed.), *English Linguistics 1500–1800* 305. Menston, England: Scolar Press, 1971.

Ramus (Pierre de La Ramée) 1559b. *Rudimenta grammaticae Latinae.* Paris: A. Wechelus. English translation: *The Rudimentes of P. Ramus his Latine Grammar.* . . . London: Robert Waldegrave, 1585. Reprinted in facsimile in: R. C. Alston (ed.), *English Linguistics 1500–1800* 306. Menston, England: Scolar Press, 1971.

Ramus (Pierre de La Ramée) 1569. *Scolae in liberates artes.* Basel: Eusebius Episcopius et Nicolai fratres haeredes, col. 167. Reprinted in facsimile (with an introduction by Walter J. Ong) Hildesheim, West Germany, and New York: Georg Olms, 1970.

Rowe, J. H. 1974. "Sixteenth and seventeenth century grammars." In: Hymes (ed), pp. 361–79.

Salmon, V. 1969. "Review of N. Chomsky, *Cartesian Linguistics* (New York, 1966)." *Journal of Linguistics* 5, pp. 165–87.

Sampson, Geoffrey 1980. *Schools of Linguistics.* Stanford, CA: Stanford University Press.

Sanctius, Franciscus (Francisco Sánchez de las Brozas) 1587. *Minerva: seu de causis linguae Latinae.* Salamanca: Apud Ioannem et Andream Renaut, Fratres.

Saussure, Ferdinand de 1959. *Course in general Linguistics.* Translated by Wade Baskin [from:

322   SHAUN F. D. HUGHES

Cours de linguistique générale, eds. Charles Bally and Albert Sechehaye in collaboration with Albert Reidlinger. *Bibliothèque scientifique*. 3rd ed. Paris: Payot, 1931]. New York: Philosophical Library.

Scoppius (Kaspar Schoppe) 1659. *Auctorium ad grammaticam philosophicam ejusque rudimenta*. Amsterdam: Apud Judocum Pluymer.

Slaughter, M. M. 1982. *Universal Languages and Scientific Taxonomy in the Seventeenth Century*. Cambridge: Cambridge University Press.

Suppe, Frederick 1977a. "Afterword—1977." In: Suppe (ed.), pp. 615–730.

Suppe, Frederick 1977b. "The search for philosophic understanding of scientific theories." In: Suppe (ed.), pp. 1–241.

Suppe, Frederick (ed.) 1977c. *The Structure of Scientific Theories*. Urbana, IL: University of Illinois Press, 2nd ed.

Uhlenbeck, E. M. 1979. "Linguistics in America 1924–1974: A detached view." In: Hoenigswald, pp. 121–44.

Vorlat, Emma 1975. *The Development of English Grammatical Theory 1586–1737 with Special Reference to the Theory of Parts of Speech*. Louvain: Leuven University Press.

Vossius, Gerardus Johannes 1635. *De arte grammatica libri septem*. Amsterdam: Apud G. Blaeu.

Wallis, John 1653. *Grammatica Linguae Anglianae*. . . . Oxford: Leon, Lichfield. Reprinted in facsimile in: R. C. Alston (ed.), *English Linguistics 1500–1800* 142. Menston, England: Scolar Press, 1969.

Wallis, John 1699. *Grammatica Linguae Anglicanae*. In: . . . *Opera Mathematica et miscellenea*. . . . 3 vols. Oxford: e Theatro Sheldoniano, 1693–99, Vol. 3, (6) 80 pp. [=5th ed.]

Wells, Rulon 1979. "Linguistics as a science: The case of the comparative method." In: Hoenigswald, pp. 23–61.

Wilkins, John 1668. *An Essay towards a real character and a philosophical language*. London: Sa. Gellibrand and John Martyn, Printer to the Royal Society. Reprinted in facsimile in: R. C. Alston (ed.), *English Linguistics 1500–1800* 119. Menston, England: Scolar Press, 1968.

CHAPTER FIFTEEN

Linguistics and Prehistory in an African Perspective: Current Methods and Argumentation

Robin Thelwall

1. Introduction

The growth of linguistics has led not only to the expansion of its subdisciplines and of its contacts with adjacent fields, but also to the uneven flow of information within those subdisciplines and fields. To take an extreme example, while in the early 1960s it might have been possible to keep abreast of most trends in descriptive and theoretical studies of English grammar, clearly today any scholar concerned with that field would need to be selective either in terms of a subdomain or in terms of selection of theoretical perspectives. While this constraint may seem obvious and unavoidable in English grammar, in the field of historical linguistics, the lack of communication between practitioners because of the separation of areally and genetically distinct zones appears to be a depressing result of barriers within a subdiscipline. Historical linguistics, as we know it, is of course built on the exegesis of Indo-European as *the* paradigm. My purpose here is to illustrate a number of historical linguistic techniques: some canonical, some controversial, in their inherent methodology or in their application. In a sense there is little new in the methods and concerns discussed, but it is hoped that the new slant on old methods or the new implications being drawn from new clusterings of methods will show the current paradigm of linguistics and prehistory in some areas of African studies. The vignette is not proposed as a model for the discipline but as a checklist of the current status and relationships of some historical linguistic techniques in a specific field. The background to my presentation, the questions to which I am personally seeking answers in the hope that these preoccupations will enable me to present a number of general methodological issues of wider interest, is a series of related, not necessarily linguistic, problems in the Nile valley and its environs.

2. Prehypothetical Questions

Some prehypothetical questions, bearing on potential applications of linguistics to history, are as follows:

1. What can genetic language classification indicate about the relationship between the present distribution of languages in this part of Africa and the past?
2. What relationships have been proposed by language and tribal history and archeological hypotheses?
3. How precise is the timescale for culture historical hypotheses and how reliable are these?
4. How reliably can the historical linguist evaluate hypotheses either from other diachronic disciplines or from the interdisciplinary zone of prehistory?

Before turning to a number of methods of inquiry that I consider germane to these queries, I would like to quote a prominent Indo-Europeanist:

> As soon as we embark on prehistory we are in the realm of hypothesis, that is, of conjectural assumptions. Conjectural assumptions are guesses. But we claim that one guess is not necessarily as good or as bad as the next. There are guesses that have a scientific value. . . . A scientific guess must serve a specific purpose, the purpose of explaining the facts. Its value derives first from the correct and complete observation of these facts, and second from the probability that no other guesses would serve this purpose as well. A prehistorian is a detective hunting for clues and fitting them together into a meaningful whole, discovering the secret of their disposition by relating them to a hypothetical picture. He is not a dreamer preoccupied with building castles in Spain. There is a good difference between the "facts" of the prehistoric archeologist and those of the prehistoric linguist. The facts of the former are concrete objects that can be handled, looked at, and put in museums. His hypothetical reconstruction consists in filling up by methodological procedures the gaps of information that are left by his fragmentary material. The prehistoric linguist never has immediate prehistoric data. All his prehistoric "facts" are unadulterated hypotheses. From the outset, he seems to be at a considerable disadvantage. But this disadvantage is outweighed by the peculiar nature of the historical material at his disposal. It permits him to reconstruct prehistoric material with a precision unequalled in any other branch of science or the arts. The particularity of linguistic facts and the characteristic processes that bring about the development of languages enable him to ask questions for which there are operational answers: he can test hypothetical predictions by accurate experiments. (Thieme 1957:180)

While Thieme may have mistakenly interpreted a naive-realist basis for archeological hypotheses, he highlights the *hypothetical* nature of the historical linguists' constructs. As a hypothetico-deductivist I would go further to emphasize not only the hypothetical nature of all constructs and metaconstructs but also the requirement of testability and thus refutability of historical linguistic hypotheses and the prehistorical hypotheses built on these and other reconstructions.

A convenient summary of the main approaches within historical linguistics may be extracted from Heine (1974:8–9). He proposes that almost all approaches to determining genetic relationship have fallen into three main types: the *Comparative Method,* which seems to be agreed upon by all linguists as providing the surest test of a genetic hypotheses; the *Method of Resemblances* (see Fodor 1966:83ff.), in which "languages are said to be related if they share a number of morphemes which are similar or identical in sound and meaning. Disagreement exists mainly as to what number is to be considered sufficient and what 'similarity' means in any case"; *The Typological Method*, much out of fashion today, but still with its adherents (if I am not mistaken, Hetzron 1972:13: "Therefore the safest criteria for language classification lie in morphology"), "is based on the assumption that related languages are structurally more similar than languages that share no common genetic origin."

Heine points out that as well as the method, the hypotheses of historical relationships are equally important, and he distinguishes three. The first one is the *Genealogical Model*, in which linguistic relationship is said to be *transitive:* if Language A is related to Language B and B is related to C, then A and C must share a common origin (Greenberg 1971, cited in Heine). Distinct from this model in that it is not predicated upon transitivity is the *Mischsprache Model*, which allows a given language to derive from more than one 'parent' language of different genetic origins. The *Substratum Model* allows two originally unrelated languages to become related if both are 'influenced' by a third language called the 'substratum language.' We may add to these three hypotheses a fourth, perhaps a variant of the third, under the heading *Areal Model*, in which a larger group of languages from several distinct genetic groups share a number of traits in common and for which a single substratum language is impossible to posit.

It should be noted that all these models and hypotheses carry ideological impedimenta, and though racial or dialectical attitudes underlying particular 'linguistic' views are generally out of fashion, each age (as the cliché has it) carries its own paradigms.

The main point of the rest of this paper is to examine the status of two techniques, *Lexicostatistics* and *Migration Theory*, in order to evaluate their contribution to the reconstruction of culture history through language, and finally to examine one area of Africa to see some types of argumentation utilizing a variety of methods and hypotheses.

3. Lexicostatistics

In the formal sense, lexicostatistics is usually said to have been developed by Swadesh, though we should note that the whole comparative method assumes part of its validity from the statistical preponderance of data conforming to hypothesized sound rules. Perhaps the biggest barrier to a balanced appraisal of lexicostatistic techniques has been an initial and specious identification of it with glottochronology. Even Hymes in an important review article fails to make clear the distinction and allows the then (and now) prevalent 'guilt by association' slur to remain: "In this paper I shall try to give a balanced appraisal to Lexicostatistics, as it has been and as it may be developed. The focus will be on glottochronology, the best known lexicostatistic method, but other topics will also be brought into view'' (1960:3).

We are in fact in the position of having no methodologically adequate definition of lexicostatistics. Heine quotes Teeter (1963:638) as saying: "By 'lexicostatistics' is meant 'the statistical manipulation of lexical similarities for the purpose of making inferences as to genetic relationship and sub-relationship among languages. . . .'' Heine ties lexicostatistics into the *Method of Resemblances,* about which Borland (1984) says: "I disagree with the repeated identification of lexicostatistics with the so-called method of resemblances. The definition by Teeter cited . . . is a very bad one which just begs this question.''

Perhaps the only linguist I know who makes explicit this distinction between method and sphere of application is Gleason (1959). He opens with a pragmatic justification for a review of historical methods:

> But we must recognize that the comparative method exacts a high price for its elegance and vigor. It is highly demanding both in time and experience. One who has never tried it cannot comprehend either the length of the processes or their complexity. The few of us who are working at the problem with African languages can produce very little with present procedures. . . . Either we must be very patient, or we must cast a sharp eye at our methods, asking whether or not the work can be reprogrammed to get more results faster and without sacrifice of vigor and validity. I believe that this reprogramming is now a demonstrated possibility. There seem to me to be three lines of attack: First: Reprogramming of the actual procedure of comparative linguistic reconstruction. I can now, in principle, feed into a machine two suitable word lists and receive from that machine a thoroughly established core of correspondences and cognates.

(We interrupt the quotation here to observe that in terms of Gleason's first line of attack the last twenty-eight years has seen remarkably little advance. Ladefoged (1969) investigated the possibility of the computer measurement of the phonetic similarity of cognate words. He came up with a measure based on a version of distinctive features, which did not accord with the intuitions or practice of historical linguistics. We may note that this was one of the problems cited by Heine (1974:8) in evaluating the Method of Resemblances. Durham and Rogers (1969) present an embryonic program for the analysis of segmental and other contexts in words for the setting up of correspondences. I suspect that the main reason why this field has not been effectively mechanized (as far as I have been able to check the literature) is primarily because of the problems of phonetic-symbol input and output. For the comparison and analysis of lexical sets the historical linguist does not just need individual computer systems that can handle pairs of languages, for instance, Coptic and German; Arabic and French; Japanese and Korean. What we need is the software capability to handle any language against any others. University College, London, has recently developed a CP/M-based program to handle any symbol, subscript, or superscript of the IPA. Similar systems may have already been developed elsewhere, but we are now in a position to demand that all courses of historical linguistics include mention of, and ideally practice in, the mechanical handling of data. The use of these methods by current scholars will geometrically accelerate research output and will also enable publication to include, easily, the data arranged to support the various elements in the reconstruction. We should soon be leaving the clerical age of comparative reconstruction. Now, back to Gleason:)

> Second: Further development of lexicostatistical methods for ascertaining internal relationships within groups of known overall relationship. These will serve both in reconnaissance work, to give us provisional results of appreciable validity and as a basis for planning further work by more complex methods, and also in organizing and interrelating the series of individual comparisons of language pairs into a genetic tree. . . . You will note that I am designating a class of methods as *lexicostatistical.* This is an extension of meaning of a term now applied to a single method, the only one of the class commonly discussed [Gleason's footnote: The term "lexico-statistical" is equally appropriate for all members of the class: "glottochronology" is not. No change in definition for the latter item is suggested]. If this usage is accepted, *lexico-statistical methods are all those which depend on the comparison of two or more vocabulary samples* selected on the basis of some lexico-statistical gloss-list, *on the counting of certain types of similarities and differences between such samples, and the calculations from these results of certain measures of relationship.* . . . Third: and intimately connected with the other two: We must improve our methods for collecting and assembling data. (Gleason 1959:22–32)

The crucial definition included in the above quotation is decisive with the exception of the mention of "the basis of some lexico-statistical gloss-list" since comparison, counting, and calculating of measures of relationship may be done just as well on the results of the comparative method (e.g., Henrici 1973; Borland 1983a) as on any 'standard' word-list. The point is that the counting and calculating methods are quite distinct from the particular data and can be applied in turn to nonlexical data (e.g., Bender 1975, 1976, and Bastin, Coupez, and De Halleux 1979, for morphostatistics). This is clear from the development of hierarchical cluster analysis techniques (see below) which were largely the result of both typological and genetic classification work in biological sciences or as general statistical work (Sokal and Sneath 1963; Everitt 1974). The long-standing assumption that lexicostatistics equals glottochronology is a clear indication that whatever the competent numeracy of some areas of linguistics, it is not yet a required part of basic training.

Before moving on to other applications of lexicostatistics it is worth commenting briefly on glottochronology. The claim of an average 'retention rate' as a constant in the formula for calculating time depth of 'splitting' has proved inadequate in a number of test cases (e.g., Fodor 1961, among others). Hattori's (1970) proposal for a retention rate estimated for the particular case of Japanese is one strategy, but the problem remains unless one can propose a systematic basis for this 'estimate.' Nevertheless, I would not reject the use of the formula out of hand (indeed, I have published glottochronological dates based on Swadesh 100-item lexicostatistics gloss-list in Thelwall 1982), but would use it in two possible ways: first where either relative sequence or absolute dating is known from other methods and where these provide a check on the local validity of glottochronology, and second where no timescale has been offered for linguistic data and where a glottochronological date provides a (highly provisional) hypothesis to orient the search for relative or absolute dating by other methods (as in Gleason's proposals for the reconnaissance value of lexicostatistics of internal relationships). Hymes's (1960:29) survey remains the most balanced review of the positive and negative results of testing glottochronology and his conclusion provides the best summary:

> I must regard the utility of the method as supported by the applications so far. Not the least utility is the heuristic value of revealing exceptions, the further study of which brings further insight. But the presence of such exceptions reminds us that the method is still in a developmental stage, and that a major obstacle to evaluating applications, and to further development, is the failure of most studies to make public their supporting data.

This last plea is something which applies equally to many recent applications of lexicostatistics to internal subgrouping within genetic groups (e.g., Ehret et al. 1974, and Thelwall 1982, among many others).

4. Lexicostatistics: The 100-Item List and Subgrouping

There seems to have been some time between the development of Swadesh's basic lists (Swadesh 1950—165 items; Lees 1953—215 items; Swadesh 1952—200 items; Swadesh 1955—100 items) and the more than sporadic application of them to subgrouping. A spate of applications in Africa developed as a result of the Ford Foundation West African Language Survey and the later East African Language Survey (e.g., Ladefoged, Glick and Criper 1972; Bender 1976). The arguments about whether there could be a universal lexicostatistical list are neatly dealt with by Hymes (1960:5): "It remains that our general understanding of the notion of basic vocabulary is not matched by specific knowledge of what constitutes it in particular cases."

In the African context two versions at least have been developed with a fair degree of thought on the premises of construction (Bender 1971; Schadeberg 1974). I would argue that the concept of a universal standard list or set of lists is chimerical. At present, an inspection of three lists shows that a common core remains, while a periphery varies. It has already been found essential to take into account particular areal factors in modifying Swadesh's original lists. A related issue that appears to be amenable to investigation is the patterns of variability in the stability internal to any particular list. Dyen, James, and Cole (1967) carried out a pioneering study of this type on the Swadesh 200-item list for a set of

Austronesian languages. We will need further investigation of these variations in order to test the hypotheses (at least) 1) that there may be a universal core of more stable items; 2) that there may be a series of semantic field groupings in the various lists; and 3) that the order of stability of these groupings (if any pattern exists) may vary by culture or genetic linguistic area. These are merely a few preliminary ideas that have come to mind in the process of writing this chapter, and there will doubtless be many more, and fruitful, aspects to the investigation of the diachronic aspects of lexicosemantic replacement. In the immediate future these kinds of investigations will enable us to quantify and order the notion of vocabulary stability and the notion of semantic change.

To turn to lexicostatistics, the application of relevant numerical manipulations to the results of 'cognate counting' has not yet resulted in any general agreement on the ground rules for what methods are available and the evaluation of different methods. Henrici (1973) seems to be the earliest application of some computer methods of cluster analysis. Bender (1976) seems to have been an attempt at developing such techniques independently, but the general availability of Sokal and Sneath (1963) and of statistical packages for university computing facilities (for a succinct review of cluster analysis see Everitt 1974) still seems not to have had widespread application (see, e.g., Bender 1976; Ehret et al. 1974; Heine 1974, but also Thelwall 1978, 1981; Schadeberg 1981a, b; Borland 1983a, b). Of course, with the application of such techniques of statistical manipulation, the notion of 'significance' acquires a measurable meaning and forces a degree of quantitative sophistication on the user which takes time to absorb.

To consider two examples, Figure 1 gives similarity matrices (= cognate counts) for two Nilo-Saharan language groups: Daju and Nubian (Thelwall 1978, 1981, 1982). If we consider the Daju group first, an examination of the numbers will show, even on cursory examination, that we have a fairly tightly knit group with straightforward genetic implications. The horizontal scale represents percentage of vocabulary. Clearly, also from simple inspection, Lagawa–Nyala–Sila form a coherent subgroup. The position of Shatt raises some questions since on the one hand its highest count is with Lagawa (66.7), but its next highest is 64.3 with Liguri and all the other counts between Shatt and the rest of the subgroup are lower than the Shatt–Liguri count. This is borne out by the cluster analyses where Nearest Neighbor places Shatt more closely to the Lagawa subgroup than to Liguri, Furthest Neighbor closer to Liguri, and the other methods (all variants on averaging) have Shatt as a separate branch from the highest node. Before examining factors extrinsic to the similarity matrix, we should note that, at present, there is no proposed measure of the 'significance' of percentage points of difference between cognate counts. This should be statistically fairly easy to propose, though I am not totally certain what the linguistic implications will be. We should intuitively expect a different 'significance' of a 3% difference (for cognate ranges of 56–82% (Daju), 32–87% (Nubian), on the one hand, and 4–12% (e.g., Tornasi with Daju/Nubian—see Thelwall 1982:169) on the other.

Figure 1. Cognate Counts and Trees for Daju and Nubian

Similarity Matrices (Cognate Counts of Swadesh 100-item list)

DAJU
Liguri
64.3 Shatt
60.2 66.7 Lagawa
56.1 62.2 82.7 Nyala
57.4 60.0 73.7 74.7 Sila

NUBIAN
Meidob
51.1 Birgid
46.2 60.2 Kadaru
44.6 57.8 86.8 Debri
40.2 49.5 56.0 56.5 Dongolawi
32.6 36.6 43.8 40.0 67.0 Nobiin

Cluster Analyses

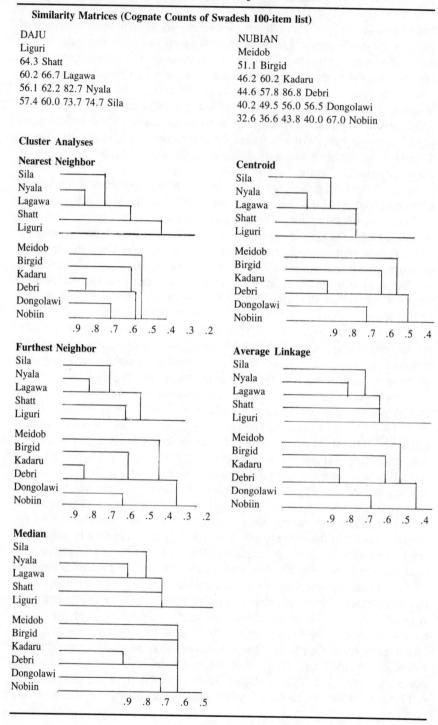

Nearest Neighbor
Sila
Nyala
Lagawa
Shatt
Liguri

Meidob
Birgid
Kadaru
Debri
Dongolawi
Nobiin
   .9 .8 .7 .6 .5 .4 .3 .2

Centroid
Sila
Nyala
Lagawa
Shatt
Liguri

Meidob
Birgid
Kadaru
Debri
Dongolawi
Nobiin
   .9 .8 .7 .6 .5 .4

Furthest Neighbor
Sila
Nyala
Lagawa
Shatt
Liguri

Meidob
Birgid
Kadaru
Debri
Dongolawi
Nobiin
   .9 .8 .7 .6 .5 .4 .3 .2

Average Linkage
Sila
Nyala
Lagawa
Shatt
Liguri

Meidob
Birgid
Kadaru
Debri
Dongolawi
Nobiin
   .9 .8 .7 .6 .5 .4

Median
Sila
Nyala
Lagawa
Shatt
Liguri

Meidob
Birgid
Kadaru
Debri
Dongolawi
Nobiin
   .9 .8 .7 .6 .5

330

And this would be so even where we can exclude borrowing or re-borrowing as factors (see also below for a discussion of chance cognation). This is certainly another important area (following Gleason's proposals) where we need to have some way of measuring the 'significance' of numerical 'differences.'

The cluster analyses which produce the trees have been developed as part of general numerical taxonomy, with the most active application being in biological sciences. Sokal and Sneath (1963) provides a detailed handbook examining aims, alternative methods, and problems of application and interpretation. Everitt (1974:97) provides a summary update of methods and concludes with the remarks:

> Cluster analysis is potentially a very useful technique, but it requires care in its application, because of the many associated problems. In many of the applications of the methods that have been reported in the literature the authors have either ignored or have been unaware of these problems, and consequently few results of lasting value can be pointed to. Hopefully future users of these techniques will adopt a more cautious approach, and in addition remember that, along with most other statistical techniques, classification procedures are essentially descriptive techniques for multivariate data, [i.e., *not* explanatory] and solutions given should lead to a proper reexamination of the data matrix rather than a mere acceptance of the clusters produced.

This further highlights Gleason's remarks about the 'reconnaissance' role of lexicostatistics in general, and Heine's on the usefulness of it as a preliminary to the selective application of the Comparative Method.

As a brief indication of the disagreement on the relative merits of different methods we may first note Mann (1976:4) who believes that

> the most stable single method is the furthest neighbour method; since however this method is based on extreme figures, there is a different danger of distribution from bad data or problematic individuals, and it is desirable to confirm any classification by the agreement of a strategy using average figures . . . the best candidate for a control method is probably the group average classification. Agreement between these two methods can probably be regarded as establishing a classification.

We must utter a warning note about the concept of 'establishing,' which is fraught with implications for the philosophy of scientific method. But this claim must be balanced by a statistician's view: "Since there are other objections to complete link clustering (furthest neighbor) see Sibson 1972; Jardine and Sibson (1968) recommend single linkage clustering as the method of greatest mathematical appeal" (Everitt 1974:62). It may be helpful to consider an analogy to the various clustering techniques: nearest neighbor (for single linkage), as its name implies, is the distance between two 'towns' gauged as the distance between nearest points while furthest neighbor is the distance between outermost points. All other methods involve intermediate values by averaging with or without weighting.

To take up Everitt's remarks in relation to the issue of the position of Shatt within the Daju group, as outlined above, preliminary analyses of sound correspondences have been carried out, some sound changes have been proposed and reconstruction of the proto-segments and thence of proto-lexicon proposed. An important factor that requires consideration in the context of subgrouping by means of the Comparative Method is the analysis of common retentions and shared innovations. The latter is frequently considered the prime factor in allocating languages to a subgroup. In the case of Daju, we have on the one hand a single sound rule, x < *r, in Shatt and Liguri alone. This is proposed as an innovation. On the other hand, Ehret (1982:388) has argued that the lexical items that distinguish Shatt and Liguri from the rest of Daju are common retentions from Proto-Daju where the rest have innovated. A return to the data and the inclusion in the argument of other aspects of the data is the only way to arrive at a solution. Even here, as we find with the subgrouping of Indo-European (Antilla 1972:309), decisions on an ultimate solution do not appear to be agreed to at present. A comparative survey of criteria employed for subgrouping in various genetic linguistic phyla is required. In the case of Nubian we have conformity of taxonomic structure between four of the different cluster analyses, but the Median averaging technique (or Weighted Pair Group Method—Sokal and Sneath 1963:201) gives a different structure. A reexamination of the data focuses attention on the position of Dongolawi. While Dongolawi's highest percentage of cognates is with Nobiin, we should note that there is an anomalous difference of 8–16% in the counts between Dongolawi and the rest (percentage points higher) and Nobiin and the rest. This difference could be treated as either retentions of a common core of Proto-Nubian and innovation by Nobiin, or as an indication of continued contact between Dongolawi and the rest of Nubian on one side and Nobiin on the other (as in a dialect chain, for example), or as an indication of subsequent (or continued) contact between Dongolawi and Nobiin which (re)introduced a set of words from Nobiin to Dongolawi. Though this problem is unresolvable at this stage on linguistic grounds alone, given the lack of adequate application of the comparative method (this is ongoing but as Gleason says above will take considerable time to complete for this specific purpose), what is hypothesized about the culture history provides a logically supportable conjecture (cf. Thieme quoted above). At the present time and at least as far back as the fourteenth century, Dongolawi has been spoken on the Nile neighboring to Nobiin further north, while all the other present-day Nubian languages are 350–900 kilometers distant. It is arguably more likely that Dongolawi moved into contact (again) with Nobiin after an earlier geographical (and linguistic) separation than either of the other two possibilities. It should be noted that the Nobiin appears to have been the politically dominant group. This is merely a hypothesis not refuted by the available (mainly nonlinguistic) evidence and requires further, more powerful linguistic testing before it can be said to have a surer basis for survival, but a hypothesis weakly tested is better than no hypothesis at all.

5. Similarity Judgments, Resemblances, and Chance and Borrowing

Bender (1969:525) sets out the 'canonical' criteria for deciding whether two vocabulary items are to score a positive or negative cognation count:

(a) $C_1V_1C_2$ is accepted as corresponding to $C_3V_2C_4$ if the vowels are identical (discounting differences of length and tone) and if one or both pairs of consonants are identical while the other pair differs by only one feature (occasionally a difference of two features is accepted). (b) $C_1V_1C_2$ is accepted as corresponding to $C_3V_2C_4$ if C_1 is identical to C_3 and C_2 is identical to C_4 regardless of the intervening vowels.

This criterion makes explicit use of a general assumption that consonants count far more in correspondences than vowels.

Extended criteria: (a) an item consisting of CV alone is counted in comparison with an identical CV standing alone or occurring in a larger item; (b) not only the first, but all CVCs are considered in longer items.

It can be seen that these criteria are more than somewhat elastic and allow for varying degrees of consistency of cognation decisions. However, these indeterminacies seem to be outweighed by the probabilities of 'mass comparison' conforming to the results of later subclassification by the comparative method, as discussed with examples in Heine (1974). A further indeterminacy which appears to be obviated by the same factor is the difference in judgments between linguists who have no familiarity with the languages in question against those who do and who could be claimed to have a better chance of utilizing intuitive awareness of comparative series in the languages in question. The probability (in the strict statistical sense) of chance cognation is something on which remarkably little has been done. Bender (1969:522) seems to be the only empirical test on a sample of languages from the world's genetic families:

Various proposals have been advanced concerning what has been referred to as "refutation of the null hypothesis" in language comparison, i.e., that the sound-meaning correspondences found for any two particular languages are within the range of what one would expect by sheer coincidence. Swadesh concludes that at the 95% confidence level, four or more cognates in a list of 100 basic vocabulary items justify accepting a hypothesis of genetic relationship. Cowan estimates that three or more cognates is sufficient at the same level. Both these proposals are based on mathematical formulations, Cowan's the more sophisticated. Approaching the problem from the empirical side, 100-item lists in 21 languages are here used to conclude that more than two solid CVC correspondences . . . raises a strong probability that more than chance is involved.

Even if we accept these estimates, we should note that first they have different potential values at different levels of cognate values. For example, a chance cognation rate of 4% has variable distorting effect at cognation rates of, for example, 70–85% against 45–60% against 10–25%. Below 10% or perhaps

20% we are in a more marginal zone for evaluating subgrouping, and unless cognate differentials are clearly patterned, they often shade into general indeterminacy with resulting cluster analyses providing wholly spurious determinacy. This latter point triggers a more general caveat at the use of numbers and statistical manipulation. It should be clear from the CVC correspondences quoted from Bender above that the essential base of words requires qualitative processing (heretofore, though, note Gleason's programmatic statements quoted earlier in this chapter) and more or less 'linguistic' judgment. After that the number game is played, but the status of the game is according to the rule 'garbage in, garbage out.' It is, however, heartening to note the (rising) rate of conformity between lexicostatistical, or resemblance method, subclassification and comparative method subclassification (see Heine 1974, as already noted). We must beware the tendency to become hypnotized by numbers and the trees generated from them. Here Thieme's remarks are again apposite.

We turn now to the most knotty remaining problem: borrowing. Now this can occur in at least two forms: first, borrowing from a genetically unrelated or distant language (group), or it may be the result of renewal of contact between members of a tightly knit genetic subgroup (e.g., as hypothesized for Dongolawi:Nobiin above). Here, as with the variability in judging 'similarity' between words, much will depend on the breadth and depth of knowledge in the geographical and linguistic zone under investigation. The assumption that 'basic' vocabulary lists of 100 to 200 items are inherently more resistant to loss and, by implication, to the borrowing of genetically unrelated (or distant) items has been little tested. A recent important contribution by Borland (1982) reassessed the work of Henrici (1973) which was in turn a reevaluation of Guthrie's (1967) Comparative Bantu. Borland compared the classifications based on Swadesh 100 and 200 and samples of 500 and 2000 of Guthrie's reconstructed roots and their distribution in twenty-eight languages. From measurement of correlation coefficients Borland (1983a:4) concludes

> The null hypothesis . . . is that there is no significant correlation between the classification made using basic and non-basic vocabulary samples . . . the values obtained above certainly suggest that the null hypothesis cannot be rejected. This means, in turn, if our earlier reasoning was correct, that there is in fact no significant difference in the susceptibility to borrowing of basic and non-basic vocabulary.

Borland warns that these conclusions are problematic because the level of significance of the correlation coefficient values is not known, but he has clearly provided evidence for a careful and statistically valid reexamination of these issues. Borrowing remains a problematic issue which can clearly affect the percentages of similarity judgments and which appears not to be reduced by applying the technique of 'basic' lexicostatistical lists.

On an issue mentioned earlier, Borland's work is crucial in showing clearly that lexicostatistical methods are neither equivalent to glottochronology nor limited to the Method of Resemblances and are equally relevant to data produced by the comparative method. It would clearly be relevant to apply them in the well-dug fields of Indo-European and Semitic.

6. Migration Theory and the Notion of Proto-Language Homelands

Dyen (1956) has proposed three premises to underlie Migration Theory:

1. The area of origin of related languages is continuous.
2. The probability of different reconstructed migrations are in inverse relation to the number of reconstructed language movements that each requires (Postulate of Least Moves).
3. In the empirical treatment of possible homelands, a homeland that is unoccupied by a daughter language is less probable than one that is occupied; the former requires at least one additional move. Therefore the homeland of any minimal group is probably that of at least one of its units.

These premises are hedged about with provisos, caused both by our relative awareness of the complexity of general sociolinguistic factors in migration and language maintenance and shift, and by our knowledge of the history of particular cases of rapid change and extensive geographical movement.

As an example of the application of Migration Theory, allied with other evidence, Thelwall and Schadeberg (1984) examines the distribution and genetic affiliation of a set of languages in a geographically distinct zone in the southwestern Sudan. Figure 2 shows the distribution and genetic affiliation in a hilly refuge zone. The Kordofanian languages are a branch of the Niger-Kordofanian phylum, which includes Bantu as a sub-branch. East Sudanic is a branch of Nilo-Saharan phylum. Kadugli is a language group that is at present unassigned to any phylum, though Schadeberg (1981c) has rejected the possibility of its affiliation to Kordofanian. Of all the languages in the Nuba Mountains, only Daju and Hill Nubian have direct members of the same group outside. On the premises of Migration Theory and on the basis of some other historical evidence, the centers of dispersal for Proto-Daju and Proto-Nubian are hypothesized as outside the Nuba Mountains. On grounds of the internal degree of differentiation as expressed by lexicostatistical cognate counts, we are able to propose 'layers' of occupation for the various language groups in the Nuba Mountains, with the explicit assumption that migration has taken place and that the layers of cognate count levels correspond to a relative chronological sequence of 'arrival.' This example is clearly a preliminary hypothesis, since there are numerous unresolved linguistic questions about the intragroup and intraphylum positions of the various languages, let alone whatever may be gleaned from historical sources, including oral tradition. However, it shows how the methods of lexicostatistics and migration theory may be employed carefully in the construction of logically more

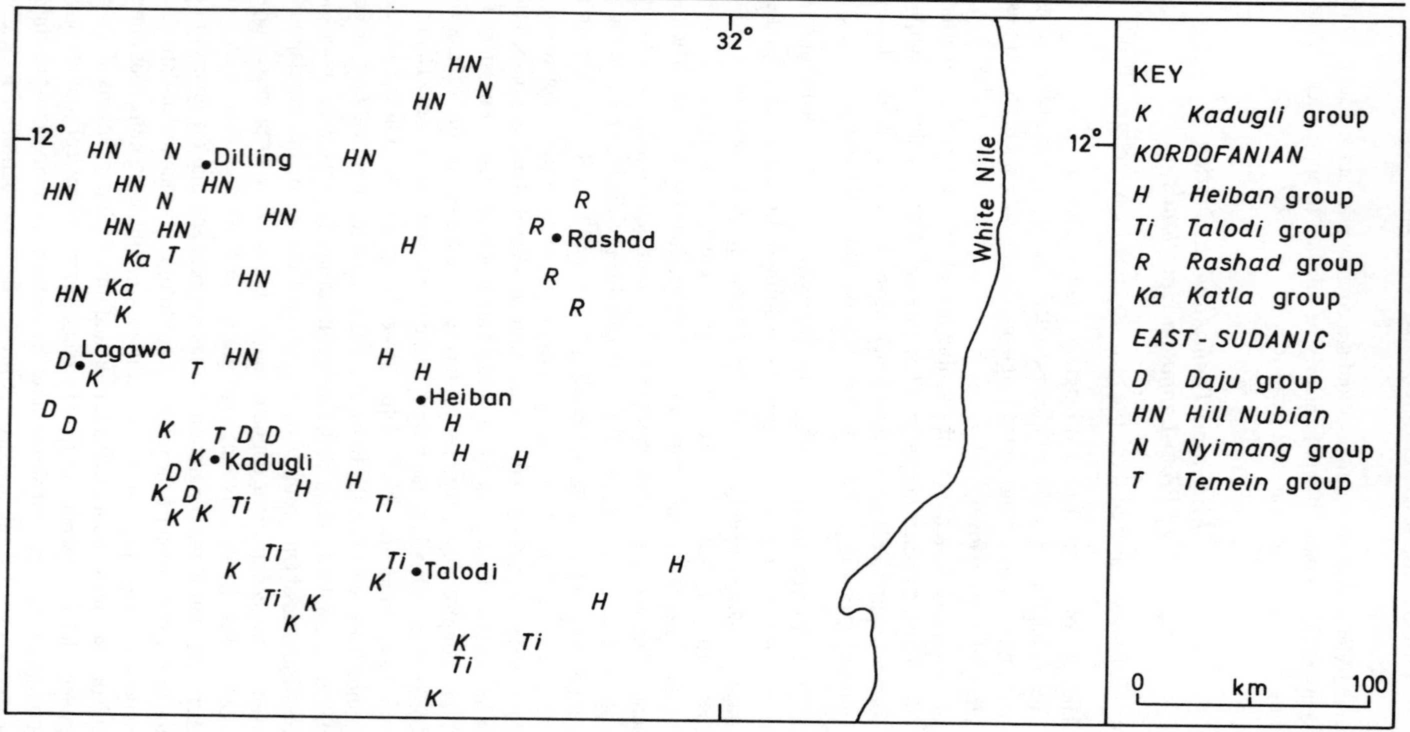

Figure 2. Distribution and Genetic Affiliation of Languages in the Nulsa Mountains

consistent hypotheses and for the clear proposal of priorities of linguistic and other research that will test the hypotheses.

An important review of migrationism in cultural and physical anthropology and historical linguistics (Adams, Van Gervan, and Levy 1978) distinguishes migrationism from diffusion and laments the paucity of explicit testable hypotheses. Levy (in Adams, Van Gervan, and Levy 1979:509) summarizes the major trends in recent linguistic migration theory:

1. There has been an increased tendency to quantify linguistic diversity for the purpose of locating original homelands.
2. Precise techniques have been developed for discontinuities in distribution.
3. The application of Wörter and Sachen techniques has been extended beyond Indo-European, with much greater success than was evident in the Indo-European applications. The use of palynological data represents a significant innovation.
4. There has been a much greater tendency to control for interlanguage borrowing in recent studies than was true earlier.

We may conclude this brief review with the comment that the most fertile synthesis in this area is being applied currently to the Americas and to Africa.

7. Nilo-Saharan: A Case Study of Multiple Techniques

The hypotheses of a Nilo-Saharan language phylum was arguably the most innovative product of Greenberg's (1963) grand review of African language classification. Applying the Method of Resemblances to both the lexicon and the grammar of an unevenly documented and scanty selection of languages, he provided one stimulus among many for what is at last becoming a respectable body of individual and comparative language studies. Lexicostatistical studies of basic vocabulary (Bender 1971; Ehret 1971; Ehret et al. 1974; Thelwall 1978; Rottland 1982, among others) have been succeeded by significant applications of the comparative method to clearly defined groups (Thayer 1976; Ehret 1980; Vossen 1982; Rottland 1982). More speculative and wider applications of diluted comparative method have been proposed recently by Bender (1981) and Ehret (1984). The current state of the genetic tree is given in Figure 3. The current genetic/geographical distribution is given in Figure 4. But the application of lexicostatistics to basic vocabulary and morphostatistics has served, as Gleason pleaded, to provide essential reconnaissance work for selective application of the comparative method to groups of languages with the most economical returns. Much of course remains to be done in this area, but the problems are more sharply delineated and the zones and periods of contact between Nilo-Saharan and other genetic families are becoming clearer. This is due not just to historical linguistics but more often to the pressures and speculations of prehistorians of all disciplines. On the nonlinguistic side, we may start with climatic history. Figure 5 (Hamilton 1982) shows that the Chad basin and a number of other lakes

Figure 3. Nilo-Saharan

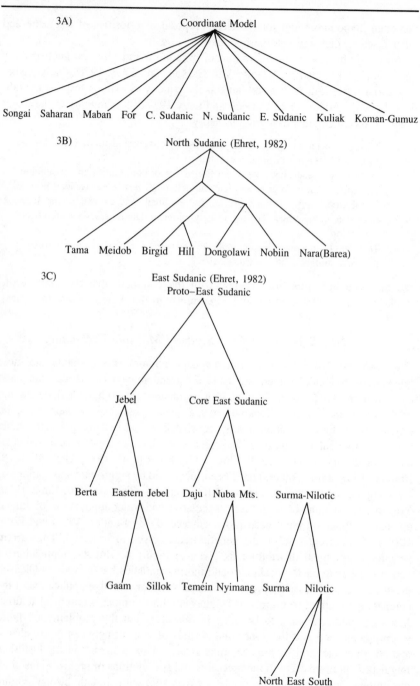

3A) Coordinate Model

Songai Saharan Maban For C. Sudanic N. Sudanic E. Sudanic Kuliak Koman-Gumuz

3B) North Sudanic (Ehret, 1982)

Tama Meidob Birgid Hill Dongolawi Nobiin Nara(Barea)

3C) East Sudanic (Ehret, 1982)
Proto–East Sudanic

Jebel Core East Sudanic

Berta Eastern Jebel Daju Nuba Mts. Surma-Nilotic

Gaam Sillok Temein Nyimang Surma Nilotic

North East South

Figure 4.   MAP OF GREENBERG'S CLASSIFICATION

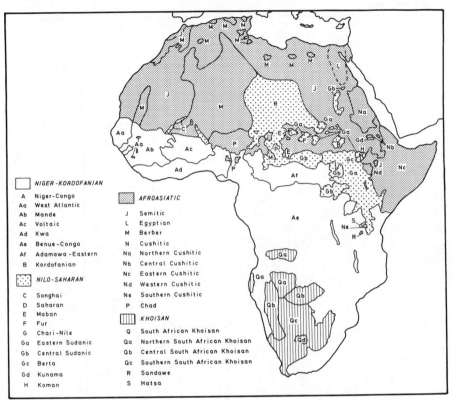

lowered their levels significantly about 4000 years ago with a continuously low level since then. This is related to a climatic shift to a steadily hotter drier period which had a major effect on the Sahara and so its southern edge. Figure 6 (Gabriel 1978) shows the extent of the Sahara at two periods. Figure 7 shows the distribution of two indices—ceramic and technological—which Sutton (1974, 1977) used to support the hypothesis of an African Aqualithic technocomplex exploiting water and embryonic agriculture. He proposed a correlation between the Aqualithic and proto-Nilo-Saharan speakers. Figure 8 (Stemler, Harlan, and DeWet 1975) shows the distribution of a particular group of sorghums which the authors proposed to correlate with a subset of the Nilo-Saharan languages. Figure 9 (Ehret 1979; Bender 1975) offers a tentative schematic homeland and migration moves for the branches of Afroasiatic.

Ehret (1979) has proposed that intensive grass collecting developed into agriculture as far back as 13,000 years ago in northern Ethiopa/northeast Sudan. The

Figure 5. AFRICAN LAKE LEVELS AND CLIMATE CHANGE (FROM HAMILTON 1982)

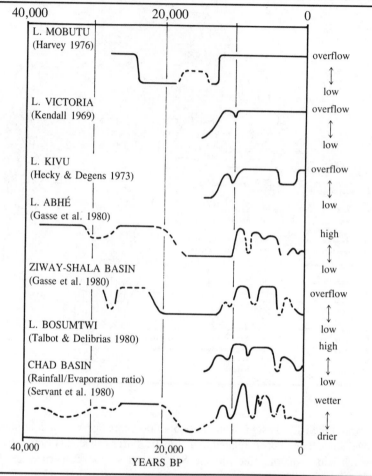

'data' and thread of argument in Ehret is typical of this field. In order to support the hypothesis that agriculture in Ethiopia and the Horn of Africa predates Near Eastern cultivation and is thus technologically independent of, and even the source for, the Near East, Ehret proposes dating for the Cushitic branch of the Afroasiatic phylum of 7000–9000BP (Before present). The lower date of 7000 years is arrived at by

> extrapolating from the rough dating of the proto–Southern Cushitic settlement in East Africa at about 4,000 years ago, a date settled on so as not to overstretch archeological dates then known. But the linguistic evidence alone favoured a deeper time span of as much as 5,000 years for the differentiation of South Cushitic populations in Kenya and Tanzania. New radiocarbon dates from East Africa now

**Figure 6.   Desert Zone with less than 50mm annual precipitation 6500–5000 BC
(Gabriel 1978)**
Desert Zone with less than 50mm annual preceipitation 5000–2000 BC (Gabriel
1978)

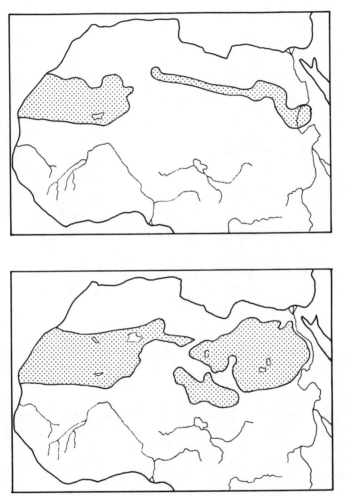

appear to confirm the longer span. Hence the proposed time scale of Cushitic
history must be adjusted upward: if proto–Southern Cushitic dates to 5,000 rather
than 4,000 years ago, then the Cushitic span as a whole would appear nearer to
9,000 than 7,000 years. (Ehret 1979:100)

It should be pointed out that Ehret (1980) has carried out a solid reconstruction of
South Cushitic, and of the borrowings between South Cushitic and a number of

Figure 7.   Artifact distribution as the base for the African Aqualithic (Sutton 1974)

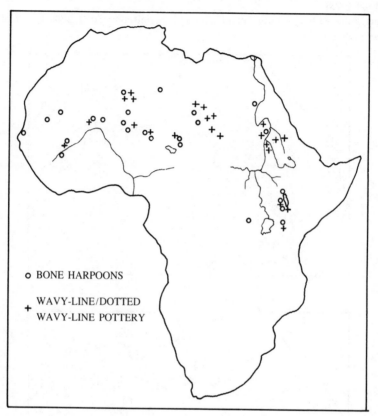

different other languages in the adjacent area. As he says, the growing volume of archeological evidence and dating does not refute his hypothesis. From the base, again by extrapolation, the period for the whole of the Afroasiatic phylum is provisionally hypothesized at 15,000 years or so. Comparison of this timescale for the attested archeological record of agriculture (or intensive exploitation of wild grasses) elsewhere in Africa and the Near East, combined with proposed reconstructions of Wörter and Sachen relating to cereals, cultivation, food processing, and animals, provides a plausible case for the independent presence (if not innovation) of agriculture in Ethiopia, and the possibility that the existence of agriculture in North Africa and the Near East are both due to the gradual expansion and migration of Afroasiatic-speaking peoples. The hypothesis appears to account for the presently available data, even if the datings are loaded with 'extrapolation.' To return to Thieme's remarks, the really important thing is that this kind of synthesis of data and argumentation should not only account for the

Figure 8.   Caudatum Sorghum distribution (after Stemler, Harlan, and DeWet 1975)

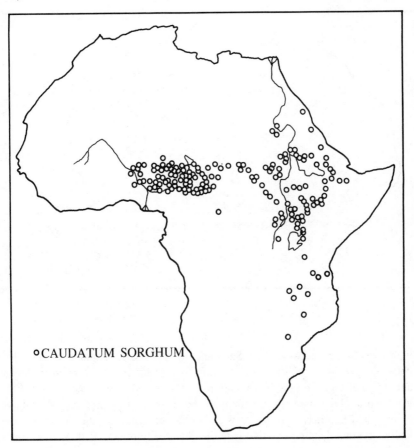

○CAUDATUM SORGHUM

available data, but also be transparent enough for inspection of the logic of the argument, and open to refutation. Testability is the key, and provides the focus for setting up the most strong hypotheses. Confrontation with the existing data is a necessary first step, and then the highlighting of new investigations, be they linguistic, archeological, or other, will provide the possibility of refutation.

Recent archeological work has shown that there is a clear archeological discontinuity between Nile (and certain Aqualithic) sites (Arkell 1953; Krzyaniak 1978; Haaland 1981; Caneva 1983) and sites east of the Nile (Fattovich et al. 1984). Subject to the need for further investigation of this discontinuity, it looks as if the hypothesis that two distinct archeological technocomplexes oriented west and east of the Nile were in evidence 3000 to 5000 years ago and correlate

Figure 9. Hypothesized homeland of Proto-Afroasiatic (Ehret 1979) and possible axes of migration (Bender 1975, after Diakonoff 1965)

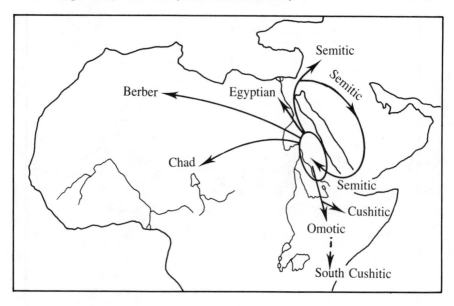

with a distinction between Nilo-Saharan and Afroasiatic language phyla. More detailed hypotheses of the possible language groups of these peoples depend among other things on the investigation of Wörter and Sachen techniques. Ehret has been applying these to comparative reconstructions from Central Sudanic, Nilotic, and Southern Cushitic as well as other present-day adjoining but genetically separate languages all down the Sudan/Ethiopian, Rift Valley zones. While his results must in many cases be considered more, rather than less, speculative, in cases where his own, or others', application of the comparative method has subsequently been carried out, a high proportion of support has been shown. In the fields of agriculture and cattle and caprid keeping, arguable cultural-historical hypotheses are being proposed alongside the evidence of lexicostatistical studies of basic vocabulary. The thread of argument is often problematic, but the utilization of basic lexicostatistics, of migration theory and homeland hypotheses, are part and parcel of the need for a mass of interacting techniques and disciplines. No realistic historical linguist working in this area would claim a unique deterministic status either for basic lexicostatistics or for the genetic trees derived from cluster analysis, but Gleason's program for a review of methods has been heeded, and, it appears, without such a loss of rigor and validity that current hypotheses are unwarranted assumptions untestable by any other than the comparative method.

REFERENCES

Adams, W. Y., D. P. Van Gervan, and R. S. Levy 1978. "The Retreat from Migrationism," *Annual Review of Anthropology* 7, pp. 483–532.

Antilla, R. 1972. *An Introduction to Historical and Comparative Linguistics*. New York: Macmillan.

Arkell, A. J. 1953. *Shaheinab*. London: Oxford University Press.

Bastin, Y., A. Coupez, and B. De Halleux 1979. "Statistique Lexicale et grammaticale pour la classification historique des langues bantoues." *Bulletin de Séance de L'Academie Royale des Sciences d'Outre-mer*, pp. 375–87.

Bender, M. L. 1969. "Chance CVC correspondences in unrelated languages." *Language* 45, pp. 519–31.

Bender, M. L. 1971. "The languages of Ethiopia: A new lexicostatistic classification and some problems of diffusion." *Anthropological Linguistics* 13:5, pp. 165–288.

Bender, M. L. 1975. *Omotic: A New Afroasiastic Language Family*. University Museum Studies. Carbondale, IL: Southern Illinois University Press.

Bender, M. L. (ed.) 1976. *The Non-Semitic Languages of Ethiopia*. East Lansing, MI: Michigan State University Press (African Studies Center).

Bender, M. L. 1981. "Some Nilo-Saharan isoglosses." In: T. C. Schadeberg and M. L. Bender (eds.), *Nilo-Saharan*. Dordrecht, Holland: Foris, pp. 253–67.

Bender, M. L., J. D. Bower, R. L. Cooper, and C. A. Ferguson (eds.) 1976. *Language in Ethiopia*. London: Oxford University Press.

Borland, C. H. 1982. "How basic is 'basic' vocabulary?" *Current Anthropology* 23:3, pp. 315–16.

Borland, C. H. 1983a. "Computational comparative historical linguistics and the evidence for basic vocabulary." Paper given at the 10th Conference of Association for Literary and Linguistic Computing, London.

Borland, C. H. 1983b. *Conflicting Methodologies of Shona Dialect Classification*. Unpublished manuscript, University of Cape Town.

Borland, C. H. 1984. Personal communication.

Caneva, I. (ed.) 1983. "Pottery using gatherers and hunters at Saggai (Sudan): Preconditions for food production," *Origini* 12, pp. 7–278.

Diakonoff, I. M. 1965. *The Semito-Hamitic Languages*. Moscow: Nauka.

Durham, S. P., and D. E. Rogers 1969. "An application of computer programming to the reconstruction of a proto-language." Paper read at the International Conference on Comparative Linguistics, Stockholm.

Dyen, I. 1956. "Language distribution and migration theory." *Language* 32, pp. 611–26.

Dyen, I., A. T. James, and J. W. L. Cole 1967. "Language divergence and estimated word retention rate." *Language* 43, pp. 150–71.

Ehret, C. 1971. *Southern Nilotic History*. Evanston, IL: Northwestern University Press.

Ehret, C. 1979. "On the antiquity of agriculture in Ethiopia." *Journal of African History* 20, pp. 161–77.

Ehret, C. 1980. *The Historical Reconstruction of Southern Cushitic: Phonology and Vocabulary*. Berlin: Reimer.

Ehret, C. 1982. "Nilotic and the limits of Eastern Sudanic." In: A. Vossen and B. Bechhaus-Gerst (eds.), *Nilotic Studies*. Berlin: Reimer.

Ehret, C. forthcoming. "The consonants of Proto-Nilo-Saharan." In: R. Thelwall (ed.), *Nilo-Saharan II*, Coleraine, N. Ireland: University of Ulster.

Ehret, C., T. Coffman, L. Fliegelman, A. Gold, M. Hubbard, D. Johnson, and D. Saxon 1974. "Some thoughts on the early history of the Nile-Congo watershed." *Ufahamu* 5:2, pp. 85–112.

Everitt, B. 1974. *Cluster Analysis*. London: Heineman/SSRC.

Fattovich, R., A. E. Marks, and Abbas Mohammed Ali 1984. "The archeology of the Eastern Sahel, Sudan: Preliminary results." *African Archeological Review* 2, pp. 2–21.

Fodor, I. 1961. "The validity of glottochronology on the basis of the Slavonic languages." *Studia Slavica* 7:4, pp. 295–346.

Fodor, I. 1966. *The Problems in the Classification of the African Languages.* Budapest: Center for Afro-Asian Research of the Hungarian Academy of Sciences.

Gabriel, B. 1978. "Klima- und Landschaftswandel der Sahara." In: *Sahara: 10,000 Jahre zwischen Weide und Wüste.* Köln: Museen der Stadt.

Gleason, H. A. 1959. "Counting and calculating for historical reconstruction." *Anthropological Linguistics* 1:2, pp. 22–32.

Greenberg, J. H. 1963. *The Languages of Africa.* The Hague: Mouton.

Greenberg, J. H. 1971. "Nilo-Saharan and Meroitic." In: T. A. Sebeok (ed.), *Current Trends in Linguistics*, Vol. 7. *Linguistics in Sub-Saharan Africa.* The Hague: Mouton, pp. 421–2.

Guthrie, M. 1967. *Comparative Bantu.* Farnborough, England: Gregg Press.

Haaland, R. 1981. *Migratory Herdsmen and Cultivating Women: The Structure of Neolithic Seasonal Adaptation in the Khartoum Nile Environment.* Bergen, Norway: no publisher.

Hamilton, A. C. 1982. *The Environmental History of East Africa.* London: Academic Press.

Hattori, S. 1953. "On the method of glottochronology and the time-depth of proto-Japanese." *Gengo Kenkyu* 22, 23: pp. 29–77.

Heine, B. 1974. "Historical linguistics and lexicostatistics in Africa." *Journal of African Languages* 11:3, pp. 7–20.

Henrici, A. 1973. "Numerical classification of Bantu." *African Languages Studies* 14, pp. 81–104.

Hetzron, R. 1972. *Ethiopian Semitic: Studies in Classification.* Manchester: Manchester University Press.

Hymes, D. 1960. "Lexicostatistics so far." *Current Anthropology* 1:1, pp. 3–44.

Jardine, N., and R. Sibson 1968. "The construction of hierarchic and non-hierarchic classifications." *Computer Journal* 11, pp. 117–84.

Krzyzaniak, L. 1978. "New light on early food production in the Central Sudan." *Journal of African History* 19:1, pp. 159–72.

Ladefoged, P. 1969. *Ugandan Languages.* London: Oxford University Press.

Ladefoged, P., R. Glick, and C. Criper 1972. *Language in Uganda.* London: Oxford University Press.

Lees, R. B. 1953. "The basis of glottochronology." *Language* 29, pp. 113–27.

Mann, M. 1976. *Some Fusional Classification Strategies: Effects of a Biased Selection of Individuals.* Unpublished manuscript, University College London.

Rottland, F. 1982. *Die Südnilotischen Sprachen.* Berlin: Reimer.

Schadeberg, T. C. 1975. *Preliminary Report on Comparative Survey of Kordofanian Languages.* Unpublished manuscript, Afrikaanse Taalkunde, Leiden.

Schadeberg, T. C. 1981a. *A Survey of Kordofanian 1: The Heiban Group.* Sprache und Geschichte in Afrika Beiheft 1. Hamburg: Buske.

Schadeberg, T. C. 1981b. *A Survey of Kordofanian 2: The Talodi Group.* Sprache und Geschichte in Afrika Beiheft 1. Hamburg: Buske.

Schadeberg, T. C. 1981c. "The Classification of the Kadugli Language Group." In: T. C. Schadeberg and M. L. Bender (eds.), *Nilo-Saharan.* Dordrecht, Holland: Foris.

Schadeberg, T. C. and M. L. Bender (eds.) 1981. *Nilo-Saharan.* Dordrecht, Holland: Foris.

Sibson, R. 1972. "Order invariant methods for data analysis." *Journal of the Royal Statistical Society* Series B, 34, pp. 311–49.

Sokal, R. R., and P. H. A. Sneath 1963. *Principles of Numerical Taxonomy,* London: W. H. Freeman.

Stemler, A. B. L., J. R. Harlan, and J. M. Dewet 1975. "Caudatum sorghums and speakers of Chari-Nile languages in Africa," *Journal of African Languages* 16:2, pp. 161–83.

Sutton, J. E. G. 1974. "The Aquatic Civilization of Middle Africa." *Journal of African History* 15:4, pp. 527–46.

Sutton, J. E. G. 1977. "The African Aqualithic." *Antiquity* 51, pp. 25–34.

Swadesh, M. 1950. "Salish internal relationships." *International Journal of American Linguistics* 16, pp. 157–67.

Swadesh, M. 1952. "Lexicostatistic dating of prehistorical ethnic contacts." *Proceedings of American Philosophical Society* 96, pp. 452–63.

Swadesh, M. 1955. "Towards a greater accuracy in lexicostatistic dating." International Journal of American Linguistics 21: pp. 121–37.

Teeter, K. V. 1963. "Lexicostatistics and genetic relationship." *Language* 39:4, pp. 638–48.

Thayer, L. 1976. *A Comparative-Historical Phonology of the Chari Languages*, Naples: Istituto Orientale di Napoli.

Thelwall, R. E. W. 1978. "Lexicostatistical relations between Nubian, Daju, and Dinka." Cairo: Institut Francais d'Archeologie Orientale (Études Nubiennes).

Thelwall, R. E. W. 1981. "Lexicostatistical subgrouping and lexical reconstruction of the Daju group." In: T. C. Schadeberg and M. L. Bender (eds.), *Nilo-Saharan*. Dordrecht, Holland: Foris, pp. 167–84.

Thelwall, R. E. W. 1982. "Linguistic aspects of Greater Nubian history." In: C. Ehret and M. Posnansky (eds.), *The Archeological and Linguistic Reconstruction of African History*. Berkeley, CA: University of California Press, pp. 39–52.

Thelwall, R., and T. C. Schadeberg 1984. "The linguistic situation in the Nuba Mountains." *Sprache und Geschichte in Afrika* 6, pp. 100–50.

Thieme, P. 1957. "Review of *Indo-European languages and Archeology* by H. Hencken." *Language* 33:2, pp. 183–90.

Vossen, R. 1982. *The Eastern Nilotes. Linguistic and Historical Reconstructions*. Berlin: Reimer.

Author Index

Subject Index